RUNNING

MS
DOS®

RUNNING

MS DOS®

By VAN WOLVERTON

The Definitive Guide
to MS-DOS® and PC-DOS,®
Now Completely Revised
to Include Version 4 and
the New DOS Shell

Microsoft PRESS®

PUBLISHED BY
Microsoft Press
A Division of Microsoft Corporation
16011 NE 36th Way, Box 97017, Redmond, Washington 98073-9717

Library of Congress Cataloging in Publication Data
Wolverton, Van, 1939–
Running MS-DOS.
Includes index.
1. MS-DOS (Computer operating system)   2. PC DOS (Computer
operating system)   I. Title.
QA76.76.063W65   1989   005.4'46   88-34519
ISBN 1-55615-186-1 (paper)   1-55615-193-4 (cloth)

Printed and bound in the United States of America.

1 2 3 4 5 6 7 8 9   FGFG   3 2 1 0 9 8

Distributed to the book trade in the
United States by Harper & Row.

Distributed to the book trade in
Canada by General Publishing Company, Ltd.

Distributed to the book trade outside the
United States and Canada by Penguin Books Ltd.

Penguin Books Ltd., Harmondsworth, Middlesex, England
Penguin Books Australia Ltd., Ringwood, Victoria, Australia
Penguin Books N.Z. Ltd., 182–190 Wairau Road, Auckland 10, New Zealand

British Cataloging in Publication Data available

Project Editor: JoAnne Woodcock   Technical Editor: Jim Johnson

For Jeanne, who makes it all worthwhile

CONTENTS

PART 3: APPENDIXES

ACKNOWLEDGMENTS

It's been more than four years since the first edition of this book hit the shelves, and the world of computers has changed mightily. The person who bought the first edition of this book most likely had a 64 K IBM PC with two diskette drives. Those of you who buy this edition probably have an IBM PC/AT with a megabyte or more of memory and a 30- or 40-megabyte fixed disk—or, even more likely, a computer made by some other company, but whose behavior is nonetheless indistinguishable from the IBM version.

But all those machines use MS-DOS, so I'd like to thank all those folks who have labored to put a DOS machine on everyone's desk. Thanks, too, to IBM and Microsoft for starting things off back in 1981.

Both DOS and this book are in their fourth version. That's uncommon longevity in the quicksilver world of personal computers. The staying power of DOS is due to the remarkable proliferation of IBM and IBM-compatible computers. The staying power of this book is due, in large part, to the inspiration and efforts of three remarkable women.

My mother, Bee Forsyth Wolverton, preached the gospel of clear writing as far back as I can remember, and emphasized her message by setting—as she continues to set—a dauntingly high example. My editor, JoAnne Woodcock, cossets and cajoles me through each revision, using her skill, judgment, and patience to improve the book each time; she is without peer. And most of all, Jeanne Elizabeth Wolverton whipped the first edition into shape before anyone else ever saw it, and continues to keep me on the right track; she has been my first editor for nearly 30 years, and I've still got a lot to learn from her.

So, a special thanks to those three women who have contributed so much to this book. And a personal thanks to the people of Montana who have made Jeanne and me feel so welcome. It's good to be back.

Van Wolverton
Rubicon
Sawmill Gulch Road
Alberton, MT 59820
December 1988

INTRODUCTION

I t may be tempting to skip these opening words and "get to the meat of it," but please read this introduction anyway. The information included here is both useful and brief.

You may want to know whether this book applies to you. It does, if your computer uses MS-DOS. The book itself was written with an IBM Personal Computer but, with the exception of a few commands, the contents of the book apply equally to any machine that uses MS-DOS.

You bought this book—or at least took the time to pick it up and glance through it—despite the hefty manual you got with your copy of DOS. Why? What else can a book like this offer? It can offer simplicity. The DOS manual is thorough and complete. It is your official, comprehensive reference guide to DOS, but it also includes a good deal of technical information you don't really need in order to *use* DOS.

This book does not show you how to set up your computer, nor does it describe in detail the pieces of the system, such as the keyboard or the display. These matters should be covered thoroughly in the manuals that came with your computer.

The book assumes neither that you are, nor that you aspire to become, a programmer. It doesn't try to explain how DOS works, and it leaves to the DOS manual the task of explaining some of the more technical features. The book does assume that you have access to an IBM Personal Computer or one of the many other machines that run MS-DOS, and that you want to put the machine to work. It includes dozens of examples, and is organized by what you want the computer to do, not by how DOS itself is structured. The examples reflect real-life situations.

You don't have to be a mechanical engineer to drive a car well, but you do need experience. You don't have to be a computer scientist to use DOS well, either, and this book starts you on your way.

WHAT'S IN THE BOOK, AND WHERE

This book covers all versions of DOS, through 4.01, used with machines that have a fixed disk drive and one or two diskette drives or that have two diskette drives.

Part 1, Chapters 1 through 4, describes the pieces of the computer system, defines some terms and concepts, and provides hands-on examples that show you the major capabilities of DOS.

Part 2, the bulk of the book, includes Chapters 5 through 17. These chapters show you how to operate your computer system and manage all its parts with the DOS commands.

Chapters 5, 6, and 7 show you how to manage your files, diskettes, and computer devices. Chapter 8 describes the DOS multilevel filing system that allows you to set up a personalized computer file system that matches the way you work. Chapter 9 shows you how to manage the files and directories on a fixed disk.

Chapters 10 and 11 make up an extended example that shows you how to create and modify files of text with Edlin, the DOS text editor. Chapter 12 shows you how to create your own commands to automate tasks you perform frequently.

Chapter 13 shows you how to use a special set of commands called filter commands to control where the other DOS commands get their input and where they send their output. Chapters 14 and 15 show you how to create more advanced commands of your own. Chapter 16 shows you how to tailor your system to suit your needs. It includes several useful techniques that can make DOS immediately useful in its own right. Chapter 17 shows you how to use the DOS Shell, a program introduced in version 4 that helps you manage your files, disks, and application programs.

Appendix A tells you about preparing a fixed disk for use. Appendix B offers some suggestions about using the installation program that comes with version 4. If you have version 3.3 or an earlier version of DOS, Appendix C shows you how to copy the DOS diskettes and install DOS on a fixed disk. Appendix D shows you how to control the way DOS displays the date, and how to type, display, and print characters from international alphabets. Appendix E, the Glossary, defines the terms used in the book, plus a few others you may have seen or heard. Finally, Appendix F, the DOS Command Reference, describes the DOS commands and includes page references to the detailed discussions and examples in the preceding chapters.

If you plan to use your computer for word processing, spreadsheets, database management, or perhaps a household accounting package and some games, this book is probably all you'll need. Not only does it show you how to use DOS so you can run your programs, it shows you how DOS can make your computer a more valuable tool without additional software.

ABOUT THE EXAMPLES

The best way to learn how to put DOS to work is to use it. This book, therefore, is devoted primarily to examples. Terms and concepts are defined as you need them to follow the examples. Because the book covers several versions of DOS and several types of machines, there are variations in some examples; these alternatives are identified. Unless an example specifically states it is for an earlier version, the DOS displays shown in this book are the IBM version 4.01 responses. If you are using a different version, the responses you see may vary somewhat. Do not be concerned.

What to Type and When

There's an awkward mismatch between a computer and a book that shows you how to use it. The computer is dynamic: It displays messages, moves data back and forth between disks and memory, prints words and pictures, and chirps now and then to announce completion of another task. When you use the computer, you enter into a dialogue: You type something, the computer responds, you type something else, and so on, back and forth, until your work is done.

A book, however, is static. It can only show snapshots of your dialogue with the system, yet it must describe that dialogue well enough so that you can take part in it. In this book, we have to show what you type and how the computer responds. We have to distinguish parts of this dialogue, such as the names of files and messages displayed on the screen, from the surrounding prose. Here are the conventions we've adopted to cover those situations:

- Hands-on examples are shown in different type, on separate lines, just as you would see them on your display. The characters you type are printed in lowercase colored type; DOS doesn't care whether you type in uppercase or lowercase, but lowercase seems to be easier. Here is an example showing these conventions:

```
C>format b:
Insert new diskette for drive B:
and press ENTER when ready...
```

- Occasionally, similar information occurs in text. In these instances, the interaction between you and DOS is printed in italics to distinguish it from the surrounding text. For example, you may see: "Type *n* when DOS displays *Format another (Y/N)?*"

- Many DOS commands include options, or parameters, that allow you to specify a particular disk drive, file, or piece of equipment, or to use a particular form of the command. Options are shown in angle brackets (<>) when they represent a variable entry, such as the name of a file. When they must be entered exactly, they are shown in the form you must use. For example, here are some options of the Format command used in the preceding examples (don't worry about understanding the command at this point):

format <drive> /V:<label> /1 /4 /8

Now it's time to meet DOS. This book was written to be used at the system, so put it beside your keyboard, turn to Chapter 1, and get ready to put DOS to work.

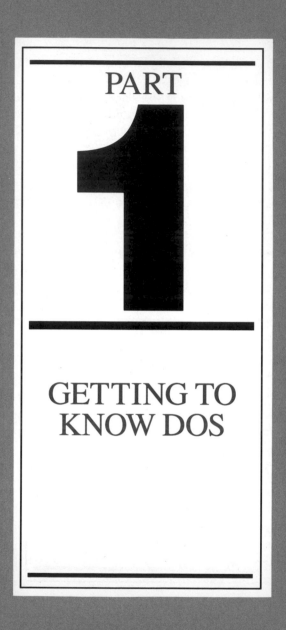

PART

1

GETTING TO
KNOW DOS

Part 1 describes the terms and the basic operating principles of DOS. The chapters show you how to start DOS and how to control the system with DOS commands. The information is primarily tutorial, and many examples are included. Later parts of the book contain all detailed reference information that describes the DOS commands and their capabilities.

Part 1 introduces you to the concept of an operating system: What it is, what it does, and why you need it. Together, these chapters give you the foundation for using DOS effectively in your daily work with the computer.

WHAT IS DOS?

Y ou've got your computer and you've probably got one or two programs, such as a word processor or a spreadsheet, to use with it. But what is this thing called DOS? Why do you hear so much about it, and why have hundreds of pages of instructions been written for it?

DOS IS A PROGRAM

DOS is a program, but it's not just any program. Chances are none of your other programs would work without it, because DOS controls every part of the computer system. DOS not only makes it possible for your other programs to work, it also gives you complete control over what your computer does, and how. DOS is the link between you and your computer.

To appreciate the role DOS plays, take a quick look at the pieces of your computer system and what they do.

HARDWARE MAKES IT POSSIBLE

Your computer equipment, called *hardware,* probably includes a keyboard, display, printer, and one or more disk drives. The purposes of the first three are straightforward: You type instructions at the keyboard, and the system responds by displaying or printing messages and results.

The purpose of a disk drive isn't quite so obvious, but it quickly becomes apparent as you use the system: A disk drive records and plays back information, much as a tape deck records and plays back music. The computer's information is recorded in files on disks; you'll find that disk files are as central to your computer work as paper files are to more traditional office work.

SOFTWARE MAKES IT HAPPEN

No matter how powerful the hardware, a computer can't do anything without programs, called *software*. There are two major types of software: *system programs,* which control the operation of the computer system, and *application programs,* which perform more obviously useful tasks, such as word processing.

Each program uses the hardware. It must be able to receive instructions from the keyboard, display and print results, read and write files from and to a disk, send and receive data through the computer's communications connection, change the colors on a color display, and so on through all the capabilities of the hardware.

So that each program doesn't have to perform all these functions for itself, a system program called the *operating system* manages the hardware. The operating system allows an application program to concentrate on what it does best, whether it's moving paragraphs about, tracking accounts receivable, or calculating stress in a bridge beam. DOS is an operating system.

DOS IS A DISK OPERATING SYSTEM

The operating system for many computers, including the IBM personal computers, is the Disk Operating System from Microsoft. It is called a disk operating system because much of its work involves managing disks and disk files.

What Does an Operating System Do?

An operating system plays a role something like a symphony conductor. When the score calls for the violins to play, the conductor cues the violins; when the score says the cellos should play more softly, the tympani should stop, or the entire orchestra should pick up the tempo, the conductor so instructs the musicians.

The players in the orchestra and their instruments represent the hardware. The experience and skill of the conductor represent the operating system. The score represents an application program.

When one score is replaced by another—Vivaldi's Mandolin Concerto is put aside and replaced by Haydn's *Surprise* Symphony, for example—the same musicians use the same instruments, and the same conductor uses the same experience and skills. A different sound, a different mood, perhaps, but the elements are the same.

When one application program is replaced by another—for example, an accounting program is put aside and replaced with a word processor—the same hardware carries out the instructions of the same operating system. A different program, a different purpose, perhaps, but the elements are the same.

DOS coordinates the computer system, just as the conductor coordinates the orchestra. Your application programs run in concert with DOS, trusting it to keep the system humming.

Much of what DOS does, such as how it stores a file on a disk or prints on the printer, is invisible to you. But DOS lets you control the things you care about, such as which program to run, what report to print, or what files to erase. These functions share an important characteristic: They need disks and disk drives.

Disk Drives

Personal computers use two main types of disk: a flexible disk in a protective plastic jacket, called a *diskette,* which you can remove from the drive, and a permanently mounted unit called a *fixed disk.* There are two types of diskette: 5.25 inches square in a flexible plastic jacket, and 3.5 inches square in a rigid plastic shell.

A fixed disk holds much more information than a diskette—from 15 to 100 times as much, or even more—and is much faster. Most personal computers have either one fixed disk and one diskette drive, or two diskette drives.

To distinguish among the types of disk, this book uses *diskette* to mean either type of flexible disk, *fixed disk* to mean only a fixed disk, and *disk* to refer to both.

Disk Files

Just as you organize and store your written records in paper files, you organize and store computer information in disk files.

A disk file—usually called a file—is a collection of related information stored on a disk. It could be a letter, an income tax return, or a list of customers. It could also be a program, because the programs you use are stored in files.

Virtually all your computer work revolves around files. Because one of the major functions of DOS is to take care of files, much of this book is devoted to showing you how to create, print, copy, and otherwise manage files. As you go through the practice sessions in the following chapters, you'll notice references to some versions of DOS that have more file-handling abilities than other versions.

Different Versions of DOS

DOS has been revised a number of times since its release in 1981; the first version was numbered 1.00. DOS is revised to add more capability, to take advantage of more sophisticated hardware, and to correct errors. When you start up your system, DOS may display the version number that you are using.

When a new version of DOS appears, a change in the number following the decimal point—3.20 to 3.30, for example—marks a minor change that leaves DOS substantially the same as the previous version. A change in the number preceding the decimal point marks a major change. Version 2.00, for example, offered almost three times as many commands as version 1.10.

This book covers all versions of DOS. Even though newer versions have much more capability, they remain compatible with earlier versions. Thus, if you start with version 2.1, you can still use all your knowledge and experience, plus all your files and diskettes, when you move to a newer version.

For simplicity, this book usually refers to DOS by major version numbers only; for example, version 3 or version 4, rather than version 3.1 or version 4.00. It also omits references to versions of DOS earlier than version 3, but much of the information applies to these versions too. Remember, version 2 is just as much a part of DOS as version 4. It's simply older and, though it includes most of the features described here, it doesn't provide them all.

What Is Compatibility?

You may have seen the terms DOS-compatible or IBM-compatible used in an article or advertisement. What does compatible mean? Although some technical issues are involved, the most meaningful measure of compatibility is the extent to which you can use the diskettes from one system in another:

- If two systems are totally compatible, you can freely exchange diskettes. This situation is common among IBM-compatible computers.

- If two systems are incompatible, you cannot exchange diskettes because neither system can read files stored by the other. That's why you can't use a diskette from an Apple computer in an IBM Personal Computer.

- If two systems are partially compatible, you can interchange some diskettes, particularly those that contain files of information rather than programs.

This last level, of partial compatibility, is what is usually meant by the term MS-DOS–compatible and is one of the advantages of using an operating system that runs on so many different machines.

To maintain consistency, this book describes how DOS works on the IBM PS/2 (all models), IBM PC/AT, IBM PC/XT, and IBM PC. If your computer is a compatible machine, however, the descriptions apply equally to your system.

WHAT CAN YOU DO WITH DOS?

DOS coordinates the operation of the computer for your application programs. That's valuable—essential, really—but DOS has much more to offer. You can use DOS, controlling it with instructions called *commands,* to manage your files, control the work flow, and perform useful tasks that might otherwise require additional software.

For example, DOS includes a program called Edlin that lets you create and revise files of text. Although it's not a word processor, Edlin is fine for short memos and lists. Using Edlin, you can write short documents in less time than it might take to start your word-processing program and store the file.

You can tailor DOS to your specific needs by creating powerful commands made up of other DOS commands, and you can even create your own small applications. For example, this book shows you how to create a simple file manager—a program that lets you search a file for specific information—using nothing but DOS commands.

Beginning with version 4, DOS also includes a separate program, called the *Shell,* that lets you choose commands and files from on-screen lists called *menus.* If you want, you can use the Shell for routine work, or you can dispense with it and work directly with DOS by typing commands.

Your knowledge of DOS can range from just enough to use a single application program to mastery of the full range of capabilities in the later versions. But no matter how far you go, you needn't learn to program. It's all DOS, and it's all in this book.

CHAPTER SUMMARY

This quick tour of DOS may have introduced several new terms and concepts. Here are the key points to remember:

- A computer system needs both hardware (equipment) and software (programs).

- DOS (the Microsoft Disk Operating System) coordinates the operation of all parts of the computer system.

- A file is a collection of related information stored on a disk. Most of your computer work will involve files.

- Besides running your application programs, DOS is valuable in its own right.

The next chapter starts you off at the keyboard.

CHAPTER

2

STARTING DOS

N ow that you have been introduced to some of the things DOS does for you, it's time to start your system and do something. Whenever you start your computer, whether it is to use a word processor, an accounting program, or DOS itself, you begin by *loading* DOS into the computer's memory, its workplace. Loading the DOS program and starting it running is sometimes called "booting the system" or "booting the disk." This term is borrowed from the phrase "pulling yourself up by your bootstraps," because DOS essentially pulls itself up by its own bootstraps, loading itself from disk into memory, where it then waits for a command from you.

The examples in this chapter assume you have set up your system and are familiar with its control switches. If you're using a fixed disk, the examples also assume you have prepared the fixed disk so DOS can use it. If your computer system is new, you haven't yet prepared the fixed disk, and you need some assistance, refer to the section on Fdisk in your DOS manual. If you need to copy DOS from the original diskettes to your fixed disk, either because the disk is new or because you are upgrading to a more recent version of DOS, turn to Appendix B for instructions on version 4; turn to Appendix C for instructions on versions 3 and earlier.

ENTERING DOS COMMANDS

The instructions you give DOS are called *commands*. For the first few commands you enter in this session, you need only the standard typewriter keys on the keyboard. Two of those keys, Enter and Backspace, are shown on the keyboards in Figures 2-1 and 2-2 and are worth separate mention.

Figure 2-1. The Backspace and Enter keys on the IBM PC and PC/XT keyboards

Figure 2-2. The Backspace and Enter keys on the enhanced IBM PC/AT keyboard

The Enter Key

The Enter key is labeled with a bent left arrow (⏎) or the word *Enter*. Like the return key on a typewriter, it marks the end of a line. In general, DOS doesn't know what you have typed until you press Enter, so remember: End a command by pressing Enter.

The Backspace Key

The Backspace key is labeled with a long left arrow (←) or the word *Backspace*. It erases the last character you typed; use it to correct typing errors.

STARTING THE SYSTEM

If you're using a fixed disk with DOS on it, the DOS program must be copied into the computer's memory from the fixed disk (usually known to DOS as drive C). All you need to do before starting the system is make sure the latch on drive A (the diskette drive) isn't closed; otherwise, the system will try to load the DOS program into the computer's memory from the diskette in drive A.

If you're not using a fixed disk, the DOS program must be copied into the computer's memory from the diskette in drive A. Open the latch of drive A (either the left-hand or upper diskette drive) and put in the diskette you use to start DOS—called the *system disk* in this book—with the label up and away from the machine, as in Figure 2-3 on page 13. If you're using 5.25-inch diskettes, close the latch.

Turn on the system. The computer seems to do nothing for several seconds, but this is normal. Each time you turn on the power switch, the computer checks its memory and all attached devices to be sure everything is working properly. The system beeps once after it has made sure that all is well, the drive lights flash, and the computer begins loading DOS into memory.

As soon as the program is loaded, DOS is running and ready to go to work.

Beginning with version 4, your first glimpse of DOS may look something like the following:

```
┌─────────────┬─────────────────────────────────────────┬─────────┐
│ 10-16-89    │            Start Programs               │ 1:12 pm │
├─────────────┴─────────────────────────────────────────┼─────────┤
│ Program  Group  Exit                                   │ F1=Help │
├────────────────────────────────────────────────────────┴─────────┤
│                        Main Group                                 │
│          To select an item, use the up and down arrows.           │
│       To start a program or display a new group, press Enter.     │
│                                                                   │
│ ┌───────────────────────────────────────────────────┐            │
│ │ Command Prompt                                     │            │
│ └───────────────────────────────────────────────────┘            │
│  File System                                                     │
│  Change Colors                                                   │
│  DOS Utilities...                                                │
│                                                                   │
│                                                                   │
│                                                                   │
│                                                                   │
│                                     �                         │
│                                                                   │
│                                                                   │
│                                                                   │
│                                                                   │
│                                                                   │
│                                                                   │
│                                                                   │
├───────────────────────────────────────────────────────────────────┤
│ F10=Actions              Shift+F9=Command Prompt                  │
└───────────────────────────────────────────────────────────────────┘
```

This is the DOS Shell as it appears on a computer system that is able to display graphics (note that an arrowhead represents the mouse pointer). If your computer cannot display graphics, the letters *P*, *G*, and *x* in the words *Program*, *Group*, and *Exit* are bright, rather than underlined.

Chapter 17, "The DOS Shell," tells you about the Shell and how to use it. The remainder of this chapter and, indeed, most of this book take you outside of the Shell both to help you become comfortable with DOS on many levels and to enable users of all versions of DOS to benefit from the examples. For the time being, leave the Shell: Press the key labeled F3.

DOS responds with a display like this:

```
C:\DOS>
```

or this:

```
C>
```

Now you have a direct line to DOS.

Note: If you don't have version 4, you won't see the display shown on the facing page because your version of DOS does not include the program that runs the Shell. If you do have version 4 but don't see the Shell, either it has not been installed on the disk that starts DOS, or DOS has been instructed to avoid displaying the Shell unless you request it. Chapter 17 tells you how to start the Shell; for now, it isn't necessary.

Date

Regardless of the version you use, DOS goes through a standard routine immediately after it starts. Its first task is to find out the correct date, so it might display a message like this:

```
Current date is Tue 01-01-1980
Enter new date (mm-dd-yy): _
```

If your computer keeps track of the date and time for you, DOS doesn't need this information, but you can see this message anyway. Type:

```
C>date
```

and press Enter.

Figure 2-3. Inserting a diskette

The blinking underline that follows the colon is the *cursor*. It shows where DOS will display whatever you type next. It also tells you that DOS is waiting for you to type something—in this case, a date in response to its *Enter new date* request. Such a request is called a *prompt*; DOS frequently prompts you to enter information so that you don't have to memorize operating procedures.

To enter the date, you type the numbers that represent the month, day, and year, separated by hyphens, and then you press the Enter key. You do not type the day of the week; as you will see later in this chapter, DOS figures out the day for you and displays both the day and date whenever you ask for them.

For this example, set the date to October 16, 1989, by typing the following (be sure to press Enter after the last number):

```
Current date is Tue 01-01-1980
Enter new date (mm-dd-yy): 10-16-89
```

Note: You can also use a slash (/) or a period to separate the numbers. Whichever you use, if you don't do it exactly right (in other words, in a way that DOS recognizes), DOS displays Invalid date *and waits for you to try again. If you make a mistake or enter the wrong date, don't be alarmed. As you'll see in the next example, it's easy to fix such errors.*

After it accepts the date, DOS might display a message asking you to enter the time and again wait for you to respond. The screen should look something like this (if you don't have version 4, you don't see a lowercase *a* or *p* after the time):

```
Current date is Tue 01-01-1980
Enter new date (mm-dd-yy): 10-16-89
Current time is  0:01:30.00a
Enter new time: _
```

If you don't see the preceding time message, type *time* and press Enter.

Before you enter the correct time, try the following exercise to see how easily you can fix typing errors.

Backspacing to Correct Typing Errors

Try out the Backspace key. Type some characters, such as the following, at random, but don't press Enter:

```
Current date is Tue 01-01-1980
Enter new date (mm-dd-yy): 10-16-89
Current time is  0:01:30.00a
Enter new time: w710273_
```

This isn't a valid time; if you were to press Enter now, DOS would display the message *Invalid time* and wait for your next attempt. Correct your typing "error" by pressing the Backspace key until all the characters are erased and the cursor is back to its original position, just to the right of the colon. The screen looks like it did before:

```
Current date is Tue   01-01-1980
Enter new date (mm-dd-yy): 10-16-89
Current time is  0:01:30.00a
Enter new time: _
```

Time

You enter the time by typing the numbers that represent the current hour and minute, separated by a colon or a period. Don't worry about seconds and hundredths of seconds. For this example, set the time to 8:15 A.M. by typing the following (don't forget to press Enter):

```
Current date is Tue 01-01-1980
Enter new date (mm-dd-yy): 10-16-89
Current time is  0:01:30.00a
Enter new time: 8:15
```

Note: In versions 1 through 3, DOS works on the basis of a 24-hour clock, so you type 1:15 P.M. as 13:15 or 10:00 P.M. as 22:00. Beginning with version 4, DOS can understand either a 12-hour or a 24-hour clock, depending on the conventions of the country for which it is installed. If, as in the United States, a 12-hour clock is more familiar, you can specify A.M. or P.M. For example, you can type 1:15 P.M. either as 13:15 or as 1:15p or as 1:15pm. Don't forget the p or pm, though, or DOS will assume 1:15 A.M. Also, don't type a blank space after the number; if you do, DOS responds Invalid time *and asks you to try again.*

If your system doesn't keep the date and time current, and you just press Enter in response to the date and time prompts when you start the system, DOS starts from its baseline date and time of midnight on January 1, 1980. Skipping these steps is a quick way to start the system, but DOS marks all the disk files you create or change with the time and date. Such information is useful, so it's a good idea to set the correct date and time each time you start the system.

Startup

DOS might also display a startup message to identify itself and the version you are using and then wait for further instructions. The exact wording of the lines that give the name of the operating system and the version number depends on which computer and version of DOS you're using.

The following message (truncated here) is the opening display for the IBM version of DOS 4:

```
IBM DOS Version 4.00
          (C)Copyright International Business Machines...
          (C)Copyright Microsoft Corp 1981-1986

C>_
```

Note: You might see only the first line of this display. If you normally start version 4 of DOS with the Shell, you won't see the message shown above. Don't be concerned.

If you're not using a fixed disk, the last line is A> instead of C> because A is the letter DOS uses to identify the diskette drive from which you started the system.

The System Prompt

The C> (or A> if you're not using a fixed disk) is called the *system prompt,* because the system program (DOS) is prompting you to type a command. At this point, DOS is at what is often called *command level,* because it's ready and waiting for a command. (The Shell in version 4 refers to the system prompt as the *command prompt.*)

The system prompt also identifies the *current drive,* the drive where DOS looks for a file. DOS identifies your drives by letter. On a system with two diskette drives, the left-hand or upper drive is drive A, the right-hand or lower drive is drive B; on a system with one diskette drive and one fixed disk, the diskette drive is identified as both A and B, the fixed disk drive as drive C.

If you're using a fixed disk with the DOS programs on it and DOS is loaded from the fixed disk (drive C), DOS assumes drive C is the current drive, and the initial system prompt is C> or C:\DOS>. If you're not using a fixed disk, DOS is loaded from drive A; DOS assumes that drive A is the current drive, and the initial system prompt on your system is A>.

This book contains many examples for you to try. With a few exceptions, the examples show the system prompt as C:\DOS> because that is the normal system prompt on a computer with a fixed disk and version 4 of DOS. If you're not using a fixed disk, you're told specifically when and how to prepare for an example; if there are no instructions, simply proceed with the example, but bear in mind that where you see C:\DOS> in the book, you will see A> on your screen.

A WORD ABOUT DOS
AND YOUR COMPUTER

Both DOS and the computers it runs on have evolved in the years since the introduction of version 1 and the IBM PC (the machine for which DOS was originally created). The examples in this book are designed to work correctly with your computer and any release of DOS that supports the commands described. There are, however, some variations in computer setups and in the way DOS and its command files are organized and presented in different versions and different computer manufacturers' releases of DOS. Here are some examples:

- If you are using version 4, DOS may be set up to take you directly to the Shell—a feature not present in any prior version. If you enter the Shell, you see the display shown earlier in this chapter. To see the system prompt, represented as C:\DOS> in this book, remember to press the F3 key.

- In terms of equipment, your computer might have a fixed disk and one diskette drive, a fixed disk and two diskette drives, or two diskette drives.

- If you have a fixed disk, the files on it, including your DOS files, might be organized in any number of different ways, just as different people might organize and label paper folders in a file drawer according to their own preferences. (The reasons for this will become clear in Chapters 8 and 9, when you encounter the terms *directory* and *path*.)

- If you use DOS from diskettes, the organization of the files on your DOS diskettes—even the number of diskettes—varies, depending on the version of DOS you use, the size of your diskettes, and the manufacturer that produced your computer. For example, the IBM release of version 4 comes on five 5.25-inch diskettes; version 3.3 from the same manufacturer comes on two 5.25-inch diskettes. Similarly, the IBM release of version 3.3 on 5.25-inch diskettes comes with most of the commands on a supplemental diskette labeled *Operating*; other manufacturers' releases of this same version of DOS might include these commands on the diskette you normally use to start your system.

None of these variations affect either your use of DOS or your use of the commands described in this book.

As mentioned earlier, the examples in this book are based on version 4.0 of DOS, as it is released by IBM and as it runs on an IBM PC/AT or compatible computer with one fixed disk and one diskette drive. Although your display might differ from what is shown, especially in the chapters dealing with the DOS diskettes themselves, don't be concerned. Where necessary, the examples provide support for other systems and other versions of DOS.

Note: If you're using IBM's release of version 3.3 on a system with 5.25-inch disk drives and no fixed disk, you're asked throughout this book to start the system with the Startup diskette, then to replace the Startup diskette with the Operating diskette before using the system. That's probably how you'll routinely use your system, too, because most of the files you need in day-to-day operation are on the Operating diskette.

CHANGING THE CURRENT DRIVE

You can change the current drive by typing the letter of the new drive, followed by a colon. For example, try changing the current drive to B.

You'll need a diskette, so either find one that you have used before or use one of your DOS diskettes (be careful with it, especially if you have version 3 and have not made duplicates as described in Appendix C).

If you have one diskette drive, insert the diskette in the drive with the label up and away from the machine. If you have two diskette drives, insert the diskette in the drive that does not currently contain your DOS disk.

Now type:

`C:\DOS>b:`

If you have one diskette drive, DOS displays the message:

Insert diskette for drive B: and press any key when ready

The diskette is in the drive, so press a key. DOS responds:

`B:\>_`

Now the system prompt is B:\>, confirming that DOS will look in drive B unless told otherwise.

If you're using a fixed disk, change the current drive back to drive C by typing the following:

`B:\>c:`

`C:\DOS>_`

The system prompt returns to C:\DOS (or, depending on how your system is set up, it returns to C>).

If you're not using a fixed disk, change the current drive back to drive A by typing the following:

`B>a:`

`A>_`

The system prompt returns to A>.

CHANGING THE DATE AND TIME

The computer has an electronic clock that keeps time to the hundredth of a second. DOS uses this clock to keep track of both the time of day and the date. If you're using the system when midnight arrives, the date advances to the next day (and, if necessary, the next month and year).

In some models of computers, the clock doesn't run when the system is shut off, so each time you start the system DOS sets the date to January 1, 1980 (1-01-1980) and sets the time to midnight (0:00:00.00). That's why DOS might prompt you for the correct date and time whenever you start the system.

The clock in the IBM PS/2 series, the PC/AT, and compatible computers—plus the clock in some IBM PC and PC/XT compatibles—runs all the time, powered by its own battery. If you're using version 3.3 or 4 of DOS, or if you have a clock-calendar card and timekeeping software in your system, the date and time in this system clock remain correct without your having to do anything, even when the system is turned off.

You can change the date whenever you want with the Date command. To tell DOS you want to change the date, type:

```
C:\DOS>date
```

DOS displays the current date (here, it is the date you set earlier) and prompts you to type a new date:

```
Current date is Mon 10-16-1989
Enter new date (mm-dd-yy): _
```

Type the correct date and press the Enter key. DOS sets its calendar to the new date and displays the system prompt. If you had just pressed Enter, DOS would have left the date unchanged. You can check and change the time the same way, with the Time command. To set the clock to the correct time, type:

```
C:\DOS>time
```

DOS displays the time (based on what you set earlier) and prompts for the new time:

```
Current time is  8:22:33:55a
Enter new time: _
```

Type the correct time and press Enter.

PRINTING WHAT IS ON THE SCREEN

The screen shows you a record of your commands and the responses from DOS; it normally shows a maximum of 25 lines. When all the lines are filled, each additional line causes the entire screen to shift up, or *scroll,* to make room for the new line at the bottom; the top line disappears from view.

Because a copy of what is on the display is often useful, DOS makes it easy to print what's on the screen. Locate the key labeled PrtSc (for *Print Screen,* spelled out on some keyboards). Make sure your printer is turned on, hold down the Shift key, and press PrtSc (this combination is referred to in text as Shift-PrtSc).

Each line of the screen is printed. Another way to print what is on the screen is described in the next chapter.

Note: If Shift-PrtSc does not produce a printed copy of what's on the screen, you might need to help your printer understand the instruction. With the Hewlett-Packard LaserJet Plus, for example, you press the button labeled ON LINE, *press the* FORM FEED *button to print the page, then press* ON LINE *again to return the printer to its earlier status. If necessary, check the documentation that came with your printer.*

CLEARING THE SCREEN

Sometimes, when the screen is filled with commands and responses, you might want to clear it before continuing with your work. You can erase everything on the screen with the Clear Screen (cls) command. Try it by typing:

```
C:\DOS>cls
```

The screen is cleared, except for the system prompt in the upper left-hand corner.

TURNING THE SYSTEM OFF

If DOS is displaying the system prompt, all you have to do to shut the system down is turn off the power switch. You can do it anytime, except when the light on a disk drive is on; turning the power off while a drive is in use can cause you to lose the data on the disk. (If you're using an application program and decide to shut the system down, first follow the program's instructions for saving your work and quitting. When the program returns you to the DOS prompt, you can shut down without risking loss of data.)

Some devices attached to your system may have special requirements for shutting down, such as a specific sequence in which they should be turned off. Be sure you know any special instructions for the devices attached to your system.

After you shut the system down, be sure to remove any diskettes you are using and store them where they will be safe. Remove your diskettes before you turn off the power, as long as the disk drive is not in use.

CHAPTER SUMMARY

You have completed your first session with DOS. It wasn't very long, but you started the system, entered a few DOS commands, and printed what was on the screen. These are the key points:

- You control DOS by typing commands.

- DOS doesn't know what you have typed until you press the Enter key.

- The Backspace key erases the last character you typed.

- The system prompt tells you that DOS is at the command level, ready to accept a command from you.

- The letter in the system prompt identifies the current drive; you can change the current drive by typing the new drive letter, followed by a colon.

- The computer keeps track of the date and time. You can also set them with the Date and Time commands.

- Pressing Shift-PrtSc prints the contents of the screen.

- Typing *cls* clears the screen.

CHAPTER

3

TAKING A TEST DRIVE

W hen you test-drive a car, you already know how to start it. The test drive helps you become familiar with the controls, the steering, the brakes, the overall feel of the car. You learned how to start DOS in the previous chapter. Now it's time for a test drive—time to begin learning to control DOS, how to steer it in the direction of one task or another, and how to call a halt if you either want or need to.

That's what this chapter is all about. It introduces you to the directory of files that DOS keeps on each disk and shows you how to use the special keys on your keyboard. You use these keys to tell DOS to cancel lines or commands, to freeze the display, and to restart DOS itself.

Note: Part of this chapter deals with keys that have special meaning for DOS. If your keyboard does not have the key used in an example, check your system's documentation for equivalent keys.

The examples in this chapter show you the names of some files that DOS uses to do the work you request. Exactly what you see depends on your version of DOS, the size (3.5 inches or 5.25 inches) and capacity of your DOS diskettes, and whether or not you have a fixed disk. Assuming that you have installed version 4 of DOS as described in Appendix B (or an earlier version as described in Appendix C), you can ensure that your practice session runs smoothly by following these instructions:

- If you have a fixed disk, start DOS as you normally do. If you have version 4, press F3 if necessary to leave the Shell.

- If you don't have a fixed disk and are using version 4 of DOS on 5.25-inch diskettes, start DOS and replace your Startup diskette with your Working 1 diskette.

- If you don't have a fixed disk and are using version 4 of DOS on 3.5-inch diskettes (one or two diskettes, depending on their capacity), start DOS and leave your Startup diskette in drive A.

- If you don't have a fixed disk and are using version 3, start the computer with your copy of the system diskette in drive A. If necessary, enter the appropriate date and time so that DOS responds with the system prompt. If you are using IBM's version 3.3 on 5.25-inch diskettes, take the Startup diskette from drive A and put in the Operating diskette.

- If you don't have a fixed disk and are using a version of DOS earlier than 3.1, start the computer and leave your copy of the system diskette in drive A.

Don't worry about leaving your computer on while you read the text between examples; DOS is patient.

THE DIRECTORY

Recall from Chapter 1 that information stored on a disk is stored as a file. DOS automatically keeps and updates a list of every file you save on every disk you use. This list is called the *directory.*

If you create and save a new file, DOS adds it to the list. If you revise an old file, DOS keeps track of that, too. The directory eliminates the need for you to keep a separate record of everything you save on each disk. You can tell DOS you want to see the directory whenever DOS is displaying the system prompt.

The example in the next section serves the double purpose of showing you a directory and showing you around some of DOS itself. As you use the system more, you'll come to recognize many of the DOS files as DOS commands. Before you look at a directory, though, you should know a little about how DOS saves your files.

Whenever you create a file, you give it a descriptive name, called the *file name,* of up to eight characters. If you want, you can add a suffix, called the *extension,* of up to three more letters. (Chapters 4 and 5 present more on files.)

Whenever you ask DOS to show you the directory of a disk, DOS lists your files by file name (and extension, if there is one). It also shows you the size of each file, in units called *bytes,* and gives you the date and the time the file was either created or last changed; that's why DOS might prompt you for the date and time.

Note: A byte is the amount of storage required to hold one character in computer memory or on disk. Here are a few familiar items and their sizes, in bytes: the letters abcd, *4 bytes (1 byte per letter); the words* United States, *13 bytes (blanks count); a double-spaced, typewritten page, 1500 bytes; this book, 1,000,000 bytes (approximately).*

Depending on the version of DOS you're using and the type of drives you have (diskette, fixed disk, or both), your diskettes can hold anywhere from 163,840 to 1,474,560 bytes. Your fixed disk, if you have one, can hold 10,240,000 or 20,480,000— even 40,960,000 bytes or more. For convenience, large quantities are usually given in kilobytes (K) or megabytes (MB). One kilobyte equals 1024 bytes, and one megabyte equals 1000 kilobytes, so disk capacity can range from 160 K to 40 MB or more.

Because a large disk is capable of holding so much information, DOS has a way of letting you divide all this storage space into smaller, more manageable units called *subdirectories.* As you'll see in Chapter 8, ''A Tree of Files,'' creating subdirectories is the equivalent of placing dividers in a drawer of your filing cabinet. Although you won't deal with subdirectories until later in this book, if you have a fixed disk—and especially if you are using version 4—DOS itself probably resides in a subdirectory named *DOS.* This organization doesn't affect your work in any way, but does explain why your system prompt might be displayed as *C:\DOS>.* DOS is telling you, through the system prompt, that its attention is currently focused on the DOS subdirectory.

DISPLAYING THE DIRECTORY OF A DISK

To display the directory of the disk in the current drive, you simply type *dir*, the name of the Directory command. Type the command and press Enter (remember, if you don't have a fixed disk, your system prompt is A>):

```
C:\DOS>dir
```

If you have a fixed disk, the directory probably scrolled off the screen faster than you could read it. There are several ways to handle that, but one of the simplest uses what's called a command *parameter*. As you'll see in the next chapter, a command parameter lets you refine the action of a command. Here, with the Directory command, you can use a parameter typed as */p* to tell DOS to *pause* after displaying a screenful of directory entries. Try it; type:

```
C:\DOS>dir /p
```

This time, scrolling stops when the screen is full. Press any key to see the remainder of the directory listing, one screenful at a time.

In this example, you've seen a list of DOS files. Figure 3-1 shows the first screenful of file names you see on a computer with a fixed disk and IBM's version 4 of DOS.

```
Volume in drive C is FIXED DISK
Volume Serial Number is 1608-5A30
Directory of  C:\DOS

    .              <DIR>      10-16-89    6:05p
    ..             <DIR>      10-16-89    6:05p
DOSSHELL BAT         214      10-16-89    6:05p
COMMAND  COM       37637      06-17-88   12:00p
COUNTRY  SYS       12838      06-17-88   12:00p
DISKCOPY COM       10428      06-17-88   12:00p
DISPLAY  SYS       15741      06-17-88   12:00p
FDISK    COM       70151      06-17-88   12:00p
FORMAT   COM       22923      06-17-88   12:00p
KEYB     COM       14759      06-17-88   12:00p
KEYBOARD SYS       23360      08-03-88   12:00p
REPLACE  EXE       17199      06-17-88   12:00p
SYS      COM       11472      06-17-88   12:00p
ASSIGN   COM        5785      06-17-88   12:00p
ATTRIB   EXE       18247      06-17-88   12:00p
BASIC    COM        1065      06-17-88   12:00p
BASICA   COM       36285      06-17-88   12:00p
COMP     COM        9491      06-17-88   12:00p
DEBUG    COM       21606      06-17-88   12:00p
DISKCOMP COM        9889      06-17-88   12:00p
```

Figure 3-1. A partial directory display of IBM's version 4

If you're using diskettes or a different version of DOS, your directory listing differs—perhaps a little, perhaps a lot, but the display should include such file names as COMMAND.COM, DISKCOPY.COM, and FORMAT.COM. For comparison purposes, Figure 3-2 shows a directory of the Operating diskette for IBM's version of DOS 3.3. As you can see, the number and names of the files, their sizes, and the dates vary from one version of DOS to another. Don't be concerned. Such variations have no effect on the way you use DOS or the way DOS responds to commands.

Note: The Directory command is used in examples throughout the book. Unless stated otherwise, the IBM version 4 display is shown.

```
Volume in drive A has no label
Directory of  A:\

APPEND    EXE     5825    3-17-87   12:00p
ASSIGN    COM     1561    3-17-87   12:00p
ATTRIB    EXE     9529    3-17-87   12:00p
BACKUP    COM    31913    3-18-87   12:00p
BASIC     COM     1063    3-17-87   12:00p
BASICA    COM    36403    3-17-87   12:00p
CHKDSK    COM     9850    3-18-87   12:00p
COMMAND   COM    25307    3-17-87   12:00p
COMP      COM     4214    3-17-87   12:00p
DEBUG     COM    15897    3-17-87   12:00p
DISKCOMP  COM     5879    3-17-87   12:00p
DISKCOPY  COM     6295    3-17-87   12:00p
EDLIN     COM     7526    3-17-87   12:00p
FIND      EXE     6434    3-17-87   12:00p
FORMAT    COM    11616    3-18-87   12:00p
GRAFTABL  COM     6128    3-17-87   12:00p
GRAPHICS  COM     3300    3-17-87   12:00p
JOIN      EXE     8969    3-17-87   12:00p
LABEL     COM     2377    3-17-87   12:00p
MORE      COM      313    3-17-87   12:00p
PRINT     COM     9026    3-17-87   12:00p
RECOVER   COM     4299    3-18-87   12:00p
RESTORE   COM    34643    3-17-87   12:00p
SHARE     EXE     8608    3-17-87   12:00p
SORT      EXE     1977    3-17-87   12:00p
SUBST     EXE     9909    3-17-87   12:00p
TREE      COM     3571    3-17-87   12:00p
XCOPY     EXE    11247    3-17-87   12:00p
BASIC     PIF      369    3-17-87   12:00p
BASICA    PIF      369    3-17-87   12:00p
MORTGAGE  BAS     6251    3-17-87   12:00p
       31 File(s)      55296 bytes free
```

Figure 3-2. A directory display of IBM's version 3.3 Operating diskette

The lines at the top of the directory give information about the disk itself and are explained in detail in Chapter 6, ''Managing Your Diskettes.'' The last line shows the number of files and the number of bytes that are still unused.

Figure 3-3 shows a breakdown of one entry from a directory. The file name is DISKCOPY; note it is eight letters long, the maximum length of a DOS file name. The next item, COM, is the file's extension. The next item tells you the file is 10,428 bytes long—about the number of characters you see on seven double-spaced, typed pages. The final two entries give the date and time the file was either created or last changed.

Figure 3-3. A directory entry

SOME IMPORTANT KEYS

In the examples in the previous chapter, you used the standard typewriter portion of the keyboard—including the Backspace and Enter keys—to enter commands. Several other keys have important meanings to DOS; you'll find yourself using them frequently while you're using DOS. Figures 3-4 and 3-5 show where these keys are located on two common versions of the IBM keyboard.

Figure 3-4. Some important keys on the IBM PC and PC/XT keyboards

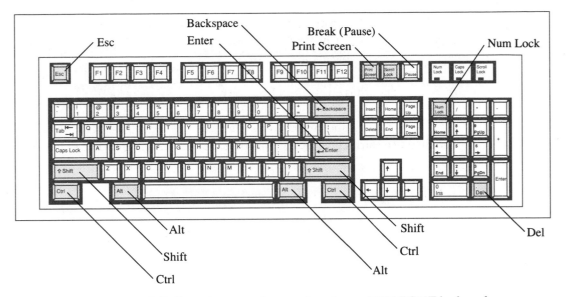

Figure 3-5. Some important keys on the enhanced IBM PC/AT keyboard

Shift

The Shift keys are labeled with an open arrow or the word *Shift*. Like the Shift keys on a typewriter, they have no effect by themselves; they shift the keyboard to upper-case letters and special characters.

Esc

Short for *Escape*. This key cancels a line you have typed. To see how it works, type several characters (but don't press Enter):

```
C:\DOS>Now is the time
```

To erase this line, you could repeatedly press the Backspace key; press the Escape key instead:

```
C:\DOS>Now is the time\
```

DOS displays a reverse slash (\) to indicate that the line was canceled, and moves the cursor to the beginning of the next line. DOS doesn't repeat the system prompt, but the cursor indicates it is still ready for you to type a command. Press the Enter key, and DOS displays the system prompt and the cursor on the next line:

```
C:\DOS>_
```

Pressing the Escape key is the quickest way to cancel a line you have typed.

Ctrl

Short for *Control*. This key has no effect by itself, but it is used like the Shift keys to change the effect of pressing another key. The combination of the Control key and some other key is represented in this book by Ctrl- followed by the other key. Ctrl-Break, for example, means "hold down the Control key, then press and release the Break key." The Control key combinations and what they do are described in a moment.

Num Lock

Short for *Numeric Lock*. This key does two things. It switches the effect of the keys in the calculator-style number pad at the right side of the keyboard back and forth between cursor movement and numbers. On the PC and PC/XT keyboard, it is also used in combination with the Control key to freeze the display. To test the first function, press Num Lock and then press the 4 key in the numeric pad several times:

```
C:\DOS>444_
```

The keys produce numbers on the screen. Now press Num Lock again and press the same 4 key you pressed before:

```
C:\DOS>44_
```

Pressing Num Lock a second time switched the keys to their cursor-movement functions. The 4 key is labeled with a left arrow in addition to the number 4; pressing it moves the cursor left, in the direction of the arrow, and erases a character just as the Backspace key does. Press Num Lock and the same 4 key again:

```
C:\DOS>444_
```

You switched back to numbers. Press Num Lock one more time to switch back to cursor movement, press Esc to cancel the line, and press the Enter key to return to the system prompt:

```
C:\DOS>444\
```

```
C:\DOS>_
```

You won't often use the arrow keys for cursor movement with DOS, but many application programs, such as word processors, require frequent cursor movements.

Break

This key is labeled either *Scroll Lock* and *Break* or *Pause* and *Break*. When labeled *Scroll Lock* and *Break* (as on the PC and PC/XT keyboard), this key has no effect on DOS by itself, but it is used with the Control key to cancel a command you have entered. If labeled *Pause* and *Break* (as on the PC/AT keyboard), this key temporarily pauses the display; when used with the Control key, it cancels a command.

Alt and Del

Short for *Alternate* and *Delete*. These keys have no effect on DOS by themselves but are used with the Control key to restart DOS.

PrtSc or Print Scrn

Short for *Print Screen*. This key is used with the Shift and Control keys to print the contents of the screen. You used Shift-PrtSc in the previous chapter; you'll use Ctrl-PrtSc, and see the difference, in a short while. (If you have an IBM PS/2 keyboard, you don't have to press Shift with PrtSc.)

CONTROL KEY FUNCTIONS

Figure 3-6 shows the effects produced by holding down the Control key and pressing another key. You'll probably use these combinations fairly often with DOS, so the next few topics show you examples of each combination. When you are being shown exactly what to type, the names of the keys are separated by hyphens and enclosed in angle brackets to represent pressing a Control key combination. Thus, when you see <Ctrl-Break> in a command, it means "press Ctrl-Break."

Before trying the examples, you should also note that DOS displays the Control key as the symbol ^ . DOS does not acknowledge all Control key commands on the screen, but when it does, it uses the symbol ^ in combination with a letter. Control-Break, for example, shows on the screen as ^C and can also be typed by holding down the Control key and typing the letter C.

Ctrl-Num Lock or Pause	Halts whatever the system is doing until you press another key. Typically used to freeze the display when information is scrolling by too fast or scrolling off the top of the screen. Can also be typed as Ctrl-S (Ctrl plus the letter S).
Ctrl-Break	Cancels whatever the system is doing. Use this when you really don't want the computer to continue what it's doing. Can also be typed as Ctrl-C (Ctrl plus the letter C).
Ctrl-PrtSc	Pressing this key combination once causes DOS to start printing every line as it is displayed; pressing Ctrl-PrtSc a second time stops simultaneous displaying and printing. Can also be typed as Ctrl-P (Ctrl plus the letter P).
Ctrl-Alt-Del	Restarts DOS. This combination is unique; no other keys can be used to do the same thing.

Figure 3-6. Control key combinations

Freezing the Display

As mentioned earlier, DOS lets you temporarily halt the display by pressing Ctrl-Num Lock or the Pause key. When you do this, the display remains frozen, giving you time to read it. To start the display moving again, you simply press any key.

To test this function, type the following to display the directory. When the entries start appearing on the screen, press Pause or Ctrl-Num Lock to freeze the display:

```
C:\DOS>dir
```

Press any key, and the display resumes. You can press Ctrl-Num Lock to stop and start the display as many times as you like, so you can view displays that are many screens long.

Pressing Ctrl-S has the same effect as pressing Ctrl-Num Lock.

Canceling a Command

If you enter a command and then change your mind or realize that you meant to enter some other command, you can cancel the command you entered by pressing Ctrl-Break. To test this function, type the Directory command again. This time, press Ctrl-Break when DOS begins to display the directory entries:

```
C:\DOS>dir

 Volume in drive C is FIXED DISK
 Volume Serial Number is 1608-5A30
 Directory of  C:\DOS

 .              <DIR>      01-04-80   12:01p
 ..             <DIR>      01-04-80   12:01p
 COMMAND   COM     37637 06-17-88   12:00p
 VDISK     SYS      6376 06-17-88   12:00p
 ANSI      SYS      9148 06-17-88   12:00p
 ENHDISK   SYS      1569 12-17-85   12:00p
 CLOCK     SYS      1462 12-17-85   12:00p
 FORMAT    COM     22923 06-17-88   12:00p
 CHKDSK    COM     17771 06-17-88   12:00p
 SYS       COM     11472 06-17-88   12:00p
 DISKCOMP COM^C

C:\DOS>_
```

Your display probably stopped somewhere else in the directory, but when you press Ctrl-Break, DOS stops what it is doing, displays ^C at the stopping point, and returns to the command level.

Pressing Ctrl-C has the same effect as pressing Ctrl-Break.

Printing and Displaying Simultaneously

In the previous chapter you printed the contents of the screen by pressing Shift-PrtSc. There's another way to print from the screen: Pressing Ctrl-PrtSc tells DOS to start printing everything it displays. DOS continues to print and display simultaneously until you press Ctrl-PrtSc again.

To test this function, make sure your printer is turned on, press Ctrl-PrtSc, then enter the Directory command:

```
C:\DOS><Ctrl-PrtSc>dir
```

DOS again displays the directory of the system disk, but this time each line is printed as it is displayed. (If you're using a LaserJet or similar printer, you might have to press Ctrl-P instead.)

The directory is displayed more slowly than when you use the Directory command alone, because DOS waits until a line is printed before displaying and printing the next line. You can cancel the Directory command before the complete directory is printed by pressing Ctrl-Break. Remember to press Ctrl-PrtSc as well, to end the simultaneous displaying and printing.

If you want to print something without printing the command that creates the display, type the command first, then press Ctrl-PrtSc, and then press Enter. For example, when you printed the directory in the preceding example, the Directory command was the first line printed. To avoid printing the command, type:

```
C:\DOS>dir<Ctrl-PrtSc>
```

Now printing begins with the first line of the directory; the Directory command isn't printed. Cancel the command by pressing Ctrl-Break.

Be sure to press Ctrl-PrtSc again to stop printing; otherwise, DOS continues to print everything it displays, even if you go on to an entirely different task.

Shift-PrtSc versus Ctrl-PrtSc

These two methods of printing from the screen work differently and have different uses. Shift-PrtSc prints everything on the screen and stops. Ctrl-PrtSc, as you just saw, alternates displaying and printing, line by line. If everything you want is on the screen, use Shift-PrtSc; it's faster. But if you want to keep a running record of a series of commands and responses, or you want to print something longer than one screenful, use Ctrl-PrtSc.

Ctrl-PrtSc is better for printing long displays, because you can press it once to tell DOS to start simultaneous displaying and printing. Then you simply enter a command—such as the Directory command—to create the display, and press Ctrl-PrtSc again when you want to stop printing. If you use Shift-PrtSc for printing displays more than one screen long, you have to display the first screen, print it, then display the second screen, print it, and so forth until everything you want has been printed.

Restarting the System

Suppose you find yourself in a situation where your computer is not responding as you think it should, or it complains about something you don't know how to handle, or you decide it would be best to scrap what you're doing and start over from the beginning. You don't have to turn the power switch off and on to restart your system; you can do it by pressing Ctrl-Alt-Del.

Try it. If you have version 4 and your Working 1 diskette is in drive A, replace it with your Startup diskette. If you're using IBM's version 3.3 with no fixed disk, first replace the Operating diskette in drive A with the Startup diskette.

Hold down both Ctrl and Alt and press Del.

The screen clears, the drive lights blink, the system beeps, and DOS is loaded just as it was when you turned the power on. Restarting with Ctrl-Alt-Del takes less time, though, because the computer doesn't test all its devices and memory as it does whenever you switch the power off and on. If you're using version 4 and the Shell appears, press F3 to leave the Shell.

A SHORT DIVERSION

The system prompt is an economical way for DOS to show you the current drive and to let you know that you can enter a command. But the combination of a letter (for the current drive) and the greater-than sign (>) is only one possible system prompt. An advanced DOS command, Prompt, lets you change the system prompt to almost anything you want.

For example, you might prefer a more courteous machine. Type the following and press Enter (< space > means press the spacebar):

```
C:\DOS>prompt May I help you?<space><Enter>
```

Now the system prompt isn't quite so cryptic:

```
May I help you? _
```

Each time DOS returns to the command level, it displays this polite phrase. Try it by pressing the Enter key once or twice to cause DOS to display the system prompt again. Although your new prompt looks quite different from A > (and actually conveys less information), the meaning is the same: DOS is at the command level, ready for you to enter a command.

To see just how much you can cram into the system prompt, type the following example as a single line (again, < space > means press the spacebar). Although the example is shown on two separate lines, don't press the Enter key until you come to < Enter > at the end of the second line:

```
May I help you? prompt The time is<space>$t$_The date is<space>
$d$_The current disk is<space>$n$_Your command:<space><Enter>
```

Now the system prompt is three lines of data followed by a request for a command:

```
The time is 16:26:03.54
The date is Thu 04-27-1989
The current disk is C
Your command: _
```

You would probably quickly tire of all this, but the exercise shows how much flexibility DOS gives you. You don't have to take advantage of it all, but it's there if you want it.

To return the system prompt to a more normal form, simply type the Prompt command by itself:

```
The time is 16:26:03.54
The date is Thu   04-27-1989
The current disk is C
Your command: prompt
```

Note: If your system prompt changed to C> instead of C:\DOS>, don't worry. Restart your computer, and your old system prompt will reappear.

CHAPTER SUMMARY

Each diskette has a directory that lists the name, extension, and size of each file, and the date and time the file was created or last changed. You can see the directory by typing *dir* and pressing Enter.

- The Escape key cancels a line you have typed.

- Pause or Ctrl-Num Lock freezes the display. Ctrl-S has the same effect.

- Ctrl-Break cancels a command. Ctrl-C has the same effect.

- Ctrl-PrtSc turns simultaneous displaying and printing on and off. Ctrl-P has the same effect.

- Ctrl-Alt-Del restarts DOS.

Now that you're more familiar with the keyboard, the next chapter gives you a closer look at diskettes and files.

CHAPTER

4

A LOOK AT FILES AND DISKETTES

T he computer's memory is temporary; it is cleared each time you turn off the computer. The only way you can save data permanently is to store the data in a file on a disk. When DOS needs data that is stored in a file, it reads the data from the disk into memory. If you change the data and want to keep the changed version, you must store the revised version on disk before turning off the system.

TYPES OF FILES

In general, a file contains either a program or data. A *program* is a set of instructions for the computer. *Data* is the text and numbers, such as a project proposal, a table of tax rates, or a list of customers, that the program needs to do your work.

Two types of files are important to your work: text files and command files. They are quite different, so it's important to look more closely at the kind of information these files contain and at how the files are used.

Text Files

Text files are data files that contain characters you can read (everyday letters, numbers, and symbols). Word-processing programs store their documents in text files, as does Edlin, the DOS text editor. Many files you use in your work with the computer—and all the files that you will create and use in this book—are text files.

The definition of a text file may seem self-evident at first, but it actually introduces you to an important characteristic of computer information storage. Your computer keeps information in two very different forms: One is text, the characters contained in text files; the other is machine-readable code, which looks meaningless to most people but is quite meaningful to computers.

Command Files

Command files contain the instructions DOS needs to carry out commands. These instructions can be a program, such as Diskcopy, or, as you will see in Chapter 12, "Creating Your Own Commands," they can be a series of DOS commands that you put together to perform a specific task, then store in a text file.

Not all DOS commands are stored in separate command files, however. Some commands, such as the Directory command, are built into the main body of DOS. When you load DOS into memory, you load these commands with it. When you want to use these commands, DOS has them on tap for immediate use—it does not need to look up a separate command file to carry them out.

These built-in commands are called *permanent,* or *internal,* commands. In contrast, the commands that are kept in command files until they are requested by you are called *temporary,* or *external,* commands. When you use a permanent command, you simply request the command and DOS carries it out. When you use a temporary command, DOS must load the command file from disk into memory before it can carry out the command.

An application program, such as a word processor, is stored in a command file; it stores your work, such as documents, in data files.

HOW FILES ARE NAMED

No matter the type of file, each file must have a file name. Recall that a file name can be up to eight characters long. You can use almost any character on the keyboard when you name your files, but it's a good idea to give your files names, such as BUDGET or LETTER2, that describe their contents.

To identify a file more completely, a three-character suffix called the file *extension* can be added to the file name; this suffix is separated from the file name by a period. So that you and DOS can tell your files apart, each file on a disk must have either a different name or a different extension; REPORT.JAN and REPORT.FEB, for example, are different files to DOS, even though their file names are the same.

Specifying the Drive

When you name a file in a command, DOS must know which drive contains the disk with the file on it. If you don't specify a drive letter, DOS looks on the disk in the current drive (the drive letter shown in the system prompt). If the disk containing the file is not in the current drive, you can precede the file name with the letter of the drive and a colon. For example, if you specify the file as *b:report.doc*, DOS looks for it on the disk in drive B.

PREPARING FOR THE EXAMPLES

The following pages show a number of examples to help you become more comfortable with files and diskettes. With DOS, as with most other computer applications, doing is often the easiest and most effective way of learning.

If you have a fixed disk, make sure the latch on drive A is open, turn on or restart the computer, and go through the startup routine until you see the system prompt (C:\DOS> or C>). (If you are using version 4 and the DOS Shell starts automatically, startup instructions from here on assume that you press F3 to leave the Shell.)

If your system doesn't have a fixed disk, start or restart your computer and go through the startup routine until you see the A> prompt. In addition, if you're using version 4 on 5.25-inch diskettes, replace the Startup diskette with the Working 1 diskette. Or, if you're using IBM's version 3.3, replace the system diskette with the Operating diskette.

Don't Worry About Memorizing

You'll use several commands in this chapter, but you needn't remember exactly how to use each one; all the commands are described in more detail in the remaining chapters of the book. The purpose of this chapter is to introduce you to files and diskettes.

QUALIFYING A COMMAND

Up to now, all the commands you have entered consisted of a single word or abbreviation, such as *time* or *dir*. Most commands, however, let you add one or more qualifiers to make the action more specific. These qualifiers are called *parameters*.

Some commands require parameters; others allow you to add parameters if you want. The Directory command, for example, does not require parameters, but it lets you add the name of the specific file you want to see; you'll use some such parameters in the following examples. The descriptions of the commands in later chapters show their parameters, both required and optional.

DISPLAYING SPECIFIC DIRECTORY ENTRIES

In the previous chapter you used the Directory command to display the directory entries of the files on a disk. You can display the directory entry of a single file, or the directory entries for a set of files, by adding a parameter to the Directory command.

Displaying the Directory Entry Of a Single File

To display the directory entry for a specific file, you simply type the file name (and its extension, if there is one) after the command name. For example, the command to copy the contents of one diskette to another is called Diskcopy. Its command file is DISKCOPY.COM. To display the directory entry for DISKCOPY.COM, type the following command, including the blank following the command name. (If you're not using a fixed disk, remember that your system prompt is A>, not C:\DOS.)

```
C:\DOS>dir diskcopy.com
```

DOS displays only the directory entry of the file you specified:

```
Volume in drive C is FIXED DISK
Volume Serial Number is 1608-5A30
Directory of  C:\DOS

DISKCOPY COM      10428 06-17-88  12:00p
        1 File(s)    14219264 bytes free

C:\DOS>
```

If the file you name isn't on the disk, or if you don't type the file name exactly as it is stored, DOS responds *File not found*.

Displaying the Directory Entries
Of a Set of Files

What if you remember most of a file name, or the file name but not the extension? DOS helps you out by giving you two wildcard characters, ∗ and ?, that you can substitute for actual characters in a file name. Like wild cards in a poker game, the wildcard characters can represent any other character. They differ only in that ? can substitute for one character, while ∗ can substitute for more than one character.

Suppose you remember only that a file's name begins with the letter F. It takes only a moment to check all the files that begin with F.

Use the DOS directory as an example. Type the following command:

```
C:\DOS>dir f*
```

DOS displays the directory entries of all file names that begin with F:

```
Volume in drive C is FIXED DISK
Volume Serial Number is 1608-5A30
Directory of  C:\DOS

FORMAT   COM     22932 06-17-88   12:00p
FDISK    COM     70151 06-17-88   12:00p
FIND     EXE      5983 06-17-88   12:00p
FASTOPEN EXE     16302 06-17-88   12:00p
FILESYS  EXE     11125 06-17-88   12:00p
         5 File(s)    14219264 bytes free
```

```
C:\DOS>
```

(This listing shows the names of all the DOS files that begin with F. If you're using DOS on diskettes, your list might differ, but you should see FORMAT.COM.)

Wildcard characters can simplify the task of keeping track of your files. Chapter 5, "Managing Your Files," includes several examples of using wildcard characters.

Now it's time to stop practicing and to create some files of your own.

PREPARING A DISKETTE FOR USE

Before DOS can store a file on a new diskette, it must prepare the diskette for use. This preparation, in which DOS writes certain information for its own use on the diskette, is called *formatting*. You tell DOS to do this formatting with the Format command. You'll need two formatted diskettes for the examples in this book. Now is a good time to format them, so get out two blank diskettes and two blank labels before proceeding.

Type the following:

```
C:\DOS>format b:
```

This command tells DOS to format the diskette in drive B.

Formatting a diskette erases any files that may be stored on it, so DOS gives you a chance to make sure you haven't put the wrong diskette in the specified drive by displaying a message, then waiting for you to type something:

```
Insert new diskette for drive B:
and press ENTER when ready . . . _
```

If you discover that you put in the wrong diskette, no problem: Just take out the wrong one and put in the right one before you press the Enter key.

If you can't find a diskette to format, and you want to cancel the command, again, no problem: You don't have to turn the system off; just press Ctrl-Break.

But you do want to format the diskette now. If you have one diskette drive, place a blank diskette in drive A and close the drive latch if necessary. If you have two diskette drives, place a blank diskette in drive B and close the latch.

Press Enter. DOS displays a message telling you formatting is in progress. Depending on your version of DOS, the message might be simply *Formatting...*, or it might be a constantly changing display that looks like this:

```
8 percent of disk formatted
```

or this:

```
Head:    0 Cylinder:      1
```

In any case, the light on the drive goes on, and DOS begins writing on the diskette. When DOS is finished, it tells you *Format complete*. If you have version 4, it then displays the message:

```
Volume label (11 characters, ENTER for none)? _
```

A volume label is a name you give a formatted disk to help identify it and the files it contains. The name can be up to 11 characters long, including blanks, but cannot include certain characters DOS reserves for special uses: characters such as a period (used between a file name and an extension), an asterisk or a question mark (used as wildcard characters), or a forward slash (used when typing command parameters).

You don't have to assign a volume label to a disk, but because DOS displays the volume label at the beginning of any directory listing you request, the few seconds you spend thinking up and typing a volume label when you format a disk can, in the long run, save you time by helping to identify what the disk contains. (If you don't have version 4, you can assign a volume label after formatting with the Label command; you'll find out about this in Chapter 6, "Managing Your Diskettes.")

If you have version 4, assign a volume label to the disk you just formatted. Type a simple, but descriptive name, such as:

```
Volume label (11 characters, ENTER for none)? examples 1
```

and press Enter.

In any version of DOS, you then see some information about the diskette, followed by a final message:

```
1213952 bytes total disk space
1213952 bytes available on disk

    512 bytes in each allocation unit
   2371 allocation units available on disk

Volume Serial Number is 0423-14EF

Format another (Y/N)?
```

The numbers shown are for the 1.2 MB diskette drive on the IBM PC/AT and compatible machines. Depending on the type of diskette drives you have and the version of DOS you're using, the total disk space in your report might be 1,457,664, or 1,213,952 (as shown), or 730,112, or 362,496, or 322,560, or 179,712, or 160,256 bytes.

The messages about allocation units and the volume serial number are provided by DOS beginning with version 4. Allocation units are groups of bytes used by DOS in storing information; the volume serial number is assigned as part of the formatting procedure. Neither is likely to be significant in your day-to-day use of DOS.

The final message, *Format another (Y/N)?*, means that DOS is now waiting for you to say whether you want to format another diskette. Type *y*. The message asking you to put the diskette in drive B and strike Enter is repeated, so go through the same process to format the second diskette. When DOS finishes, it asks you again whether you want to format another.

Now type *n*. DOS displays the system prompt (C:\DOS>), telling you the Format command is ended and that DOS is waiting for you to type another command.

You now have two formatted diskettes. It's time to put one of them to use by creating a file; if you removed the diskette you just formatted, put it in your diskette drive (drive B if you have two diskette drives).

CREATING A TEXT FILE

An easy way to create a text file is by using the DOS Copy command. As you might guess from its name, the Copy command can be used to make a copy of a file. It can also be used to copy characters from the keyboard into a file.

DOS refers to the parts of your computer, such as the keyboard, display, and printer, as *devices*. To DOS, devices, like files, have names. The keyboard is known to DOS as CON (for CONsole).

You are going to create a file by telling DOS to copy what you type from the keyboard onto the blank diskette in drive B.

Note: If you have one diskette drive, recall that DOS treats it as both drive A and drive B. In the remaining examples, DOS will sometimes display Insert diskette for drive A: *or* Insert diskette for drive B:, *followed by* and press any key when ready. *When you see this message, simply press the spacebar or any other key and continue with the example.*

To create a file named NOTE.DOC on the diskette in drive B, type the following example. End each line by pressing Enter; where you see a blank line, press Enter to tell DOS to insert an extra line:

```
C:\DOS>copy con b:note.doc
October 16, 1989

Dear Fred,
Just a note to remind you
that our meeting is at 9.

Jack
```

That's the end of the file. To tell DOS that it's the end of the file, press Ctrl-Z (hold down the Control key and press Z), then press Enter:

```
<Ctrl-Z><Enter>
```

When you press Ctrl-Z, DOS displays ^Z (the ^, remember, represents the Control key). After you press Enter, DOS acknowledges that it copied a file:

```
        1 File(s) copied
```

```
C:\DOS>_
```

To verify that the file is there, display the directory of the diskette in drive B:

```
C:\DOS>dir b:
```

Sure enough, NOTE.DOC is on the diskette:

```
 Volume in drive B is EXAMPLES 1
 Volume Serial Number is 0423-14EF
 Directory of  B:\

NOTE      DOC        94  10-16-89    2:05p
        1 File(s)    1213440 bytes free
```

```
C:\DOS>_
```

This method of creating a text file is quick and convenient, and is used in examples throughout the book.

Displaying a Text File

Because you can read the characters in text files, you'll often want to display one on the screen. It's even easier to display a text file than it is to create it. Just use the DOS Type command. To display your file, type the following:

```
C:\DOS>type b:note.doc
```

DOS displays each line and returns to the command level:

```
October 16, 1989

Dear Fred,
Just a note to remind you
that our meeting is at 9.

Jack

C:\DOS>_
```

This is the quickest way to see what's in a file; you'll probably use the Type command frequently. Displaying a file isn't always helpful, though, because not all files are text files; they don't all contain readable characters. See for yourself. If you're using version 4 on 5.25-inch diskettes without a fixed disk, place the diskette you labeled Working 2 in drive A. If you're using IBM's version 3.3 of DOS on 5.25-inch diskettes, place the Operating disk in drive A. If you're using any other version of DOS, make sure the system diskette is in drive A. Now type:

```
C:\DOS>type more.com
```

Yes, the display is correct. It's hard to tell from that jumble what is in the file, because the file contains a program stored in machine code, not text.

Printing a Text File

One of the main reasons you write documents, of course, is to have a printed copy. You can print your file by copying it to the printer. You've already copied from the keyboard to a disk. Now, copy from the disk to the printer. The printer is known to DOS as PRN. Make certain the printer is turned on, and type the following:

```
C:\DOS>copy b:note.doc prn
```

The file is printed. When you print a file, you'll probably want to position the paper by hand before you enter the command, so that the printing will begin where you want it to on the page.

There's an easier way, however, to print a file: the Print command.

Note: If you're using version 4 without a fixed disk, DOS needs the command file named PRINT.COM for this example. If you installed DOS with the Shell, PRINT.COM is on your Shell diskette. If you did not install the Shell and see the message Bad command or filename *when you try to print in this example, check each of your diskettes for PRINT.COM by inserting them in drive A and typing* dir print.com. *When you find the file, leave that disk in drive A.*

To print your file with the Print command, type the following:

```
C:\DOS>print b:note.doc
```

If DOS responds:

```
Name of list device [PRN]: _
```

press the Enter key. DOS displays one or both of the following messages and prints your file:

```
Resident part of PRINT installed

  B:\NOTE.DOC is currently being printed
```

```
C:\DOS>_
```

These messages are explained in more detail in Chapter 5, "Managing Your Files."

The Print command makes most printers advance to the next page after printing. Although this file is too short to show it, you can continue to use the system to do other work while the Print command is printing a file.

Copying a Text File

The Copy command is one of the more versatile DOS commands. You have already used it to create and print a text file. The Copy command also duplicates files.

To copy the file named NOTE.DOC into another file named LETTER.DOC, type:

```
C:\DOS>copy b:note.doc b:letter.doc
```

When you press Enter, DOS copies the file; then it acknowledges that it did so:

```
        1 File(s) copied
```

```
C:\DOS>_
```

Display the directory of the diskette in drive B again to verify the copy:

```
C:\DOS>dir b:
```

Now you have two text files:

```
 Volume in drive B is EXAMPLES 1
 Volume Serial Number is 0423-14EF
 Directory of  B:\

NOTE      DOC        94 10-16-89    2:05p
LETTER    DOC        94 10-16-89    2:05p
        2 File(s)     1212928 bytes free

C:\DOS>
```

If you wanted, you could make changes to one file and still have a copy of the original version on disk. You'll find the Copy command quite useful when you need several files that differ only slightly, or when you have several small files that can be combined in different ways to create other files: often-used paragraphs, for example, that can be recombined in different letters, contracts, or other documents.

Erasing a Text File

Just as you get rid of paper files, you can erase disk files. To erase NOTE.DOC from the diskette in drive B, type:

```
C:\DOS>erase b:note.doc

C:\DOS>_
```

Now check the directory one more time:

```
C:\DOS>dir b:

 Volume in drive B is EXAMPLES 1
 Volume Serial Number is 0423-14EF
 Directory of  B:\

LETTER    DOC          94 10-16-89    2:05p
         1 File(s)      1213440 bytes free

C:\DOS>_
```

It's gone.

SOME ADVANCED FEATURES

Several commands and features give you much greater control over the way DOS does its work. For example, you can:

- Sort lines of data—for example, sort alphabetically the list of directory entries produced by the Directory command.

- View a long display one screenful at a time, without having to freeze the display by pressing Ctrl-Num Lock or Pause.

- Tell DOS to send the results, or *output,* of a command to the printer instead of to the display, simply by adding a few characters to the command.

- Search lines of data for a series of characters.

The examples in this section give you a glimpse of these advanced features; the features are described in detail, with many additional examples, in later chapters.

You'll notice that these advanced features cause more disk activity and take a bit longer than the other DOS commands. That's because DOS creates temporary files to help it carry out the advanced features.

Sorting Lines of Data

You have probably arranged card files or lists in some sequence, such as alphabetic or numeric order. The Sort command sorts, or arranges, lines of data such as a list of names for you. To see how this works, sort the lines of the text file B:LETTER.DOC. (If you're using version 4 on 5.25-inch diskettes, put the Working 2 diskette in drive A.)

Type the following:

```
C:\DOS>sort < b:letter.doc
```

The less-than symbol (<) tells DOS to send a copy of the file B:LETTER.DOC to the Sort command, which then displays the lines of the file rearranged (sorted) into alphabetic order:

```
Dear Fred,
Jack
Just a note to remind you
October 16, 1989
that our meeting is at 9.

C:\DOS>_
```

Although you probably don't want to sort the lines of your letters, you can put whatever you like in a text file—for example, a list of customers or employees. The Sort command is a powerful addition to your kit of computer tools.

Viewing a Long Display
One Screenful at a Time

When you displayed a directory in Chapter 3, lines might have scrolled off the top of the screen because the display was too long to fit. You saw that you can freeze the display by pressing Ctrl-Num Lock or Pause. There's an easier way to stop scrolling: The More command displays one screenful, with — *More* — at the bottom of the screen, then waits for you to press any key to continue to the next screenful. Display the directory of the current disk again, this time using the More command. (If you're using IBM's version 3.3, place your copy of the Operating diskette in drive A.)

Type the vertical bar by holding down a Shift key and pressing the key labeled with a ¦ character:

```
C:\DOS>dir ¦ more
```

DOS displays the first screenful, but the last few lines aren't displayed yet (notice the — *More*— in the last line):

```
Volume in drive C is FIXED DISK
Volume Serial Number is 1608-5A30
Directory of  C:\DOS

.              <DIR>       10-16-89    6:05p
..             <DIR>       10-16-89    6:05p
DOSSHELL BAT         214 10-16-89    6:05p
COMMAND  COM       37637 06-17-88   12:00p
COUNTRY  SYS       12838 06-17-88   12:00p
DISKCOPY COM       10428 06-17-88   12:00p
DISPLAY  SYS       15741 06-17-88   12:00p
FDISK    COM       70151 06-17-88   12:00p
FORMAT   COM       22923 06-17-88   12:00p
KEYB     COM       14759 06-17-88   12:00p
KEYBOARD SYS       23360 08-03-88   12:00p
REPLACE  EXE       17199 06-17-88   12:00p
SYS      COM       11472 06-17-88   12:00p
ASSIGN   COM        5785 06-17-88   12:00p
ATTRIB   EXE       18247 06-17-88   12:00p
BASIC    COM        1065 06-17-88   12:00p
BASICA   COM       36285 06-17-88   12:00p
COMP     COM        9491 06-17-88   12:00p
DEBUG    COM       21606 06-17-88   12:00p
-- More --
```

To see the rest of the directory, press any key. If DOS once again displays — *More*— at the bottom of the screen, press Ctrl-Break to end the command and return to the system prompt.

The More command displays long output one screenful at a time, giving you a chance to view it all at your convenience.

Note: When you use the More command, you might see directory entries for files with odd names, such as 1106002B and 11060104 or %PIPE1.$$$ and %PIPE2.$$$. These are temporary files that DOS creates, then erases when it no longer needs them.

Sending Command Output to the Printer

In earlier examples, you printed the output of the Directory command by pressing Shift-PrtSc and Ctrl-PrtSc. There's a more direct way to print the output of a command: Simply follow the command with a greater-than symbol (>) and the name of the printer, PRN. To print the directory of the disk in the current drive, make sure the printer is turned on and type:

```
C:\DOS>dir > prn
```

If you don't want to wait for the whole directory to be printed, cancel the printing by pressing Ctrl-Break.

This same technique can be used to send the output of a command to some other device or to a file, by substituting the device name or file name for PRN.

Finding a Series of Characters in a File

How many times have you searched through a pile of letters or notes, looking for a particular item or reference? If you have to look through DOS files or the output of DOS commands, the Find command will do the looking for you. For example, suppose you want to see the directory entries of all DOS files with SK in their names. Try the following (the quotation marks tell DOS which letters—known technically as a *character string,* or just *string*—to look for).

If you don't have a fixed disk and are using version 4 on 5.25-inch diskettes, first make sure that your copy of the Working 2 diskette is in drive A. If you have version 3.3, make sure that the system (or Operating) diskette is in drive A. Type:

```
C:\DOS>dir | find "SK"
```

DOS displays only the entries with SK in their names (your list might differ):

```
DISKCOPY COM     10428 06-17-88   12:00p
FDISK    COM     70151 06-17-88   12:00p
DISKCOMP COM      9889 06-17-88   12:00p
CHKDSK   COM     17771 06-17-88   12:00p
VDISK    SYS      6376 06-17-88   12:00p

C:\DOS>
```

The Find command is even more useful when you use it to search for a series of characters in a text file. If a file contains a list of names and telephone numbers, for example, you can quickly display one particular entry, or all entries that contain a particular series of characters (such as an area code), or even all entries that *don't* contain a particular series of characters. Chapter 13, ''Taking Control of Your System,'' shows you how to create such an automated index of names and telephone numbers with nothing but DOS commands.

Combining Features

These advanced features of DOS can also be used together in a single command, giving you even more flexibility in controlling DOS. Combining these features makes it possible to do a great deal with just one command. For example, suppose you want to print the directory entries of all files on the disk in the current drive whose names include the letter F; further, you want the entries sorted according to the size of the files. Type the following:

```
C:\DOS>dir | find "F" | sort /+16 > prn
```

This whole command translates easily into: Look at the directory, find all files with the letter F in their names, sort those files starting at the 16th column (where the size begins), and send the results to the printer. DOS does as it is told; it prints the directory entries of the sorted files in order, from the smallest (5983 bytes) to the largest (70151 bytes):

```
FIND      EXE      5983 06-17-88   12:00p
NLSFUNC   EXE      6910 06-17-88   12:00p
GRAFTABL  COM     10271 06-17-88   12:00p
FILESYS   EXE     11125 06-17-88   12:00p
FASTOPEN  EXE     16302 06-17-88   12:00p
IFSFUNC   EXE     21653 08-03-88   12:00p
FORMAT    COM     22923 06-17-88   12:00p
FDISK     COM     70151 06-17-88   12:00p
         66 File(s)    14213120 bytes free
```

(Your list might differ, but the files should still be sorted from smallest to largest.)

You may rarely search your directories this carefully, but such combinations make DOS a powerful tool for handling text files.

CHAPTER SUMMARY

This chapter concludes the portion of the book designed to give you a feel for running DOS, including some of its advanced features. The key points to remember include:

- The computer's memory is cleared each time you turn the system off. To save your work permanently, you must store it in a file on a disk.

- A text file contains ordinary characters you can read.

- A command file contains instructions that DOS uses to carry out a command.

- A file name can be up to eight characters long; you can add an extension of up to three characters, separated from the file name by a period.

- Each file on a disk must have a different name or a different extension.

The remainder of the book shows you how to use DOS to manage your files, disks, and devices; use the text editor; and create your own commands.

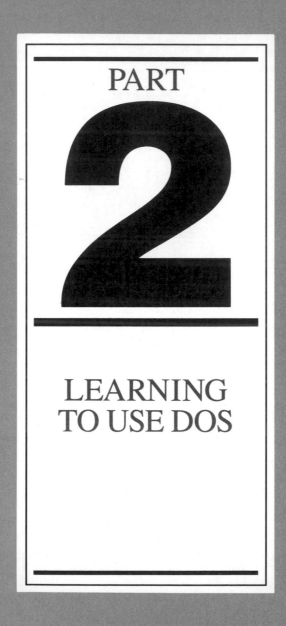

PART

2

LEARNING
TO USE DOS

P art 2 shows you how to use DOS to manage your work with the computer. The chapters in Part 2 include extensive examples that use real-life situations to illustrate each DOS command, but the information is organized so that you can quickly find a particular topic to refresh your memory.

The material in these chapters covers all versions of DOS. Chapter 9 covers the use of a fixed disk in detail.

Chapters 12 through 16 show you how to use the advanced features of DOS. Chapter 17 introduces you to the version 4 DOS Shell.

CHAPTER
5
MANAGING YOUR FILES

T he previous chapters defined a file as a named collection of related information stored on a disk, and showed you several ways to create, copy, display, print, and otherwise work with your computer files. This chapter describes the DOS filing system in detail, showing you more about how files are named and how you can use DOS to manage your computer files.

Note: A few of the examples in the remaining chapters of this book may look familiar, because they repeat some of the examples in Chapters 2, 3, and 4. This repetition is intentional, so that Chapters 5 through 16 present a complete guide to DOS commands. You won't have to refer back to Chapters 2, 3, or 4 for command descriptions.

THE DOS FILE COMMANDS

To be useful, a filing system—whether it contains disk files or paper files—must be kept orderly and up to date. Using the DOS file commands, you can manage your disk files much as you manage your paper files. This chapter covers the DOS commands you use most often on a day-to-day basis. It shows you how to:

- Display specific directory entries with the Directory command.
- Display a file with the Type command.
- Copy a file with the Copy command.
- Combine files with the Copy command.
- Send a copy of a file to a device with the Copy command.
- Remove a file from a disk with the Erase command.
- Change the name of a file with the Rename command.
- Compare two files with the Compare command.
- Print a file with the Print command.
- Control whether a file can be changed with the Attribute command.

FILE NAMES AND EXTENSIONS

As Chapter 4 pointed out, files are named so that you (and DOS) can tell them apart; each file on a disk must have a different name. You know that a file name can be up to eight characters long, made up of any letters or numbers; you can also use the following symbols:

    ` ~ ! @ # $ % ^ & ( ) _ - { } ´

You can add a suffix—called an *extension*—to the file name to describe its contents more precisely. The extension can be up to three characters long and can include any of the characters that are valid for the file name. It must be separated from the name by a period. The extension distinguishes one file from another just as the name does: REPORT and REPORT.JAN, for example, are two different files, as are REPORT.JAN and REPORT.FEB. Figure 5-1 shows some valid and invalid file names.

These File Names Are Valid	These Are Invalid...	Because
B	1988BUDGET	Name too long
87BUDGET	BUDGET.1988	Extension too long
BUDGET.87	.88	No file name
BUDGET.88	SALES 87.DAT	Blank not allowed
BDGT(88)	$1,300.45	Comma not allowed

Figure 5-1. Some valid and invalid file names

Try to make file names and extensions as descriptive as possible. A short file name might be easy to type, but you can have difficulty remembering what the file contains if you haven't used it for a while. The more descriptive the name, the more easily you can identify the contents of the file.

Special Names and File Name Extensions

Some names and file name extensions have special meanings to DOS. As you'll see in Chapter 7, ''Managing Your Devices,'' DOS refers to the parts of your computer system by certain reserved names known as *device names*. The keyboard and screen, for example, are named CON, and the system clock is called CLOCK$. You cannot use any of these device names as file names.

Similarly, certain file name extensions have special meanings to DOS. These extensions either are created by DOS or cause DOS to assume the file contains a particular type of program or data. You should avoid giving files any of these extensions. A number of the most important ones are listed in Figure 5-2 on the following page.

Some application programs also use special extensions. For example, Microsoft Word, the Microsoft word processor, uses DOC to identify a document, BAK to identify a backup version of a document, and STY to identify a file that contains a style sheet of print specifications. Again, avoid using extensions that have special meaning for your application programs; these extensions are usually listed in the documentation that comes with each program.

Name	Meaning to DOS
BAS	Short for *BASIC*. Contains a program written in the BASIC programming language. You run the program while using BASIC.
BAT	Short for *batch*. Identifies a text file you can create, which contains a set of DOS commands that are run when you type the name of the file.
COM	Short for *Command*. Identifies a command file that contains a program DOS runs when you type the file name.
EXE	Short for *Executable*. Like COM, identifies a command file that contains a program DOS runs when you type the file name.
SYS	Short for *System*. Identifies a file that can be used only by DOS.

Figure 5-2. Some special DOS file name extensions

Specifying the Drives

You can tell DOS to look for a file in a specific drive by typing the drive letter and a colon before the file name. If you specify a file as *b:report*, for example, DOS looks in drive B for a file named REPORT; if you specify the file as *report*, DOS looks for the file in the current drive.

PREPARING FOR THE EXAMPLES

If your system isn't running, start it (from the fixed disk if you're using one). If you do not have a fixed disk and are using version 4 on 5.25-inch diskettes, replace the Startup diskette with the Working 1 diskette. If you are using IBM's version 3.3 on a system without a fixed disk, replace the Startup diskette with the Operating diskette.

You need one empty, formatted diskette for the examples in this chapter. Put the formatted diskette in the diskette drive (drive B if you have two diskette drives), and type the following to create a sample text file named REPORT.DOC on the diskette; be certain to press Enter at the end of each line. Where you see ^Z, either hold down the key labeled Ctrl and press Z or press the function key labeled F6:

```
C:\DOS>copy con b:report.doc
This is a dummy file.
^Z
```

If you have only one diskette drive, DOS asks you to make sure the correct diskette is in the diskette drive:

```
Insert diskette for drive B: and press any key when ready
```

The correct diskette is in the drive, so just press the spacebar or any other key. DOS acknowledges:

```
1 File(s) copied
```

```
C:\DOS>_
```

Change the current drive to B by typing:

```
C:\DOS>b:
```

DOS changes the system prompt to show that drive B is now the current drive:

```
B:\>_
```

Now you're ready to create some more sample files.

Creating the Sample Files

Type the following Copy commands (described in detail later in this chapter) to create some other sample files.

```
B:\>copy report.doc report.bak
        1 File(s) copied

B:\>copy report.doc bank.doc
        1 File(s) copied

B:\>copy report.doc budget.jan
        1 File(s) copied

B:\>copy report.doc budget.feb
        1 File(s) copied

B:\>copy report.doc budget.mar
        1 File(s) copied
```

Now check the directory.

```
B:\>dir
```

It should list six files:

```
Volume in drive B has no label
Volume Serial Number is 1A2C-13F5
Directory of  B:\

REPORT    DOC       23 10-16-89    9:16a
REPORT    BAK       23 10-16-89    9:16a
BANK      DOC       23 10-16-89    9:16a
BUDGET    JAN       23 10-16-89    9:16a
BUDGET    FEB       23 10-16-89    9:16a
BUDGET    MAR       23 10-16-89    9:16a
        6 File(s)     1210880 bytes free
```

Remember, the time and date in your list will be different, but the file names and sizes (23 bytes) should be the same.

WILDCARD CHARACTERS

To make it easier to manage your disk files, most file commands let you use wildcard characters to handle several files at once. That way, when you want to do the same thing to several files—change their names, perhaps, or erase them—you don't have to enter a separate command for each file. You can use wildcard characters to tell DOS you mean a set of files with similar names or extensions. Just as a wild card in a poker game can represent any other card in the deck, a wildcard character can represent any other character in a file name or extension.

There are two wildcard characters, the asterisk (*) and the question mark (?). The following examples use the Directory command to illustrate ways you can use wildcard characters to specify groups of files.

Using the Asterisk Wildcard Character: *

The asterisk makes it easy to carry out commands on sets of files with similar names or extensions; it can represent up to all eight characters in a file name or up to all three characters in an extension. If you use the asterisk to represent the name or extension, you are specifying all file names or all extensions.

The following examples illustrate several ways to use the asterisk to find selected directory entries. You can use the asterisk with other DOS commands as well.

To specify all files named BUDGET, regardless of extension, type the following:

```
B:\>dir budget.*
```

DOS displays the directory entry of each sample file named BUDGET, regardless of its extension:

```
Volume in drive B has no label
Volume Serial Number is 1A2C-13F5
Directory of  B:\

BUDGET    JAN          23 10-16-89    9:16a
BUDGET    FEB          23 10-16-89    9:16a
BUDGET    MAR          23 10-16-89    9:16a
         3 File(s)      1210880 bytes free
```

To specify all file names beginning with B, type the following:

```
B:\>dir b*
```

If you don't specify an extension, the Directory command displays the entry for each file that matches the name, regardless of extension (it's the equivalent of specifying the extension as ∗). There are four such files:

```
Volume in drive B has no label
Volume Serial Number is 1A2C-13F5
Directory of  B:\

BANK      DOC      23 10-16-89    9:16a
BUDGET    JAN      23 10-16-89    9:16a
BUDGET    FEB      23 10-16-89    9:16a
BUDGET    MAR      23 10-16-89    9:16a
        4 File(s)     1210880 bytes free
```

To specify all files with the same extension, regardless of name, you replace the name with ∗. For example, to specify each file with the extension DOC, type:

```
B:\>dir *.doc
```

DOS displays just those entries:

```
Volume in drive B has no label
Volume Serial Number is 1A2C-13F5
Directory of  B:\

REPORT    DOC      23 10-16-89    9:16a
BANK      DOC      23 10-16-89    9:16a
        2 File(s)     1210880 bytes free
```

Using the Question Mark Wildcard Character: ?

The question mark replaces only one character in a file name or extension. You'll probably use the asterisk more frequently, using the question mark only when one or two characters in the middle of a name or extension vary.

To see how the question mark works, type the following:

```
B:\>dir budget.?a?
```

This command specifies all files named BUDGET that have extensions beginning with any character, followed by the letter *a*, and ending with any character. DOS displays two entries:

```
Volume in drive B has no label
Volume Serial Number is 1A2C-13F5
Directory of  B:\

BUDGET    JAN      23 10-16-89    9:16a
BUDGET    MAR      23 10-16-89    9:16a
        2 File(s)     1210800 bytes free
```

A Warning About Wildcard Characters

Be careful using wildcard characters with commands that can change files. Suppose you spent several days entering a year's worth of budget data into 12 files named BUDGET.JAN, BUDGET.FEB, BUDGET.MAR, and so on. On the same disk you also have three files you don't need named BUDGET.OLD, BUDGET.TST, and BUDGET.BAD. The disk is getting full, so you decide to delete the three unneeded files. It's 2 A.M., you're tired, and you're in a hurry, so you quickly type *erase budget.** and press Enter. You have told DOS to do more than you wanted.

You may realize immediately what you have done, or it may not dawn on you until you try to use one of the 12 good budget files and DOS replies *File not found.* You display the directory; there isn't a single file named BUDGET, because you told DOS to erase them all.

With commands that can change a file (Erase or Copy), use wildcard characters with extreme caution.

DISPLAYING DIRECTORY ENTRIES

As you have seen, the Directory command (dir) displays entries from the directory that DOS keeps on each disk. Each entry includes the name and extension of the file, its size in bytes, and the date and time it was created or last updated. You can use the Directory command to display all entries, or just the entries of selected files.

In the descriptions of the commands here and throughout the remaining chapters, you are shown the general form of the command—the name of the command and most or all its parameters—before you try the examples. If a parameter has an exact form, such as /W, the form is shown. If a parameter is something you specify, such as a file name, it is named and shown enclosed in angle brackets: for example, <filename>.

The Directory command has three qualifiers, or parameters: filename, /W, and /P. Written out, the command format, including the parameters, looks like this:

dir <filename> /W /P

When using the Directory command, if you:

- Include a <filename>, for example, *dir budget.jan*, DOS searches the disk in the current drive and displays the entry for that file. If DOS does not find the file, it displays *File not found.*

- Include both a drive letter and a <filename>, for example, *dir b:budget.jan*, DOS displays the directory entry for the file you specify from the disk in the drive you specify.

- Include a <filename> with wildcard characters, DOS displays the entries for all files whose name and extension match the wildcard characters; for example, you used *dir budget.** earlier to display the entries for BUDGET.JAN, BUDGET.FEB, and BUDGET.MAR.

- Omit a <filename>, but include a drive letter, for example, *dir b:*, DOS displays all the entries from the disk in the drive you specify.

- Omit a <filename>, for example, *dir*, DOS displays all directory entries on the disk in the current drive.

Because a list of directory entries can be quite long, the Directory command includes two parameters you can use to keep the list from scrolling off the screen:

- /W (Wide) tells DOS to display only the file names and extensions in five columns across the screen. This display contains less information than a complete directory listing, because it omits the file sizes, dates, and times, but it makes a long list of entries more compact.

- /P (Pause) tells DOS to display the entries one screenful at a time; a message at the bottom of the screen tells you to press any key to continue.

Examples of Displaying Directory Entries

Because you have already used the Directory command several times, only the options are shown here. First, use the /W parameter to see a wide directory display showing the files on your sample diskette. Type:

```
B:\>dir /w
```

DOS arranges just the name and extension of each file in five columns across the screen (only three of the five columns are shown here):

```
Volume in drive B has no label
Volume Serial Number is 1A2C-13F5
Directory of  B:\

REPORT   DOC     REPORT   BAK     BANK     DOC...
BUDGET   MAR
         6 File(s)      1210880 bytes free
```

Your sample diskette doesn't contain enough files to show how many file names a wide directory display can contain, so the following illustration shows a wide listing for part of a much longer directory. (This directory shows some DOS version 4 files as they are stored on a fixed disk; again, only three of the five columns are shown.)

```
Volume in drive C is FIXED DISK
Volume Serial Number is 1608-5A30
Directory of  C:\DOS
 .                  . .                DOSSHELL BAT...
DISKCOPY COM    DISPLAY  SYS    FDISK    COM...
KEYBOARD SYS    REPLACE  EXE    SYS      COM...
BASIC    COM    BASICA   COM    COMP     COM...
EDLIN    COM    FILESYS  EXE    FIND     EXE...
LABEL    COM    MEM      EXE    MODE     COM...
SHARE    EXE    SORT     EXE    SUBST    EXE...
CHKDSK   COM    PCIBMDRV MOS    PCMSDRV  MOS...
SHELL    CLR    SHELL    HLP    SHELL    MEU...
DOSUTIL  MEU    ANSI     SYS    APPEND   EXE...
 .
 .
 .
        66 File(s)    13006848 bytes free
```

Such a display doesn't contain as much information as the standard directory display, but it packs a lot of entries onto the screen. The wide format is particularly handy when all you want is a quick look at the names of the files on a crowded disk.

Pausing the Directory Display

To display the directory of a disk one screenful at a time, you use the /P option. DOS displays the first screenful of entries, followed by either *Press any key to continue...* or *Strike a key when ready...*, depending on your version of DOS. To see the next screenful, press any key. This option lets you view the entire directory without using Ctrl-Num Lock or Pause to freeze the display periodically.

Your sample disk contains less than one screenful of file names, but you can try using the /P parameter to list your DOS files.

If you are using DOS from a fixed disk, try either of these commands (they differ only in ensuring that you see a listing of DOS files):

    B:\>dir c: /p

or:

    B:\>dir c:\dos /p

If you have two diskette drives and are using DOS from diskettes, try typing:

    B:\>dir a: /p

Depending on your version of DOS, your DOS diskette may or may not contain more than a screenful of files; if it does, you see the pause message described above and can continue the display by pressing any key. If you do not see the message, keep this parameter in mind for a later time when you need to see a listing of all the files on a crowded disk, one screenful at a time.

DISPLAYING A FILE

Many of the files you use are text files, and there will be times when you want to check the contents of a file but don't need a printed copy. DOS gives you a quick way to see what's in a file: the Type command. (The name Type is a carryover from the days when most computers had only typewriter-like consoles.)

When you use the Type command, DOS displays the file without stopping; if the file is longer than one screenful and you want to read the entire file, freeze the display by pressing Ctrl-Num Lock or Pause.

The Type command has one parameter:

type <filename>

<filename> is the name of the file to be displayed. The Type command displays just one file at a time, so you can't use wildcard characters in the file name. If you do use a wildcard character, DOS displays *Invalid filename or file not found* and returns to command level. If the file you name doesn't exist, DOS displays *File not found* followed by the file name you typed and, again, returns to command level.

An Example of Displaying a File

To display the file named REPORT.DOC on the diskette in the current drive, verify that your sample disk is in drive B and type:

```
B:\>type report.doc
```

DOS displays the file:

```
This is a dummy file.

B:\>
```

You'll probably use the Type command frequently to check your text files.

MAKING COPIES OF FILES

Just as you sometimes make copies of your paper files, you'll find yourself needing copies of your disk files.

You may want to share a file with a colleague who has a computer, you may want to alter the copy slightly to produce a different version, or you may want to store a copy for safekeeping. The Copy command can make a copy of a file on the same disk (with a different file name) or on a different disk (with any valid file name).

When used to make copies of files, the Copy command has two major parameters, <file1> and <file2>. The format of the Copy command is:

copy <file1> <file2>

<file1> is the name of the file to be copied (the *source* file) and <file2> is the name of the copy to be made (the *target* file). You can use wildcard characters to copy a set of files.

Note: Three additional, seldom-used parameters (/A, /B, and /V) are described in Appendix F, the DOS command reference.

When copying files, if you:

- Specify a <file1> (including the drive letter) that is not on the disk in the current drive and omit <file2>, DOS copies <file1> to the disk in the current drive and gives the copy the same name as the original. Example (if the current drive is B): *copy a:report.mar.*

- Specify only a drive letter as <file2>, the file is copied from the disk in the current drive to the disk in the drive you specify and is given the same name as <file1>. Example: *copy report.feb a:.*

- Specify a <file1> that doesn't exist, DOS responds by displaying the file name you typed, followed by *File not found,* followed by the name you typed for <file1> and *0 File(s) copied,* and returns to command level.

- Specify a <file2> that doesn't exist, DOS creates it.

- Specify a <file2> that does exist, DOS replaces its contents with <file1>. This is the same as erasing the existing target file, so be careful not to give the target the same name as an existing file you want to keep.

The following practice session illustrates different ways to copy files; it also indicates the type of situation in which you might want to use each form of the command.

Examples of Copying Files

You want to change a document you already have on disk, but you want to keep the original, as well as the changed version. For example, to make a copy of the file REPORT.DOC on the same diskette and to name the copy RESULTS, type:

```
B:\>copy report.doc results
```

DOS acknowledges *1 File(s) copied.*

To verify that both files, REPORT.DOC and RESULTS, are on the diskette, display the directory by typing:

```
B:\>dir
```

DOS now shows seven files on the diskette:

```
Volume in drive B has no label
Volume Serial Number is 1A2C-13F5
Directory of  B:\

REPORT    DOC        23 10-16-89    9:16a
REPORT    BAK        23 10-16-89    9:16a
BANK      DOC        23 10-16-89    9:16a
BUDGET    JAN        23 10-16-89    9:16a
BUDGET    FEB        23 10-16-89    9:16a
BUDGET    MAR        23 10-16-89    9:16a
RESULTS              23 10-16-89    9:16a
         7 File(s)     1210368 bytes free
```

Any time you want to verify the results of an example, use the Directory command to see what files are on the diskette.

Suppose you want to copy a file from another diskette and store it, under the same file name, on the diskette in the current drive.

For example, your current drive is drive B. To copy a file from a different drive to the diskette in drive B, all you need to specify is the drive letter and name of the source file, because DOS assumes you want to copy the source file to the disk in the current drive and give the target file the same name.

DOS includes a number of external command files, including FORMAT.COM, the file for the Format command. Copy FORMAT.COM to the disk in the current drive. If you have a fixed disk and do not know where the FORMAT.COM file is stored, type:

```
B:\>dir c:\dos\format.com
```

If DOS responds with a directory listing for the file, type:

```
B:\>copy c:\dos\format.com
```

If DOS responds *File not found*, try:

```
B:\>dir c:\format.com
```

and then type:

```
B:\>copy c:\format.com
```

(If DOS responds *File not found* to both of these commands, you can use the Change Directory command described in Chapter 8, ''A Tree of Files,'' to search for FORMAT.COM. It's not necessary, however; simply read these examples and remember their use for another time.)

If you're using DOS from diskettes, use the Directory command to check the diskette in drive A for the file named FORMAT.COM. When the appropriate DOS diskette is in drive A, type:

```
B:\>copy a:format.com
```

DOS copies FORMAT.COM to the diskette in drive B and gives it the same name.

Now return to the files on your sample diskette. Suppose you want to change a file and store the new version under the same file name and on the same diskette as the original, but be able to distinguish between the two versions. Simply make a copy of the file on the same diskette, with the same file name but a different extension. You can use the asterisk wildcard character to tell DOS to use the same file name. For example, to make a copy of BUDGET.MAR and call it BUDGET.APR, type the following:

```
B:\>copy budget.mar *.apr
```

DOS acknowledges that it copied one file.

You have several files named REPORT stored on disk. Suppose you want to keep the originals, but make copies of them all for a new project; to avoid confusion, you want to give the copies a new file name but keep the same extension. For example, to make a copy of each file named REPORT, giving each copy the name FORECAST, type the following:

```
B:\>copy report.* forecast.*
```

DOS displays the name of each source file as it makes the copies:

```
REPORT.DOC
REPORT.BAK
        2 File(s) copied
```

You can copy all the files on a diskette by specifying the source file as *.* and specifying the target as just a drive letter. This procedure is not the same as copying the diskette with the Diskcopy command; the difference is explained under the heading ''Copying a Complete Diskette'' in Chapter 6, ''Managing Your Diskettes.''

In addition to the Copy command, version 3.2 of DOS introduced two additional commands for copying files selectively: Replace, which lets you copy only files that already exist on the target disk; and Xcopy, which lets you copy only files that haven't been backed up. Both of these commands are described in Chapter 9, ''Managing Your Fixed Disk.''

SENDING FILES TO DEVICES

In Chapter 4, you printed a file by using the Copy command to send a copy of the file to the printer. You can also send a copy of a file to any other output device. If, for example, you copy a file to a communications connection, or *port,* on the computer, the file goes to whatever device is attached to the port—such as a telecommunications line to another computer.

When it is used to send a copy of a file to an output device, the Copy command has two parameters:

copy <filename> <device>

<filename> is the name of the file to be sent; <device> is the name of the device to which the file is to be sent.

Be sure <device> exists. If you try to send a file to a device that doesn't exist or isn't ready, DOS might stop running. You won't hurt anything, but you'll have to restart the system.

An Example of Sending Files to a Device

To send a copy of each sample file with the extension DOC to the printer, make certain your printer is turned on and type:

```
B:\>copy *.doc prn
```

DOS displays the name of each file as it sends the file to the printer:

```
REPORT.DOC
BANK.DOC
FORECAST.DOC
         1 File(s) copied
```

The files are printed with no separation between them. DOS reports only one file copied because, in effect, only one output file was created: the printed copy of the three files.

COMBINING FILES

Sometimes, it's useful to combine several files. Perhaps you have several short documents, and you decide it would be easier and more convenient to work with one document that includes all the shorter ones. If you have several sets of files with similar names or extensions, you can combine each set into a new file, creating several new files. The Copy command lets you copy several files into a new file without destroying the original versions.

When it is used to combine files, the Copy command has two parameters:

copy <source> <target>

<source> represents the files to be combined. You can use wildcard characters to name the source files to be combined, or you can list several file names, separating them with a plus sign (+). If any file in the list doesn't exist, DOS goes on to the next name without telling you the file doesn't exist.

<target> represents the file that results from combining the source files. If you specify a target, DOS combines the source files into the target file. If you don't specify a target but do specify individual source files, DOS combines all the source files into the first source file in the <source> list, changing its contents.

Examples of Combining Files

Suppose you have two files you want to use as the basis for a single new file, but you want to keep the originals intact. For example, to combine the files BANK.DOC and REPORT.DOC into a new file named BANKRPT.DOC, type:

```
B:\>copy bank.doc+report.doc bankrpt.doc
```

DOS displays the names of the source files as it copies them:

```
BANK.DOC
REPORT.DOC
        1 File(s) copied
```

Again, DOS reports one file copied because the command created only one file.

You can copy several files into an existing file. To combine BUDGET.JAN, BUDGET.FEB, and BUDGET.MAR into the first file, BUDGET.JAN, type:

```
B:\>copy budget.jan+budget.feb+budget.mar
```

DOS displays the name of each source file as it copies:

```
BUDGET.JAN
BUDGET.FEB
BUDGET.MAR
        1 File(s) copied
```

Now, suppose you've been keeping monthly budget files. It's the end of the year. You still need separate monthly files for comparison with next year's figures, but right now, you want to work with all the files together. To combine all the files named BUDGET into a file named ANNUAL.BGT, type:

```
B:\>copy budget.* annual.bgt
```

DOS responds:

```
BUDGET.JAN
BUDGET.FEB
BUDGET.MAR
BUDGET.APR
        1 File(s) copied
```

Or, suppose you want to combine pairs of files with the same file names, but different extensions. You can combine them under the same file names, with new extensions, and end up with both the original and combined versions.

If you have entered all the examples, among the files on the diskette in drive B are REPORT.DOC and REPORT.BAK, FORECAST.DOC, and FORECAST.BAK. To combine each pair of files with the same name and the extensions DOC and BAK into a single file with the same name and the extension MIX, type:

```
B:\>copy *.bak+*.doc *.mix
```

DOS displays the names of the files as it copies them:

```
REPORT.BAK
REPORT.DOC
FORECAST.BAK
FORECAST.DOC
        2 File(s) copied
```

This time DOS reports two files copied because the command created two files: REPORT.MIX and FORECAST.MIX.

ERASING FILES

Just as you have to clean out a file drawer once in a while, you'll occasionally have to clear your disks of files you no longer need. The Erase command (you can type it either as *erase* or as *del*, for *delete*) erases one or more files from a disk.

The Erase command has two parameters:

erase <filename> /P

<filename> is the name of the file to be erased. If you use wildcard characters, DOS erases all files that match <filename>. If the file doesn't exist, DOS displays *File not found* and returns to command level.

/P tells DOS to prompt you for verification before deleting the file. If you use wildcard characters to delete more than one file, DOS prompts you to verify deletion of each file. (Version 4 only)

Warning: Whenever you type an Erase command that uses wildcard characters, use the /P parameter or double-check the command on the screen before you press the Enter key. If you don't use these precautions, you don't get a second chance. If your version of DOS doesn't include the /P parameter, make sure you have specified the correct drive letter (if necessary), file name, and extension; be certain that you know exactly which files will be erased and that you want all of them to be erased.

There is only one exception to this warning: If you tell DOS to erase all the files in a directory by typing erase *.*, *DOS prompts* All files in directory will be deleted! Are you sure (Y/N)? *before erasing the files. DOS erases the files only if you respond* y. *(Versions earlier than 4 just ask* Are you sure (Y/N)?*)*

Examples of Erasing Files

To erase the file named BUDGET.APR on the diskette in the current drive, type:

```
B>erase budget.apr
```

As soon as you press the Enter key, the file's gone.

The next example erases all files on the sample diskette whose extension is BAK.

If you have version 4, use the /P parameter to ask DOS to prompt you for verification; type the following:

```
B:\>erase *.bak /p
```

If you have an earlier version of DOS, the /P parameter is unavailable, so type:

```
B:\>erase *.bak
```

With the /P parameter, DOS responds by displaying the name of the first file whose extension is BAK and asking you whether to delete it:

```
B:\REPORT.BAK,     Delete (Y/N)?_
```

Type *y* and press Enter to delete it. Now DOS shows you the name of the next file and again asks you:

```
B:\FORECAST.BAK,     Delete (Y/N)?_
```

Type *y* and press Enter again to delete the file. If you had typed *n* in response to either prompt, DOS would have left the file alone and moved on to the next file (if any) that matched the file name you typed as part of the Erase command. The /P option is thus handy when you want to erase several—but not all—files that have similar names or extensions. The prompt lets you avoid the work of entering a separate command for each file.

But what if your version of DOS doesn't have the /P option? If you typed the Erase command as *erase *.bak*, your disk drive became active for a brief time after you pressed the Enter key, and then the system prompt returned to the screen. In that short time, DOS erased the two sample files whose extension was BAK without telling you the names of the files. This example underscores the need for you to be sure you have typed the correct file name and the correct drive letter or extension (if necessary) whenever you use wildcard characters with the Erase command.

Whether or not you use the /P parameter, be particularly careful when you use the question mark in a file extension. To see why, create two additional test files by typing the following:

```
B:\>copy results *.1
     1 File(s) copied

B:\>copy results *.12
     1 File(s) copied
```

This gives you three files with the same name but different extensions: RESULTS, RESULTS.1, and RESULTS.12. Now type a Directory command, using a single question mark as the extension. Before you press Enter, decide which files you believe DOS will list.

```
B:\>dir results.?
```

DOS lists two files:

```
Volume in drive B has no label
Volume Serial Number is 1A2C-13F5
Directory of  B:\

RESULTS   1           23 10-16-89    9:16a
RESULTS               23 10-16-89    9:16a
          2 File(s)   1184256 bytes free
```

If you expected to see only RESULTS.1, the response to this Directory command is a surprise. If you had typed an Erase command, instead of a Directory command, the files you see listed are the files DOS would have erased. An unexpected directory listing can be momentarily confusing, but unintentionally erasing files is definitely an unpleasant surprise. Use the /P parameter if you aren't sure what the effect of an Erase command will be.

To erase both of the files you just created but leave your original RESULTS file untouched, type the following command:

B:\>erase results.1?

Typing *1* as the first character of the extension ensures that the file RESULTS isn't affected. Note, however, that even though you included a question mark (which takes the place of a single character) after the 1, DOS erased RESULTS.1 as well as RESULTS.12. Be careful whenever you use wildcard characters with commands that change or erase files.

CHANGING FILE NAMES

There will be times when you want to change the name of a file. You might simply change your mind, or perhaps you'll have changed the contents of a file so much that you want to give it a name that more closely describes its new contents. The Rename command changes a file's name or extension, or both. You can use wildcard characters to rename a set of files.

The Rename command has two parameters:

rename <oldname> <newname>

<oldname> is the name of an existing file. If the file doesn't exist, DOS displays *Duplicate file name or file not found* and returns to command level.

<newname> is the name you want to give to the file specified by <oldname>. If there is already a file with the new name, DOS displays *Duplicate file name or file not found* and returns to command level. Two files on the same disk can't have the same name, and DOS would have to erase the existing file to carry out the command, so this built-in safeguard keeps you from inadvertently erasing one file in the process of renaming another.

You can abbreviate the Rename command as *ren.*

The Rename command simply changes the name of a file; it doesn't copy a file to a different disk. Both the old name and the new name must refer to the same drive. If you specify a drive letter with the new name, DOS responds *Invalid parameter*.

Examples of Changing File Names

To change the name of the file ANNUAL.BGT to FINAL on the disk in the current drive, type:

```
B:\>ren annual.bgt final
```

DOS changes the name and displays the system prompt.

To change the extension of the file BUDGET.MAR from MAR to 003, on the disk in the current drive, you can use the * wildcard character for the new file name. Type the following:

```
B:\>ren budget.mar *.003
```

The file is now named BUDGET.003.

To change the extension DOC to TXT for all files on the disk in the current drive, use the * for both the old and new file names. Type the following:

```
B:\>ren *.doc *.txt
```

Verify this change with the Directory command by typing:

```
B:\>dir *.txt
```

DOS shows four files, all of which used to have the extension DOC:

```
Volume in drive B has no label
Volume Serial Number is 1A2C-13F5
Directory of  B:\

REPORT   TXT       23 10-16-89   9:16a
BANK     TXT       23 10-16-89   9:16a
FORECAST TXT       23 10-16-89   9:16a
BANKRPT  TXT       47 10-16-89  10:51a
         4 File(s)    1185280 bytes free
```

If you use the Directory command now to display the entries of all files with the extension DOC, DOS responds *File not found*.

PREPARING FOR THE REMAINING EXAMPLES

The remaining examples in this chapter show you how to use some external DOS commands. These commands are on your fixed disk, if you're using one, or on the DOS diskette in drive A. Before continuing with the examples, you must enable DOS to find the command files it needs.

If you're using a fixed disk, change the current drive to C by typing:

`B:\>c:`

and leave your practice diskette in drive B.

If you're not using a fixed disk, change the current drive to A by typing:

`B:\>a:`

and leave your practice diskette in drive B. The examples use the command files named ATTRIB.EXE, COMP.COM, and PRINT.COM. Use the Directory command to check the DOS diskette in drive A for these files. If DOS responds *File not found*, check your other DOS diskette(s) for the files you need. Begin the examples with the diskette containing ATTRIB.EXE in drive A.

Now the current drive is the one containing some or all of the command files DOS will need to carry out your requests, and drive B contains the diskette with the files on which DOS will act. To tell DOS where to find the practice files, you'll preface their file names with the drive letter, *b:*.

CONTROLLING WHETHER A FILE CAN BE CHANGED

Your disks will contain many files. Some, such as program files (including DOS, application programs, and programs you write yourself), you will seldom, if ever, erase. Although you probably have backup copies, some of these files might exist only on your working disks; erasing them could represent a serious loss.

Similarly, you will probably have other files, such as spreadsheets, for periodic calculations or reports, and word-processing style sheets or form letters, that you seldom change. Because these files can represent a significant investment of time and information, inadvertently changing them would be a serious loss.

The Attribute (attrib) command lets you protect yourself from inadvertently erasing or changing a file. You do this by making the file *read-only,* which means that you (or anyone else using the file) can read it but cannot erase or change it. Before a read-only file can be changed or erased, the protection must be removed, again with the Attribute command.

Because you can affect the read-only status of a file with only one command, it's easy to temporarily protect files that may change later—the most recent version of a text file or spreadsheet, for example. This protection can be particularly useful if someone else is going to use the same disk or computer that you use.

When used to control the read-only status of a file, the Attribute command has three parameters:

attrib +R −R <filename>

+R tells DOS to make <filename> read-only—that is, to deny all attempts to change or erase <filename>.

–R tells DOS to let <filename> be changed or erased.

<filename> is the name of the file whose read-only status is to be affected. If you enter the command with <filename> only, DOS displays the name of the file and, if the file is read-only, displays an *R* to the left of the file name. You can check or change the read-only status of a series of files by using wildcard characters.

The display of the Directory command doesn't show whether a file is read-only; you must use the Attribute command.

Note: Starting with version 3.3 of DOS, you can use the Attribute command to affect the read-only status of groups of files stored in units called subdirectories. *(Subdirectories, and this use of the Attribute command, are described in Chapter 8, "A Tree of Files.") In addition, starting with version 3.2 of DOS, you can also use the Attribute command to control the* archive *status of a file, which controls how the file is treated by the Backup and Xcopy commands, which you use to make archive copies of your files. (This use of the Attribute command is described in Chapter 9, "Managing Your Fixed Disk," as are the Backup and Xcopy commands.)*

Example of Controlling Whether a File Can Be Changed

Type the following command to tell DOS to display the status of the files with the extension TXT on the disk in drive B:

```
C:\DOS>attrib b:*.txt
```

DOS responds:

```
A              B:\REPORT.TXT
A              B:\BANK.TXT
A              B:\FORECAST.TXT
A              B:\BANKRPT.TXT
```

None of the file names is preceded by an R; this tells you none is read-only.

If you're not using version 3.2 or a later version of DOS, your display doesn't include the *A* to the left of each file name, and you can skip the rest of this paragraph. If you do see the *A*, the letter shows that the file's archive status is on; this means that the file has not been backed up by the Backup command or copied by the Xcopy command since it was created or last changed. The importance and use of a file's archive status is described in Chapter 9, "Managing Your Fixed Disk."

To make BANK.TXT read-only, type:

```
C:\DOS>attrib +r b:bank.txt
```

DOS responds by displaying the system prompt. Now, when you check the status again, DOS shows that BANK.TXT is read-only. Type the following:

```
C:\DOS>attrib b:*.txt

    A               B:\REPORT.TXT
    A       R       B:\BANK.TXT
    A               B:\FORECAST.TXT
    A               B:\BANKRPT.TXT
```

If you try to erase BANK.TXT, DOS displays an error message:

```
C:\DOS>erase b:bank.txt
Access denied
```

The result would be the same if you edited the file with a word processor; when you tried to store the revised version, DOS or the word processor would issue an error message. You could, however, save the revised version with a different name.

Remove the read-only protection and verify that it is gone by typing:

```
C:\DOS>attrib -r b:bank.txt

C:\DOS>attrib b:bank.txt

    A               B:\BANK.TXT
```

COMPARING FILES

Note: Some versions of DOS prior to version 3 do not include the Compare command. If you're not sure whether you have this command, check your DOS diskettes for the command file by typing dir comp.com. *If you don't have the Compare command, you have a similar command named FC (for* File Compare*); it is described in Appendix F.*

Sometimes you'll want to know whether two files are exactly the same. Suppose you have two files named BUDGET on different disks. They're the same length, but are they different budgets, or two copies of the same one? You could display or print both files and compare them, but that could take quite a while and you still might miss some small difference. It's quicker and more accurate to use Compare (comp).

The Compare command has two parameters:

comp <file1> <file2>

<file1> and <file2> are the file names of the files to be compared. If you omit <file2>, DOS prompts you for it. If you omit both <file1> and <file2>, DOS prompts you for both.

If the files are different lengths, DOS displays *Files are different sizes* and asks you if you want to compare any more files. If the files are the same length, the Compare command compares them byte-by-byte. If the files are identical, DOS tells you so by displaying *Files compare ok.*

If the files are the same length but DOS finds a difference, DOS displays a message that shows the characters that differ, and how far each is from the beginning of the file. If DOS finds 10 mismatches, it displays *10 Mismatches - ending compare*, and asks if you want to compare any more files.

Examples of Comparing Files

Note: If you are using DOS from diskettes, verify that the DOS diskette in drive A contains the file named COMP.COM before continuing.

To compare REPORT.TXT with BUDGET.FEB, type:

```
C:\DOS>comp b:report.txt b:budget.feb
```

The files are identical, so DOS replies as follows:

```
B:REPORT.TXT and B:BUDGET.FEB

EOF mark not found
Files compare OK
Compare more files (Y/N) ?_
```

Don't be concerned by *EOF mark not found*—DOS is simply telling you that it didn't include your end-of-file indicator (^Z) as a character in the files. Type *y* to tell DOS you want to compare more files. DOS prompts you for the names of the files. To compare REPORT.TXT with REPORT.MIX, type the file names as follows:

```
Enter primary filename
b:report.txt

Enter 2nd filename or drive id
b:report.mix
```

DOS determines that the two files are different lengths, and it doesn't even begin to compare them:

```
B:REPORT.TXT and B:REPORT.MIX

Files are different sizes
Compare more files (Y/N) ?_
```

Type *n* and DOS returns to command level.

You can use wildcard characters to compare two sets of files with one command. To compare all files with the extension TXT and all files with the same file name but the extension MIX, type the following:

```
C:\DOS>comp b:*.txt b:*.mix
```

There are four files with the extension TXT, but only two with the extension MIX. DOS tells you which files don't exist and which ones it tried to compare:

```
B:REPORT.TXT and B:REPORT.MIX

Files are different sizes

B:BANK.TXT and B:BANK.MIX

File not found - B:BANK.MIX

B:FORECAST.TXT and B:FORECAST.MIX

Files are different sizes

B:BANKRPT.TXT and B:BANKRPT.MIX

File not found - B:BANKRPT.MIX
Compare more files (Y/N) ?_
```

Type *n* to return DOS to command level.

Because all the sample files are identical, you'll have to create one that is different, but still the same length (23 bytes), to see how DOS notifies you about differences. To create a different file, named DIFF, type the following:

```
C:\DOS>copy con b:diff
This is not the same.
^Z
        1 File(s) copied
```

Now compare REPORT.TXT with DIFF by typing:

```
C:\DOS>comp b:report.txt b:diff
```

DOS quickly finds and reports 10 errors:

```
B:REPORT.TXT and B:DIFF

Compare error at OFFSET 8
File 1 = 61
File 2 = 6E
Compare error at OFFSET 9
File 1 = 20
File 2 = 6F
Compare error at OFFSET A
File 1 = 64
File 2 = 74
Compare error at OFFSET B
File 1 = 75
File 2 = 20
Compare error at OFFSET C
File 1 = 6D
File 2 = 74
```

```
Compare error at OFFSET D
File 1 = 6D
File 2 = 68
Compare error at OFFSET E
File 1 = 79
File 2 = 65
Compare error at OFFSET 10
File 1 = 66
File 2 = 73
Compare error at OFFSET 11
File 1 = 69
File 2 = 61
Compare error at OFFSET 12
File 1 = 6C
File 2 = 6D
10 Mismatches - ending compare
Compare more files (Y/N) ?_
```

Type *n* to return DOS to command level.

The messages that show the differing characters and their locations use numbers that are combinations of the digits 0 through 9 and the letters A through F. These characters are from the base-16 number system, usually called *hexadecimal,* in which A through F are used to represent the decimal numbers 10 through 15. If you must know what the differing characters are or must calculate their exact locations, you need a chart of the American Standard Code for Information Interchange (ASCII), which shows how characters are encoded, and you need a guide to hexadecimal arithmetic. The manuals that came with your computer might contain both. In addition, the book *Supercharging MS-DOS* (Microsoft Press, 1989) describes both the ASCII code and hexadecimal numbers.

PRINTING FILES

You can print files at the same time you're using the computer to do other things. The Print command keeps a list—called the *print queue*—of files to be printed, and it prints the files in the order in which they appear in the queue. The print queue normally can hold up to 10 files.

In addition to printing files, the Print command lets you change some characteristics of its operation—notably, the size of the print queue and the printer that DOS uses. For a description of these uses of the Print command, see ''Changing Operation of the Print Command'' later in this chapter.

Because the computer can really do only one thing at a time, DOS prints when nothing else is happening, such as when you pause to think between keystrokes. You'll notice that printing slows and sometimes even stops when something else is going on—especially when DOS is using a disk drive.

You use the Print command to add a file to the print queue, delete a file from the queue, cancel all printing, and display the names of the files in the queue. When used to print a file, the Print command has four parameters:

print <filename> **/P /C /T**

<filename> is the name of the file to be added to or deleted from the print queue. You can enter more than one file name with a Print command; just type the list of file names, separating each from the next with a blank.

/P (Print) tells DOS to add <filename> to the print queue. DOS assumes this parameter if all you specify is <filename>.

/C (Cancel) tells DOS to remove <filename> from the print queue. If the file is being printed, printing stops and the paper is advanced to the top of the next page.

/T (Terminate) stops all printing. If a file is being printed, printing stops and the paper is advanced to the top of the next page. All files are removed from the print queue.

If you enter the Print command with no parameters, DOS displays the list of files in the print queue.

Examples of Printing a File

DOS advances the paper to the next page each time it prints a new file, so the examples here use several sheets of printer paper. Check what each example does before you try it, so that you can be ready to stop the printing process; you'll save both time and paper. First, a bit of preparation.

Most of the sample files you created in this chapter consist of a single line and would print too quickly for you to try using all the Print parameters in the following examples. Increase the size of the file REPORT.TXT using Edlin, the DOS text editor; it's described in Chapters 10 and 11.

Note: If you're using DOS from diskettes, you'll need the files named EDLIN.COM and PRINT.COM for these examples. Check your DOS diskette(s) for these files, and place the appropriate diskette in drive A before requesting either Edlin or the Print command. Begin with the diskette that contains EDLIN.COM in drive A.

To increase the size of the file REPORT.TXT, type the following lines:

```
C:\DOS>edlin b:report.txt
End of input file
*1,1,2,199c
*e
```

The Edlin command copies the first (and only) line 199 times, so REPORT.TXT now consists of 200 identical lines. (If you're using DOS from diskettes, you don't need Edlin anymore. If necessary, replace the DOS diskette in drive A with the diskette that contains PRINT.COM.)

Command files don't contain printable characters, so erase FORMAT.COM from the diskette in drive B by typing the following (*don't* forget the *b:*):

```
C:\DOS>erase b:format.com
```

Finally, make sure the printer is turned on and that the paper is adjusted to the top of a page. This completes the preparation for the Print command examples.

To print the file REPORT.TXT, type:

```
C:\DOS>print b:report.txt
```

The first time you enter the Print command after starting the system, DOS might prompt you for the name of the printer to use:

```
Name of list device [PRN]: _
```

The brackets around PRN mean that DOS will use the device named PRN if you press the Enter key. Unless you have more than one printer attached to your system, or you are using a printer with a serial interface, just press the Enter key. If you have never printed with your printer, press the Enter key.

When you respond to the prompt, DOS loads the Print command file from the system disk and keeps it in memory until you either turn the system off or restart DOS. DOS reports that the program is loaded:

```
Resident part of PRINT installed
```

When DOS begins to carry out your Print command, it displays the names and print status of the files in the print queue:

```
B:\REPORT.TXT is currently being printed
```

There is one file in the print queue (REPORT.TXT), and it's now being printed.

When you printed a file in Chapter 4 by copying it to the printer, DOS didn't display the system prompt—and you couldn't use the system—until the file had been printed. This time, the system prompt returned as soon as printing started. As soon as DOS starts printing a file with the Print command, DOS is ready to accept another command from you.

Note: If you're using a laser printer, or if your computer is part of a network, the following descriptions of the /C and /T parameters don't apply. Check the network or laser printer manual to see how to stop printing a file or, in the case of a network, how to delete files from its print queue. The laser printer doesn't beep or advance to the next page at the times described in the following paragraphs. You may have to push the buttons labeled ON LINE and FORM FEED to clear the page from the printer; check the manual for instructions. Laser printers are also very fast, so you may just prefer to skip these examples.

If you decide you don't want to print a file after all, you can remove it from the print queue with the /C parameter; type the following command while REPORT.TXT is being printed:

```
C:\DOS>print b:report.txt /c
```

DOS displays a terse acknowledgment of your command:

PRINT queue is empty

and stops sending lines to your printer, even though your printer will probably continue to operate until it finishes printing the characters it has already received. At that point, the printer beeps and advances the paper to the next page. If you check the last line of the printout, you see a message like this:

```
This is a dummy file.
This is a dummy file.
This is a dumm

File B:\REPORT.TXT canceled by operator
```

You can put more than one file into the print queue with a single Print command. To tell DOS to print both REPORT.TXT and BUDGET.JAN, type:

```
C:\DOS>print b:report.txt b:budget.jan
```

DOS starts printing REPORT.TXT and displays the print queue:

```
        B:\REPORT.TXT is currently being printed
        B:\BUDGET.JAN is in queue
```

If you want to stop printing entirely, you can remove all files from the print queue with the /T parameter. Type the following, again while REPORT.TXT is being printed:

```
C:\DOS>print /t
```

Again, DOS displays the acknowledgment *PRINT queue is empty*. This time, it prints the message *All files canceled by operator* at the point where it stopped printing and, again, advances the paper to the next page, removes all remaining files from the queues, and causes the printer to beep.

You can also put several files in the print queue at once by using wildcard characters. To print all the files whose extension is TXT, type:

```
C:\DOS>print b:*.txt
```

Now DOS tells you that there are four files in the queue (the order might vary):

```
        B:\BANK.TXT is currently being printed
        B:\REPORT.TXT is in queue
        B:\FORECAST.TXT is in queue
        B:\BANKRPT.TXT is in queue
```

DOS prints the files in the order shown. Stop all printing again by typing:

```
C:\DOS>print /t
```

Again, DOS stops printing the current file, prints the cancellation message, advances the paper to the next page, causes the printer to beep, removes all remaining files from the queue, and acknowledges on the screen *PRINT queue is empty*.

The following example uses several sheets of paper. If you're not using continuous form paper or an automatic sheet feeder, you shouldn't try this example because it might print on the platen of your printer. Skip to the heading ''Changing Operation of the Print Command.''

The print queue normally holds up to 10 files. To fill it, tell DOS to print all the files on the diskette in drive B; there are 13 files, so DOS puts the first 10 in the queue. Type the following:

```
C:\DOS>print b:*.*
```

DOS tells you the queue is full and displays the list of files in the queue (again, the order might vary):

```
PRINT queue is full

        B:\REPORT.BAK is currently being printed
        B:\DIFF is in queue
        B:\BANK.TXT is in queue
        B:\BUDGET.JAN is in queue
        B:\BUDGET.FEB is in queue
        B:\BUDGET.003 is in queue
        B:\RESULTS is in queue
        B:\REPORT.TXT is in queue
        B:\FORECAST.TXT is in queue
        B:\BANKRPT.TXT is in queue
```

You really don't need to print all these files. Stop all printing by typing:

```
C:\DOS>print /t
```

DOS empties the queue and alerts you as before:

```
PRINT queue is empty
```

Changing Operation of the Print Command

DOS initially limits the print queue to 10 files, but you can increase the size of the queue and can also tell DOS to use a printer other than the standard printer, PRN (more details on printers are in Chapter 7, ''Managing Your Devices'').

You can change Print command operations only the first time you use the Print command during a session at your computer; if you try to use these options again before restarting DOS or turning the computer off, DOS displays the message *Invalid parameter* and ignores the command.

When used to change the size of the print queue or the name of the printer, the Print command has two parameters:

print /D:<printer> /Q:<size>

/D:<printer> tells DOS to use the printer named <printer>. If you omit /D:<printer>, DOS uses the standard printer named PRN.

/Q:<size> tells DOS the number of files the print queue can hold; the minimum number is 4 and the maximum number is 32. If you omit /Q:<size>, the print queue holds 10 files.

If you wanted to increase the size of the print queue to 15 files, you would type *print /q:15*. If you wanted to tell DOS to use the printer named LPT2, you would type *print /d:lpt2*. You can combine the /D and /Q parameters in the same Print command, but you cannot combine them with other parameters unless you are entering the Print command for the first time since starting DOS.

The Print command lets you print text files without losing the use of your system during printing; it can make both you and your system more productive.

Several infrequently used parameters that give you more precise control over how the print program interacts with DOS are described in Appendix F.

CHAPTER

6

MANAGING YOUR DISKETTES

Diskettes are the computer's filing cabinets. Managing your computer filing system includes not only keeping track of your files, as described in the previous chapter, but also taking care of your diskettes. There are many ways to prepare and store information on diskettes; the concepts underlying diskette handling, however, apply to all microcomputers.

Several DOS commands deal with entire diskettes, not with individual files. For example, you must prepare a new diskette for use; this process is called formatting (or, less commonly, initializing). Or, if you need an exact copy of a diskette, you don't copy each file separately; you copy the entire diskette with one command.

This chapter suggests ways to handle your diskettes, briefly describes how DOS stores files on diskettes, and shows you how to do the following:

- Prepare a diskette for use with the Format command.

- Create another system diskette with the Format command.

- Duplicate a diskette with the Diskcopy command.

- Compare the contents of two diskettes with the Diskcomp command.

- Analyze and report on the use of diskette storage space with the Check Disk command.

- Assign, change, or delete the volume label (identifying name) of a disk with the Label command.

- Display the volume label of a disk with the Volume command.

The Label and Volume commands can be used with either diskettes or a fixed disk. Two additional commands, Backup and Restore, can also be used with diskettes or a fixed disk to make backup copies of files and to restore them if they're needed. Because Backup and Restore are typically used to deal with the files on a fixed disk, these commands are described in Chapter 9, ''Managing Your Fixed Disk.''

HANDLING DISKETTES

Diskettes are remarkably durable, especially the 3.5-inch type in a hard plastic shell. The useful life of diskettes depends on how often you use them, of course, but even more important is how you treat them. Handle your diskettes with the same care you use when handling valuable recording tapes or photographs:

- Avoid touching the diskette surfaces that show through the openings in the protective jacket. Dirt, fingerprints, or dust can shorten the life of a diskette and can damage or destroy the data.

- Keep diskettes away from magnets and other sources of magnetic influence, such as telephones, electric motors, and television sets.

- Keep food and drinks away from diskettes. The same goes for cigarettes, cigars, pipes, and ashtrays.

- Don't fold, spindle, or mutilate diskettes. Don't pile other objects on them.

- Don't write on diskette labels with a pencil, ballpoint pen, or other sharp instrument; use a felt-tipped marker.

- Store your diskettes in a safe place when you're not using them. Protect them from extreme heat or cold, humidity, or contact with other objects.

Many products are available for storing diskettes, including plastic boxes, vinyl pockets that fit a three-ring binder, and hanging file folders. All offer good protection; they aren't necessary, but they make it easier for you to organize your diskettes and store them safely, rather than leaving them scattered around your desk.

Although an office is a mild environment compared to a factory or a shop floor, data on a diskette can be damaged by such innocuous objects as a paper clip that has been stored in a magnetic paper-clip holder, a magnetized letter opener, an electric pencil sharpener, or a telephone-answering machine. If you put a letter down on top of a diskette lying on your desk, it's all too easy to put a hot coffee cup or heavy object on the letter without realizing that the diskette is underneath.

The safest places for a diskette are in the computer and in protective storage. Information and time are two of your most valuable assets: A damaged diskette can cost you both, so protect your diskettes accordingly.

BACK UP YOUR DISKETTES

Even though you treat your diskettes with care, they can still be mislaid or damaged by accident. Files can be inadvertently changed or erased, and eventually diskettes simply wear out. Making backup copies of your diskettes limits the amount of information and time you lose if something goes wrong. The time it takes to make these copies could be one of your better investments.

Unless a program diskette is copy protected so that you cannot duplicate the original, make a copy of the program before you ever use it—even if you plan to install the program on your fixed disk. Store the original diskette in a safe place, and use the copy. If something happens to the copy, make another copy from the original. Always keep the original stored safely.

Your collection of data files will grow as you use application programs, such as a word processor or spreadsheet. Back up a data diskette whenever the value of the information it contains—or the time it would take to re-create it—is greater than the value of a blank diskette and the few minutes it takes to make a copy. Keep your backup copies in a safe place and use your computer with the comforting thought that, should something unforeseen happen, you're protected.

HOW INFORMATION IS STORED ON A DISKETTE

Information is stored on a diskette much as music or video is recorded on tape. A description of how DOS uses a diskette helps you understand the commands you use to manage your diskettes.

What Is a Diskette?

What we call a diskette actually consists of two parts: a disk of thin plastic coated with magnetic material, and a protective plastic jacket or hard shell. Figure 6-1 shows a 5.25-inch diskette in its flexible jacket, and Figure 6-2 shows both the front and back of a 3.5-inch diskette in its hard shell.

The dashed lines in Figures 6-1 and 6-2 show how the coated disk lies inside the protective jacket. The magnetic coating itself is visible through the openings in the jacket of a 5.25-inch diskette (shaded in Figure 6-1). The spring-loaded shutter that normally covers the opening in a 3.5-inch diskette is moved aside by the diskette drive to provide access to the magnetic coating. The hole in the center of the disk goes around the drive motor, which spins the disk so that data can be written (recorded) or read (played back).

The write-protect notch or slide lets you protect all the files on a diskette from being erased or changed. To protect a 5.25-inch diskette, cover the write-protect notch

Figure 6-1. A 5.25-inch diskette

Figure 6-2. A 3.5-inch diskette

with one of the small tabs of tape included with the box of diskettes. To protect a 3.5-inch diskette, move the write-protect slide down (toward the edge of the diskette) until the hole through the diskette shell is open. To permit files on the diskette to be changed or erased, remove the tape or move the slide up until the hole is closed. Protect your DOS diskettes in this way; protect each of your application program diskettes, too, unless the application program manual tells you otherwise.

How Does DOS Keep Track of Files?

Information is recorded on a diskette in narrow concentric circles called *tracks*; there are 40 such tracks on a standard 360-kilobyte (360 K) diskette and 80 tracks on the high-capacity 5.25-inch and 3.5-inch diskettes used on the IBM PC/AT, IBM PC Convertible, IBM PS/2 models, and compatible systems. A track is divided into smaller areas called *sectors,* each of which can hold 512 bytes. Figure 6-3 on the following page shows how tracks and sectors are laid out on a diskette. For simplicity, the illustration shows only four tracks.

The side, track, and sector numbers of the beginning of a file are stored as part of the directory entry for the file. You don't see this information when you use the Directory command, but DOS can find any sector on a diskette by its side, track, and sector numbers, just as you can find any seat in a stadium or a theater by its section, row, and seat numbers.

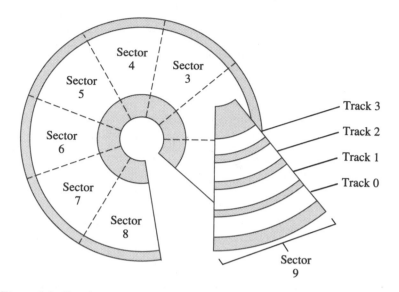

Figure 6-3. Tracks and sectors on a diskette

Diskette Capacity

Tracks on a standard diskette are numbered 0 through 39 (making 40 in all); sectors are numbered 1 through 9, for a total of 360 sectors (40 tracks times 9 sectors per track) on each side. Most personal computers that run DOS have double-sided drives, which use both sides of a diskette, but some earlier models had single-sided drives that used only one side. A standard double-sided (or 360 K) diskette has an actual capacity of 368,640 bytes (though not all of it is available for files); a single-sided (or 180 K) diskette has a capacity of 184,320 bytes.

The high-capacity 5.25-inch diskettes used on the IBM PC/AT and compatible systems have 80 tracks (numbered 0 through 79), each of which has 15 sectors. A sector still stores 512 bytes, so the two sides of a high-capacity (or 1.2 MB) diskette can hold 1,228,800 bytes.

The 3.5-inch diskettes used on the IBM PS/2 computers and compatible systems are also double-sided diskettes with 80 tracks per side. Depending on disk capacity, however, they have either 9 or 18 sectors per track—again with 512 bytes per sector. The 9-sectored (or 720 K) diskettes can hold 737,280 bytes; the 18-sectored (or 1.44 MB) diskettes can hold 1,474,560 bytes.

Volume Label

Any disk can be assigned a name, or *volume label,* to identify its contents. The volume label can be up to 11 characters long, and you can use the same characters allowed in a file name, plus a space. You can assign a volume label when you format a disk or at any time later on. DOS stores the volume label on the disk and displays it when you use the Directory, Check Disk, Label, or Volume commands. The volume label is for identification only; you can't use it in a command to specify a disk.

PREPARING FOR THE EXAMPLES

The examples in this chapter require one diskette that doesn't contain any files you want to keep (the examples erase any data on the diskette). Put the diskette in your diskette drive; if you have two diskette drives, put the diskette in drive B. If you're using DOS on diskettes, be sure the DOS disk in drive A contains the file named FORMAT.COM.

PREPARING A DISKETTE FOR USE

As you've seen, the Format command prepares a diskette for use. The diskette can be either new or previously formatted. However, formatting erases any existing files, so be certain not to format a diskette that contains files you need.

In carrying out the Format command, DOS also checks for flaws on the recording surface of the diskette and marks any bad sectors so they won't be used. After formatting, DOS displays a message that tells you the maximum number of bytes the diskette can hold, how many bytes (if any) are defective, and how many bytes are available for storing files. Beginning with version 4, DOS also tells you how much storage space the diskette has in terms of *allocation units* (a term for packages of bytes DOS uses instead of reading or writing from or to disk one byte at a time), and it displays the diskette's *volume serial number* (a disk identifier DOS assigns during formatting). As mentioned earlier, this information is unlikely to be of any concern to you.

DOS knows the type of diskette drive you have and formats the diskette accordingly. That is, it can tell whether the drive uses 3.5-inch or 5.25-inch, standard or high-capacity diskettes, and formats the diskette to match the drive's maximum capabilities unless you specify otherwise.

This does not mean, however, that you can simply put any diskette in any drive and leave the details to DOS. It is up to you to provide the appropriate diskette for formatting. You cannot expect a half-gallon bucket to hold a gallon of water, nor can you expect DOS to format a standard 360 K or 720 K diskette to reliably hold 1.2 MB or 1.44 MB of information.

You can, however, format and use low-capacity diskettes in a high-capacity drive. For example, if you have a high-capacity 3.5-inch drive and run out of 1.44 MB diskettes, you can format 720 K diskettes in the drive and use them reliably in a 720 K or a 1.44 MB drive. If you have a 5.25-inch drive, you can format, read, and write standard 360 K diskettes in it. In this case, though, you should expect to use your 360 K diskettes only in another high-capacity drive; a standard 360 K drive cannot read these diskettes reliably.

The Format command reserves space on the diskette for the directory, thus reducing the amount of storage available for files. Because the size of the directory varies, depending on whether the diskette is standard or high capacity, and because early versions of DOS used either single-sided or double-sided diskettes and in some cases created only eight (rather than nine) sectors per track, the storage capacity of your diskettes depends on both the type of diskette and the version of DOS you use. Figure 6-4 shows diskette sizes, number of sectors per track, and number of bytes available for all diskette drives DOS recognizes.

Size	Sides	Tracks per Side	Sectors per Track	Total Capacity	Available for Files	System Where Used
3.5"	2	80	18	1,474,560 (1.44 MB)	1,457,664	IBM PS/2 (except Models 25 and 30); DOS version 3.3 and later
5.25"	2	80	15	1,228,800 (1.2 MB)	1,213,952	IBM PC/AT and compatibles; DOS versions 3 and later
3.5"	2	80	9	737,280 (720 K)	730,112	IBM PS/2 Model 30, IBM PC Convertible, and compatibles; DOS versions 3.2 and later
5.25"	2	40	9	368,640 (360 K)	362,496	IBM PC, PC/XT, and compatibles; DOS versions 2 and later
5.25"	2	40	8	327,680 (320 K)	322,560	IBM PC, PC/XT, and compatibles; all DOS versions
5.25"	1	40	9	184,320 (180 K)	179,712	IBM PC, PC/XT, and compatibles; DOS versions 2 and later
5.25"	1	40	8	163,840 (160 K)	160,256	IBM PC, PC/XT, and compatibles; all DOS versions

Figure 6-4. Storage capacity of different diskettes

Format Command Parameters

When used to prepare a non-system (data) diskette, the Format command has six parameters:

format <drive> /1 /4 /8 /F:<size > /V:<label>

<drive> is the letter, followed by a colon, of the drive that contains the diskette to be formatted (such as *b:*). With version 3.1 or earlier, if you omit <drive>, DOS formats the diskette in the current drive. If you omit <drive> and you're using version 3.2, 3.3, or 4, DOS responds either *Drive letter must be specified* or *Required parameter missing* (depending on the version you have) and returns to the system prompt.

/1 formats only one side of a diskette in a standard 360 K double-sided drive.

/4 formats a 360 K diskette in a high-capacity, 5.25-inch drive.

/8 formats eight sectors per track.

/F:<size>, new with version 4, formats a diskette for the capacity indicated by <size>. You can specify any appropriate diskette capacity from 160 K to 1.44 MB, and you can type <size> in any of the forms shown in Figure 6-5. If you are using version 3.2 or 3.3, two alternate parameters, /N:<sectors> and /T:<tracks>, enable you to specify diskette capacity by giving DOS the number of sectors and tracks to format; examples are given in Appendix F.

Disk Capacity	Type in Any of the Following Forms (No Blank Preceding K, KB, M, or MB)					
160 K	160	160K	160KB			
180 K	180	180K	180KB			
320 K	320	320K	320KB			
360 K	360	360K	360KB			
720 K	720	720K	720KB			
1.2 MB	1200	1200K	1200KB	1.2	1.2M	1.2MB
1.44 MB	1440	1440K	1440KB	1.44	1.44M	1.44MB

Figure 6-5. Ways to type <size> as part of the version 4/F:<size> parameter of the Format command

/V:<label>, in version 4, assigns the diskette the volume label <label>. This parameter speeds formatting by letting you specify the volume label ahead of time and thus skip the usual request for a volume label that DOS otherwise displays at the end of the format procedure. If you have an earlier version of DOS, your equivalent parameter is typed as /V (without <label>) and works in reverse, telling DOS to request a volume label at the end of the format procedure.

Warning: If you're not using version 3.2 or later and you type a Format command without specifying a drive letter, DOS formats the disk in the current drive. If the current drive is a diskette drive that contains your system disk and you haven't covered the write-protect notch, DOS erases every file on your system diskette. If the current drive is a fixed disk, formatting erases every file on it: not just the DOS files, but every program and data file you have stored. Although newer versions of DOS provide some protection against inadvertently formatting the wrong disk, the consequences are severe enough that you should be certain you know which disk is going to be formatted before you press the Enter key after a Format command.

Examples of Preparing a Diskette

If you're not using a fixed disk, your system prompt is A>, not C:\DOS>, as shown in the examples. This difference has no effect on what you type or how DOS responds, so follow the examples as printed; just remember the difference in the system prompt.

Format the diskette in drive B and give it a volume label. If you have version 4, type the following:

```
C:\DOS>format b: /v:dosdisk
```

If you have an earlier version, type:

```
C:\DOS>format b: /v
```

DOS asks you to put the diskette in drive B:

```
Insert new diskette for drive B:
and press ENTER when ready... _
```

Make sure the right diskette is in the drive, then press Enter.

If you're using version 4, DOS reports on its progress with the message *xx percent of disk formatted.* If you're using version 3.1 or an earlier version, DOS displays *Formatting...* while it formats the disk. If you're using version 3.2 or 3.3, DOS displays *Head: 0 Cylinder: 0* and changes the head and cylinder numbers to show you its progress (*cylinder* is another way of referring to a track).

When DOS has formatted the diskette, it displays *Format complete.* If you have version 4, this message is followed by a report on available storage space and, on a separate line, the DOS-assigned volume serial number (which, if you're curious, is based on the current date and time). As you'll see in a moment, DOS has also used the parameter */v:dosdisk* to name the diskette DOSDISK. At the end of the report, DOS asks if you want to format another diskette:

```
Format another (Y/N)?_
```

Type *n*.

If you have an earlier version of DOS, the *Format complete* message is followed by a prompt for the volume label:

```
Volume label (11 characters, ENTER for none)? _
```

Name the diskette DOSDISK by typing the following:

```
dosdisk
```

DOS displays the report of available storage on the diskette and asks if you want to format another. Reply *n*.

Now, regardless of your version of DOS, display the directory of the disk: It's empty, but you can see the volume label on the first line.

```
C:\DOS>dir b:

 Volume in drive B is DOSDISK
 Volume Serial Number is 2F49-1AFF
 Directory of  B:\

File not found
```

(If you don't have version 4, the display doesn't include the volume serial number.)

MAKING A SYSTEM DISKETTE

Sometimes, to leave room for a large application program, you might need to format a diskette that you can use to start DOS and your application, but that doesn't include all of the DOS command files.

You could copy your system diskette with the Diskcopy command described below and then erase the files you don't need, but there's a simpler way: The /S option of the Format command formats a diskette and copies the files that must be on a system diskette. These include COMMAND.COM and a few hidden files that are necessary for DOS to operate and must be stored in specific locations on the diskette. A system diskette created in this way contains none of the command files for the DOS external commands, such as Format, but you can use this diskette to start DOS and to use any of the internal commands, such as the Directory command.

COPYING A COMPLETE DISKETTE

The Diskcopy command makes an exact duplicate of any diskette, including the hidden system files on a system diskette. If the target diskette isn't formatted, version 4 and IBM's earlier versions of DOS format it before copying; Diskcopy in other versions of DOS may require formatted diskettes of the same size and capacity. Diskcopy works only with diskettes of the same size and capacity. For example, you cannot use it to copy to or from a 360 K diskette and a formatted 1.2 MB, 5.25-inch diskette, nor can you use it to copy from a fixed disk.

The Diskcopy command has three parameters:

diskcopy <source> <target> /1

<source> is the letter, followed by a colon, of the drive that contains the diskette to be copied (such as *a:*).

<target> is the letter, followed by a colon, of the drive that contains the diskette that is to receive the copy (such as *b:*). If you have only one diskette drive, <source> and <target> can be the same letter (for example, *diskcopy a: a:*).

If you omit <target>, DOS copies from the diskette in <source> to the diskette in the current drive; if you omit <target> and you specify the current drive as <source>, DOS assumes you want to use only the current drive and prompts you to switch diskettes during the copy. If you don't specify <source> or <target>, DOS assumes you want to use only the current drive and prompts you to switch diskettes during the copy.

/1 copies only the first side of a diskette if you have double-sided drives.

Assuming that the source and target diskettes are the same size and capacity, DOS gives the target diskette the same number of sides and sectors as the source diskette. If the source diskette, for example, has nine sectors per track and the target diskette was formatted with eight, DOS formats the target diskette with nine sectors per track before copying.

Examples of Copying a Diskette

This example copies an existing diskette, duplicating information from the source onto the target diskette. If you are using version 4 from a fixed disk, use the diskette you labeled Select Copy during the installation procedure as the source; if that diskette is not available, use a data diskette—the one you used for the examples in Chapter 5 will do. If you have an earlier version of DOS, use your copy of one of the DOS diskettes. Place your source diskette in drive A (replace the diskette you just formatted if you have one diskette drive).

If you do *not* have a fixed disk, check that the DOS diskette in drive A contains the file DISKCOPY.COM. The diskette will serve the dual purpose of ensuring that DOS can find the command file it needs and that you have a disk to copy.

Be sure that your source and target diskettes are the same capacity. Use the diskette you just formatted as the target if you can; otherwise, find an unformatted diskette or one that matches the capacity of your source diskette. Now, follow the instructions under the heading that describes your system.

If You Have One Diskette Drive

Because you have only one diskette drive, DOS must use it for both the source and target diskettes, prompting you to exchange diskettes as required. The source diskette described above should be in the diskette drive.

To copy the diskette, type:

```
C:\DOS>diskcopy a: b:
```

DOS prompts you to put in the source diskette:

```
Insert SOURCE diskette in drive A:

Press any key to continue . . .
```

You put the diskette in already, so press any key. DOS tells you how many tracks, sectors, and sides it's copying, then prompts you to put the target diskette in the drive:

```
Insert TARGET diskette in drive A:

Press any key to continue . . .
```

Remove the source diskette, put in the target diskette, and press a key. DOS might prompt you to exchange diskettes until it has copied the diskette. Then it asks if you want to copy another:

```
Copy another diskette (Y/N)? _
```

Reply *n.*

If You Have Two Diskette Drives

If you're using DOS on a system with two diskette drives, your source diskette should be in drive A. If you don't have a fixed disk, verify that the diskette containing DISKCOPY.COM is in drive A.

To copy the diskette in drive A to the target diskette, type:

```
A>diskcopy a: b:
```

DOS prompts you to put in the diskettes. The correct diskettes are in the two drives, so just press a key. DOS tells you how many tracks, sectors, and sides it's copying, then asks if you want to copy another; reply *n.*

COMPARING TWO DISKETTES

Note: The command for comparing two diskettes might not be included in your version of DOS. You can check for it in your DOS manual, or you can check for the file named DISKCOMP.COM. If you don't have the Diskcomp command, skip to the heading "Checking the Condition of a Disk."

Sometimes you'll want to know whether two diskettes are identical—for example, you might have copied a diskette with the Diskcopy command, and you want to be certain the duplicate is an exact copy of the original. Diskcomp compares two diskettes track-by-track. The Diskcomp command can only be used with diskettes of the same size and capacity; you cannot use it to compare a fixed disk with a diskette.

Note: Just because two diskettes contain the same files, they're not necessarily identical, because the files might be stored in different sectors. If you want to compare all the files on two diskettes, rather than the diskettes themselves, use the Compare (comp) command (described in Chapter 5) and specify all files (∗.∗).

The Diskcomp command has four parameters:

diskcomp <drive1> <drive2> /1 /8

<drive1> and <drive2> are the drive letters, each followed by a colon, of the drives containing the diskettes to be compared (such as *a:* and *b:*). If you omit <drive2>, DOS compares the diskette in <drive1> to the diskette in the current drive. If you omit both <drive1> and <drive2>, DOS assumes you want to use only the current drive and prompts you to switch diskettes during the comparison.

/1 compares only the first side of double-sided diskettes.

/8 limits the comparison to eight sectors, even if <drive1> contains a nine-sector diskette.

If DOS finds any differences, it displays the side and track of each; for example:

```
Compare error on
side 0, track 33
```

Examples of Comparing Two Diskettes

Follow the instructions under the heading that describes your system.

If You Have One Diskette Drive

To compare the source diskette to the copy you just made, type:

```
C:\DOS>diskcomp a: b:
```

DOS prompts you to put in the first diskette:

```
Insert FIRST diskette in drive A:

Press any key to continue . . .
```

Make sure the copy you just made is in the drive, then press a key:

```
Comparing 40 tracks
9 sectors per track, 2 side(s)
```

DOS prompts you to put in the second diskette:

```
Insert SECOND diskette in drive A:

Press any key to continue . . .
```

Remove the diskette, put in the source diskette you used for the Diskcopy example, and then press a key. If necessary, DOS continues to prompt you to exchange diskettes until it finally tells you it's done and asks if you want to compare more diskettes:

```
Compare OK
Compare another diskette (Y/N) ?_
```

Reply *n.*

If You Have Two Diskette Drives

To compare the diskette in drive B (the copy you just made) to the diskette in drive A (the diskette you used as your source), type:

```
A>diskcomp a: b:
```

DOS prompts you to put in the diskettes:

```
Insert FIRST diskette in drive A:

Insert SECOND diskette in drive B:

Press any key to continue . . .
```

The diskettes are already in the drives, so press a key. DOS reports how many tracks, sectors, and sides it is comparing, then reports the results of the comparison and asks if you want to compare more diskettes:

```
Comparing 40 tracks
9 sectors per track, 2 side(s)

Compare OK

Compare another diskette (Y/N) ?_
```

Reply *n.*

CHECKING THE CONDITION OF A DISK

Computers aren't infallible; malfunctions can produce errors in the directory of a disk. Such errors are rare, but the Check Disk (chkdsk) command helps by making sure that all files are recorded properly.

Check Disk analyzes the directory on a disk, comparing the directory entries with the locations and lengths of the files, and reports any errors it finds. The Check Disk report includes the following:

- The total amount of space on the disk.

- The number of files and directories and how much space they take up.

- How much space on the disk remains available for files.

- In version 4, the size of each allocation unit, the number of such units on the disk, and the number available for storage.

- The size of the computer's memory up to 640 K and how many bytes remain free for use.

You can also ask the command to display the name of each file on the disk and to check whether any files are stored inefficiently.

If possible, DOS stores files in adjacent, or *contiguous,* sectors. As files are deleted and new files are stored, however, they can become fragmented (stored in nonadjacent sectors). A fragmented file isn't a cause for worry; the worst that can happen is that DOS will take slightly longer to read the file. If several files on a diskette are fragmented, you can restore them to contiguous sectors by copying all the files to an empty, formatted diskette with the Copy command. (Remember, don't use the Diskcopy command, because it makes a faithful sector-by-sector copy of the diskette, storing the files in exactly the same—nonadjacent—sectors in which they are stored on the original diskette.)

The Check Disk command has four parameters:

chkdsk <drive> <filename> /V /F

<drive> is the letter, followed by a colon, of the drive that contains the disk to be checked. If you omit <drive>, DOS checks the disk in the current drive.

<filename> is the name of the file whose storage you want DOS to check. DOS displays a message if the file is stored in noncontiguous sectors. You can use wildcard characters to check a set of files.

/V displays the name of each directory and file on the disk.

/F tells DOS to correct any errors it finds in the directory if you so specify when the error is found.

Examples of Checking a Disk

Whether you have one or two diskette drives, check the diskette in drive B by typing:

```
C:\DOS>chkdsk b:
```

Press any key if DOS prompts you to insert a diskette in drive B.

DOS displays its report. (The report you see might be somewhat different. This is for the IBM version 4 Select Copy diskette.)

```
Volume Serial Number is 1BC6-425F

    361472 bytes total disk space
     69632 bytes in 3 hidden files
    274432 bytes in 16 user files
     17408 bytes available on disk

       512 bytes in each allocation unit
       706 total allocation units on disk
        34 available allocation units on disk

    655360 total bytes memory
    526224 bytes free
```

To check the diskette in drive B, and to check whether all files on it are stored in contiguous sectors, type:

```
C:\DOS>chkdsk b:*.*
```

DOS displays the same report as the preceding, but adds the following message:

```
All specified file(s) are contiguous
```

If any files were stored in noncontiguous sectors, DOS would display their names and the number of noncontiguous blocks of storage in place of this message.

To check the diskette in drive B and, at the same time, display the name of each file on it, type:

```
C:\DOS>chkdsk b: /v
```

DOS displays the name of each file on the diskette, then appends its usual report of disk space and memory available. If the list of files scrolls off the top of the screen, remember that, to view it all, you can freeze the display by pressing Ctrl-Num Lock or the Pause key.

Note: If you had organized the files on a diskette into groups called directories, the /V parameter of the Check Disk command would list the directories, as well as the files grouped within them. Directories are covered in Chapter 8, "A Tree of Files."

You can combine the Check Disk parameters in one command; for example, *chkdsk b: *.* /v* would check the diskette in drive B, check all files on it for fragmentation, and display the names of all files.

If the Check Disk command finds an error, it displays a message such as *xx lost allocation units found in yy chains. Convert lost chains to files (Y/N)?* Although this message might look confusing, it simply means that Check Disk has found some storage units on the disk that have been used but, because of a program or system problem, aren't linked with any particular files. If you type the Check Disk command with the /F parameter and then type *y* when the *Convert lost chains...* message appears, DOS turns these "lost" units into files with the filename and extension FILE000X.CHK (where X is a number such as 1, 2, or 3). Depending on the type of error that caused these units to be lost, DOS may or may not be able to recover the data in them. When the Check Disk command is complete, you can look at the contents of these files with the Type command and determine whether or not they contain information you want to save. If you don't want to save the information, delete the files to make the storage space available for new files.

ASSIGNING OR CHANGING A DISK'S VOLUME LABEL

The Label command assigns, changes, or deletes the volume label of a diskette or fixed disk. It has two parameters:

label <drive> <newlabel>

<drive> is the letter, followed by a colon, of the drive (such as *b:*) that contains the disk whose volume label is to be altered.

<newlabel> is the volume label to be assigned to the disk in the drive specified by <drive>.

If you omit <drive>, DOS assumes you want to alter the label of the disk in the current drive. If you omit <newlabel>, DOS prompts you to enter the new label.

Examples of Changing a Disk's Volume Label

At the beginning of this chapter, you used the /V option of the Format command to assign the volume label DOSDISK to your practice diskette. Later, you used the same (or possibly a different) diskette with the Diskcopy command. Diskcopy creates an exact duplicate of a source diskette, including the volume label, so your target diskette from the Diskcopy example is not named DOSDISK. To check this, type the following:

```
C:\DOS>label b:
```

DOS responds:

```
Volume in drive B has no label
Volume Serial Number is 1BC6-425F
Volume label (11 characters, ENTER for none)?
```

But volume labels are useful, so name the diskette DOSCOPY. Type:

doscopy

and press Enter.

If the diskette had a volume label and you wanted to delete it, you would reply to the prompt by pressing the Enter key without typing a name. DOS would then ask *Delete current volume label (Y/N)?* You would reply *y* to delete the volume label.

DISPLAYING A DISK'S VOLUME LABEL

The Volume (vol) command displays the volume label (and volume serial number in version 4) of a fixed disk or a diskette. If you assign descriptive volume labels to your diskettes when you format them, you can use the Volume command to make sure that you're using the correct diskettes. It's faster and easier than checking the directory.

The Volume command has one parameter:

vol <drive>

<drive> is the letter, followed by a colon, of the drive (such as *b:*) that contains the diskette whose volume label is to be displayed. If you omit <drive>, DOS displays the volume label of the disk in the current drive.

To display the volume label of the diskette in drive B, type:

C:\DOS>vol b:

DOS displays the volume label:

```
Volume in drive B is DOSCOPY
Volume Serial Number is 1BC6-425F
```

If the diskette had no volume label, DOS would respond *Volume in drive B has no label.*

7

MANAGING YOUR DEVICES

Data flows into and out of a computer system through pieces of equipment called *devices*. Devices are categorized by whether they handle data coming in (input) or going out (output), or both. The keyboard, for example, is an input device; the computer gets information from it. A printer is an output device; the computer sends information to it. A disk drive is both an input device and an output device; the computer can either read a file from a disk or write a file onto a disk.

Some devices, such as the keyboard, don't usually need much attention from you because DOS requires no special instructions to operate them. Beginning with version 4, however, you can fine-tune their performance, as you'll see later in this chapter. Other devices, such as a color display or a printer, sometimes require you to tell DOS how you want to use them. For example, if you have both a monochrome display and a color display, you can change from one to the other simply by telling DOS which one to use.

Displays, keyboards, printers, and the computer's communications channels, called *ports,* can all be used in a variety of ways. This chapter shows you how to do the following with the DOS commands that help you manage your system:

- Check on system memory with the Mem command.

- Clear the screen with the Clear Screen command.

- Set the speed at which your keyboard repeats a key that is held down with the Mode command.

- Switch displays, control color, and specify the number of characters and lines on the screen with the Mode command.

- Control the width and line spacing of your printer with the Mode command.

- Define the settings of the communications ports with the Mode command.

- Copy from a device to a file or to another device with the Copy command.

- Enable DOS to print graphics with the Graphics command.

- Enable DOS to display special graphics characters on a color/graphics display in graphics mode with the Load Graphics Table (Graftabl) command.

DOS also includes a group of commands that let you change the keyboard layout, available characters, and other operating characteristics to match the requirements of other languages and countries. If you need to use your computer with more than one language, Appendix D, ''DOS Is an International System,'' shows you how to use these commands.

DEVICE NAMES

Just as files have names, so do devices. You can use a device name in many DOS commands just as you would use a file name. DOS assigns all device names, however. You can't name a device yourself. Figure 7-1 on the following pages shows the devices that make up a typical system, with the names assigned to them by DOS.

CON is short for *Console*. It is both an input device and an output device and refers to both the keyboard (input) and the display (output). Because the keyboard is input only and the display is output only, DOS can tell which one to use by the way you use the name CON in a command.

PRN is short for *Printer*. It is an output device and refers to the parallel printer that DOS uses unless you specify otherwise (much as DOS looks for files on the current drive unless you specify otherwise). You can attach as many as three parallel printers (named LPT1, LPT2, and LPT3); PRN usually means LPT1.

AUX is short for *Auxiliary*. It is for both input and output and refers to the communications port that DOS uses unless you instruct otherwise. You can attach one or two communications ports, named COM1 and COM2, with any version of DOS; if you're using version 3.3 or later, you can attach up to four communications ports (COM1 through COM4). Unless you or a program specifies otherwise, DOS assumes that AUX means COM1. On a typical system, COM1 could be used for a modem, and COM2 could be used for a serial printer—or vice versa.

DOS reserves these names for use with devices only; you cannot give any of these names to a file.

PREPARING FOR THE EXAMPLES

Devices often need very specific setup instructions and operating parameters. The examples in this chapter work with IBM and IBM-compatible personal computers. If you're not using one of these machines, you might need to use different instructions to manage your devices. Refer to your documentation for specific information.

When you try the examples, make sure the devices you name are attached to the system and are turned on. You won't hurt anything by entering a command naming a device that isn't present or isn't ready, but the command may cause an error that requires you to restart DOS.

If you're using DOS from diskettes, you'll need the diskette(s) containing the files MEM.EXE (version 4 only), MODE.COM, GRAPHICS.COM, and GRAFTABL.- COM. Before using the Mem, Mode, Graphics, or Graftabl commands, check that the appropriate DOS diskette is in drive A.

Figure 7-1. DOS device names

CHECKING SYSTEM MEMORY WITH THE MEM COMMAND

Even though computer memory isn't a device as you would normally think of the term, it can be both handy and reassuring to know how much memory a system contains, what programs have been loaded into memory, and how much can be used by another program. Beginning with version 4 of DOS, you can use the Mem command to request a report on memory and memory usage. Type:

```
C:\DOS>mem
```

DOS quickly produces a report like this one:

```
655360 bytes total memory
655360 bytes available
526224 largest executable program size
```

Here, DOS is reporting that the computer has 640 K (655,360 bytes) of memory and that more than 500 K is available for another program (a word processor, perhaps). If your computer system contains either extended or expanded memory installed in such a way that DOS can find and use it, the report will also include a summary of how much extra memory is in the system and how much of that memory is available for use.

The Mem command also includes two parameters, /PROGRAM and /DEBUG. These parameters cause DOS to produce a much more detailed report showing the names, sizes, and types of programs that have been loaded into memory and telling you what portion of memory they've been assigned to. Unless you're interested in programming or in learning about the inner workings of your computer, most of this information probably won't seem very meaningful.

CLEARING THE SCREEN

Sometimes you might want to erase distracting clutter from the screen: old directory listings, perhaps, or the display of commands DOS has already completed for you. You can clean things up with the Clear Screen (cls) command, which erases everything on the screen and then displays the system prompt in the upper left corner.

The Clear Screen command has one form:

cls

To test it, type its name:

```
C:\DOS>cls
```

The screen is cleared, except for the system prompt.

FINE-TUNING THE KEYBOARD

Beginning with version 4 of DOS, you can adjust the *typematic* feature of your keyboard. This is the feature that repeats a keystroke again and again on the screen (*xxxxxxxx*...) as long as you press and hold the key that produces the keystroke. To change the way your keyboard operates, you use the Mode command, an all-purpose device-control command that lets you tell DOS not only about your keyboard but about many other parts of your computer system, including your display and printer.

To refine the use of your keyboard, the Mode command has three parameters:

mode con rate=<speed> delay=<pause>

con is the name of the console device (here, the keyboard).

rate=<speed> specifies the speed at which DOS is to repeat the same keystroke. You can specify any number from 1 through 32.

delay=<pause> specifies how long DOS is to wait before starting to repeat the keystroke. You can specify *1* for a 0.25-second delay; *2* for a 0.5-second delay; *3* for a 0.75-second delay; or *4* for a 1-second delay.

You must specify both a rate and a delay. For example, the average keyboard repeats about 20 times per second with a delay of 0.5 second before repeating begins. To see the effect of this version of the Mode command, slow the keyboard considerably. Type:

```
C:\DOS>mode con rate=1 delay=4
```

and try pressing the X key to see the result.

If you are a fast typist, impatient with a too-slow keyboard, set the rate for a high value, such as 32, and set the delay to a low number, such as 1. To slow keyboard repetition, lower the rate and, if you want, increase the delay time.

CONTROLLING THE DISPLAY

A number of different displays and display adapters (the printed-circuit cards that are inserted into the system unit to operate the display) are used with IBM personal computers and compatible machines. Figure 7-2 on the following page describes the most commonly used types of displays and display adapters.

The DOS Mode command has several display-related options. Which option you use depends on the type of display you have and how much you want to see on the screen.

Normally, a computer screen displays 80 columns (characters) across and 25 lines down. If you have an EGA or a VGA display you can, beginning with version 4, change the size of the characters on your display and the number of lines on the screen. When used in this way, the Mode command has three parameters:

mode con cols=<columns> lines=<lines>

Short Name	IBM Product Name	Description
MDA	Monochrome Display Adapter	Text only, medium resolution, one color (usually green on a dark background). Introduced with the IBM PC.
CGA	Color/Graphics Adapter	Text and graphics, low resolution, up to 16 colors. Introduced with the IBM PC.
Hercules	None (works with mono-chrome display)	Displays graphics on monochrome display. (Not compatible with CGA. An application program must specifically support the Hercules board, but most major applications do because of its popularity.)
EGA	Enhanced Graphics Adapter	Text and graphics, medium resolution, up to 64 colors. Introduced with the IBM PC/AT.
MCGA	Multicolor Graphics Array	Text and graphics, low to medium resolution, up to 256 colors. Introduced with the IBM PS/2 models.
VGA	Video Graphics Array	Text and graphics, medium to high resolution, up to 256 colors. Introduced with the IBM PS/2 models.

Figure 7-2. IBM and IBM-compatible displays and adapters

con is the name of the console device (here, the display).

cols=<columns> sets the number of characters displayed on each line. <columns> can be either 40 (for extra-large characters) or 80 (for normal-sized characters).

lines=<lines> sets the number of lines on the screen. <lines> can be 25, 43, or 50, but not all display adapters can handle all three choices.

To set the screen to display 40 characters per line, type:

```
C:\DOS>mode con cols=40
```

To display 80 characters per line and 43 lines per screen, type:

```
C:\DOS>mode con cols=80 lines=43
```

Note: If you try this command and DOS displays the message Function not supported on this computer, *the command does not work on your computer system. If you see the message* ANSI.SYS must be installed to perform requested function, *you need to identify a program named ANSI.SYS to DOS, in a startup file named CONFIG.SYS. Chapter 16, "Tailoring Your System," tells you how to do this.*

In version 4 and earlier versions of DOS, you can use two other parameters of the Mode command to control the number of characters per line on a display attached to a color/graphics adapter (CGA). When used to control the number of columns on a display attached to a color/graphics adapter, the Mode command has one form:

mode <characters>

<characters> is either 40 or 80.

To display 40 columns on a display attached to a color/graphics adapter, type:

`C:\DOS>mode 40`

DOS clears the screen and displays the system prompt in large characters in the upper left corner of the screen.

CONTROLLING MONOCHROME AND CGA DISPLAYS

If you have two displays, one attached to a monochrome display adapter and the other to a color/graphics adapter, DOS uses the monochrome display when you start the system. The Mode command lets you switch from one display to the other. It also lets you specify the number of columns on the display attached to the color/graphics adapter, and specify whether DOS tries to display in color. If you have a non-color display attached to the color/graphics adapter, disabling color can make the display easier for you to read.

When used to switch and control displays, the Mode command has one form:

mode <method>

<method> is one of the following:

mono	Display attached to monochrome display adapter
bw40	Color display, 40 columns, color disabled
bw80	Color display, 80 columns, color disabled
co40	Color display, 40 columns, color enabled
co80	Color display, 80 columns, color enabled

If you're using a color display, you can type the following to switch to the monochrome display:

`C:\DOS>mode mono`

DOS displays the system prompt on the monochrome display.

To specify the color display, 80 columns, and color enabled, type:

`C:\DOS>mode co80`

DOS clears the screen and displays the system prompt in the upper left corner of the CGA display.

CONTROLLING THE PRINTER
WIDTH AND SPACING

A dot-matrix printer normally prints a maximum of 80 characters per line and 6 lines per inch. It can also print in a smaller type, called *condensed,* that fits 132 characters on a line. This ability to change widths is often useful for printing spreadsheets and other documents wider than 80 characters. The printer can also print 8 lines per inch, to fit more lines on a page.

Note: If you have a letter-quality or laser printer, the documentation that came with the printer tells you how to define the printer to DOS and how to control the printer's characteristics, such as line and character spacing. The examples here most likely won't work, unless your laser printer can emulate an Epson dot-matrix printer.

If your printer is attached to a parallel port, you can use the Mode command to specify the line width (80 or 132) and spacing (6 or 8).

When used to control a dot-matrix printer attached to a parallel port, the Mode command has three parameters, which you type in one of the following two forms. The first form applies only to version 4; the second applies to any version of DOS:

mode <printer> cols=<width> lines=<spacing>

or:

mode <printer> <width>,<spacing>

<printer> is the name of the printer, followed by a colon (*lpt1 :, lpt2:,* or *lpt3:*). <width> is either 80 or 132.

<spacing> is either 6 or 8. Notice the comma preceding <spacing> in the second form of the command.

You must always include <printer>. You can omit either <width> or <spacing>, and DOS will leave the current width or spacing unchanged. In the second form of the command, however, if you omit <width> you must still type the comma before <spacing> to tell DOS you omitted <width>.

Note: To avoid cluttering the following pages, the examples show commands as they can be typed with any version of DOS. If you have version 4, bear in mind any alternatives shown in command descriptions like the one above. You might find these alternatives easier to use or remember when working with your system later on.

Examples of Controlling
A Dot-Matrix Printer

Make sure the printer is turned on before entering the following examples.

To cause a printer attached to LPT1 to print in small type (up to 132 characters per line if the printer can do so), type the following:

```
C:\DOS>mode lpt1: 132
```

DOS replies with a display like this one:

```
LPT1: not rerouted
LPT1: set for 132
No retry on parallel printer time-out
```

(If you don't have version 4, you see only the line *LPT1: set for 132*. Don't be concerned about the other information. As you'll see in later examples too, version 4 of DOS often provides more detailed reports than do earlier versions. The commands, however, work the same unless you're told otherwise.)

To test the new printer setting, print and display the directory by typing:

```
C:\DOS><Ctrl-PrtSc>dir
```

The directory is printed with the new line width. (You can cancel the Directory command by pressing Ctrl-Break.) Press Ctrl-PrtSc to stop simultaneous printing.

To set the spacing of the printer attached to LPT1 to 8 lines per inch and leave the width unchanged, type:

```
C:\DOS>mode lpt1: ,8
```

DOS replies with a message like this:

```
LPT1: not rerouted
Printer lines per inch set
No retry on parallel printer time-out
```

(Again, if you don't have version 4, your message is shorter.)

To see the effect of this setting, again start printing and displaying the directory simultaneously by typing:

```
C:\DOS><Ctrl-PrtSc>dir
```

This time the directory is printed both in small type (from the previous example) and with closer line spacing. Press Ctrl-PrtSc again to stop simultaneous printing.

To restore the printer to normal width and line spacing, type:

```
C:\DOS>mode lpt1: 80,6
```

DOS replies:

```
LPT1: not rerouted
LPT1: set for 80
Printer lines per inch set
No retry on parallel printer time-out
```

The printer is back to its normal settings.

CONTROLLING THE SERIAL COMMUNICATIONS PORT

Serial communications is controlled by several characteristics, or communications parameters, that define how fast and in what form data is transmitted. Different devices often require different parameter settings; the parameters of your serial port must match those of the device or computer service with which you want to communicate. Before you can use a communications port, you must set these parameters with the Mode command.

The communications parameters you can set include:

- *Baud,* how quickly characters are sent or received.

- *Parity,* the kind of error-checking technique used.

- *Data bits,* the number of electrical signals required to define a character.

- *Stop bits,* the number of electrical signals that mark the end of a character.

A more complete definition of these parameters is beyond the scope of this book. Figure 7-3 lists the parameters you can set with the Mode command. The documentation of the device or computer service you want to use shows the required setting; compare these settings with those shown in Figure 7-3 to see which, if any, parameters you must change.

When used to set the parameters of a serial communications port, the Mode command has the form:

mode <port> baud=<baud> parity=<parity> data=<databits> stop=<stopbits>

or:

mode <port> <baud>,<parity>,<databits>,<stopbits>

<port> is the name, followed by a colon, of the communications port—*com1:* through *com4: (com1:* or *com2:* if you're using a version earlier than 3.3). The remaining parameters, separated by commas, are those described in Figure 7-3.

Name	Valid Settings	How You Specify	Value DOS Assumes
Baud	110, 150, 300, 600, 1200, 2400, 4800, 9600, 19,200*	You can abbreviate the first two digits (11 for 110, 24 for 2400)	None (you must set a value)
Parity	None, Odd, Even, Mark†, or Space†	N, O, E, M, or S	Even (E)
Databits	5†, 6†, 7, or 8	5, 6, 7, or 8	7
Stopbits	1, 1.5†, or 2	1, 1.5, or 2	2 if baud = 110, 1 otherwise

*19,200 is available from version 3.3 only and can be used only with a computer capable of that speed, such as some IBM PS/2 models.
† Version 4 only.

Figure 7-3. Serial communications parameters

You must specify a value for <baud> each time you enter this form of the Mode command. DOS assumes the values for the other parameters listed in the last column of Figure 7-3 unless you specifically change them; you needn't specify these parameters unless the device or service with which you want to communicate requires values different from those that DOS assumes.

If you omit any parameter from the second form of the Mode command shown above, you must still type the comma that precedes it, to show DOS that you omitted the parameter.

Examples of Controlling the Serial Port For Communications

These examples show you different uses of the Mode command. Don't enter them unless you have a serial communications port.

To set the baud rate for COM1 to 1200 and let DOS assume values for the other parameters, you would type:

```
C:\DOS>mode com1: 1200
```

DOS replies by reporting the current setting of each parameter:

```
COM1: 1200,e,7,1,-
```

This report shows that <baud> is 1200, <parity> is even, <databits> is 7, and <stopbits> is 1. The hyphen at the end tells you DOS will not keep trying to send to a device that isn't ready, but will stop after a brief time.

To set <baud> for COM1 to 2400, <parity> to none, leave <databits> set to 7, and set <stopbits> to 2, you would type:

```
C:\DOS>mode com1: 2400,n,,2
```

Note the two commas before the 2, telling DOS that you omitted <databits>. DOS confirms the settings:

```
COM1: 2400 ,n,7,2,-
```

CONNECTING A SERIAL PRINTER

If you want to use a serial printer attached to a communications port, you must use the Mode command to tell DOS to send printer output to the communications port instead of to the regular (parallel) printer port; this is called *redirecting* or *rerouting* the printer output. (You might recall from the earlier examples of controlling a dot-matrix printer that the DOS responses to the Mode command included the line *LPT1: not rerouted*. Here, you can see the meaning of that message: DOS was reporting that output to the regular printer port was not redirected to a serial port.)

Before you redirect the printer output, you must first set the parameters of the serial communications port to the values required by the printer, as described in the preceding topic.

When used to redirect printer output to a serial communications port, the Mode command has one form:

mode <printer>=<port>

<printer> is the name of the printer (*lpt1:, lpt2:,* or *lpt3:*) whose output is to be redirected.

<port> is the name of the serial communications port (*com1:* or *com2:* in all versions of DOS, *com1:* through *com4:* in 3.3 and later versions). You must enter both parameters.

Example of Connecting a Serial Printer

To redirect printer output from LPT1 to serial port COM1, you would first set the serial port to match the communications parameters of your printer, then type:

```
C:\DOS>mode lpt1:=com1:
```

DOS would acknowledge:

```
LPT1: rerouted to COM1:
```

Now all output that would normally go to LPT1: would be sent to COM1: instead. To cancel the redirection and restore the printer output to LPT1:, you would type:

```
C:\DOS>mode lpt1:
```

FINDING OUT ABOUT YOUR SYSTEM

You have, up to this point, seen a number of ways to use the Mode command to control the devices on your system. But just as it's useful to know how to control your devices, it's also helpful to know what devices DOS is prepared to use and how it "sees" them. Beginning with version 4, you can use the Mode command not only to describe devices to DOS but to find out about them.

To check on the status of any or all devices on your system, you use the command:

mode <device>

<device> is the name of a particular device you want to check on. If you omit <device>, DOS reports on the devices it recognizes.

To check on the status of a single device, you type *mode* and the name of the device. For example, if the display were set to show 80 characters per line and 43 lines per screen, the command:

```
C:\DOS>mode con
```

would produce a report like this:

```
Status for device CON:
----------------------
COLUMNS=80
LINES=43
Code page operation not supported on this device
```

(The message *Code page operation not supported on this device* simply means that DOS, on this computer, has not been told to recognize international language, date, decimal, and currency conventions. If you need this capability, refer to Appendix D, "DOS Is an International System.")

To check on all the devices on your system, you would type:

```
C:\DOS>mode
```

and DOS would respond with a report like this:

```
Status for device LPT1:
----------------------
LPT1: not rerouted
RETRY=NONE
Code page operation not supported on this device
Status for device LPT2:
----------------------
LPT2: not rerouted
Status for device LPT3:
----------------------
LPT3: not rerouted
Status for device CON:
----------------------
Code page operation not supported on this device
```

Although parts of the report might look unfamiliar, here's what it means:

- The report covers four devices: three output ports, LPT1, LPT2, and LPT3, and the display, CON.

- The message *LPTx: not rerouted* simply means that information sent to any of these output channels has not been diverted to another port.

- The message *RETRY=NONE* means that, if the device connected to the port is busy, DOS will not keep trying to send information to the device (a printer, for example).

- The *Code page . . .* message is explained above.

COPYING FROM A DEVICE TO A FILE OR ANOTHER DEVICE

As you saw in earlier examples, you can use the Copy command to copy from a device to a file. You have used this technique several times to create sample files by copying from the keyboard to a file, and you will find it handy for creating short text files.

You can also copy from one device to another. Copying from the keyboard to the printer, for example, is a quick and convenient way to print short notes or lists.

When you copy from one device to a file or another device, DOS continues to copy until it comes to the character (Ctrl-Z) that marks the end of a file. Whenever you copy from the keyboard, you can send this end-of-file character by pressing the key labeled F6 and then pressing the Enter key (or, as you've done before, by pressing Ctrl-Z and Enter).

When used to copy from a device to a file or another device, the Copy command has two parameters:

copy <source> <target>

<source> is the name of the source device.
<target> is the name of the target file or device.

Examples of Copying from a Device To a File or Another Device

To copy from the keyboard (CON) to the printer (PRN), make certain the printer is turned on and type:

```
C:\DOS>copy con prn
```

Now everything you type will be both displayed and sent to the printer. Type a few lines, and then end the copy by pressing F6 or Ctrl-Z (shown as ^Z in the example because that's how DOS displays it):

```
These lines are being
copied from the
keyboard to the printer.
^Z
        1 File(s) copied

C:\DOS>_
```

Note: If you're using a Hewlett-Packard LaserJet Plus or a similar laser printer, this example will produce a printed copy if you press the ON LINE *button and then the* FORM FEED *button. Be sure to do this after you type the example; otherwise, it might appear at the beginning of the next document you print.*

To copy from the serial communications port (AUX) to the printer (PRN), you would first set the serial port to match the communications parameters of whatever is attached to it, then you would type:

```
C:\DOS>copy aux prn
```

Everything received at the communications port would be printed until the end-of-file character was received.

PRINTING GRAPHICS IMAGES

Pressing Shift-PrtSc prints the text displayed on either a monochrome or color display, but it does not print graphics images from a display that is attached to a graphics adapter. The Graphics command enables DOS to print these graphics images on any of several different printers.

You need enter the Graphics command only once. After you enter it, pressing Shift-PrtSc prints everything on the screen of the active display, including graphics images. Low-resolution graphics images are printed across the paper; color on non-color printers is simulated with shading. High-resolution graphics images are printed sideways (rotated 90 degrees) and enlarged.

The Graphics command loads a program that increases the amount of memory that DOS uses.

The Graphics command has four main parameters:

graphics <printer> /R /B /LCD

<printer> is one of the IBM printers or a compatible model. It can be any of the following:

- For the IBM Personal Computer Color Printer, the options are: *color1* for a black ribbon or the black band of a color ribbon; *color4* for a red-green-blue ribbon; *color8* for a cyan-magenta-yellow ribbon.

- For the IBM Personal Computer Compact Printer, specify *compact* (versions prior to 4).

- For an IBM Graphics printer, Proprinter, Pageprinter, or Quietwriter, specify *graphics.*

- For an IBM Quietwriter or Proprinter with an 11-inch carriage, specify *graphicswide* (version 4 only).

- For the IBM PC Convertible Printer, specify *thermal* (versions 3.3 and later).

If you don't specify <printer>, DOS assumes *graphics.*

/R tells DOS to print the screen as you see it—in other words, light characters on a dark background.

/B tells DOS to print the background color if you have specified *color4* or *color8* for <printer>. If you don't specify /B, DOS doesn't print the background color.

/LCD tells DOS to print the contents of the liquid crystal display of the IBM PC Convertible computer.

When you enter the Graphics command, DOS loads the program, adds it to the parts of the system kept in memory, and displays the system prompt. You needn't enter the command again until the next time you start DOS.

If you're using a color display and have a printer that can print graphics, you can test the Graphics command by entering the command and appropriate parameters, then displaying a graphics image and pressing Shift-PrtSc.

DISPLAYING GRAPHICS CHARACTERS

Even when the color/graphics adapter is in graphics mode, it normally cannot display the 128 special characters that include accented characters, Greek letters, box-drawing graphics, and others. The Graftabl command enables DOS to display these characters when the color/graphics adapter is in graphics mode.

Like the Graphics command, you need enter the Graftabl command only once. After you enter it, the additional characters can be displayed on the screen. The Graftabl command loads a small program that increases the amount of memory that DOS uses.

You don't need the Graftabl command in normal DOS operation, but there are certain times it can come in handy. For example, suppose you would like to display accented French or Spanish characters on the screen. If your display is connected to the color/graphics adapter, you would simply type *graftabl*.

Depending on your version of DOS, you see a message like this:

```
Previous Code Page: None
Active Code Page: 437
```

or this:

```
No version of Graphic Character Set Table is already loaded.
USA version of Graphic Character Set Table has just been loaded.
```

or this:

```
GRAPHIC CHARACTERS LOADED
```

In any case, all 128 special graphics characters would be available until you reset or turned off your computer. DOS includes more foreign-language capabilities; these are significantly expanded beginning with version 3.3 and changed further in version 4. For a detailed description of these capabilities, see Appendix D.

CHAPTER
8
A TREE OF FILES

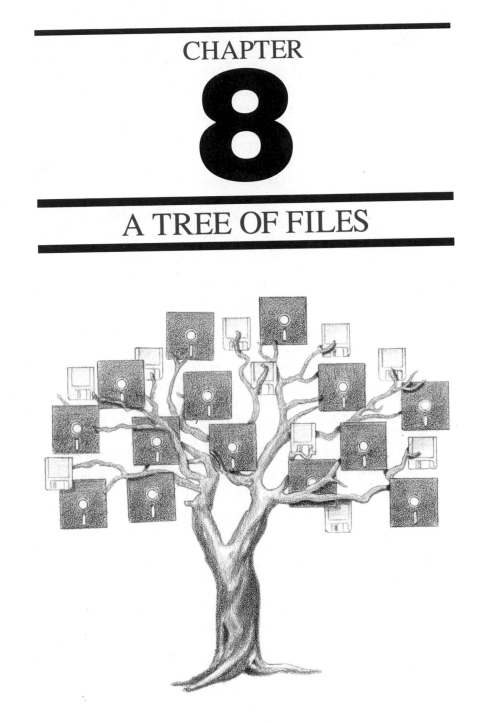

A s you have seen, when DOS formats a disk, it creates a directory that describes each of the files on the disk. The directory holds a fixed number of entries: 112 on a 360 K or 720 K diskette, 224 on a 1.2 MB or 1.44 MB diskette, and 512 or more on a fixed disk (the number varies with the size of the disk).

To make your computer filing system more flexible, DOS lets you create additional directories, called *subdirectories,* on a disk. The subdirectories divide the disk into different storage areas, each of which you can use as if it were a different disk.

To distinguish the main directory that DOS creates from the subdirectories that you create, the main directory is known as the *root directory* because a multilevel directory structure can grow from it.

As you add levels to your file structure, a block diagram would show it spreading from the root directory and branching to other directories, like a tree branching from its root. This type of file structure is often called a *tree-structured* file system and is the reason for the name root directory.

DEFINING A SUBDIRECTORY

To DOS, a subdirectory is simply a file that contains directory entries; these entries are identical in form to the entries in the main directory, but there is no limit to the number of entries you can put in a subdirectory.

You name a subdirectory as you name any other file, but because the subdirectory defines other files, you cannot use the normal file commands to copy or erase a subdirectory. This chapter shows you how to use several commands that enable you to do the following:

- Create a subdirectory with the Make Directory command.

- Change or display the name of the current directory with the Change Directory command.

- Delete a subdirectory with the Remove Directory command.

- Display a list of all the directories on a disk with the Tree command.

- Tell DOS where to look for a command file, if it's not in the current directory, with the Path command.

- Tell DOS where to look for a data file, if it's not in the current directory, with the Append command (3.3 and later versions).

Using these features of DOS, you can create and manage a computer filing system that is tailored to the way you work.

PREPARING FOR THE EXAMPLES

The examples in this chapter require one formatted diskette. If you're using a fixed disk or have a one-drive system, put the diskette in the diskette drive. If you're using two diskette drives, put the formatted diskette in drive B. If any files from earlier examples are stored on the diskette, erase them by typing the following; be sure to include the *b:* in the command:

```
C:\DOS>erase b:*.*
```

If you have only one diskette drive, DOS asks you to make sure the correct diskette is in the drive:

```
Insert diskette for drive B: and press any key when ready
```

Press any key.

DOS asks you to confirm that you want to erase all the files:

```
All files in directory will be deleted!
Are you sure (Y/N)?_
```

Before you respond, check the command you entered and be certain that you typed the drive letter (*b:*). If you didn't, press Ctrl-Break to cancel the Erase command, and retype the command correctly. If you did type the drive letter, respond *y*. Because a mistake here could cause the loss of valuable files, you must also press the Enter key after typing *y* before DOS will carry out the command.

After you have erased the files, change the current drive to B by typing:

```
C:\DOS>b:
```

This completes the preparation.

CREATING A MULTILEVEL FILE STRUCTURE

Suppose you work at a small company and provide services to two departments, Marketing and Engineering. You keep all your papers in a file drawer. You keep miscellaneous items in the front of the drawer, and dividers labeled MKT and ENG separate the parts where you store papers that relate to each department. Figure 8-1 on the following page shows how the file drawer might look.

Now that you're going to be using a computer, you can set up your computer filing system to match your paper files by creating two subdirectories named MKT and ENG. You can store miscellaneous computer files in the main, or root, directory of the disk, and you can store the files relating to each department in separate subdirectories. Figure 8-2 shows the filing cabinet and a block diagram of this corresponding DOS file structure.

Figure 8-1. File drawer with dividers

Figure 8-2. Two-level file systems

Creating a Subdirectory

The Make Directory (md, or mkdir) command creates a subdirectory. The only parameter you must include is the name of the subdirectory you want to create. The command is described later in more detail; for now, type the following to create two subdirectories named MKT and ENG:

```
B:\>md mkt
```

```
B:\>md eng
```

You can see the subdirectories you just created by displaying the entries in the root directory. Type:

```
B:\>dir
```

DOS shows two files named MKT and ENG:

```
Volume in drive B has no label
Volume Serial Number is 1359-1AEF
Directory of  B:\

MKT            <DIR>      10-16-89    8:14a
ENG            <DIR>      10-16-89    8:14a
          2 File(s)   1212928 bytes free
```

Note that the directory identifies the files as subdirectories by displaying <DIR> after their names. The backslash (\) in the third line of the display is the character that DOS uses to refer to the root directory of a disk. You've seen the backslash as part of the system prompt throughout this book; you'll see more of it and its uses in later examples.

Because MKT is a subdirectory, you can display its contents with the Directory command, just as you can display the contents of the root directory. Type the following command:

```
B:\>dir mkt
```

DOS displays the contents of MKT:

```
Volume in drive B has no label
Volume Serial Number is 1359-1AEF
Directory of  B:\MKT

.             <DIR>      10-16-89    8:14a
..            <DIR>      10-16-89    8:14a
          2 File(s)   1212928 bytes free
```

Even though you just created it, MKT seems to contain subdirectories named . (one period) and .. (two periods). These really aren't subdirectories; they're abbreviations you use to refer to other directories. You'll see how these abbreviations are used a bit later.

The Path to a Directory

The second line of the preceding directory display tells you that you're looking at the directory of B:\MKT. The \ (backslash) refers to the root directory, and MKT is the name of the subdirectory whose contents you're displaying. Together, they are called the *path name* of the directory, or just the *path,* because they describe the path DOS follows to find the directory. The path names of the two subdirectories you created, \MKT and \ENG, tell DOS that the subdirectories are in the root directory.

You can also include a path name with a file name, to tell DOS where to find a file. The path name goes just before the file name (after the drive letter, if one is included) and is separated from the file name by a backslash. For example, if the subdirectory \MKT contained a file named BUDGET.JAN, the full path and file name would be \MKT\BUDGET.JAN.

The Current Directory

Just as DOS keeps track of the current drive, it also keeps track of the current directory. If you use DOS from diskettes or if DOS is in the root directory of your fixed disk, the current directory when you start up is the root directory of the current drive. If you use a fixed disk and DOS is in a directory of its own, the current directory when you start up is probably the DOS directory, as shown in the system prompt (C:\DOS>) in most of the examples in this book.

Just as you can change the current drive, you can change the current directory, so that you don't have to type the path name each time you want to work with a directory other than the current directory.

The Change Directory (cd, or chdir) command changes or displays the name of the current directory. If you enter the command with no parameter, it displays the name of the current directory. To see what the current directory is, type:

    B:\>cd

The current directory is the root directory, so the response is short:

    B:\

It tells you that any command you enter will apply to the root directory of the diskette in drive B, unless you specify a different path name. Change the current directory to the subdirectory named MKT by typing:

    B:\>cd mkt

If your system prompt normally shows the current directory, DOS acknowledges:

    B:\MKT>

as soon as it carries out the Change Directory command.

If your system prompt doesn't display the current directory, DOS acknowledges merely by displaying the system prompt. But if you display the current directory again by typing:

```
B>cd
```

DOS responds:

```
B:\MKT
```

Note: Whenever you work with subdirectories, it's useful to have the current directory displayed as part of the system prompt. If your system prompt does not include the current directory, try changing it: type prompt pg. *Chapter 12, "Creating Your Own Commands," tells you how to make this instruction a normal part of your system's startup routine. Chapter 16, "Tailoring Your System," shows you many other types of information you can include in the system prompt.*

You've changed the current directory to \MKT, so any command you enter applies to the subdirectory MKT in the root directory. Type the Directory command again:

```
B:\MKT>dir
```

DOS displays the entries in the subdirectory \MKT:

```
Volume in drive B has no label
Volume Serial Number is 1359-1AEF
Directory of  B:\MKT

.            <DIR>      10-16-89    8:14a
..           <DIR>      10-16-89    8:14a
         2 File(s)    1212928 bytes free
```

This is the same display you saw earlier when you typed *dir mkt*, but this time you didn't have to name the subdirectory because you had changed the current directory to \MKT.

Using Subdirectories

Your diskette now has the directory structure shown in Figure 8-2. You can use each of these directories as if it were a separate disk. The current directory is \MKT. Create a file in the root directory by typing the following lines:

```
B:\MKT>copy con \sample.txt
This is a sample file.
^Z
        1 File(s) copied
```

Notice that you included the backslash to tell DOS to put the file in the root directory. You also use the backslash to display the contents of the root directory when it's not the current directory. Type the following:

```
B:\MKT>dir \
```

Again DOS displays the entries in the root directory:

```
Volume in drive B has no label
Volume Serial Number is 1359-1AEF
Directory of  B:\

MKT              <DIR>       10-16-89    8:14a
ENG              <DIR>       10-16-89    8:14a
SAMPLE   TXT           24 10-16-89    8:17a
          3 File(s)      1212416 bytes free
```

The root directory contains two subdirectories and the file you just created.

Copying from One Directory to Another

Because you can treat directories as if they were separate disks, you can copy a file from one directory to another. Copy SAMPLE.TXT from the root directory of drive B to a file named ACCOUNT in the current directory (\MKT) by typing:

```
B:\MKT>copy \sample.txt account
       1 File(s) copied
```

You included the path (the backslash, meaning the root directory) in front of SAMPLE.TXT to tell DOS where to find the file; you didn't have to include a path for ACCOUNT because you were putting it in the current directory. Now display the current directory by typing the following:

```
B:\MKT>dir

 Volume in drive B has no label
 Volume Serial Number is 1359-1AEF
 Directory of  B:\MKT

 .               <DIR>       10-16-89    8:14a
 ..              <DIR>       10-16-89    8:14a
 ACCOUNT               24 10-16-89    8:17a
          3 File(s)      1211904 bytes free
```

The file is there. You can copy files from one directory to another as easily as you can copy them from one disk to another.

Just as DOS doesn't confuse two files with the same name on different disks, it doesn't confuse two files with the same name in different directories. DOS can tell the latter apart because their paths are different. You can demonstrate this by copying the file named ACCOUNT from \MKT to the subdirectory \ENG, giving it the same file name. Type the following:

```
B:\MKT>copy account \eng
        1 File(s) copied
```

You didn't include the file name after the path name of the target directory because you wanted to give the copy the same name as the original. Assure yourself that the file was copied correctly by displaying the directory of \ENG:

```
B:\MKT>dir \eng

 Volume in drive B has no label
 Volume Serial Number is 1359-1AEF
 Directory of  B:\ENG

 .           <DIR>      10-16-89    8:14a
 ..          <DIR>      10-16-89    8:14a
 ACCOUNT            24 10-16-89    8:17a
        3 File(s)     1211392 bytes free
```

You now have two files named ACCOUNT on the same disk; but they are in different subdirectories, and their different path names make them as different to DOS as if you had given them different file names.

Time Out for a Quick Review

Before completing your multilevel file structure, take a few minutes to review the following definitions. They summarize the terms and concepts introduced in the preceding examples.

Directory entry: A description of a file that includes the name, extension, and size of the file, and the date and time it was created or last updated.

Directory: A list of directory entries. You'll also see it used with a sense of place: "Which directory am I in?"

Root directory: The list of directory entries that DOS creates and maintains on each disk. It is called the root directory (or simply the root) because the entire directory structure on the disk grows from it. Because the root has no name to DOS, it is represented by a backslash (\ ).

Subdirectory: A file that contains directory entries. Like the term directory, it is also sometimes used with a sense of place: "Which subdirectory is that file in?"

Path name: The list of directory names that defines the path to a subdirectory. The directory names are separated by backslashes (\ ). The root directory is represented by a backslash at the beginning of the path. If a file name is included at the end of the path, it is separated from the last directory name by a backslash.

Current directory: The directory that DOS assumes you want to use unless you specify another in a command. The current directory is similar in concept and effect to the current drive.

ADDING MORE LEVELS TO YOUR FILE STRUCTURE

The subdirectories you create can contain any type of file, including other subdirectories. Like putting dividers between other dividers in a file drawer, this further structuring narrows the subject of a storage area. Suppose you do the following type of work for the Marketing and Engineering departments:

MARKETING	ENGINEERING
Word processing	Word processing
Budgets	Budgets
Customer lists	Project scheduling
Sales forecasts	

You decide to set up your file structure to match your work.

The following list shows the additional subdirectories you could create to match your computer files to the work you do (MKT and ENG are the departmental subdirectories you created earlier):

In MKT:	In ENG:
WP	WP
BUDGET	BUDGET
CUSTOMER	SCHEDULE
SALES	

You would then have created the file structure shown in Figure 8-3.

Making a Subdirectory The MD Command

As you saw earlier, the Make Directory (md, or mkdir) command creates a subdirectory. The Make Directory command has two parameters:

md <drive><path>

<drive> is the letter, followed by a colon, of the drive (such as *b:*) that contains the disk on which the subdirectory is to be created. If you omit <drive>, DOS creates the subdirectory on the disk in the current drive.

<path> is the path name of the directory in which the subdirectory is to be created. If you omit <path>, the subdirectory is created in the current directory.

The current directory is \MKT. If your system prompt doesn't show this, check it by typing:

```
B>cd
```

Figure 8-3. Three-level file systems

For the example in this chapter, you want four subdirectories in \MKT named WP, BUDGET, CUSTOMER, and SALES. Type the following Make Directory commands to create the subdirectories:

```
B:\MKT>md wp

B:\MKT>md budget

B:\MKT>md customer

B:\MKT>md sales
```

Display the directory of \MKT by typing:

```
B:\MKT>dir

    Volume in drive B has no label
    Volume Serial Number is 1359-1AEF
    Directory of  B:\MKT

    .            <DIR>        10-16-89    8:14a
    ..           <DIR>        10-16-89    8:14a
    ACCOUNT                24 10-16-89    8:17a
    WP           <DIR>        10-16-89    8:21a
    BUDGET       <DIR>        10-16-89    8:21a
    CUSTOMER     <DIR>        10-16-89    8:21a
    SALES        <DIR>        10-16-89    8:21a
            7 File(s)     1209344 bytes free
```

The directory shows the file you copied a few minutes ago (ACCOUNT) and the four subdirectories you just created.

Your file structure calls for subdirectories named WP and BUDGET in both \MKT and \ENG. Remember, DOS can distinguish between \MKT\WP and \ENG\WP, \MKT\BUDGET and \ENG\BUDGET, because their paths are different.

To create the subdirectory \ENG\WP, type:

```
B:\MKT>md \eng\wp
```

You included the path (\ENG) because the current directory is \MKT. The Make Directory command doesn't change the current directory, so it's still \MKT, but you can verify that the subdirectory \ENG\WP was created by displaying the contents of \ENG. Include the path here, too, by typing:

```
B:\MKT>dir \eng

 Volume in drive B has no label
 Volume Serial Number is 1359-1AEF
 Directory of  B:\ENG

 .             <DIR>      10-16-89    8:14a
 ..            <DIR>      10-16-89    8:14a
ACCOUNT                24 10-16-89    8:17a
WP             <DIR>      10-16-89    8:22a
         4 File(s)    1208832 bytes free
```

Now you're going to start moving around from subdirectory to subdirectory, so before creating the last two subdirectories in \ENG, here's a closer look at your navigator, the Change Directory command.

Changing the Current Directory
The CD Command

You have already used the Change Directory (cd, or chdir) command to change and display the current directory. The Change Directory command has two parameters:

cd <drive><path>

<drive> is the letter, followed by a colon, of the drive (such as *b:*) that contains the disk on which the current directory is to be changed. If you omit <drive>, DOS changes the current directory on the disk in the current drive.

<path> is the path name of the directory that is to become the current directory. If you omit <path>, DOS displays the current directory on <drive>.

If you omit both <drive> and <path> (enter the command with no parameters), DOS displays the current directory of the disk in the current drive.

Keeping Track of Where You Are

As a note earlier in this chapter showed, you can change the system prompt to display not only the current drive but other information, such as the current directory.

Up to this point, the system prompt has shown the current drive and directory in abbreviated form (such as *B:\MKT>*). In the remainder of the chapter, you'll be changing directories fairly often, so change the prompt to one that helps you identify the current directory at a glance. Type the following, including a blank at the end of the line, just before you press the Enter key:

```
B:\MKT>prompt Current Directory is $p$_Command: <Enter>
```

Now the system prompt becomes:

```
Current Directory is B:\MKT
Command: _
```

You could restore the system prompt to its more familiar form by typing the Prompt command with no parameters (*prompt*) or by typing *prompt pg*, but leave it this way for the rest of the chapter. The prompt takes up a bit more space, but it helps you keep track of where you are—a useful feature, especially if you are still adjusting to the idea of moving from one directory to another.

Using the Subdirectory Markers

Remember those markers (. and ..) listed in each subdirectory? They're designed to let you move quickly up and down a directory structure, particularly when several levels make the path names long.

The .. represents the directory that contains the current directory (sometimes called the *parent* of the current directory). The current directory is \MKT; to move the current directory up (toward the root directory) one level, type:

```
Current Directory is B:\MKT
Command: cd ..

Current Directory is B:\
Command: _
```

The system prompt still shows you the current directory but, as you can see, the current directory has changed to the root directory, which is one level above \MKT.

To complete your file structure, you need two more subdirectories in \ENG. Change the current directory to \ENG and create \ENG\BUDGET and \ENG\SCHEDULE by typing the following:

```
Current Directory is B:\
Command: cd eng

Current Directory is B:\ENG
Command: md budget

Current Directory is B:\ENG
Command: md schedule
```

This completes the structure of your multilevel file system.

You have nine subdirectories, plus the root directory, any of which you can use as if it were a separate disk. To show you how easy this is, the next few examples have you put sample files in several of the subdirectories. Figure 8-4 shows how your final file system will look, including the path names of all directories (above the boxes) and the names of the files you'll add (inside the shaded boxes).

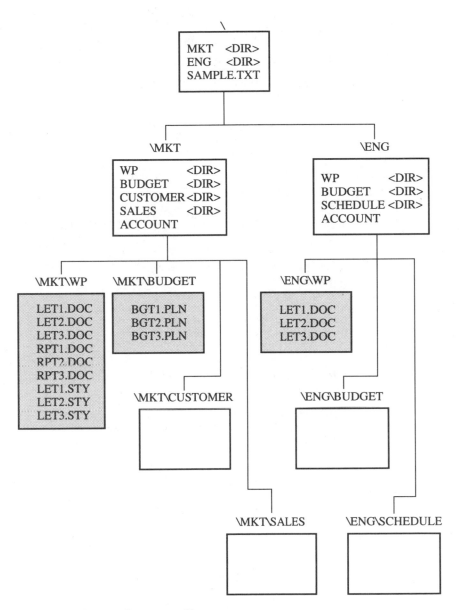

Figure 8-4. Two-department file structure

To create the sample files in \ENG\WP, first change the current directory to \ENG\WP and copy the file named ACCOUNT from \ENG, naming it LET1.DOC, by typing the following:

```
Current Directory is B:\ENG
Command: cd wp

Current Directory is B:\ENG\WP
Command: copy \eng\account let1.doc
        1 File(s) copied
```

Note that you must use \ENG in the command, even though \ENG\WP is a subdirectory of \ENG.

Now copy LET1.DOC twice, to create LET2.DOC and LET3.DOC, and display the directory by typing:

```
Current Directory is B:\ENG\WP
Command: copy let1.doc let2.doc
        1 File(s) copied

Current Directory is B:\ENG\WP
Command: copy let1.doc let3.doc
        1 File(s) copied

Current Directory is B:\ENG\WP
Command: dir

 Volume in drive B has no label
 Volume Serial Number is 1359-1AEF
 Directory of  B:\ENG\WP

 .              <DIR>       10-16-89    8:22a
 ..             <DIR>       10-16-89    8:22a
 LET1     DOC          24 10-16-89    8:17a
 LET2     DOC          24 10-16-89    8:17a
 LET3     DOC          24 10-16-89    8:17a
        5 File(s)     1206272 bytes free
```

From this subdirectory, you can copy all three of these files to \MKT\WP with one command. Type the following:

```
Current Directory is B:\ENG\WP
Command: copy *.* \mkt\wp
```

DOS lists the source files as it copies them:

```
LET1.DOC
LET2.DOC
LET3.DOC
        3 File(s) copied
```

These files could be word-processing files that contain letters. Now create three
more files in \MKT\WP that could represent word-processing files that contain
reports. First, change the directory to \MKT\WP, then copy the three files whose
names begin with LET, changing their names so they begin with RPT. Type:

```
Current Directory is B:\ENG\WP
Command: cd \mkt\wp

Current Directory is B:\MKT\WP
Command: copy let?.doc rpt?.doc
```

DOS again lists the source files as it makes the copies:

```
LET1.DOC
LET2.DOC
LET3.DOC
        3 File(s) copied
```

To complete the files in this subdirectory, copy the same three files again, this
time changing their extension to STY, which could identify word-processing files that
contain style sheets for formatting and printing documents. Type the following:

```
Current Directory is B:\MKT\WP
Command: copy let?.doc let?.sty
```

Now display the directory to verify that all nine files are there by typing:

```
Current Directory is B:\MKT\WP
Command: dir

 Volume in drive B has no label
 Volume Serial Number is 1359-1AEF
 Directory of  B:\MKT\WP

 .            <DIR>      10-16-89    8:21a
 ..           <DIR>      10-16-89    8:21a
 LET1    DOC        24   10-16-89    8:17a
 LET2    DOC        24   10-16-89    8:17a
 LET3    DOC        24   10-16-89    8:17a
 RPT1    DOC        24   10-16-89    8:17a
 RPT2    DOC        24   10-16-89    8:17a
 RPT3    DOC        24   10-16-89    8:17a
 LET1    STY        24   10-16-89    8:17a
 LET2    STY        24   10-16-89    8:17a
 LET3    STY        24   10-16-89    8:17a
        11 File(s)     1201664 bytes free
```

To complete the file system, you need three files in \MKT\BUDGET named
BGT1.PLN, BGT2.PLN, and BGT3.PLN. Use the Copy command to copy the files and
change their names by typing the following:

```
Current Directory is B:\MKT\WP
Command: copy let?.doc \mkt\budget\bgt?.pln
```

DOS lists the source files as it makes the copies:

```
LET1.DOC
LET2.DOC
LET3.DOC
          3 File(s) copied
```

Your file system now has the directories and files shown in Figure 8-4.

Removing a Subdirectory
The RD Command

As you work with a multilevel filing system, you might find that you no longer need a particular subdirectory, or that you want to combine the files from several subdirectories into one and then delete the unneeded subdirectories from your file structure. The Remove Directory (rd, or rmdir) command removes a subdirectory. A subdirectory cannot be removed if it contains any files or subdirectories.

The Remove Directory command has two parameters:

rd <drive><path>

<drive> is the letter, followed by a colon, of the drive that contains the disk with the subdirectory to be removed. You can omit <drive> if the subdirectory is on the disk in the current drive.

<path> is the path name of the subdirectory to be removed. You must specify <path> because DOS will not remove the current directory.

Suppose you decide you don't need the subdirectory \ENG\WP. Tell DOS to remove it by typing:

```
Current Directory is B:\MKT\WP
Command: rd \eng\wp
```

DOS responds *Invalid path, not directory, or directory not empty* because \ENG\WP isn't empty: You put three files, LET1.DOC, LET2.DOC, and LET3.DOC, in it.

This example points out the difference in the ways you handle files and subdirectories. As you saw in earlier chapters, you use the Erase command to erase a file from a disk. To remove a directory, however, you use the Remove Directory command.

In the next example, you will erase three files with the Erase command, and then remove a directory with the Remove Directory command. First, change the current directory to \ENG, and then delete the files with the Erase command by typing:

```
Current Directory is B:\MKT\WP
Command: cd \eng

Current Directory is B:\ENG
Command: erase wp\*.doc
```

You changed the current directory to \ENG, rather than to \ENG\WP, because DOS won't remove the current directory. Now that \ENG\WP is empty, type the Remove Directory command and verify the change by displaying the directory.

```
Current Directory is B:\ENG
Command: rd wp

Current Directory is B:\ENG
Command: dir

 Volume in drive B has no label
 Volume Serial Number is 1359-1AEF
 Directory of  B:\ENG

.               <DIR>      10-16-89    8:14a
..              <DIR>      10-16-89    8:14a
ACCOUNT                 24 10-16-89    8:17a
BUDGET          <DIR>      10-16-89    8:24a
SCHEDULE        <DIR>      10-16-89    8:24a
         5 File(s)     1202176 bytes free
```

The subdirectory \ENG\WP is gone.

If you want to remove a directory but need some of the files it contains, copy the files you need to another subdirectory, then erase all the files and remove the unneeded directory.

The Path to a Command
The PATH Command

In a multilevel filing system, you'll probably change the current directory as you use data files in different subdirectories. But you'll use command files too, such as the external DOS commands and application programs. When you type a command, DOS looks for the command file in the current directory. If you have changed the current directory, chances are the new current directory doesn't contain the command file you need.

The Path command lets you tell DOS where to look for a command file if it's not in the current directory. You can name one or more directories—the root directory or any subdirectory for the disk in any disk drive. This command lets you work in any subdirectory you want and still be able to use any command file.

The Path command has three parameters:

path <drive><path> ;

<drive> is the letter, followed by a colon, of the drive (such as *b:*) with the disk that contains the command file. If you omit <drive>, DOS looks on the disk in the current drive for the directory specified by <path>.

<path> is the path name of the directory that contains the command file.

You can specify several command paths in one command, separating them with semicolons. If you enter a Path command with no parameters (just type *path*), DOS displays the command paths you have defined. If you type *path* followed only by a semicolon, DOS cancels any command paths you have already defined.

If you have a fixed disk, the root directory probably contains a special file named AUTOEXEC.BAT that DOS reads each time you start or restart your computer. AUTOEXEC.BAT contains instructions that help DOS work well for you. One of those instructions is probably a Path command that enables you to use application programs, as well as external DOS commands, no matter what the current directory is. For example, suppose you use Microsoft Word, Lotus 1-2-3, R:BASE System V, and MaxThink, and your DOS files are in a directory named \DOS. Your Path command might look like this:

```
path c:\dos;c:\word;c:\123;c:\rbfiles;c:\max
```

The order in which the directory names are specified determines the order in which DOS searches for the command file that runs the particular program. Because the drive letter and root-directory symbol (\) precede each subdirectory name, DOS knows where to find each program, and you can use any program in any of these directories even if the current drive isn't C.

If you have a fixed disk and DOS has no trouble starting application programs or carrying out external commands when drive B is the current drive, you can be sure you have an AUTOEXEC.BAT file with a Path command in it. You can check on your own command path by typing *path* with no parameters. Type:

```
Current Directory is B:\
Command: path
```

If you do have any problems, Chapter 12, "Creating Your Own Commands," tells you how to create or modify an AUTOEXEC.BAT file.

And what if you don't have a fixed disk? You use the Path command to tell DOS to look on drive A for its command files. The following few examples use external command files. The current drive is B, so use the Path command to tell DOS where to find its external commands. Type:

```
Current Directory is B:\
Command: path a:\
```

Displaying the Directory Structure
The Tree and Check Disk commands

When you create a file structure with several levels, you might not remember exactly what subdirectories you created or where you created them, nor might you always be able to remember which subdirectories contain which files. You could use the Change Directory and Directory commands to move from one subdirectory to the next and to display the contents of each, but there are quicker ways: the Tree and Check Disk commands. Which of these commands you use depends on your version of DOS. If you have IBM's release of DOS version 2.0 or later, or Microsoft's release of DOS version 3.2 or later, you can use the Tree command. Otherwise, you can use Check Disk.

The Tree command has two main parameters:

tree <drive> /F

<drive> is the letter of the drive, followed by a colon, that contains the disk whose directory structure is to be displayed.

/F displays a list of the files in each directory.

Checking the Directory Structure of a Disk

Note: The following two examples use the Tree command. If your version of DOS does not include this command, a later example shows you how to use the Check Disk command to see a list of directories and files on a disk.

Suppose you're about to create a new file and you want to check on the most appropriate subdirectory for it. As its name implies, the Tree command shows you the structure of the directory tree on whichever disk you specify. For example, check the directories on your sample disk. To be sure you see the entire structure, first change to the root directory. Type:

```
Current Directory is B:\ENG
Command: cd \
```

Now ask DOS to show you the names and relative levels of the directories on the disk. (If you're not using a fixed disk, place the diskette with the file TREE.COM in drive A.) Type:

```
Current Directory is B:\
Command: tree
```

If you're using version 4 of DOS, you see a report like this:

```
Directory PATH listing
Volume Serial Number is 1359-1AEF
B:.
├───MKT
│   ├───WP
│   ├───BUDGET
│   ├───CUSTOMER
│   ├───SALES
└───ENG
    ├───BUDGET
    └───SCHEDULE
```

If you're using an earlier version of DOS, you see a report like the following (some blank lines that appear on the screen have been removed to condense the display):

```
DIRECTORY PATH LISTING
Path: \MKT
Sub-directories:   WP
                   BUDGET
                   CUSTOMER
                   SALES
Path: \MKT\WP
Sub-directories:   None
Path: \MKT\BUDGET
Sub-directories:   None
Path: \MKT\CUSTOMER
Sub-directories:   None
Path: \MKT\SALES
Sub-directories:   None
Path: \ENG
Sub-directories:   BUDGET
                   SCHEDULE
Path: \ENG\BUDGET
Sub-directories:   None
Path: \ENG\SCHEDULE
Sub-directories:   None
```

But suppose a report on the directory structure isn't detailed enough. You want to know the name of each file in each subdirectory—perhaps because there is one file in particular you need to work on. To do this, you use the /F parameter, which shows not only the directory structure of the disk, but the names of the files in each directory. For example, version 4 of DOS produces a report like this when you type *tree/f*:

```
Directory PATH listing
Volume Serial Number is 1359-1AEF
B:.
|    SAMPLE.TXT
|
|---MKT
|    |    ACCOUNT
|    |
|    |---WP
|    |        LET1.DOC
|    |        LET2.DOC
|    |        LET3.DOC
|    |        RPT1.DOC
|    |        RPT2.DOC
|    |        RPT3.DOC
|    |        LET1.STY
|    |        LET2.STY
|    |        LET3.STY
|    |
```

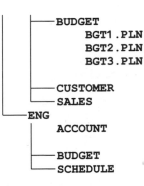

```
        ─── BUDGET
                BGT1.PLN
                BGT2.PLN
                BGT3.PLN

        ─── CUSTOMER
        ─── SALES
    ─ENG
            ACCOUNT

        ─── BUDGET
        ─── SCHEDULE
```

Now the tree shows the names of your files beneath the names of the subdirectories that contain them.

If your version of the Tree command doesn't produce the graphic type of report shown above, or if your version of DOS doesn't include a Tree command, you can use the /V parameter of the Check Disk command to see a list of files and directories. (If you're not using a fixed disk, check that the file CHKDSK.COM is on the disk in drive A.) Type:

```
Current Directory is B:\
Command: chkdsk /v
```

DOS responds:

```
Volume Serial Number is 1359-1AEF
Directory B:\
Directory B:\MKT
        B:\MKT\ACCOUNT
Directory B:\MKT\WP
        B:\MKT\WP\LET1.DOC
        B:\MKT\WP\LET2.DOC
        B:\MKT\WP\LET3.DOC
        B:\MKT\WP\RPT1.DOC
        B:\MKT\WP\RPT2.DOC
        B:\MKT\WP\RPT3.DOC
        B:\MKT\WP\LET1.STY
        B:\MKT\WP\LET2.STY
        B:\MKT\WP\LET3.STY
Directory B:\MKT\BUDGET
        B:\MKT\BUDGET\BGT1.PLN
        B:\MKT\BUDGET\BGT2.PLN
        B:\MKT\BUDGET\BGT3.PLN
Directory B:\MKT\CUSTOMER
Directory B:\MKT\SALES
Directory B:\ENG
        B:\ENG\ACCOUNT
Directory B:\ENG\BUDGET
```

```
Directory B:\ENG\SCHEDULE
         B:\SAMPLE.TXT
 1213952 bytes total disk space
    4096 bytes in 8 directories
    7680 bytes in 16 user files
 1202176 bytes available on disk
     512 bytes in each allocation unit
    2371 total allocation units on disk
    2348 available allocation units on disk

  655360 total bytes memory
  526192 bytes free
```

Here, the directories are identified by *Directory* preceding the path and file name. File names are indented below the name of the directory that contains them; the file in the root directory (SAMPLE.TXT) is listed at the end, above the usual Check Disk reports on disk space and memory.

A printed copy of either of these reports can be helpful, especially if your filing system has several levels. For a fixed disk with several hundred files, however, bear in mind that either a Tree or a Check Disk report showing both directories and files could be several pages long. Here are some ways you can print the reports of either or both the Tree and Check Disk commands.

If you want to print a list of both directories and files, use the Tree command with the /F parameter or the Check Disk command with the /V parameter. If you have version 4 and your printer is not an IBM or IBM-compatible printer, either use the Check Disk command or use an additional parameter of the Tree command: /A. (For example, type *tree b: /f /a.*) The /A parameter, described in Appendix F, tells DOS to use hyphens, backslashes, and other characters available on your printer. Without the /A parameter, your printout might include accented letters, small open circles, or other such characters in place of the horizontal and vertical lines showing the branches of your directory tree.

For example, to print a complete report for the disk in drive B, type:

```
Current Directory is B:\
Command: tree /f > prn
```

or:

```
Current Directory is B:\
Command: tree /f /a > prn
```

or:

```
Current Directory is B:\
Command: chkdsk /v > prn
```

To print only a list of directories on the disk in drive B, you can use either of the following commands.

With the Tree command, type:

```
Current Directory is B:\
Command: tree > prn
```

With the Check Disk command, you use techniques described in Chapter 13, "Taking Control of Your System" to filter out all the file names from the output of the Check Disk command, leaving just the subdirectory names, which are then sent to the printer. Try it. (Notice that a slash, not a backslash, precedes the *v*.) Type:

```
Current Directory is B:\
Command: chkdsk /v ¦ find "Di" > prn
```

The printed output of this command shows only the names of the directories (the lines that contain *Di*).

Any of these guides to your filing system can help you keep track of both files and subdirectories and can help you use your system more efficiently.

The Path to a Data File
The APPEND Command

If you're using 3.3 or a later version of DOS, you can use the Append command to tell DOS where to look for a data file if it's not in the current directory. Just as with the Path command, you can name one or more directories on any disk drive.

The Append command has three main parameters related to helping DOS find data files:

append <drive><path> ;

<drive> is the letter, followed by a colon, of the drive (such as *c:*) with the disk that contains the data files. If you omit <drive>, DOS looks in the directory specified by <path> on the current drive.

<path> is the path name of the directory that contains the data files.

You can specify several data paths in one command, separating them with semicolons. If you enter an Append command with no parameters (just type *append*), DOS displays the data paths you have defined. If you type *append* followed only by a semicolon, DOS cancels any data paths you have defined.

It's easy to try the Append command. The current directory is \ENG, and the file RPT1.DOC is in the directory \MKT\WP. First, try to display the file by using the Type command:

```
Current Directory is B:\
Command: type rpt1.doc
```

DOS replies *File not found* because RPT1.DOC isn't in the current directory. Now type two Append commands to set the data path to \MKT\WP and display the data path:

```
Current Directory is B:\
Command: append \mkt\wp

Current Directory is B:\
Command: append
APPEND=\MKT\WP
```

Now try the Type command again:

```
Current Directory is B:\
Command: type rpt1.doc
This is a sample file.
```

This time DOS finds the file because you told it where to look. Cancel the data path by typing *Append* with just a semicolon, then check the data path again:

```
Current Directory is B:\
Command: append ;

Current Directory is B:\
Command: append
No Append
```

The Path and Append commands are valuable tools for improving the efficiency and convenience of using a fixed disk. Appendix F, the DOS command reference, includes a complete description of each.

If you're going to continue using your system, restart your computer or type the following to restore the system prompt:

```
Current Directory is B:\
Command: prompt

B>
```

CHAPTER SUMMARY

Although this chapter introduced several new terms and concepts, it doesn't take many commands to set up a multilevel file system. The structure shown in Figure 8-3, for example, required only the following 11 commands (don't enter them; this list is just to show you the commands you entered):

md mkt	md sales
md eng	md \eng\wp
cd mkt	cd \eng
md wp	md budget
md budget	md schedule
md customer	

You might not create a file structure with this many levels on a diskette, although it's certainly possible if you use high-capacity diskettes. As you noticed, subdirectories require a great deal of work from the diskette drive. But you might find that two or three subdirectories reduce the number of diskettes you use, or that they let you use your system more efficiently. The examples in this chapter showed you how to use all the commands you need to create and manage a multilevel filing system.

If you're using a fixed disk, save the diskette that contains the file system you created in this chapter. You'll use it to copy sample files in the next chapter, ''Managing Your Fixed Disk.''

CHAPTER
9

MANAGING YOUR FIXED DISK

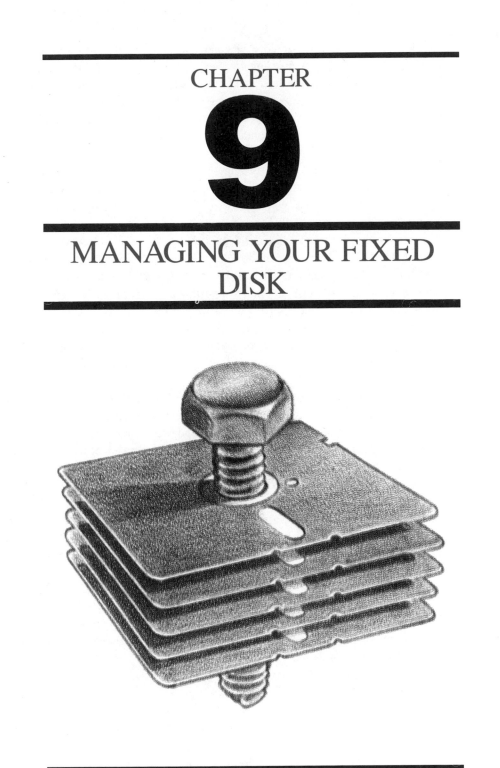

A fixed disk holds far more data than a diskette does, and DOS uses it much more quickly. As its name implies, you don't remove the disk; it is permanently fixed in the drive. Like a diskette, a fixed disk stores data in tracks and sectors; unlike a diskette, however, a fixed disk stores data on several magnetically coated, rigid metal—not plastic—disks that are enclosed in a nonremovable case.

A fixed-disk drive usually contains two or more separate disks that give it a total storage capacity of 20 to 40 megabytes, but fixed disks with even higher capacities are becoming more common. Several computers offer a fixed disk that can hold 300 megabytes or more. This chapter focuses on how to use your fixed disk efficiently. If you don't have a fixed disk, you can skip to Chapter 10, ''Creating and Editing Files of Text.''

Managing your fixed disk requires more thought and planning than managing your diskettes, simply because of the sheer number of files involved. But properly organized and managed, your fixed disk is a fast and effective tool you use with a minimum of fuss. Two tasks are more important than any others in managing your fixed disk efficiently. One is setting up a filing system that lets you take advantage of the disk's capacity without losing track of all your files. The other is backing up the files periodically, both to protect yourself against loss of data in the event your fixed disk is inadvertently erased or damaged, and to clear out old files you no longer use regularly.

The previous chapter covered setting up a multilevel filing system. Everything you learned there applies to managing your fixed disk properly. This chapter covers the additional tasks of organizing directories and files on your fixed disk, using some commands that are tailored for keeping track of large numbers of files, and backing up files to diskettes and restoring them to the fixed disk.

In most ways, you treat a fixed disk as if it were a large diskette, using the DOS directory commands to create, change, and remove directories, and the DOS file commands to copy, erase, rename, and otherwise work with your files. The Volume and Label commands described in Chapter 6, ''Managing Your Diskettes,'' can also be used with a fixed disk. But two diskette commands—Diskcopy and Diskcomp—don't work with the fixed disk because they are specifically designed to work only with entire diskettes.

Warning: It's possible to erase all the files on the fixed disk by inadvertently formatting it. A way to protect yourself against this is described under ''Renaming the Format Command'' in Chapter 16, ''Tailoring Your System.''

This chapter suggests some guidelines to simplify the job of managing your fixed disk; it shows you how to:

- Control the archive attribute of a file with the Attribute command.

- Copy files selectively with the Replace and Xcopy commands.

- Back up files from one disk to another with the Backup command.

- Restore files from a backup disk with the Restore command.

- Put all the DOS files in a directory named \DOS and thus reduce clutter in the root directory (versions earlier than 4.0).

- Install a new version of DOS on your fixed disk, using the System and Copy commands (versions earlier than 4.0).

PUTTING APPLICATION PROGRAMS ON THE FIXED DISK

The examples in this chapter use part of the directory structure and sample data files you created in the previous chapter. When you actually set up a directory structure, you'll undoubtedly want to copy the command and data files of your application programs onto the fixed disk. Depending on how you set up your directories and how many application programs you use, you might put the application programs in the root directory, in another subdirectory, or in a separate subdirectory for each application.

In general, however, you shouldn't put all your programs in the root directory or in a single large program directory. You'll have the same problem you would if you tossed all your program diskettes into a big drawer. Remember, too, that DOS itself is a collection of command (program) and data files. Like application program files, the DOS files can be stored in a variety of places on your fixed disk—for example, in the root directory, in a subdirectory named \DOS, or even in a sub-subdirectory named \PROGRAMS\DOS. Version 4 of DOS suggests that you allow it to install itself in a subdirectory named \DOS (or in another subdirectory you name). Earlier versions, however, might be installed in any of the locations mentioned above.

If all your DOS programs are in the root directory, you should consider moving them to a DOS directory so they'll be easy to find and won't clutter up your root directory and directory displays. Instructions for doing this are at the end of this chapter in the section "DOS and Your Fixed Disk." If you haven't yet prepared your fixed disk, turn to Appendix A, "Preparing Your Fixed Disk," and then follow the instructions on installing DOS in Appendix B (version 4) or Appendix C (versions prior to 4) before you continue with this chapter.

PREPARING FOR THE EXAMPLES

The examples in this chapter rely on the information presented in the previous chapter, ''A Tree of Files,'' and use the directory structure and files you created there. If you haven't completed those examples, do so before continuing.

The examples in this chapter require the sample subdirectories and files in Figure 9-1. You will create these on the fixed disk in a subdirectory named \TEMP, which will keep all your examples in one place for easy removal. If you already have a \TEMP directory, use a different name.

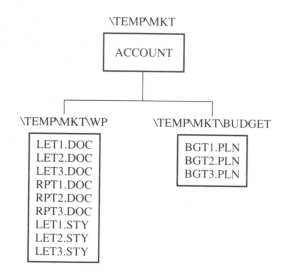

Figure 9-1. Subdirectories and files for fixed-disk examples

If your system prompt doesn't show the current directory, change it to an abbreviated version of the *Current Directory is...* prompt you used in the last chapter. Type:

```
C>prompt $p$g<Enter>
C:\DOS>
```

Now your system prompt shows both the current drive and the current directory and will help you keep track of where you are in your directory structure.

To create the \TEMP subdirectory, type:

```
C:\DOS>md \temp
```

Now change the current directory to \TEMP by typing:

```
C:\DOS>cd \temp
```

Moving Files to Your Fixed Disk

The remainder of your preparation depends on which version of DOS you're using. If you have version 3.2 or later, follow the instructions under the heading ''Moving Files with the Xcopy Command.'' If you have a version of DOS prior to 3.2, follow the instructions under the heading ''Moving Files with the Copy Command.''

Moving Files with the Xcopy Command

If you're using version 3.2 or later of DOS, moving everything from your practice diskette to the \TEMP directory is simple. All you need is one Xcopy command, which copies subdirectories and files from the source disk to the target disk. The Xcopy parameter you use here, /S, copies all subdirectories as well as all files. Xcopy is described in more detail later. For now, put the diskette that contains your sample files in drive A and type:

```
C:\TEMP>xcopy a: /s
```

DOS responds:

```
Reading source file(s)...
A:SAMPLE.TXT
A:MKT\ACCOUNT
A:MKT\WP\LET1.DOC
A:MKT\WP\LET2.DOC
A:MKT\WP\LET3.DOC
A:MKT\WP\RPT1.DOC
A:MKT\WP\RPT2.DOC
A:MKT\WP\RPT3.DOC
A:MKT\WP\LET1.STY
A:MKT\WP\LET2.STY
A:MKT\WP\LET3.STY
A:MKT\BUDGET\BGT1.PLN
A:MKT\BUDGET\BGT2.PLN
A:MKT\BUDGET\BGT3.PLN
A:ENG\ACCOUNT
        15 File(s) copied
```

You don't need the file named SAMPLE.TXT, or the directory named \ENG and the file it contains, so remove them by typing:

```
C:\TEMP>erase sample.txt
```

```
C:\TEMP>erase eng\account
```

```
C:\TEMP>rd eng
```

You're through.

Moving Files with the Copy Command

Put the diskette that contains your sample files in drive A and type the following commands to duplicate the diskette's directory structure on your fixed disk:

```
C:\TEMP>md mkt

C:\TEMP>md mkt\wp

C:\TEMP>md mkt\budget
```

Now type the following to copy the files from the diskette to the fixed disk; press any key when DOS prompts you for the diskette for drive A:

```
C:\TEMP>copy a:\mkt\account mkt
        1 File(s) copied

C:\TEMP>copy a:\mkt\wp\*.* mkt\wp
A:\MKT\WP\LET1.DOC
A:\MKT\WP\LET2.DOC
A:\MKT\WP\LET3.DOC
A:\MKT\WP\RPT1.DOC
A:\MKT\WP\RPT2.DOC
A:\MKT\WP\RPT3.DOC
A:\MKT\WP\LET1.STY
A:\MKT\WP\LET2.STY
A:\MKT\WP\LET3.STY        *
        9 File(s) copied

C\TEMP>copy a:\mkt\budget\*.* mkt\budget
A:\MKT\BUDGET\BGT1.PLN
A:\MKT\BUDGET\BGT2.PLN
A:\MKT\BUDGET\BGT3.PLN
        3 File(s) copied
```

This completes the preparation.

CHANGING THE ARCHIVE ATTRIBUTE OF A FILE

In Chapter 5, following the heading "Controlling Whether a File Can Be Changed," you saw how to use the Attribute command to control the read-only attribute of a file or a group of files. If you're using 3.2 or a later version of DOS, you can also use the Attribute command to control the *archive attribute* of a file.

The archive attribute, like the read-only attribute, is a part of the directory entry that isn't displayed by the Directory command but can be examined or changed by DOS or any other program. This attribute is turned off by the Backup and Xcopy commands, which are described later in this chapter, and by some programs that back up files from a fixed disk. The archive attribute is turned on by Edlin, Microsoft Word, and most other programs that change a file.

The archive attribute therefore tells DOS (or any other program that checks it) whether a file has been changed since the last time it was backed up. The archive attribute is used principally by the Backup and Xcopy commands—and by backup programs—to determine which files must be backed up.

Because of the way it is stored in the directory entry, you might sometimes see the archive attribute called the *archive bit;* rest assured that the terms mean the same.

The Attribute command, which lets you control the read-only or archive attributes, can have six parameters:

attribute +R −R +A −A <filename> /S

+R turns on the read-only attribute (as you saw in Chapter 5), and −R turns it off.

+A turns on the archive attribute. This tells DOS (or any other program) that the file has been changed since it was backed up to an archival storage medium, such as a diskette or a tape. You can use this parameter with 3.2 and later versions.

−A turns off the archive attribute. This tells DOS (or any other program) that the file has not been changed since it was backed up for archival storage. You can use this parameter with 3.2 and later versions.

<filename> is the name of the file whose attributes are to be changed or displayed. You can use wildcard characters to specify a group of files.

/S tells DOS to apply the Attribute command to each subdirectory contained in <filename>. If you specify <filename> as the root directory of a disk and include /S, the Attribute command is applied to every subdirectory on the disk. You can use this parameter with 3.3 and later versions.

If you omit all parameters except <filename>, DOS displays the name or names of the files, with an A in column 3 if the file has the archive attribute and an R in column 8 if the file is read-only.

Examples of Changing The Archive Attribute

First, change the current directory to \TEMP\MKT\WP and check the attributes of the files in the current directory by typing the following Change Directory and Attribute commands:

```
C:\TEMP>cd mkt\wp

C:\TEMP\MKT\WP>attrib *.*
    A           C:\TEMP\MKT\WP\LET1.DOC
    A           C:\TEMP\MKT\WP\LET2.DOC
    A           C:\TEMP\MKT\WP\LET3.DOC
    A           C:\TEMP\MKT\WP\RPT1.DOC
    A           C:\TEMP\MKT\WP\RPT2.DOC
    A           C:\TEMP\MKT\WP\RPT3.DOC
    A           C:\TEMP\MKT\WP\LET1.STY
    A           C:\TEMP\MKT\WP\LET2.STY
    A           C:\TEMP\MKT\WP\LET3.STY
```

DOS displays the name of each file with an A in column 3 because the files have never been backed up.

To turn off the archive attribute of all files with the extension DOC and check the result, type:

```
C:\TEMP\MKT\WP>attrib -a *.doc

C:\TEMP\MKT\WP>attrib *.*
                C:\TEMP\MKT\WP\LET1.DOC
                C:\TEMP\MKT\WP\LET2.DOC
                C:\TEMP\MKT\WP\LET3.DOC
                C:\TEMP\MKT\WP\RPT1.DOC
                C:\TEMP\MKT\WP\RPT2.DOC
                C:\TEMP\MKT\WP\RPT3.DOC
   A            C:\TEMP\MKT\WP\LET1.STY
   A            C:\TEMP\MKT\WP\LET2.STY
   A            C:\TEMP\MKT\WP\LET3.STY
```

Now only those files whose extension is STY have the archive attribute.

If you're using 3.3 or a later version of DOS, you can use the /S parameter to apply the Attribute command to all subdirectories. To turn off the archive attribute of all files in the directories \TEMP\MKT, \TEMP\MKT\WP, and \TEMP\MKT\BUDGET and then check the results in all three directories, type the following commands to change the directory to \TEMP\MKT, turn off the archive attribute of all files in all subdirectories, and check the attributes of all files in all subdirectories:

```
C:\TEMP\MKT\WP>cd ..

C:\TEMP\MKT>attrib -a *.* /s

C:\TEMP\MKT>attrib *.* /s
                C:\TEMP\MKT\WP\LET1.DOC
                C:\TEMP\MKT\WP\LET2.DOC
                C:\TEMP\MKT\WP\LET3.DOC
                C:\TEMP\MKT\WP\RPT1.DOC
                C:\TEMP\MKT\WP\RPT2.DOC
                C:\TEMP\MKT\WP\RPT3.DOC
                C:\TEMP\MKT\WP\LET1.STY
                C:\TEMP\MKT\WP\LET2.STY
                C:\TEMP\MKT\WP\LET3.STY
                C:\TEMP\MKT\BUDGET\BGT1.PLN
                C:\TEMP\MKT\BUDGET\BGT2.PLN
                C:\TEMP\MKT\BUDGET\BGT3.PLN
                C:\TEMP\MKT\ACCOUNT
```

The response to the second Attribute command shows that you turned off the archive attribute of all the files in \TEMP\MKT\WP, \TEMP\MKT\BUDGET, and \TEMP\MKT.

Type the following command to turn on the archive attributes of all files in all subdirectories in \TEMP\MKT. (Examples later in the chapter expect them to be on.)

```
C:\TEMP\MKT>attrib +a *.* /s
```

COPYING SELECTED FILES

In earlier chapters, you saw that you can copy files with similar names or extensions by using the Copy command and wildcard characters. If you're using 3.2 or a later version of DOS, you have even more flexibility in copying files:

■ The Replace command lets you replace all files in every subdirectory of a target disk that have the same name as the files on a source disk. The Replace command also lets you copy only the files on a source disk that *don't* exist on the target disk or in a target directory. Beginning with version 4, the Replace command also lets you update files by replacing only those on the target disk that are *older* than those of the same name on the source disk.

■ The Xcopy command, as you saw in preparing for this chapter's examples, lets you copy whole subdirectories and the files in them. It also lets you copy only files that have changed since they were last backed up, or those that have changed since a particular date.

Replacing Files on a Disk

The Replace command, like the Copy command, copies files from one disk or directory to another. The Replace command, however, is more selective:

■ If used without the /A or /U parameters, the Replace command copies only source files that also exist on the target; it *replaces* files, hence its name.

■ If used with the /A parameter, it lets you reverse the operation of the Replace command and tell it to copy only source files that *don't* exist on the target; with this option, it only *adds* files.

■ If used with the /U parameter, the Replace command lets you copy only source files that are newer than files of the same name on the target; with this option, it *updates* files.

As a further refinement, the Replace command also lets you copy files not only from the source directory, but also from all the subdirectories the source contains.

The Replace command has eight parameters:

replace <source> <target> /A /S /R /P /U /W

<source> is the name of the file to be copied. You can use wildcard characters to replace a set of files that have similar file names or extensions.

<target> specifies where <source> is to be copied. You can include a drive letter and a path name.

/A (for *add*) copies only the files specified in <source> that don't exist in <target>. This lets you add files to <target> without replacing files that already exist.

If you don't specify /A, only files specified in <source> that also exist in <target> are copied. If you specify /A, you cannot specify /S or /U.

/S (for *search*) applies the Replace command to all subdirectories contained in <target>. If you specify <target> as the root directory of a disk, the command is applied to every subdirectory on the disk. If you specify /S, you cannot specify /A.

/R replaces files in <target> that are read-only.

/P prompts you for confirmation before it replaces or adds each file.

/U (for *update*) replaces only those files on the target disk that are older than the corresponding files on the source disk. If you specify /U, you cannot specify /A.

/W (for *wait*) prompts you to press a key before the Replace command begins. This lets you put in the correct diskette before starting to replace or add files.

To see how the Replace command works, copy the file named LET1.DOC from \TEMP\MKT\WP to \TEMP\MKT\BUDGET and check the directory by typing:

```
C:\TEMP\MKT>copy wp\let1.doc budget
          1 File(s) copied

C:\TEMP\MKT>dir budget

 Volume in drive C is FIXED DISK
 Volume Serial Number is 1608-5A30
 Directory of  C:\TEMP\MKT\BUDGET

 .              <DIR>      10-16-87    8:21a
 ..             <DIR>      10-16-87    8:21a
 BGT1    PLN          24  10-16-87    8:17a
 BGT2    PLN          24  10-16-87    8:17a
 BGT3    PLN          24  10-16-87    8:17a
 LET1    DOC          24  10-16-87    8:17a
          6 File(s)     15157248 bytes free
```

Now use the Replace command with no parameters to replace all files in \TEMP\MKT\BUDGET whose name begins with LET and whose extension is DOC that also exist in \TEMP\MKT\WP. Type:

```
C:\TEMP\MKT>replace wp\let*.doc budget
```

DOS responds:

```
Replacing C:\TEMP\MKT\BUDGET\LET1.DOC

1 file(s) replaced
```

The Replace command copied only the file—the one you copied at the beginning of this example—that already existed in \TEMP\MKT\BUDGET. The message tells you that DOS *replaced* one existing file.

Now type the Replace command again, but this time include the /A parameter, which tells DOS to copy only those files that do *not* exist in the target; you're doing the opposite of what you did with the previous Replace command:

```
C:\TEMP\MKT>replace wp\let*.doc budget /a
```

DOS responds:

Adding C:\TEMP\MKT\BUDGET\LET2.DOC

Adding C:\TEMP\MKT\BUDGET\LET3.DOC

2 file(s) added

This time the Replace command copied the files that it didn't copy in the previous example. The message tells you that DOS *added* files to the target directory.

Finally, if you have version 4 of DOS, see how you can update files. Begin by creating a newer version of LET1.DOC in the directory \TEMP\MKT\WP:

```
C:\TEMP\MKT>copy con wp\let1.doc
This is a newer file.
^Z
        1 File(s) copied
```

Now you have one version of the file in \TEMP\MKT\BUDGET and a newer version with the same file name in \TEMP\MKT\WP. Update all files in the BUDGET subdirectory by typing:

```
C:\TEMP\MKT>replace wp\let*.doc budget /u
```

DOS responds:

Replacing C:\TEMP\MKT\BUDGET\LET1.DOC

1 file(s) replaced

This time, DOS compared matching file names and updated only the one, LET1.DOC, that had a more recent version in the source directory than in the target.

Copying Files with the Xcopy Command

In preparing for this chapter, you used the Xcopy command to move an entire directory structure from one disk to another. If the corresponding subdirectories don't exist on the target disk or directory, the Xcopy command creates them.

Unlike Copy and Replace, Xcopy can be used to copy only files whose archive attribute is on, or to copy only files that have been changed since a date you specify.

The Xcopy command has 10 parameters:

xcopy <source> <target> /A /M /D:<date> /E /P /S /V /W

<source> is the name of the file to be copied. You can include a path name, and you can use wildcard characters to copy a set of files with similar file names or extensions.

<target> specifies where <source> is to be copied. You can include any combination of drive letter, path name, and file name. If you specify different drives, the target directory does not have to have the same name as the source directory.

/A copies only those files whose archive attribute is on, and leaves the archive attribute of the source unchanged.

/M copies only those files whose archive attribute is on, and turns off the archive attribute of the source. This tells DOS (or any other program) that the file hasn't been changed since it was last backed up and therefore doesn't need to be backed up again.

/D:<date> copies only files created or changed on or after <date>. (The date of creation or last change is the date shown in the directory entry for any file. Enter <date> just as you would for the Date command.)

/E creates subdirectories in <target> even if they're empty in <source>.

/P prompts for confirmation before each file specified in <source> is copied.

/S applies the Xcopy command to all subdirectories contained in <source>. If you specify <source> as the root directory of a disk, the Xcopy command is applied to every subdirectory on the disk.

/V verifies that the copy of the file on <target> was stored correctly. This can slow the operation of the Xcopy command somewhat, but it's good insurance if you're copying critical data and must be certain that it was copied correctly.

/W prompts you to press a key before the Xcopy command begins. This wait gives you a chance to put in the correct diskette before starting to copy files.

For this example, you create a temporary subdirectory named FRED in the root directory and dispose of it at the end of the example. First, change the current directory to \TEMP:

```
C:\TEMP\MKT>cd ..
```

Now type the following Make Directory command:

```
C:\TEMP>md \fred
```

and add the following sample file to \TEMP:

```
C:\TEMP>copy con test.doc
This is a test file.
^Z
        1 File(s) copied
```

All the files in \TEMP and its subdirectories have the archive attribute turned on. For the first Xcopy command, use the /A parameter to copy all the files in \TEMP whose extension is DOC and whose archive attribute is turned on:

```
C:\TEMP>xcopy *.doc \fred /a
```

DOS responds by displaying the name of each source file as it is copied:

```
Reading source file(s)...
TEST.DOC
        1 File(s) copied
```

DOS copied TEST.DOC, the only file in \TEMP whose extension is DOC. Verify this by displaying the directory of \FRED:

```
C:\TEMP>dir \fred

 Volume in drive C is FIXED DISK
 Volume Serial Number is 1608-5A30
 Directory of  C:\FRED

 .              <DIR>       10-16-89   12:28p
 ..             <DIR>       10-16-89   12:28p
 TEST    DOC          22    10-16-89   12:35p
        3 File(s)     14096384 bytes free
```

Now type the same Xcopy command, but add the /S parameter to copy all files whose extension is DOC and whose archive attribute is turned on, not only in \TEMP but also in all its subdirectories:

```
C:\TEMP>xcopy *.doc \fred /a /s
Reading source file(s)...
TEST.DOC
MKT\WP\LET1.DOC
MKT\WP\LET2.DOC
MKT\WP\LET3.DOC
MKT\WP\RPT1.DOC
MKT\WP\RPT2.DOC
MKT\WP\RPT3.DOC
MKT\BUDGET\LET1.DOC
MKT\BUDGET\LET2.DOC
MKT\BUDGET\LET3.DOC
        10 File(s) copied
```

This time DOS copied 10 files; it also copied the subdirectories named MKT\WP and MKT\BUDGET. Verify this by displaying the directory of \FRED\MKT:

```
C:\TEMP>dir \fred\mkt

 Volume in drive C is FIXED DISK
 Volume Serial Number is 1608-5A30
 Directory of  C:\FRED\MKT

 .              <DIR>       10-12-89   12:28p
 ..             <DIR>       10-12-89   12:28p
 WP             <DIR>       10-12-89   12:39p
 BUDGET         <DIR>       10-12-89   12:39p
        4 File(s)     14071808 bytes free
```

The Xcopy command created the subdirectories named WP and BUDGET in \FRED, then copied the files whose extension is DOC and whose archive attribute is on from \TEMP\MKT\WP to \FRED\MKT\WP and from \TEMP\MKT\BUDGET to \FRED\MKT\BUDGET.

The value of the archive attribute, however, is that it can tell you which files have changed since they were last backed up, if the archive attribute is turned off when a file is backed up and it is turned on when a file is changed. The /M parameter, like the /A parameter, tells Xcopy to copy only those files whose archive attribute is on; but it also turns the archive attribute off on the source file, so that you can mark the files as backed up. Type another Xcopy command to copy the files whose extension is DOC, but this time use /M instead of /A:

```
C:\TEMP>xcopy *.doc \fred /m /s
```

DOS responds just as it did to the previous Xcopy command, because it copied the same 10 files, but this time it turned their archive attributes off. It's easy to check this; retype the last Xcopy command:

```
C:\TEMP>xcopy *.doc \fred /m /s
        0 File(s) copied
```

This time no files were copied because the previous command turned off the archive attributes of the files.

Now suppose you change one of the files. A new file's archive attribute is on, just as if it were an existing file you changed with Edlin or a word processor, so type the following to create a different version of \TEMP\TEST.DOC:

```
C:\TEMP>copy con test.doc
A new version of TEST.DOC.
^Z
        1 File(s) copied
```

Type the same Xcopy command you typed twice before; the first time Xcopy copied 10 files, the second time it copied no files, and this time it should copy one file:

```
C:\TEMP>xcopy *.doc \fred /m /s
Reading source file(s)...
TEST.DOC
        1 File(s) copied
```

Xcopy copied only the file whose archive attribute was on.

Type the following commands to dispose of the files and directories you added for this example:

```
C:\TEMP>erase \fred\mkt\wp\*.doc

C:\TEMP>rd \fred\mkt\wp

C:\TEMP>erase \fred\mkt\budget\*.doc

C:\TEMP>rd \fred\mkt\budget

C:\TEMP>rd \fred\mkt

C:\TEMP>erase \fred\test.doc

C:\TEMP>rd \fred
```

Change the current directory back to \TEMP\MKT:

`C:\TEMP>`cd mkt

and, finally, clean up your \TEMP\MKT\BUDGET directory for later examples:

`C:\TEMP\MKT>`erase budget\let*.doc

DEVELOPING A BACKUP PROCEDURE

It could take a drawerful of diskettes to back up all the files on a fixed disk: If your average file were 10,000 bytes long (about 6½ double-spaced typed pages), a full 20 MB fixed disk would have more than 2000 files, and you would need almost sixty 360 K diskettes to back them all up. A full 40 MB fixed disk could require about one hundred fifteen 360 K diskettes, or about thirty-five high-capacity (1.2 MB) diskettes.

But you don't have to back up all your files. You needn't back up program files, for example, because you've already got the original DOS and application-program diskettes. Some data files, such as a spelling dictionary, don't usually change, so it isn't necessary to back them up either.

How often you back up your other data files, such as word-processed documents or spreadsheets, depends on how often they change. For example, spreadsheets might change often while the budget is being prepared but remain unchanged the rest of the year. The backup procedures you use depend on how you use your computer. But no matter how you decide to back up your files, be certain to do so regularly. A system failure can happen, but if you back up your files regularly, such a failure will be more of an inconvenience than a disaster.

BACKING UP FILES

The Backup command lets you select files on the basis of their path name, their file name, whether they have been changed since the last backup, or whether they have been changed since a particular date. The options can be combined, so you can back up files in just about any way you like.

The Backup command can have as many as 10 parameters:

**backup <path><filename> <drive> /A /S /M /F /D:<date>
/T:<time> /L:<logfile>**

<path> is the path name of the directory, preceded by a drive letter and a colon, if appropriate, from which files are to be backed up. If you don't specify <path>, DOS backs up files from the current drive and directory.

<filename> is the name of the file to be backed up. You can use wildcard characters to back up a set of files. If you don't specify <filename>, DOS backs up all files in the specified directory.

<drive> is the letter, followed by a colon, of the drive (such as *a:*) that contains the diskette that receives the backup files. You must specify <drive>.

/A adds the backup files to the backup diskette, rather than erasing all files on the backup diskette as the command usually does before making the backup copies.

/S backs up files from all subdirectories.

/M backs up only the files that have been modified since the last backup.

/F formats the target disk if it isn't already formatted. The /F option of the Backup command uses the Format command file (FORMAT.COM) to format the target disk, so FORMAT.COM must be in either the current directory or a directory that is in the command path. The /F parameter isn't required in version 4; DOS automatically formats the diskette if you haven't already done so.

/D:<date> backs up all files that have changed since <date>. Enter <date> just as you would for the Date command.

/T:<time> backs up all files that have changed since <time> on <date>. Enter <time> just as you would for the Time command.

/L:<logfile> creates a log file on the disk in the source drive. The log file contains the date and time of the backup procedure and, for each file that is backed up, the path name, the file name, and the number (assigned by DOS) of the diskette that contains the file. If a log file already exists, the backup information is added at the end, creating a history of backups for the source drive. If you include /L but omit the colon and <logfile>, DOS names the log file BACKUP.LOG and stores it in the root directory of the source drive.

You can combine parameters in one Backup command.

Note: Although the Backup command exists in versions of DOS numbered 2.0 and later, not all the versions include all the parameters described here, nor are all the versions and releases of DOS compatible with one another. For a list of the options available to you, check the documentation that came with your version of DOS. You must use the same version of DOS both to back up and to restore files.

Backing Up All the Files in a Directory

The simplest way to back up files is by directory. You back up all files in a directory by specifying just the path of the directory and the letter of the diskette drive that contains the backup diskette. Before you try the following examples, have ready a blank diskette that matches the capacity of your diskette drive. (Be sure the diskette is formatted if you don't have version 4.) Now, to back up all the files in the directory named \TEMP\MKT\BUDGET, type the following:

```
C:\TEMP\MKT>backup c:\temp\mkt\budget a:
```

DOS displays a warning:

```
Insert backup diskette 01 in drive A:

WARNING! Files in the target drive
A:\ root directory will be erased
Press any key to continue . . .
```

If you don't use the /A option, DOS erases any files on the backup diskette before it makes the backup copies. This warning gives you a chance to make certain the correct diskette is in the drive. Put your blank diskette in drive A and press any key.

If you have version 4 and are using an unformatted diskette, DOS begins the backup procedure by formatting the diskette. You see the usual *xx percent of disk formatted* message and, when formatting is complete, DOS asks if you want to format another. Type *n* and press Enter.

When the backup procedure begins, DOS displays the name of each file as it makes the copies:

```
*** Backing up files to drive A: ***
Diskette Number: 01

\TEMP\MKT\BUDGET\BGT1.PLN
\TEMP\MKT\BUDGET\BGT2.PLN
\TEMP\MKT\BUDGET\BGT3.PLN
```

The directory of the backup diskette shows one or two files you might not expect. Type the following:

```
C:\TEMP\MKT>dir a:
```

If you're using 3.2 or an earlier version, DOS responds:

```
Volume in drive A has no label
Directory of  A:\

BACKUPID @@@       128  10-16-89   3:19p
BGT1     PLN       152  10-16-89   8:17a
BGT2     PLN       152  10-16-89   8:17a
BGT3     PLN       152  10-16-89   8:17a
         4 File(s)     358400 bytes free
```

BACKUPID.@@@ is a small file that DOS stores on a backup diskette to identify it. Also, note that the files you backed up are larger than the originals on the fixed disk; confirm this by typing:

```
C:\TEMP\MKT>dir \temp\mkt\budget
```

```
Volume in drive C is FIXED DISK
Directory of  C:\temp\mkt\budget

.              <DIR>        10-17-89 12:11p
..             <DIR>        10-17-89 12:11p
BGT1     PLN       24  10-16-89   8:17a
BGT2     PLN       24  10-16-89   8:17a
BGT3     PLN       24  10-16-89   8:17a
         5 File(s)     17658400 bytes free
```

If you're using 3.2 or an earlier version, DOS adds 128 bytes at the beginning of each backup file. This addition contains the path and file name of the file that was backed up and is used by the Restore command when it restores files to the fixed disk. The Restore command deletes the path and file name information, so the restored version of the file is identical to the one you originally backed up. You'll work with the Restore command later in the chapter.

If you're using 3.3 or a later version, the DOS response to your directory command looks something like this:

```
Volume in drive A is BACKUP   001
Volume Serial Number is 1266-14DA
Directory of  A:\

BACKUP   001         72 10-16-89    3:19p
CONTROL  001        311 10-16-89    3:19p
        2 File(s)       1212928 bytes free
```

If you're using 3.3 or a later version, DOS stores all the backed-up files in the file named BACKUP.001 and all the path names in the file named CONTROL.001. (On a second backup diskette, the extensions would be 002; on a third backup diskette, they would be 003, and so forth.) Note that the size of BACKUP.001 corresponds to the total number of bytes in the three files it contains; CONTROL.001 contains all the extra information DOS needs to restore those files. This difference in the way backup files are stored is one reason you must use the Backup and Restore commands from the same version of DOS.

If a Backup command fills the diskette before backing up all the files you specified, DOS prompts you to put in another diskette. It displays the same warning, but refers to the second diskette as Diskette Number 02.

If another diskette is required, DOS prompts again, increasing the diskette number each time. If you were actually backing up files, you would label the diskette you just used with the contents and date and store it away in a safe place.

Backing Up All Subdirectories

You can back up the files in a directory and all its subdirectories with the /S option. For example, to back up all the files in \TEMP\MKT and its subdirectories (\TEMP\MKT\WP and \TEMP\MKT\BUDGET), specify \TEMP\MKT as the path and include the /S parameter by typing the following (be sure to use a backslash in \TEMP\MKT, but a forward slash in /S):

```
C:\TEMP\MKT>backup c:\temp\mkt a: /s
```

Again, DOS displays the warning; press any key to start the backup. DOS displays the file names as it makes the copies:

```
*** Backing up files to drive A: ***
Diskette Number: 01
\TEMP\MKT\ACCOUNT
\TEMP\MKT\WP\LET1 .DOC
\TEMP\MKT\WP\LET2 .DOC
\TEMP\MKT\WP\LET3 .DOC
\TEMP\MKT\WP\RPT1 .DOC
\TEMP\MKT\WP\RPT2 .DOC
\TEMP\MKT\WP\RPT3 .DOC
\TEMP\MKT\WP\LET1 .STY
\TEMP\MKT\WP\LET2 .STY
\TEMP\MKT\WP\LET3 .STY
\TEMP\MKT\BUDGET\BGT1 .PLN
\TEMP\MKT\BUDGET\BGT2 .PLN
\TEMP\MKT\BUDGET\BGT3 .PLN
```

This backup diskette contains all your marketing files, not just the files from one of the subdirectories. Note that you again backed up BGT1.PLN, BGT2.PLN, and BGT3.PLN. As the warning indicated, your prior backups were erased.

Backing Up Specific Files

You can back up specific files by including a file name with the Backup command. A word-processing directory, for example, might contain both documents, which can change frequently, and style sheets, which seldom change. You would back up the documents much more frequently than you would the style sheets. Type the following to change the current directory to \TEMP\MKT\WP and back up only the documents (files whose extension is DOC):

```
C:\TEMP\MKT>cd wp
```

```
C:\TEMP\MKT\WP>backup c:*.doc a:
```

DOS displays its usual warning, but wait a moment before you press any key to back up the files. It's good practice to store a printed list of the files on a backup diskette along with the diskette itself. That's easy; make sure your printer is on, and press Ctrl-PrtSc to start simultaneous printing. Now press any key. As usual, DOS displays the file names as it backs them up, but this time it prints them too:

```
*** Backing up files to drive A: ***
Diskette Number: 01

\TEMP\MKT\WP\LET1 .DOC
\TEMP\MKT\WP\LET2 .DOC
\TEMP\MKT\WP\LET3 .DOC
\TEMP\MKT\WP\RPT1 .DOC
\TEMP\MKT\WP\RPT2 .DOC
\TEMP\MKT\WP\RPT3 .DOC
```

The files whose extension is STY were not backed up because you specified only those whose extension is DOC. You can store the printed list with the backup diskette. Remember to press Ctrl-PrtSc again to stop simultaneous printing.

Backing Up Only Files That Have Changed

As your files increase, you might want to be even more selective about the ones you back up. For example, a word-processing directory might contain hundreds of documents; backing them all up could take a lot of time and several diskettes. Two options of the Backup command let you back up only the files that have changed since a directory was backed up, or only the files that have changed since a particular date.

Selecting Files That Have Changed
Since the Last Backup

The /M (Modify) option of the Backup command backs up only those files that have changed since the directory was last backed up. To see this option, you need a file that has changed since you backed up \TEMP\MKT\WP in the last example. Create a short file by copying from the console:

```
C:\TEMP\MKT\WP>copy con new.doc
This file has changed
since the last backup.
^Z
        1 File(s) copied
```

Now tell DOS to back up only the files whose extension is DOC that have changed since the directory was last backed up:

```
C:\TEMP\MKT\WP>backup c:*.doc a: /m
```

DOS displays its warning and, when you press a key, it displays the files backed up:

```
*** Backing up files to drive A: ***
Diskette Number: 01

\TEMP\MKT\WP\NEW.DOC
```

Only the new file is backed up.

Selecting Files That Have Changed
Since a Particular Date

The /D:<date> option backs up only those files that have changed since a particular date. To see this, you'll need a file with a different date. Change the system date with the Date command. Type the following:

```
C:\TEMP\MKT\WP>date
Current date is Mon 10-16-1989
Enter new date (mm-dd-yy): 1-1-90
```

Now create a file named DATE.DOC by copying from the console:

```
C:\TEMP\MKT\WP>copy con date.doc
This file was last changed
on 1-1-90.
^Z
        1 File(s) copied
```

Use the /D:<date> option to back up the files that have changed since December 31, 1989, by typing the following. Use whatever date format DOS used in response to your Date command:

```
C:\TEMP\MKT\WP>backup c:*.doc a: /d:12-31-89
```

After the warning, DOS displays the file it backs up:

```
*** Backing up files to drive A: ***
Diskette Number: 01

\TEMP\MKT\WP\DATE.DOC
```

Only the file changed after the date you specified is backed up. You can use the /T:<time> option to specify a time in addition to using the /D:<date> option to specify the date.

Adding Files to a Backup Diskette

Each form of the Backup command you have used so far starts by erasing any files on the backup diskette. There might be times, however, when you want to back up files from several different directories on one diskette or add a file or two to an existing backup diskette. The /A option adds a file to a backup diskette.

Your backup diskette now contains \TEMP\MKT\WP\DATE.DOC. To back up the files in \TEMP\MKT\BUDGET, adding them to the backup diskette, type the following command:

```
C:\TEMP\MKT\WP>backup c:\temp\mkt\budget a: /a
```

This time DOS doesn't need to warn you that it's going to erase any files from the backup diskette. If you're using 3.3 or a later version, DOS prompts with a message like this:

```
Insert last backup diskette in drive A:
Press any key to continue . . .
```

Press a key to start the backup.

With all versions, DOS then starts backing up the files and displaying their names on the screen:

```
*** Backing up files to drive A: ***
Diskette Number: 01

\TEMP\MKT\BUDGET\BGT1.PLN
\TEMP\MKT\BUDGET\BGT2.PLN
\TEMP\MKT\BUDGET\BGT3.PLN
```

If your backup procedure involves periodically backing up a few files from several different directories, you can use the /A option to put all the backup files on one diskette. A word of caution about this technique: With versions of DOS through 3.2, if a file you add to a backup diskette has the same name and extension as a file already on the diskette, DOS changes the extension of the added file to @01, regardless of what it was before.

RESTORING FILES TO THE FIXED DISK

It's easy to restore a file from a backup diskette to the fixed disk. Simply put the backup diskette in the diskette drive and type the Restore command, specifying the name of the file to be restored. The Restore command needs the path and file name information added to files by the Backup command, so you can restore only files that were backed up with the Backup command. Remember, too, that you should use the same version of DOS for both the Backup and Restore commands.

The Restore command can have as many as 11 parameters:

restore <drive> <path><filename> /S /P /M /N /B:<date> /A:<date> /E:<time> /L:<time>

<drive> is the letter, followed by a colon, of the drive (such as *a:*) that contains the backup diskette. You must include <drive>.

<path> is the path name, preceded by a drive letter and a colon, if appropriate, of the directory to which the file is to be restored. If you omit <path>, the file is restored to the current directory.

<filename> is the name of the file to be restored. You can use wildcard characters to restore a set of files. You must specify either <path> or <filename>.

/S restores files to all subdirectories.

/P tells DOS to prompt you for confirmation before restoring files that have changed since they were last backed up.

/M restores files that were *modified* (or deleted) since they were backed up.

/N restores files that have been deleted from the original source disk since they were backed up.

/B:<date> restores only those files that were changed on or *before* <date>. Enter <date> just as you would for the Date command.

/A:<date> restores only those files that were changed on or *after* <date>. Enter <date> just as you would for the Date command.

/E:<time> restores only those files that were changed at or *earlier than* <time> on <date>. Enter <time> just as you would for the Time command.

/L:<time> restores only those files that were changed at or *later than* <time> on <date>. Enter <time> just as you would for the Time command.

Note: Although the Restore command exists in versions of DOS numbered 2.0 and later, not all the versions include all the parameters described here. For a list of the options available to you, check the documentation that came with your version of DOS.

Warning: Don't use the Backup or Restore commands if you have entered an Assign, Join, or Substitute command to alter the way DOS interprets drive letters. Because these commands can mask the type of drive, DOS could damage or delete the files you specify in the commands or other files on the disk. For more information on Assign, Join, and Substitute, see "Commands for Occasional Use" in Chapter 16.

Preparing for the Restore Command Examples

Type the following to change the date, back up all the files in \TEMP\MKT\WP, and then erase all the files in \TEMP\MKT\WP:

```
C:\TEMP\MKT\WP>date
Current date is Mon 01-01-1990
Enter new date: 10-16-89

C:\TEMP\MKT\WP>backup c:\temp\mkt\wp a:

Insert backup diskette 01 in drive A:

WARNING! Files in the target drive
A:\ root directory will be erased
Press any key to continue . . .

*** Backing up files to drive A: ***
Diskette Number: 01

\TEMP\MKT\WP\LET1.DOC
\TEMP\MKT\WP\LET2.DOC
\TEMP\MKT\WP\LET3.DOC
\TEMP\MKT\WP\RPT1.DOC
\TEMP\MKT\WP\RPT2.DOC
\TEMP\MKT\WP\RPT3.DOC
\TEMP\MKT\WP\LET1.STY
```

```
\TEMP\MKT\WP\LET2.STY
\TEMP\MKT\WP\LET3.STY
\TEMP\MKT\WP\NEW.DOC
\TEMP\MKT\WP\DATE.DOC

C:\TEMP\MKT\WP>erase *.*
All files in directory will be deleted!
Are you sure (Y/N)?y
```

This completes the preparation.

Restoring One File

Inadvertently erasing or changing a file is probably the most common reason for restoring a file. You restore a file by specifying the source drive and the target drive, path name, and file name with the Restore command. (You must include the path name if you are restoring a file to a directory other than the current directory; the path name must be the same as the path from which the file was originally backed up.)

For example, to restore \TEMP\MKT\WP\LET1.STY, type:

```
C:\TEMP\MKT\WP>restore a: let1.sty
```

Note that the drive and path can be omitted because the file is being restored to the current directory.

DOS prompts you for the backup diskette:

```
Insert backup diskette 01 in drive A:
Press any key to continue . . .
```

The correct diskette is in the drive, so press any key. DOS displays the name of the restored file:

```
*** Files were backed up 10-16-1989 ***

*** Restoring files from drive A: ***
Diskette: 01
\TEMP\MKT\WP\LET1.STY
```

You can display the directory to verify that it's back.

Restoring a Set of Files

You can use wildcard characters to restore a set of files. To restore all the files whose extension is DOC that you backed up from the current directory (\TEMP\MKT\WP), type the following:

```
C:\TEMP\MKT\WP>restore a: *.doc
```

When DOS prompts you for the backup diskette, press any key. DOS displays the names of the files it restores. Again, you can display the directory to verify that the files were restored.

Restoring All the Files in a Directory

If you enter the Restore command with a path name and the Wildcard specification ∗.∗, DOS restores all files belonging in that directory. For example, to restore all the files you backed up from \TEMP\MKT\WP, type:

```
C:\TEMP\MKT\WP>restore a: \temp\mkt\wp\*.*
```

Again, press any key when DOS prompts for the diskette. DOS restores all the files you backed up from \TEMP\MKT\WP, not just those whose extension is DOC.

Restoring All Subdirectories

Just as the /S option of the Backup command backs up the files in a directory and all its subdirectories, the /S option of the Restore command restores the files in a directory and all its subdirectories. To restore the files in \TEMP and all its subdirectories, you would type *restore a: \ temp\ ∗.∗ /s.*

Selecting Files To Be Restored

A file you restore replaces a file with the same name on the fixed disk. You might not want this replacement, especially if you have changed the file on the fixed disk since the backup diskette was made. You can protect yourself from unwanted changes by using the /P (*prompt*) option of the Restore command, which tells DOS to prompt for confirmation if the file on the fixed disk has changed since the backup was made.

Warning: If you're using version 3.2 or earlier and are restoring files that were backed up with a previous version of DOS, be sure to use the /P parameter. If DOS asks whether to restore files named MSDOS.SYS, IO.SYS, IBMBIO.COM, or IBMDOS.COM, reply n *(no). Otherwise, you would replace parts of your DOS program with portions of an earlier version, and DOS wouldn't start from your fixed disk.*

To see how the /P parameter works, change LET3.DOC and LET1.STY. First, copy from the console to create a new version of LET3.DOC:

```
C:\TEMP\MKT\WP>copy con let3.doc
The new version of let3.doc.
^Z
        1 File(s) copied
```

Copy this file to LET1.STY, making it a new file too:

```
C:\TEMP\MKT\WP>copy let3.doc let1.sty
        1 File(s) copied
```

Now restore the entire directory with the /P option:

```
C:\TEMP\MKT\WP>restore a: \temp\mkt\wp\*.* /p
```

DOS asks for the diskette and begins restoring files in the usual way, but finds a file on the fixed disk that has changed since its backup copy was made.

```
*** Files were backed up 10-16-1989 ***

*** Restoring files from drive A: ***
Diskette: 01
\TEMP\MKT\WP\LET1.DOC
\TEMP\MKT\WP\LET2.DOC

WARNING! File LET3.DOC
was changed after it was backed up
Replace the file (Y/N)?
```

This message (yours might vary) gives you a chance to decide whether you want to restore the file. Suppose that you don't want to restore this file; type *n* (and press Enter if you don't have version 4). DOS resumes displaying the names of the files it restores, starting with the one that follows LET3.DOC:

```
n \TEMP\MKT\WP\RPT1.DOC
\TEMP\MKT\WP\RPT2.DOC
\TEMP\MKT\WP\RPT3.DOC

WARNING! File LET1.STY
was changed after it was backed up
Replace the file (Y/N)?
```

Now suppose you do want to replace the version on the fixed disk with the backup version; type *y* and press Enter. DOS again resumes displaying the names of the files it restores, starting with LET1.STY:

```
y \TEMP\MKT\WP\LET1.STY
\TEMP\MKT\WP\LET2.STY
\TEMP\MKT\WP\LET3.STY
\TEMP\MKT\WP\NEW.DOC
\TEMP\MKT\WP\DATE.DOC
```

This completes the examples for backing up and restoring files.

DELETING THE SAMPLE FILES AND DIRECTORIES

If you don't want to keep the files and subdirectories you created for these examples, the following commands erase the files and remove the directories. Be certain to type the Erase commands exactly as shown to avoid the possibility of erasing other files. If you created a temporary subdirectory with a name other than \TEMP, don't forget to type its name in place of \TEMP.

Change the current directory to \TEMP\MKT:

```
C:\TEMP\MKT\WP>cd \temp\mkt
```

Erase the file ACCOUNT in \TEMP\MKT:

```
C:\TEMP\MKT>erase account
```

Erase the files in \MKT\WP:

```
C:\TEMP\MKT>erase wp\*.*
All files in directory will be deleted!
Are you sure (Y/N)?y
```

Remove \TEMP\MKT\WP:

```
C:\TEMP\MKT>rd wp
```

Erase the files in \TEMP\MKT\BUDGET:

```
C:\TEMP\MKT>erase budget\*.*
```

Remove \TEMP\MKT\BUDGET:

```
C:\TEMP\MKT>rd budget
```

Change the current directory to \TEMP:

```
C:\TEMP\MKT>cd \temp
```

Erase the file TEST.DOC:

```
C:\TEMP>erase test.doc
```

Remove \MKT:

```
C:\TEMP>rd mkt
```

Change the current directory to root:

```
C:\TEMP>cd \
```

Remove \TEMP:

```
C:\>rd \temp
```

The fixed disk now contains only the directories and files it had before you started the examples in this chapter.

DOS AND YOUR FIXED DISK

Now that you're familiar with directories and the commands you use to manage them, it's time to look at your own system and see if you can put some of your knowledge to work. The final part of this chapter shows how you can organize your fixed disk to keep your root directory from becoming filled with an assortment of unrelated files.

Setting Up Your Directories

Because a fixed disk can hold so many files, it's important to create a directory structure that lets you keep track of your files and programs. You can set up your subdirectories to match the way you use your computer, organizing them by department, application program, people's names, or any other way that's comfortable. The topic "Setting Up a Filing System" in Chapter 16 suggests several ways you might want to set up your directories.

Until you get a directory structure established, however, files have a tendency to collect in the root directory, making it difficult to find a file you need. If you reserve the root directory for nothing but subdirectories and files that must be there, finding your way around your fixed disk becomes much easier.

If you've been using your fixed disk for some time and haven't known about or paid much attention to the idea of creating a directory structure on it, it's possible that the root directory of your fixed disk contains many files that need not be there: DOS files, for example, if DOS is not in a subdirectory of its own; program files; data files; perhaps even files inherited from a former user of the computer. Some of these files, such as the DOS command files, are essential, but need not all be in the root directory; others, such as files you've inherited, might be unnecessary to your work; still others, such as application program files and data files, might be much easier to find and keep track of in directories of their own.

Few people, and certainly no book, can tell you the best way to organize your directories and files. If your root directory contains many files that should be in subdirectories of their own, the Make Directory, Copy, Xcopy and (when you've moved files to new subdirectories) Erase commands can help you with your housekeeping. Ultimately, you are the best judge of your own work and work habits, but there are some general guidelines you can follow, either in setting up a new fixed disk or in organizing one you've been using:

- Keep your DOS command files in a subdirectory of their own. The only files that DOS requires to be in the root directory are named COMMAND.COM, CONFIG.SYS, and AUTOEXEC.BAT. Version 4 of DOS automatically offers to install itself so that these files are in the root directory but all other DOS files are in a separate subdirectory. If you have an earlier version of DOS and all of the DOS files are in your root directory, the section "Moving the DOS Files from the Root Directory to \DOS" below tells you how to set up and populate such a subdirectory.

- Some application programs also require files in the root directory; the documentation that came with the program should tell you about this, and the program itself might create the necessary files when you install it. When in doubt, follow the advice given in the documentation.

- If your fixed disk has been used by someone else, print a listing of the root directory before you try reorganizing or deleting the files in it. Be particularly careful about removing any files with the extensions COM, SYS, or EXE; remember, they are program files. If you don't know what a command file is supposed to do, ask someone who does know.

- When you install a new program, put it in its own subdirectory if you can. Some programs propose this during the installation procedure. If yours doesn't, you might still be able to put it in a subdirectory, provided it can be installed on a fixed disk and has the ability to work with different drives and subdirectories. Check the program's documentation for instructions. After a program is installed in a subdirectory, all you need do is add the subdirectory name to the command path in order to make the program's command files available at any time.

- Think about the data files you create. These are generally the files that take up the most room on a fixed disk. They are also the ones that can become the most confusing as file names begin to proliferate and come close to duplicating one another. Although this book uses files with the names LET1.DOC, LET2.DOC, and so on, real data files with such names would mean little in a root directory cluttered with a hundred other letters. On the other hand, such names might mean a great deal in subdirectories named for clients, projects, proposals, and the like. In short, pay as much attention to organizing your fixed disk as you would to organizing a large set of files in a file cabinet.

The remainder of this chapter focuses primarily on versions of DOS earlier than 4.0. It shows you how to put all the DOS files except COMMAND.COM in a subdirectory named \DOS in the root directory of your fixed disk. If your DOS files are already stored in a directory other than the root, you can go on to the next chapter.

If your root directory contains many files in addition to the DOS files, the procedures described here use some DOS commands that are introduced in later chapters. If you like to know what you're doing before you do it, you might want to wait until you have completed several more chapters and then come back here to move the DOS files. It's up to you; read through the procedure and decide whether you want to do it now or later.

Depending on how your system is set up, you might also have to change the contents of the two files named AUTOEXEC.BAT and CONFIG.SYS in the root directory. This will mean using either a text editor, such as the DOS text editor Edlin, or a word processor that lets you store a file with no formatting commands in it (word processors describe such files as "unformatted," "text-only," or "nondocument"). The use of Edlin is described in Chapters 10 and 11. Again, if you prefer to wait, by all means do so. DOS will continue to function quite well in the meantime.

A Look at Your Fixed Disk

The following descriptions assume that your fixed disk is not shared, as on a network, and is dedicated to DOS—that is, it is not used by another operating system (such as the multiple-user operating system called XENIX). If your fixed disk is shared with other users or other operating systems, or if you aren't sure, check with the person who set up the disk before trying any of the procedures here.

If DOS and your fixed disk are yours to do with as you will, it's best to know what you're working with. So first look at your root directory to see what's in it. Type:

```
C>dir /w
```

If DOS has simply been copied from your DOS diskettes to the root directory of your fixed disk, you see a fairly long display with a number of files that should be familiar by now. The display includes file names like this:

```
Volume in drive C is FIXED DISK
Directory of  C:\

MAX                BATCH              RUNNING      ...
DEVICE             CONFIG   SYS       AUTOEXEC BAK...
MKT                TEMP               WORD         ...
COMMAND   COM      AUTOEXEC BAT       CONFIG   BAK...
DIRS      BAT      APPEND   EXE       ASSIGN   COM...
BASIC     COM      BASICA   COM       CHKDSK   COM...
DISKCOMP  COM      DISKCOPY COM       EDLIN    COM...
GRAFTABL  COM      GRAPHICS COM       JOIN     EXE...
PRINT     COM      RECOVER  COM       RESTORE  COM...
SUBST     EXE      TREE     COM       XCOPY    EXE...
MORTGAGE  BAS
        51 File(s)   12466176 bytes free
```

Notice that the display shows such DOS files as CHKDSK.COM, PRINT.COM, DISKCOPY.COM, and so on—all are good indicators that your DOS files are in the root directory. If your directory looks like this, proceed with the instructions in the section that best describes what you see.

On the other hand, you might see something like this (note the DOS directory, highlighted here):

```
Volume in drive C is FIXED DISK
Directory of  C:\

MAX                BATCH              DOS          ...
RUNNING            DEVICE             CONFIG   SYS...
AUTOEXEC BAK       MKT                TEMP         ...
WORD               COMMAND  COM       AUTOEXEC BAT...
CONFIG    BAK      DIRS     BAT...
        22 File(s)   12763136 bytes free
```

If your display looks something like this, DOS is already in a directory of its own, and you can skip ahead to the next chapter.

Note: Although this display shows a directory named DOS, your DOS files might be in a directory with a different name, or they might be in a subdirectory of one of the directories shown on your screen. If you don't see the names of FORMAT.COM, DISKCOPY.COM, and other familiar DOS command files, try displaying the entries of a directory with a likely looking name, such as DOS or PROGRAMS. Another way to check is to type path *and display the entries in each directory that DOS shows in its response to the command.*

Moving the DOS Files from the Root Directory to \DOS

Note: Remember that the version 4 installation procedure puts the DOS files in a directory named \ DOS (or some other directory you choose). If you're using version 4, you can skip the rest of this chapter.

The following procedures leave all non-DOS files in the root directory. Because it's critical to store files in the correct directories, all Copy and Erase commands include both the drive letter and path name, whether or not they're normally required.

First, create a directory named \DOS in the root directory by typing the following Make Directory (md) command:

```
C>md \dos
```

Note: If you already have a directory named \ DOS that contains something other than the DOS files, either use a name other than DOS in the procedure you follow or create a different directory, copy the files from your existing \ DOS directory into it, and then delete the files from \ DOS.

To move the DOS files, you must copy them to \DOS and then delete them from the root directory. The following three procedures describe how to go about it, depending on how many non-DOS files are already in the root directory and how familiar you are with their purpose. Choose the procedure whose title best describes the contents of your root directory and your understanding of their purpose.

Few Non-DOS Files: You Know What They Are

If your root directory contains only a few files other than the DOS command files, and you know what they are and what they contain:

1. Copy all the files in the root directory to \DOS. You'll need a list of the non-DOS files being copied, so if you want, turn on your printer and press Ctrl-PrtSc for simultaneous displaying and printing. Type:

```
C>copy c:\*.* c:\dos
```

Press Ctrl-PrtSc again to turn off printing.

2. Erase all the files in the root directory:

    ```
    C>erase c:\*.*
    ```

    Respond *y* when DOS asks *Are you sure?*

3. Copy the non-DOS files back to the root directory. This example shows three separate Copy commands, one for COMMAND.COM, one for CONFIG.SYS, and one for AUTOEXEC.BAT:

    ```
    C>copy c:\dos\command.com c:\
    ```

    ```
    C>copy c:\dos\config.sys c:\
    ```

    ```
    C>copy c:\dos\autoexec.bat c:\
    ```

    Type a similar Copy command for any other file you want to move back into the root directory.

4. Delete the non-DOS files from \DOS. Again, this example shows three Erase commands, one for COMMAND.COM, one for CONFIG.SYS, and one for AUTOEXEC.BAT:

    ```
    C>erase c:\dos\command.com
    ```

    ```
    C>erase c:\dos\config.sys
    ```

    ```
    C>erase c:\dos\autoexec.bat
    ```

    Type a similar Erase command for each file in \DOS that you copied back to the root directory. When you have erased all the non-DOS files from \DOS, a listing of the entries in your root directory should include the following:

    ```
     Volume in drive C is FIXED DISK
     Directory of  C:\

    DOS           <DIR>       10-16-89   1:53p
    COMMAND  COM    25307      3-17-87  12:00p
    AUTOEXEC BAT      762     10-16-88  10:57a
    CONFIG   SYS      155     10-16-88   6:08a
    ```

    In addition to the DOS directory and these files, your directory listing might show additional directories and some other files.

Go on to the heading "Changing CONFIG.SYS."

Many Non-DOS Files: You Know What They Are

If your root directory contains a lot of files in addition to the DOS command files, but you know what these files are and what they contain, and you are certain which ones must remain:

1. Print a listing of the entries in the root directory:

    ```
    C>dir c:\ > prn
    ```

    Mark the files that must be in the root directory, such as COMMAND.COM, CONFIG.SYS, and AUTOEXEC.BAT, on the printed copy.

2. Copy the files you marked in Step 1 to \DOS. This example shows three Copy commands, for COMMAND.COM, CONFIG.SYS, and AUTOEXEC.BAT:

    ```
    C>copy c:\command.com c:\dos
    ```

    ```
    C>copy c:\config.sys c:\dos
    ```

    ```
    C>copy c:\autoexec.bat c:\dos
    ```

    Type a similar Copy command for any other file you want to keep in the root directory.

3. Now erase all the files in the root directory:

    ```
    C>erase c:\*.*
    ```

    Respond *y* when DOS asks *Are you sure?*

4. Copy the files that must be in the root directory from the \DOS directory back to the root directory:

    ```
    C>copy c:\dos\*.* c:\
    ```

5. Erase the files from \DOS:

    ```
    C>erase c:\dos\*.*
    ```

    Respond *y* when DOS asks *Are you sure?*

6. Put the DOS Startup diskette (the diskette labeled DOS if you're using 3.2 or an earlier version) in drive A and copy all the files to \DOS:

    ```
    C>copy a:*.* c:\dos
    ```

7. Copy COMMAND.COM from the system diskette to the root directory (DOS requires this file to be in the root directory of the disk from which it is started):

    ```
    C>copy a:command.com c:\
    ```

8. Delete COMMAND.COM from \DOS (it only has to be in the root directory):

```
C>erase c:\dos\command.com
```

9. Put the DOS Operating diskette (the DOS diskette labeled Supplemental Programs if you're using 3.2 or an earlier version) in drive A and copy all the files to \DOS:

```
C>copy a:*.* c:\dos
```

When you have copied all the DOS files to \DOS, a listing of the entries in your root directory should include the following:

```
Volume in drive C is FIXED DISK
Directory of  C:\

DOS           <DIR>       10-16-89    1:53p
COMMAND   COM     25307    3-17-87   12:00p
AUTOEXEC  BAT       762   10-16-88   10:57a
CONFIG    SYS       155   10-16-88    6:08a
```

In addition to the \DOS directory and these files, your directory listing should include the other directories and files you kept there.

Go on to the heading "Changing CONFIG.SYS."

You're Not Sure What the Files
In the Root Directory Are

If you don't know what the files in the root directory are or what they contain:

1. Put the DOS Startup diskette (the diskette labeled DOS if you're using 3.2 or an earlier version) in drive A and type the following command to store its directory listing in a temporary file named DOSDIR:

```
C>dir a: > c:\dosdir
```

2. Put the DOS Operating diskette (the DOS diskette labeled Supplemental Programs if you're using 3.2 or an earlier version) in drive A and make sure the printer is ready to print. Now type the following commands to print a sorted directory listing of both DOS diskettes and to erase the temporary file:

```
C>dir a: >> dosdir

C>sort < dosdir > prn

C>erase c:\dosdir
```

3. If necessary, move the paper to the top of a new page and print a sorted directory listing of the root directory of the fixed disk by typing the following command:

    `C>dir c:\ ¦ sort > prn`

    Now compare the two printed directories, marking each file name that appears in the listing of the root directory but not in the listing of the DOS diskettes.

4. Copy the files that you marked in Step 3 to \DOS. This example shows three Copy commands, for COMMAND.COM, CONFIG.SYS, and AUTOEXEC.BAT:

    `C>copy c:\command.com c:\dos`

    `C>copy c:\config.sys c:\dos`

    `C>copy c:\autoexec.bat c:\dos`

    Type a similar Copy command for each file you want to keep in the root direc-tory. If you have many files with similar names or extensions that don't duplicate DOS file names or extensions, use wildcards to reduce the number of commands.

    For example, if several files have the extension DOC, type *copy c:\ *.doc c:\dos*. Be certain to mark all files on the listing that are copied by commands using wildcards. (DOS displays their names as it copies them.) That way, you can make sure that you've copied all the files you intend to keep in the root directory. When you've finished, you can double-check your work by printing a directory listing of \DOS (type *dir c:\dos > prn*) and comparing it with the listing you marked in Step 3.

5. Now erase all the files in the root directory:

    `C>erase c:\*.*`

    Respond *y* when DOS asks *Are you sure?*

6. Copy the files that must be in the root directory from the \DOS directory back to the root directory:

    `C>copy c:\dos\*.* c:\`

7. Erase the files from \DOS:

    `C>erase c:\dos\*.*`

    Respond *y* when DOS asks *Are you sure?*

8. Put the DOS Startup diskette (the diskette labeled DOS if you're using 3.2 or an earlier version) in drive A and copy all the files to \DOS:

    `C>copy a:*.* c:\dos`

9. Copy COMMAND.COM from the system diskette to the root directory (DOS requires this file to be in the root directory of the disk from which it is started):

```
C>copy a:command.com c:\
```

10. Put the DOS Operating diskette (the DOS diskette labeled Supplemental Programs if you're using 3.2 or an earlier version) in drive A and copy all the files to \DOS:

```
C>copy a:*.* c:\dos
```

When you have copied all the DOS files to \DOS, your root directory should look something like the display shown at the end of the preceding procedure.

11. Delete COMMAND.COM from \DOS (it only has to be in the root directory):

```
C>erase c:\dos\command.com
```

Changing CONFIG.SYS

If there is a file named CONFIG.SYS in the root directory of your fixed disk, it might contain some Device commands that name DOS files. If it does, you must change these commands so that they refer to the new location of the DOS files (C:\DOS) instead of the root directory (C:\).

Check the contents of CONFIG.SYS by displaying it with a Type command:

```
C>type c:\config.sys
```

If DOS responds *File not found*, you have no file named CONFIG.SYS, so go on to ''Testing the New DOS Directory.''

If DOS displays the contents of the file, check each line to see whether it is a Device command or other configuration command (see Appendix F) that names a DOS file; for example, *device=c:\vdisk.sys* or *device= c:\mouse.sys*. If it is, use your text editor or word processor (if it lets you store a file with no formatting commands) to change each command so that it refers to \DOS, not to the root directory. (The example Device commands shown earlier would become *device=c:\dos\vdisk.sys* and *device=c:\dos\mouse.sys*.)

Testing the New DOS Directory

Double-check your work by displaying the entries in the root directory to make sure it contains only subdirectories (entries identified by *<DIR>*), COMMAND.COM, and the files you left there:

```
C>dir c:\
```

Make certain that COMMAND.COM is included, because DOS won't start without it; if the file isn't in the root directory, put the DOS system diskette in drive A and copy COMMAND.COM to the root directory.

Next, check the directory of \DOS to make sure it contains the DOS files:

```
C>dir c:\dos
```

If you're not certain you can recognize the DOS files, look for such file names as FOR-MAT.COM, MODE.COM, or SORT.EXE, or compare the directory display to the directory list you printed earlier. If you didn't print one, put the DOS system diskette in drive A, display its directory, and compare the results. It isn't necessary to do a file-by-file check, just a general comparison. If the DOS files aren't in your DOS directory, or some are missing, copy them from the DOS diskettes to \DOS (Steps 6–9 of the second procedure).

Now it's time to make sure everything works. Open the latch on drive A and press Ctrl-Alt-Del to restart the system. DOS should start just as it did before.

If the system doesn't start properly, chances are that COMMAND.COM isn't in the root directory. Close the latch on drive A (so that DOS will start from the system diskette) and press Ctrl-Alt-Del again. When DOS is running, copy COMMAND.COM from the DOS diskette to the root directory on the fixed disk and restart the system.

If DOS displays a message such as *Bad or missing VDISK.SYS*, a Device command in CONFIG.SYS probably still refers to the root directory instead of C:\DOS. Go back to the heading "Changing CONFIG.SYS" and follow the instructions there.

Adding \DOS to the Command Path

When your system is running with the DOS files in their new location, you have one more task: Put C:\DOS in the command path with the Path command, so that DOS can find its command files. You'll put this command in a file named AUTOEXEC.BAT—described under "Creating Your Own Startup Procedure" in Chapter 12—that contains commands DOS carries out each time the system is started.

First, check the contents of AUTOEXEC.BAT with the Type command:

```
C>type c:\autoexec.bat
```

If DOS responds *File not found*, type the following to create the file with the Path command you need:

```
C>copy con c:\autoexec.bat
path c:\dos
^Z
        1 File(s) copied
```

If DOS displays a series of commands in response to your Type command, edit the file using a text editor or a word processor. If there is no Path command, add the line *path c:\dos* to the file. If there is a Path command (such as *path c:* or *path c:\;c:\word*), add a semicolon and *c:\dos* to the end of the command and save the revised version of the AUTOEXEC.BAT file.

Now press Ctrl-Alt-Del to restart the system. When DOS displays the system prompt, check the command path by typing a Path command with no parameters:

`C>path`

DOS should respond by displaying the command path, which should include C:\DOS (for example, *PATH=C:\DOS* or *PATH=C:\;C:\WORD;C:\DOS*). If there is no path, or the path doesn't include C:\DOS, go back and repeat the instructions beginning with ''Adding \DOS to the Command Path.''

When you successfully add C:\DOS to the command path, DOS can find its command files no matter what the current directory is.

If the root directory in your fixed disk still contains application program files and data files, you should eventually move them to other directories. As you learn what more of the files are for and become more comfortable with the tree-structured filing system, you can create directories for these files, copy them to the new directories, and delete them from the root directory.

CHAPTER SUMMARY

If you organize your file structure to match your work, a fixed disk quickly becomes an essential part of your computer system. If, in addition, you develop a backup procedure that protects only those files whose loss would cost you time or data, backing up your fixed disk takes just a little time and a few diskettes. The relatively small investments required to organize and safeguard your data will be returned many times over in ease of use and peace of mind, especially the first time an error—by the system or by you—causes the loss of a valuable file.

You can also create your own commands to back up the fixed disk. With the techniques described in Chapters 12, 14, and 15, backing up the fixed disk can become a routine part of using your computer, simplifying the job and guaranteeing consistency no matter who backs up the files on the fixed disk.

CHAPTER
10
CREATING AND EDITING FILES OF TEXT

W hen you need to write a note or other short document, it's not always convenient to find a typewriter or to schedule the work with your word-
processing people. You could use a word-processing program, but loading
the program, writing the document, and printing the results might be more trouble
than a short document is worth. What you need is a small, fast program that's easy to
use. Edlin, the DOS text editor, is just such a program. After practicing the example in
this chapter, you'll be able to use Edlin for those reminder lists, short notes, and
memos, as well as for batch files (which you'll encounter in Chapter 12).

The example in this chapter presents a situation that could occur in any office:
You're a project leader; your team has completed several spreadsheets, a 10-page proposal, and a cover letter. You have copied these files to a diskette and want the team to
review the results one last time before the presentation next Thursday. You're going to
send a copy of the diskette to each team member, and you need a short memo to tell
them what's on it.

Note: Edlin is a unique part of DOS with its own prompt and its own commands. The ex-
ample in this and the following chapter shows you the evolution of a short text file named
MEMO.TXT. To disrupt the example as little as possible, the descriptions of Edlin com-
mands are included in the narrative portion of the text, but are not elaborated on as in the
preceding chapters. Full descriptions of all Edlin commands and parameters are in the
reference section in Appendix F of this book.

PREPARING FOR THE EXAMPLE

The example in this chapter requires one formatted diskette. If you have one diskette
drive, put the diskette in it. If you have two diskette drives, put the diskette in drive B.
Now change the current drive to drive B by typing:

```
C:\DOS>b:
```

If you have only one diskette drive, DOS prompts you to insert a diskette. The diskette is in the drive, so press any key.

Edlin is an external command file. Whenever you use Edlin, DOS must be able to
find the command program on disk. If you don't have a fixed disk, use the Directory
command, if necessary, to verify that EDLIN.COM is in the system disk in drive A,
and then tell DOS to look for commands on that diskette by typing:

```
B>path a:\
```

This completes the preparation for the example.

CREATING A NEW TEXT FILE

When you type *edlin* followed by the name of a file in response to the system prompt, DOS copies the Edlin program into memory and starts the program. Edlin checks to see if the file you named exists. If the file exists, Edlin copies the file into memory and waits for you to enter any of several commands that say, in effect, ''Edlin, do this to my file.'' If the file doesn't exist, Edlin assumes you want to create a file and give it the name you specified, and so it waits for you to enter an appropriate command.

To begin the example for this chapter, type the following to create a file called MEMO.TXT on the disk in drive B. Like DOS, Edlin accepts commands in either uppercase or lowercase letters:

```
B:\>edlin memo.txt
```

Edlin tells you that MEMO.TXT is a new file and waits for a command:

```
New file
*_
```

The asterisk (*) is the Edlin command prompt; it tells you that Edlin is ready for you to type an Edlin command, just as the system prompt tells you that DOS is ready for you to type a DOS command.

All you can do with a new file is insert lines. Most Edlin commands are single letters, so all you need type here is *i* (for Insert):

```
*i
```

Edlin responds with:

```
1:*_
```

When you use Edlin, you work with a file line by line. To help you keep track of where you are, Edlin displays a line number at the beginning of each line. These line numbers are important because many of the editing commands can be preceded either by a line number or by starting and ending line numbers that define a range of lines you want to work with. The asterisk following the line number isn't part of the line; it shows you the *current line,* and it is no more a part of your document than the system prompt or the cursor. Just as DOS remembers the current disk and uses it unless you specify otherwise, Edlin remembers the current line and uses it unless you specify otherwise.

In response to your Insert command, Edlin displays the number it will assign to the first line you enter, followed by the asterisk and the cursor. Because this is a new file, the first line number is 1. After you type the Insert command, Edlin adds each subsequent line you type to the file. You tell Edlin when to end each line by pressing Enter. Each time you press Enter, Edlin moves to the beginning of the next line and displays the new line number, the asterisk, and the cursor. When you want to stop adding lines, press Ctrl-Break (or Ctrl-C).

ENTERING LINES

It's time to enter the first few lines of the sample memo. If you make a typing error, you can backspace and correct it before pressing Enter. But don't worry if you enter a line with errors; as you'll learn, it's easy to correct them. Type the following lines, but not the line numbers; remember, they're automatically displayed by Edlin. <Ctrl-Break> means hold down the Ctrl key and press the Break key; <Enter> means press the Enter key without typing anything.

```
 1:*This diskette has 5 files on it:
 2:*FORECAST.PLN
 3:*OPTION1.PLN
 4:*OPTION2.PLN
 5:*LETTER.DOC
 6:*PROPOSAL.DOC
 7:*<Enter>
 8:*Please check the spreadsheets and print the
 9:*documents to make sure they agree with our
10:*assumptions.
11:*<Enter>
12:*Let's do this quickly, it's due Thursday.
13:*<Ctrl-Break>

*_
```

Ctrl-Break shows on your screen as ^C and tells Edlin you don't want to insert any more lines, so Edlin moves the cursor to the beginning of a new line and displays its prompt, *, telling you it's waiting for another command.

DISPLAYING LINES

There are several reasons you might want to display your file:

- To see if you have included everything you meant to include.
- To check what you have done.
- To edit your file.

The List command (l) displays one line or a range of lines. If you type a line number followed by l, Edlin displays a maximum of 23 lines (one screenful), starting with the line you specify. To see the example you just typed, use the List command to display the document, starting at line 1. Type:

```
*1l
```

Edlin responds with:

```
 1: This diskette has 5 files on it:
 2: FORECAST.PLN
 3: OPTION1.PLN
 4: OPTION2.PLN
 5: LETTER.DOC
 6: PROPOSAL.DOC
 7:
 8: Please check the spreadsheets and print the
 9: documents to make sure they agree with our
10: assumptions.
11:
12: Let's do this quickly, it's due Thursday.
*_
```

You can display a range of lines by preceding the l with the numbers, separated by a comma, of the first and last lines you want to see. For example, to display only lines 2 through 6, type:

```
*2,61
```

Edlin shows you:

```
 2: FORECAST.PLN
 3: OPTION1.PLN
 4: OPTION2.PLN
 5: LETTER.DOC
 6: PROPOSAL.DOC
*_
```

ADDING LINES TO A FILE

You can insert lines anywhere in an existing file by preceding the Insert command with a line number. Edlin inserts the new line or lines before the line you specify, and it automatically renumbers the lines following the insertion.

For example, to insert a blank line before the list of file names, type:

```
*2i
    2:*<Enter>
    3:*<Ctrl-Break>

*_
```

To insert lines at the end of a document, use the Insert command and either specify a line number larger than the last line number or use the symbol #, which means "the line after the last line." To use # to add a signature line, type:

```
*#i
       14:*<Enter>
       15:*Tom
       16:*<Ctrl-Break>

*_
```

Now suppose you decide to add a title to your memo. The beginning is line 1, so specify line 1 with the Insert command:

```
*1i
       1:*Final Project Review -- 10/16/89
       2:*<Enter>
       3:*To: Project team
       4:*<Enter>
       5:*<Ctrl-Break>

*_
```

Display the file now to see the insertions. Type:

```
*1l
```

Edlin shows you:

```
       1: Final Project Review -- 10/16/89
       2:
       3: To: Project team
       4:
       5:*This diskette has 5 files on it:
       6:
       7: FORECAST.PLN
       8: OPTION1.PLN
       9: OPTION2.PLN
      10: LETTER.DOC
      11: PROPOSAL.DOC
      12:
      13: Please check the spreadsheets and print the
      14: documents to make sure they agree with our
      15: assumptions.
      16:
      17: Let's do this quickly, it's due Thursday.
      18:
      19: Tom
*_
```

Note that Edlin has renumbered all the lines.

ENDING AN EDITING SESSION

When you end an editing session with e (the End Edit command), Edlin stores your edited file on disk and returns you to DOS. After the file has been stored, DOS displays the system prompt (B:\>). Type the End Edit command:

```
*e
```

DOS stores the file on the disk and displays the system prompt:

```
B:\>_
```

PRINTING A FILE

A file stored on diskette is of limited value if you can't print a copy of it, so DOS makes it easy to print a file. First, make sure the printer is turned on. Next, use the DOS Copy command to copy the practice file to the printer. Type the following:

```
B:\>copy memo.txt prn
```

DOS prints the file and tells you:

```
1 File(s) copied
```

Your memo is ready for distribution. For many short jobs, that's all there is to it. Using Edlin, you can create and print a file in only a few minutes.

EDITING AN EXISTING TEXT FILE

There will be times you'll want to change an existing text file—perhaps to add items to a list, delete a sentence or two from a memo, or change some wording. Use Edlin now to edit your practice file. Type *edlin*, followed by the name of the file, MEMO.TXT:

```
B:\>edlin memo.txt
End of input file
*_
```

This time you're not creating a new file, so Edlin tells you that it has read to the end of your input file and copied the file into memory, and then it displays its prompt.

DELETING LINES

You can use Edlin to delete a line by typing the number of the line followed by d (the Delete command). For example, suppose you decide not to include line 10 (LETTER.DOC) in your memo. To delete the line, type:

```
*10d
```

Edlin acknowledges by moving to the next line and displaying the * prompt.

To delete several lines, precede the d with the numbers of the first and last lines to be deleted, separating the numbers with a comma (*number,number* represents the range of lines). To delete the heading (lines 1 through 4) in your practice memo, type:

```
*1,4d
```

To verify that the lines have been deleted, type:

```
*1l
```

Edlin responds with:

```
 1:*This diskette has 5 files on it:
 2:
 3: FORECAST.PLN
 4: OPTION1.PLN
 5: OPTION2.PLN
 6: PROPOSAL.DOC
 7:
 8: Please check the spreadsheets and print the
 9: documents to make sure they agree with our
10: assumptions.
11:
12: Let's do this quickly, it's due Thursday.
13:
14: Tom
*_
```

Again, notice that Edlin has renumbered the lines.

CANCELING AN EDITING SESSION

Suppose you change a file, then decide you really don't want the changes. You can cancel the editing session with q (the Quit command) and return to DOS. The revised version of your file won't be stored on disk.

So that you don't inadvertently cancel an editing session and lose your work, Edlin prompts you to confirm the Quit command. If you type *y*, Edlin returns you to DOS without storing the revised file. If you type any other character, Edlin ignores the Quit command. With this command, you don't have to press Enter after replying to the prompt.

For example, to cancel your editing session, type:

```
*q
```

Edlin responds:

```
Abort edit (Y/N)? _
```

Type *y*. Edlin returns you to DOS, and DOS displays its system prompt:

```
B:\>_
```

Edit the file again:

```
B:\>edlin memo.txt
End of input file
*_
```

Now, display it to verify that the lines you deleted earlier are still in the version stored on disk:

```
*1l
          1:*Final Project Review -- 10/16/89
          2:
          3: To: Project team
          4:
          5: This diskette has 5 files on it:
          6:
          7: FORECAST.PLN
          8: OPTION1.PLN
          9: OPTION2.PLN
         10: LETTER.DOC
         11: PROPOSAL.DOC
         12:
         13: Please check the spreadsheets and print the
         14: documents to make sure they agree with our
         15: assumptions.
         16:
         17: Let's do this quickly, it's due Thursday.
         18:
         19: Tom
    *_
```

It's the same version you stored with the End Edit command.

SEARCHING FOR A GROUP OF CHARACTERS

As a file gets longer, the List command becomes a less and less efficient way to locate and display a particular line. If your sample memo were 80, 90, or 100 lines long, for example, it would take several List commands to display it all, because the screen normally displays only 23 lines at a time.

You can locate a line much more quickly by telling Edlin to search for a unique group (*string*) of characters the line contains. But note the word ''unique.'' You could become very frustrated if you specified a string of commonly occurring letter combinations, such as *the* or *ing*. Remember, Edlin makes no judgments. If you specified the string *the*, Edlin might dutifully show you every single *the, then, there, hither*, and *thither* in your document. To search for a string of characters, type the number of the line where Edlin should begin searching, then type *s* (for the Search command) and the string.

Suppose the sample memo was several pages long, the list of file names was on page 3, and you wanted to delete a file name. Instead of displaying several screenfuls of text to find the right line, you could use the Search command to find the first line containing the string PLN (the extension of the first three file names). Edlin displays the first line it finds that contains PLN.

Even though the memo is actually much shorter, perform this search anyway. To start searching at the beginning of the file for PLN (note the capitalization), type:

```
*1sPLN
```

Edlin displays the first line that contains PLN:

```
        7: FORECAST.PLN
    *_
```

The line Edlin finds becomes the current line. In the preceding example, the current line is 7. If no line contains the string you specified, Edlin responds *Not found.*

Suppose you know that several lines contain the same string. You can amplify the Search command to tell Edlin to display a prompt, after it shows you each line, that asks whether this is the line you want. If you respond *y*, Edlin stops the search; if you reply *n*, Edlin searches for the next line that contains the string.

To tell Edlin you want to be shown this prompt, type a question mark before the *s*. For example, suppose you know that several lines contain PLN; you want to find OPTION2.PLN, but you're not sure which line it's on. To find OPTION2.PLN, type the following:

```
*1?sPLN
```

Edlin responds as follows. Type *n* or *y* as shown here:

```
        7:*FORECAST.PLN
O.K.? n
        8: OPTION1.PLN
O.K.? n
        9: OPTION2.PLN
O.K.? y
*_
```

As with most Edlin commands, you can specify a range of lines to search. If you know that you need to search only lines 2 through 5, you can limit the search by typing *2,5sPLN*. If you don't specify a starting line, Edlin starts searching from the line that follows the current line. If you don't specify an ending line, Edlin searches to the end of the file.

EDITING A LINE

Up to this point, you have been editing the memo by inserting and deleting entire lines. You can also edit individual lines, to change the wording or to correct typing errors. Edlin gives you two ways to change a line: You can use the Replace command (not the same as the DOS Replace command) or you can use the editing keys on your keyboard.

The Replace command (r), like the Search command, tells Edlin to look for a string of characters. Each time it finds the string, however, Edlin replaces the old string with a new string of characters you have included in the Replace command.

The format of the Replace command is much like the format of the Search command: a range of line numbers, *r* for *replace,* and then the string to search for. Because the Replace command replaces one string with another, the Replace command ends with the string that is to replace the old one. If you don't specify a replacement string of characters, Edlin deletes the string and replaces it with nothing. If you do specify a new string, you must separate the two strings by pressing F6 or Ctrl-Z.

Note: When you press F6 or Ctrl-Z, Edlin displays the keystroke as ^Z. But the symbols ^ and Z aren't actual characters. If you press the left arrow key, you erase both the ^ and the Z, because the pair represents one symbol. When you see ^Z in the following examples, press F6 or Ctrl-Z.

In the sample memo, suppose you remember that the extension of your word-processing files is TXT, not DOC. You could change each line that contains DOC, but it's faster to use the Replace command to change all the occurrences of DOC with one command. If you don't specify an ending line, Edlin assumes you mean the entire file. To change DOC to TXT throughout the practice file, type:

```
*1 rDOC^ZTXT
```

Edlin displays each line it changes:

```
      10: LETTER.TXT
      11: PROPOSAL.TXT
  *_
```

As with the Search command, the last line changed (line 11 in the example) becomes the current line. If no line contains the string, Edlin responds *Not found.*

What if you want to change some, but not all, occurrences of the first string? Again, as with the Search command, you can tell Edlin to prompt you for confirmation after it displays each line that would change. When Edlin prompts you for confirmation, it shows the changed version; but the change isn't permanent yet, so you can decide whether to make the change. If you type *n*, Edlin will scrap the new version and keep the original. You ask Edlin to display the prompt by typing *?* before the command name (r).

Suppose you want to change PLN to DIF, except in the line that refers to the file OPTION1; you want to leave that one unchanged. Because one occurrence of PLN is going to stay the same, you need to tell Edlin to prompt for confirmation. Type the following to make the changes:

```
*1?rPLN^ZDIF
        7: FORECAST.DIF
O.K.? y
        8: OPTION1.DIF
O.K.? n
        9: OPTION2.DIF
O.K.? y
*_
```

To look at the results, type:

```
*1l
        1: Final Project Review -- 10/16/89
        2:
        3: To: Project team
        4:
        5: This diskette has 5 files on it:
        6:
        7: FORECAST.DIF
        8: OPTION1.PLN
        9:*OPTION2.DIF
       10: LETTER.TXT
       11: PROPOSAL.TXT
       12:
       13: Please check the spreadsheets and print the
       14: documents to make sure they agree with our
       15: assumptions.
       16:
       17: Let's do this quickly, it's due Thursday.
       18:
       19: Tom
*_
```

You can change the lines back by typing:

```
*1rDIF^ZPLN
        7: FORECAST.PLN
        9: OPTION2.PLN
```

and:

```
*1rTXT^ZDOC
       10: LETTER.DOC
       11: PROPOSAL.DOC
*_
```

The Replace command is one of Edlin's most powerful features, so use it with some care. You could change every occurrence of a string of characters in the entire file with one command—including some changes you didn't intend.

Remember, each occurrence of the string in a line is changed, so be sure you want all the changes you make. If you change a range of lines, check to make certain there aren't any occurrences that you don't want to change.

If you don't specify a starting line in the Replace command, Edlin starts with the line that follows the current line. If you don't specify an ending line, Edlin continues to the end of the file. To limit the changes to one line, specify the same line as both the beginning and the end of the range. (For example, to change LETTER to MEMO in line 10, the command would be *10,10rLETTER^ZMEMO.*)

Using the Editing Keys

Even when you change one or more lines with the Replace command, you're still probably thinking more in terms of the entire document than you are about individual lines. To make specific changes, you use several editing keys, which are shown on the representative keyboard in Figure 10-1.

Changing a Line

To tell Edlin you want to change a line, you type the line number and press Enter. Edlin displays the line, moves the cursor to the next row on the display, displays the line number again, then waits for further instructions. You can then use the editing keys to copy the characters you want, skip the characters you don't want, or insert new characters. To help you become familiar with the editing keys, Figure 10-2 on the following page summarizes the keys and their functions. You might find it helpful to review this figure before going on to the next practice session.

Figure 10-1. Editing keys

Key	Function
Right arrow	Copies one character.
Left arrow	Erases the last character you copied.
Ins	Causes characters you type to be inserted in the new line. Pressing Ins again stops the insert.
Del	Skips one character in the old line (effectively deleting it from the new line).
Backspace	Same as left arrow.
F1	Same as right arrow.
F2	Copies to a certain character in the old line (type the character after pressing F2).
F3	Copies the remaining characters in the line.
F4	Skips to a certain character in the old line (type the character after pressing F4).

Figure 10-2. Edlin editing key functions

Now use the editing keys to edit line 3 of the sample memo. To do this, type the line number, *3*, and press Enter:

```
*3
```

Edlin responds:

```
3:*To: Project team
3:*_
```

Think of the displayed line as the old line and the row underneath, with the cursor at the beginning, as the new line. You edit a line by copying the characters you want to keep from the old line to the new line, and by inserting any new characters in the new line. The editing keys tell Edlin which characters to copy.

Press the right arrow key. The first letter of the old line appears on the new line:

```
3:*To: Project team
3:*T_
```

You copied one character from the old line to the new line. Continue pressing the right arrow key. Each time you press it, you copy another character. When you reach the end of the line, pressing the right arrow key has no effect, because you have copied all the characters to the new line:

```
3:*To: Project team
3:*To: Project team_
```

If you pressed Enter now, you would be telling Edlin you had finished editing line 3. The line would remain unchanged, because you copied all the characters from the old line to the new without making any changes.

Press the left arrow key. The cursor moves one column to the left, erasing the last character you copied to the new line:

```
3:*To: Project team
3:*To: Project tea_
```

Continue pressing the left arrow key. Each time you press it, you erase another of the characters that you copied to the new line. When you reach the beginning of the line, you've erased all the characters you copied to the new line; you're now back where you started.

```
3:*To: Project team
3:*_
```

If you pressed Enter now, the line would again remain unchanged because you haven't copied any characters and Edlin assumes you don't want to change the line.

The F(unction) Keys

There are quicker ways to copy characters than by using the right arrow key.

F3: Press the key labeled F3. Because F3 copies all the original characters from the cursor location to the end of the line, all of the old line is copied to the new line. Hold down the left arrow key until the cursor is back to the beginning of the line.

F2: The F2 key copies all the characters in the original line up to a particular character you specify. F2 acts somewhat like a search command that works inside a line. To use it, press F2, then press the character at which you want the copy to stop. Edlin distinguishes between uppercase and lowercase letters, so be certain to press the exact character you want.

For example, suppose you want to change the word *Project* to *Product* in the example. To do this, you press F2 and j to copy all the characters up to the j, type *du* to replace *je*, then press F3 to copy the rest of the line. Press F2, then j:

```
3:*To: Project team
3:*To: Pro_
```

Now type *du*:

```
3:*To: Project team
3:*To: Produ_
```

The characters you type replace the corresponding characters in the old line, so in the new line, *du* has replaced *je*. Press F3 to copy the rest of the old line:

```
3:*To: Project team
3:*To: Product team_
```

Use the left arrow key to move the cursor back to the beginning of the line.

As you just saw, characters you type replace the corresponding characters from the old line. If you press the Insert key before typing the characters, however, Edlin inserts the characters into the new line without replacing any characters in the old line. To insert the word *New* after the word *To:* in line 3, for example, first copy *To:* by pressing the right arrow key four times (once for each character, including the blank after the colon):

```
3:*To: Project team
3:*To: _
```

Notice that line 3 still says *Project*. You didn't press Enter after changing it to *Product*, so the old line remains unchanged.

Now press the Insert key, type *New* (don't forget to add a blank after it), and press F3 to copy the rest of the old line:

```
3:*To: Project team
3:*To: New Project team_
```

Use the left arrow key to move the cursor back to the left margin again.

Now suppose you want to delete one or more characters in your original line. You use the Delete key, which tells Edlin to eliminate the next character in the old line. Because the character isn't copied from the old line, it is deleted from the new one.

For example, to delete *To:* from line 3, press the Delete key four times (once for each character, plus the blank). Nothing seems to happen, but when you press F3 to copy the rest of the line, you see:

```
3:*To: Project team
3:*Project team_
```

You deleted *To:*, so it's not in the new line. Move the cursor back to the left margin again.

F4: But suppose you want to delete a number of characters. Isn't there a faster way? Yes, just as the F2 key copies to a specified character in the old line, the F4 key skips to a specified character in the old line, deleting the characters it skips, all at once. The way to use F4 is the same as for F2: Press F4, then the character at which you wish to stop. Again, Edlin distinguishes between uppercase and lowercase letters, so be certain to press the exact character you want.

To delete *To: Project* in line 3, for example, you could press the Delete key 12 times, but it's quicker to use F4. Press F4, then t to skip *To: Projec*. Press the Delete key twice to delete the t and the blank. Now press F3 to copy the rest of the line:

```
3:*To: Project team
3:*team_
```

Remember, no matter how many changes you make, you can always cancel them by pressing Ctrl-Break before you press Enter. When you press Enter, the line is changed. Press Ctrl-Break to cancel the editing of line 3.

If you want to end your practice session here, type *e* to End Edit and return to DOS. Because the End Edit command saves your file on disk, you will be able to use the sample again in the next chapter, which covers more ways to revise an Edlin file.

CHAPTER SUMMARY

This concludes the first session with Edlin. The next chapter shows you how to revise a text file and describes several additional Edlin commands. If you're not going to continue with the next chapter right away, be sure to save the diskette that contains MEMO.TXT.

CHAPTER
11
USING EDLIN
TO REVISE A FILE

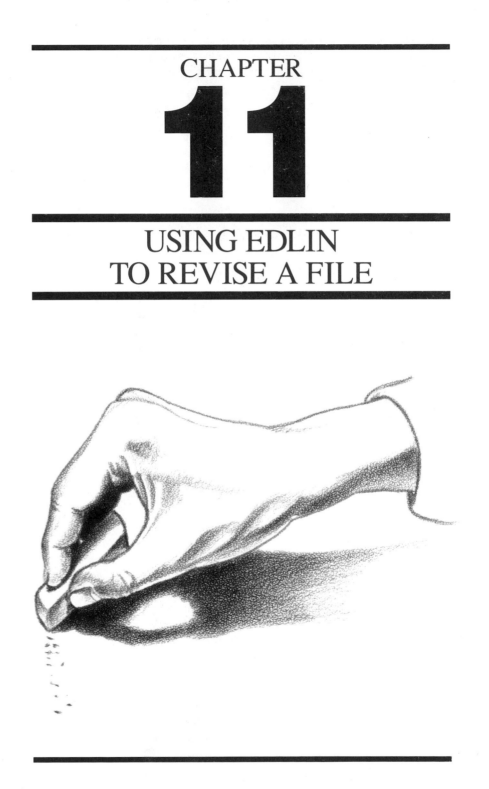

The previous chapter showed you how to create a text file, type lines into it, and revise part or all of a line. Edlin would be useful even if this were all it could do, but there's more: Edlin includes several other ways to revise, or *edit,* a text file. This chapter shows you how to use these additional capabilities of Edlin, particularly for revising files. Using these features, you can:

- Display the file a screenful at a time with the Page command.

- Enter more than one Edlin command on a line by separating the commands with semicolons.

- Move one or more lines to another place in the file with the Move command.

- Copy one or more lines to another place in the file with the Edlin Copy command.

- Combine another file with the file you're editing with the Transfer command.

PREPARING FOR THE EXAMPLE

If you are continuing directly from Chapter 10, no preparation is needed. Go on to the heading ''Printing Your File.''

If you are starting a new session, you'll need the file you created in Chapter 10. Put the diskette that contains MEMO.TXT in your diskette drive (drive B if you have two diskette drives) and change the current drive to B by typing:

```
C:\DOS>b:
```

On a system with a fixed disk, DOS will prompt for a diskette when you change the current drive. Press any key.

For a system with two diskette drives and no fixed disk, you must again tell DOS where to find the Edlin commands. Place the DOS diskette containing EDLIN.COM in drive A and type:

```
B>path a:\
```

Now type the following to edit MEMO.TXT:

```
B>edlin memo.txt
```

Edlin responds:

```
End of input file
*_
```

This completes the preparation for the example.

PRINTING YOUR FILE

Suppose you have completed your memo, but now decide to make some changes. The practice memo is short enough to change on the screen, but sometimes you'll want to print a file and mark the changes on the paper copy.

If you're working with Edlin, you don't have to return to DOS to print your file. You could press the Shift-PrtSc key combination, but this prints just one screenful (including commands and messages, as well as the file). You can print the entire file by pressing Ctrl-PrtSc or Ctrl-P (which prints everything that is displayed) and then displaying the file with the List command.

Note: If you have version 4, Edlin is a little more sophisticated than in earlier versions of DOS: If you use the first of the following commands to display (or print) a file longer than one screenful, Edlin stops after 24 lines and asks if you want to see more by displaying the message Continue (Y/N)? *This doesn't hamper your ability to print a long file by pressing Ctrl-PrtSc, but it does mean your printout contains not only the file, but the message too. If this small interruption doesn't bother you, use the command shown below to print your memo. If you prefer a cleaner printout, use the second command shown below.*

With any version of DOS, turn your printer on and type the following; remember, *1,#l* means list all lines from 1 to # (the line after the last line):

```
*1,#l<Ctrl-PrtSc><Enter>
```

Your file is printed.

To see a cleaner printout with version 4, turn your printer on and type:

```
*1,24l;25,#l<Ctrl-PrtSc><Enter>
```

In this case, you've put two commands on a single line by separating them with a semicolon. The first command, *1,24l*, tells Edlin to list the first 24 lines of the file; the second command, *25,#l*, tells Edlin to list the file from line 25 to the line following the last line.

Regardless of the command you use to print your memo, remember to press Ctrl-PrtSc (or Ctrl-P) again when you're finished, to avoid simultaneous printing of everything you display later.

ENTERING MORE THAN ONE COMMAND ON A LINE

Although the preceding example showed a way to trick Edlin in version 4 into displaying and printing a file longer than one screenful, you can enter more than one command on a line in any version of DOS.

If an action requires more than one command, you can put all the commands on the same line, separating the commands with semicolons. Edlin carries out each command as if it had been entered on a separate line. Some of the examples later in this chapter use this technique.

REVISING YOUR MEMO

Assume you have finished the memo but decide to add instructions for reviewing the documents, and you want to make a few other changes to the memo as well. Figure 11-1 shows a copy of the file marked with the changes you plan to make; it won't take long to make these changes.

```
 1:*Final Project Review -- 10/16/89
 2:
 3: To: Project team   UPPERCASE
 4:
 5: This diskette has 5 files on it:
 6:
 7: FORECAST.PLN
 8: OPTION1.PLN   HIGHER SALES
 9: OPTION2.PLN   NO STAFF INCREASE
10: LETTER.DOC
11: PROPOSAL.DOC
12:
                                          MAKE
13: Please check the spreadsheets and   print the
14: documents to make sure they agree with our
15: assumptions.
16:
17: Let's do this quickly, it's due Thursday.
18:
19: Tom           {  YOU CAN REVIEW THE DOCUMENTS ON THE SCREEN.
        TO BE     {  TO CHECK THE PROPOSAL, TYPE:
      INSERTED    {  TYPE B: PROPOSAL | MORE
       BEFORE     {  THIS DISPLAYS ONE SCREEN AT A TIME.
      LINE 16     {  PRESS THE SPACE BAR TO DISPLAY THE
                  {  NEXT SCREEN, OR CTRL-BREAK TO STOP.
```

Figure 11-1. Sample memo marked with changes

First, to change *Project team* in line 3 to uppercase, type *3* to tell Edlin you want to edit line 3. When Edlin responds with the original line and the new line number, copy the first five characters by pressing the right arrow key five times; then type the uppercase characters to replace the lowercase ones:

```
*3
        3:*To: Project team
        3:*To: PROJECT TEAM
*_
```

Here is a quick way to confirm your change. Type the line number and press Enter. Edlin assumes you want to edit the line again and displays the newly revised line for you. Press Enter again. The second Enter tells Edlin to save the line without any further changes. Confirm the changes to line 3:

```
*3<Enter>
        3:*To: PROJECT TEAM
        3:*<Enter>
*_
```

Next, the revisions in Figure 11-1 show that you want to add descriptions to the file names in lines 8 and 9. To add text at the end of a line: Type the line number, press Enter, press F3 to copy the entire line, type the added text, and press Enter again. Add three blanks and the words *Higher sales* to line 8 as follows. Type:

```
*8
        8:*OPTION1.PLN
        8:
```

Press F3 to copy the line:

```
        8:*OPTION1.PLN
        8:*OPTION1.PLN
```

Press the spacebar three times, type *Higher sales*, and press Enter:

```
        8:*OPTION1.PLN
        8:*OPTION1.PLN    Higher sales
*_
```

When you have finished editing a line, you can press Enter when Edlin displays its next prompt and Edlin will assume you want to edit the next line. You want to add text at the end of line 9, so press Enter, press F3 to copy the entire line, and add three blanks followed by *No staff increase*:

```
*<Enter>
        9:*OPTION2.PLN
        9:*OPTION2.PLN    No staff increase
*_
```

Check your progress by listing the file:

```
*1l
        1: Final Project Review -- 10/16/89
        2:
        3: To: PROJECT TEAM
        4:
        5: This diskette has 5 files on it:
        6:
        7: FORECAST.PLN
        8: OPTION1.PLN    Higher sales
        9:*OPTION2.PLN    No staff increase
       10: LETTER.DOC
       11: PROPOSAL.DOC
       12:
       13: Please check the spreadsheets and print the
       14: documents to make sure they agree with our
       15: assumptions.
       16:
       17: Let's do this quickly, it's due Thursday.
       18:
       19: Tom
     *_
```

Now you want to delete the last two words, *print the*, of line 13 and replace them with one word, *make*. Type *13* and press Enter; press F3 to copy the entire line, then use the left arrow key to erase *print the*:

```
*13
       13:*Please check the spreadsheets and print the
       13:*Please check the spreadsheets and _
```

Type *make* and press Enter:

```
       13:*Please check the spreadsheets and print the
       13:*Please check the spreadsheets and make
     *_
```

You want to delete more words, *documents to make*, at the beginning of the next line; press Enter to edit line 14:

```
*<Enter>
       14:*documents to make sure they agree with our
       14:*_
```

To make the change, you can either press the Delete key 18 times or skip to the second s (*sure*) in the line. It's faster to skip, so press F4 and press s. Nothing happens on the screen, because you haven't copied any characters yet. You want to skip to the second s, so press F4 and press s again. Press F3 to copy the rest of the line, but don't press Enter just yet:

```
       14:*documents to make sure they agree with our
       14:*sure they agree with our_
```

The words at the beginning have been deleted, and now the line is short enough to include the only word in the next line, *assumptions.*

To make your memo look nicer, type *assumptions* (don't forget a blank at the beginning and a period at the end) and press Enter:

```
14:*documents to make sure they agree with our
14:*sure they agree with our assumptions.
*_
```

Line 15 contains only one word, *assumptions*, which you already moved up to the previous line. You've completed all the revisions up to this point; it's also where you want to insert instructions for displaying the files. Edit the line. It's the next line, so just press Enter and, instead of copying any characters, start entering the new text, which will replace the old:

```
*<Enter>
15:*assumptions.
15:*You can review the documents on the
*_
```

Now insert the remaining new lines before line 16. Type:

```
*16i
16:*screen. To check the proposal, type:
17:*<Enter>
18:*TYPE B:PROPOSAL | MORE
19:*<Enter>
20:*This displays one screen at a time.
21:*Press the spacebar to display the
22:*next screen, or Ctrl-Break to stop.
23:*<Ctrl-Break>
*_
```

Ctrl-Break in line 23 tells Edlin you have finished inserting lines. You have completed your revisions, so it's time to look at your edited memo. Your file, however, is now more than 25 lines long, and 25 lines is the maximum normally displayed on a computer monitor.

If you have version 4, remember that you can display a range of lines by typing the List command as *<from>, <to> l*, where *<from>* is the number of the first line to display and *<to>* is the number of the last line to display. To have Edlin display a long file screen by screen, type *l* as the beginning line number and # as the ending line number, as described earlier in the example showing how to print your file. Edlin shows 24 lines of the file at a time, ending each display with the message *Continue (Y/N)?* Type *y* to continue viewing the file, or type *n* to cancel the display. Try it now to see your memo; type:

```
*1,#l
```

Edlin displays:

```
 1: Final Project Review -- 10/16/89
 2:
 3: To: PROJECT TEAM
 4:
 5: This diskette has 5 files on it:
 6:
 7: FORECAST.PLN
 8: OPTION1.PLN    Higher sales
 9: OPTION2.PLN    No staff increase
10: LETTER.DOC
11: PROPOSAL.DOC
12:
13: Please check the spreadsheets and make
14: sure they agree with our assumptions.
15: You can review the documents on the
16: screen. To check the proposal, type:
17:
18: TYPE B:PROPOSAL ¦ MORE
19:
20: This displays one screen at a time.
21: Press the spacebar to display the
22: next screen, or Ctrl-Break to stop.
23:*
24: Let's do this quickly, it's due Thursday.
Continue (Y/N)?_
```

To see the rest, type *y* to display the rest of the file:

```
Continue (Y/N)?y
25:
26: Tom
*_
```

If you don't have version 4, type the List command as you've done before:

```
*l
```

Edlin displays the first 23 lines of the file. To see the rest, use the List command again, this time starting the display with the next line, 24:

```
*24l
```

Your revised memo, complete with instructions, is ready for your team. Just store the memo, print a copy for each member of the project team, tuck one in each diskette envelope, and deliver them.

To save the memo, type:

```
*e
```

Edlin stores the file on disk and returns you to DOS:

```
B:\>
```

BACKUP FILES

When you edit an existing file, Edlin works with a copy that it has placed in your computer's memory. The original version remains, unchanged, on the disk. When you end an editing session on the working copy of an existing file, Edlin changes the extension of the unchanged original to BAK (for backup) and stores the revised version on the disk in addition to the BAK version. If there is already a file with the same name and an extension of BAK, Edlin erases the old BAK file before renaming the version it copied into memory for you to work with. If you need the original version, you can use the BAK file. (If you're using 3.2 or an earlier version, you'll have to change its extension, because Edlin in those versions won't edit a file with an extension of BAK. You can use the Rename command—for example, you would change MEMO.BAK to MEMO.OLD by typing *ren memo.bak memo.old*.)

PAGING THROUGH A FILE

If you typed *e* to End Edit at the conclusion of the previous session, tell DOS you want to use Edlin to edit MEMO.TXT by typing:

```
:\B>edlin memo.txt
```

Edlin responds:

```
End of input file
*_
```

Earlier, you displayed the file screen by screen with the List command, either by typing *1,#l* or by increasing the line number by 23 (the number of lines per screen) each time (*1l* for the first screenful, then *24l* for the second screenful, and so on). The Page command (p) gives you a way to page through a file without worrying about line numbers. Start with line 1 and page through the practice memo:

```
*1p
 1: Final Project Review -- 10/16/89
 2:
 3: To: PROJECT TEAM
 4:
 5: This diskette has 5 files on it:
 6:
 7: FORECAST.PLN
 8: OPTION1.PLN   Higher sales
 9: OPTION2.PLN   No staff increase
10: LETTER.DOC
11: PROPOSAL.DOC
12:
13: Please check the spreadsheets and make
14: sure they agree with our assumptions.
```

```
15: You can review the documents on the
16: screen. To check the proposal, type:
17:
18: TYPE B:PROPOSAL | MORE
19:
20: This displays one screen at a time.
21: Press the spacebar to display the
22: next screen, or Ctrl-Break to stop.
23:*
*_
```

To see the next group of lines (in this case, the lines remaining in the file), type:

```
*p
24: Let's do this quickly, it's due Thursday.
25:
26:*Tom
*_
```

If you don't specify a line number, the Page command displays the current line and the following 22 lines. The Page command changes the current line to the last line displayed, so you can page through a file just by typing *p* for each screenful.

MOVING LINES

You can move a paragraph or other block of lines from one place to another in the file with the Move command (m). First, you specify the starting and ending line numbers of the block to be moved, then you specify the number of the line before which the block should be placed, separating the numbers with commas.

For example, suppose you want to move lines 5 through 12 from where they are to just before the last sentence (line 24). To move the lines and to verify the move, type the following. Notice that you are giving Edlin two commands on one line, separating the commands with a semicolon:

```
*5,12,24m;1p
```

You see:

```
1: Final Project Review -- 10/16/89
2:
3: To: PROJECT TEAM
4:
5: Please check the spreadsheets and make
6: sure they agree with our assumptions.
7: You can review the documents on the
8: screen. To check the proposal, type:
9:
10: TYPE B:PROPOSAL | MORE
11:
12: This displays one screen at a time.
```

```
13: Press the spacebar to display the
14: next screen, or Ctrl-Break to stop.
15:
16: This diskette has 5 files on it:
17:
18: FORECAST.PLN
19: OPTION1.PLN    Higher sales
20: OPTION2.PLN    No staff increase
21: LETTER.DOC
22: PROPOSAL.DOC
23:*
*_
```

Note that Edlin renumbers the lines, just as when you insert or delete lines.

If you omit either the starting or ending line number, Edlin assumes you mean the current line. To move one line that is not the current line, specify it as both the beginning and end of the block (for example, to move line 26 to just before line 5, the command would be *26,26,5m*). After the lines are moved, the first line that was moved becomes the current line.

COPYING LINES

You can copy a block of lines to another place in the file with the Copy command (c). To do so, specify the beginning and ending line numbers of the block and the number of the line before which the block is to be copied, just as you did with the Move command. Copy differs from Move in that the block you specify remains in its original location and is repeated in the new location.

For example, suppose you want to copy the line that begins with *This diskette has* plus the list of files (lines 16 through 22) to the end of the document so that you can use these lines as a label. Type the following Copy and Page commands to copy the lines and verify the copy (remember that # means the line that follows the last line):

```
*16,22,#c;16p
```

You see:

```
16: This diskette has 5 files on it:
17:
18: FORECAST.PLN
19: OPTION1.PLN    Higher sales
20: OPTION2.PLN    No staff increase
21: LETTER.DOC
22: PROPOSAL.DOC
23:
24: Let's do this quickly, it's due Thursday.
25:
26: Tom
27: This diskette has 5 files on it:
```

```
28:
29: FORECAST.PLN
30: OPTION1.PLN    Higher sales
31: OPTION2.PLN    No staff increase
32: LETTER.DOC
33:*PROPOSAL.DOC
*_
```

You can make several copies of a block of lines with one Copy command by adding a comma and the number of copies just before the *c*. For example, to make five more copies of the same block of lines, type the following:

```
*16,22,#,5c;27p;p
```

If you omit the starting or ending line number, Edlin assumes the omitted line number is the current line. To copy one line other than the current line, specify it as both the start and end of the block. After the lines are copied, the last copy of the last line that was moved becomes the current line.

COPYING ANOTHER FILE

You can copy another file into the file you're editing. Suppose you have a file that contains the name and address of each member of the project team. If you want to include the address list in this memo, you don't have to type it again; you can merge the two files with the Transfer command (t).

To see how this works, quit the edit of this file, use Edlin to create a small file named ADDRESS on the diskette in drive B, then return to editing MEMO.TXT and display the first 23 lines of the file. To do this, type:

```
q
Abort edit (Y/N)? y
B:\>edlin address
New file
*i
        1:*XXX ADDRESS LIST XXX
        2:*<Enter>
        3:*<Ctrl-Break>

*1,1,2,3c;1p
        1: XXX ADDRESS LIST XXX
        2: XXX ADDRESS LIST XXX
        3: XXX ADDRESS LIST XXX
        4: XXX ADDRESS LIST XXX
        5:*
*e

B>edlin memo.txt
End of input file
*p
```

The first 23 lines of MEMO.TXT are on the screen.

To copy another file with the Transfer command, you specify the line before which the file is to be placed, then type *t* and the name of the file. Do not use commas.

To copy the file named ADDRESS to just before line 3 and see the result, type:

```
*3taddress;1p
        1: Final Project Review -- 10/16/89
        2:
        3: XXX ADDRESS LIST XXX
        4: XXX ADDRESS LIST XXX
        5: XXX ADDRESS LIST XXX
        6: XXX ADDRESS LIST XXX
        7:
        8: To: PROJECT TEAM
        9:
       10: This diskette has 5 files on it:
       11:
       12: FORECAST.PLN
       13: OPTION1.PLN    Higher sales
       14: OPTION2.PLN    No staff increase
       15: LETTER.DOC
       16: PROPOSAL.DOC
       17:
       18: Please check the spreadsheets and make
       19: sure they agree with our assumptions.
       20: You can review the documents on the
       21: screen. To check the proposal, type:
       22:
       23:*TYPE B:PROPOSAL ¦ MORE
    *_
```

If you don't specify the line number, Edlin copies the file to just above the current line and the first line of the copied file becomes the current line.

EDITING FILES TOO LARGE TO FIT INTO MEMORY

Although you'll probably find Edlin handy mostly for short documents, you can also use Edlin to edit very large files—even those that are larger than the amount of available memory. When you edit a very large file, Edlin starts loading the file into memory, stopping when it has filled 75 percent of the available memory; this leaves room for you to add to the file. If you insert enough additional text to fill the remaining 25 percent of available memory, or if you want to work with the part of the file that was not loaded, you can move the part of the file in memory onto disk, to make room for loading the next part of the file.

Two Edlin commands control this process: Write Lines (w), which stores (writes) the part of the file in memory (<number> of lines) onto disk; and Append Lines (a), which loads the next part of the file (<number> of lines) from disk into memory. The practice file is not large enough to demonstrate these commands, so simply keep them in mind for your own later use.

CHAPTER SUMMARY

Although Edlin is a simple text editor and lacks many of the features required of a word processor, its speed and simplicity make it an excellent tool for creating and revising short text files. The examples in this and the preceding chapter showed you how you can use Edlin to write a short memo. The remaining chapters of this book describe some of the advanced features of DOS, many of which require short files of text. You'll find that Edlin is admirably suited to taking advantage of these features.

CHAPTER

12

CREATING YOUR OWN COMMANDS

A s the preceding chapters show, DOS gives you a great deal of control over your computer system. But DOS is necessarily general purpose, because many people use it for many different tasks. So that you can adapt the computer to your work, DOS lets you combine existing DOS commands to create your own special-purpose commands.

The technique is simple: To make your own command, you create a text file that contains DOS commands. You can give such a file—called a *batch file*—any valid name except the name of an existing command; the extension of the file must be BAT. To use your command, simply type the name of the batch file; DOS carries out the commands contained in the file as if you had typed each of them separately. Commands you create this way are called *batch commands*.

This chapter describes how to create batch files and how to carry out batch commands. It also describes the Remark command, which is intended for batch files, and it shows you how to modify the DOS startup procedure if there are certain commands you always carry out when you start your system.

A BATCH OF WHAT?

The term *batch* has its origins in the early days of large computers, when most work was done by submitting a deck of punched cards to the data-processing department. The punched cards had to contain all the instructions required for the program to run correctly. There was no chance to interact with the system. The data-processing personnel ran these jobs in batches and delivered the output.

In effect, you do the same thing when you use a batch command, because a batch file contains all the instructions needed to carry out a job. Batch, then, is used to describe a computer job that runs without interruption, as opposed to an interactive job—such as word processing—that consists of an exchange of instructions and responses between you and the computer.

You can use batch files to automate frequently used command sequences and to make the system more accessible to colleagues who use application programs but might not know DOS as well as you do.

HOW DOS SEARCHES
FOR A COMMAND

If you type something when DOS is displaying the system prompt, DOS assumes you have typed a command name. It then follows a particular sequence in trying to carry out the command:

1. It checks to see if you typed the name of a built-in command, such as *dir* or *copy*. If you did, DOS runs the program that carries out that command.

2. If what you typed isn't the name of a built-in command, DOS checks to see if you typed the name of a file with the extension COM or EXE (a command file). If you did, DOS loads the program contained in the file and runs it.

3. If what you typed isn't the name of a command file, DOS checks to see if you typed the name of a file with the extension BAT (a batch file). If you did, DOS carries out the commands in the batch file.

The sequence is important, because it explains why DOS won't carry out a command file with the same name as a built-in command, and why it won't carry out a batch file that has the same name as either a built-in command or a command file.

PREPARING FOR THE EXAMPLES

If you're using a fixed disk, create a directory named \RUNNING by typing the following:

```
C:\DOS>md \running
```

Now change the current directory to \RUNNING by typing:

```
C:\DOS>cd \running

C:\RUNNING>
```

Because you'll be creating your own commands in this chapter, the system prompt is shown as a simple C> to keep it unobtrusive. If your system prompt normally shows the current directory, you can simplify it temporarily by typing:

```
C:\RUNNING>prompt
```

When you next start or restart your computer, the system prompt will revert to showing both the current drive and the current directory. Go on to the heading ''Creating the Sample Files.''

If you're not using a fixed disk, leave your system diskette in drive A and put a formatted diskette in drive B. Type the following to change the current drive to B:

```
A>b:

B>_
```

The system prompt in the examples will be C>, not B>.

Creating the Sample Files

You will use three sample files in this chapter:

```
LETR1.DOC
LETR2.DOC
LETR3.DOC
```

Type the following to create the sample files (remember, press either F6 or Ctrl-Z, and then press Enter, where you see ^Z):

```
C>copy con letr1.doc
This is the sample file.
^Z
         1 File(s) copied

C>copy letr1.doc letr2.*
         1 File(s) copied

C>copy letr1.doc letr3.*
         1 File(s) copied

C>_
```

CREATING A BATCH FILE

A batch file is simply a text file, with an extension of BAT, that contains DOS commands. It's a simple matter to create a batch file. You can create one just as you create any other text file: Copy from the console to a text file, or use Edlin or a word processor (if it can store files without inserting its own formatting codes).

The examples in this chapter have you copy from the console to create short batch files. The only drawback to using this technique is that you can't go back to correct an error after you press Enter at the end of a line. If you make a typing error while entering an example, either press Ctrl-Break and reenter the batch file, or use Edlin to correct the error in the file.

Suppose one of the application programs you use is a word processor, and you name the files that contain letters LETR1.DOC, LETR2.DOC, LETR3.DOC, and so forth. You use the Directory command fairly often to display the names of those particular files. Instead of typing *dir letr*.doc* each time, you could put the Directory command in a batch file named DIRLET.BAT.

Type the following to create the batch file:

```
C>copy con dirlet.bat
dir letr*.doc
^Z
         1 File(s) copied

C>_
```

The first line you typed names the batch file; the second line contains the command DOS carries out. Test your batch command by typing its name:

```
C>dirlet
```

```
C>dir letr*.doc

 Volume in drive C is FIXED DISK
 Volume Serial Number is 1608-5A30
 Directory of  C:\RUNNING

LETR1    DOC        26 10-16-89   3:13p
LETR2    DOC        26 10-16-89   3:13p
LETR3    DOC        26 10-16-89   3:13p
                3 File(s)   13277184 bytes free
```

It's possible that you'll see a double prompt, like this:

```
C>
C>_
```

when your batch file finishes running. Don't worry about it. If you object to the duplication for aesthetic reasons, press Ctrl-Z at the end of the last line of each batch file you copy from CON, instead of on a line by itself.

The first line displayed after you type your batch command is the Directory command that you entered into your batch file. DOS displays the commands in a batch file as they are carried out; it's as if you typed the command itself.

You could make the batch command even easier to type by naming the batch file just LDIR.BAT. In the long run, however, it's usually better to make the name long enough to give a good hint of what the command does, especially if you create a large number of batch files.

Displaying Messages from a Batch File

The Remark (rem) command doesn't cause DOS to do anything, but it is a valid command. You can include a message with the Remark command. The command form is:

rem <message>

Although this command isn't especially useful at the DOS command level, it lets you display a message from a batch file. To see how the Remark command works, create another version of DIRLET.BAT that displays a descriptive message; type the following:

```
C>copy con dirlet.bat
rem DIRECTORY OF LETTERS
dir letr*.doc
^Z
        1 File(s) copied
```

The new version of DIRLET.BAT replaces the first version you created a few minutes ago. Test this new version by typing:

```
C>dirlet
```

The Remark command you included causes DOS to display the message before it displays the directory:

```
C>rem DIRECTORY OF LETTERS

C>dir letr*.doc

 Volume in drive C is FIXED DISK
 Volume Serial Number is 1608-5A30
 Directory of  C:\RUNNING

LETR1     DOC        26 10-16-89    3:13p
LETR2     DOC        26 10-16-89    3:13p
LETR3     DOC        26 10-16-89    3:13p
         3 File(s)     13277184 bytes free

C>_
```

Carrying Out the Same Batch Command With Different Data

You have seen that most DOS commands include one or more parameters that you can use to make your instructions more specific. When you enter a Directory command, for example, you can specify a file name to display some portion of the files on a disk and the /W option to display the wide form of the directory. The Copy command is another example. It requires two parameters: the name of the file to be copied, and the name to be given to the new copy.

Parameters let you use the same DOS command with different data. You can give your batch files the same capability with a feature called a *replaceable parameter*.

A replaceable parameter is a special symbol you put in a batch file. When you use the batch file, DOS replaces the symbol with a parameter you include when you type the batch command. The symbol consists of a percent sign followed by a one-digit number, such as %1. You can use the numbers 1 through 9 in replaceable parameters, and you can include more than one replaceable parameter in a batch file. (DOS also recognizes %0 as a replaceable parameter but reserves this parameter to mean the drive, path, and file name of the batch file itself.)

The number of the symbol identifies which parameter replaces the symbol. If a batch command takes two parameters, for example, DOS replaces %1, wherever it occurs in the batch file, with the first parameter you type with the batch command, and it replaces %2 with the second parameter you type. Replaceable parameters can be used anywhere in a batch command.

For example, suppose you wanted a batch command that would print a file by copying it to the printer. (You already have a DOS Print command, but go through the example anyway; it illustrates the use of replaceable parameters.) All the batch file needs is a Copy command and one replaceable parameter that identifies the file to be printed. The batch command is called *Prnt* to avoid confusion with the Print command. Type the following:

```
C>copy con prnt.bat
copy %1 prn
^Z
        1 File(s) copied
```

To test your Prnt batch command, make certain the printer is turned on and type the following:

```
C>prnt letr1.doc
```

DOS displays the command after replacing %1 with the batch-command parameter, LETR1.DOC, and prints the file:

```
C>copy letr1.doc prn
        1 File(s) copied
```

Figure 12-1 shows several versions of PRNT.BAT that you might create for printing other documents. Each version contains at least one replaceable parameter; the last version contains two. To the left of each version is an example of how the batch command would be typed, and to the right are the corresponding commands that would be carried out after DOS replaced the replaceable parameters. The batch-command parameters, the replaceable parameters in each version of the batch file, and the result after DOS replaces them with the batch-command parameters, are in *italics*.

Batch Command You Would Type	Contents of PRNT.BAT	Commands That Would Be Carried Out
C>prnt *memo.doc*	copy *%1* prn	copy *memo.doc* prn
C>prnt *memo*	copy *%1*.doc prn	copy *memo*.doc prn
C>prnt *memo rept*	copy *%1*.doc prn	copy *memo*.doc prn
	copy *%2*.doc prn	copy *rept*.doc prn

Figure 12-1. Replaceable parameters in a batch file

Replaceable parameters make batch files much more flexible. Your batch commands needn't be limited to handling the same files or devices all the time—they can be used just like DOS commands to operate with any file or device.

Canceling a Batch Command

Just as with other DOS commands, you press Ctrl-Break to cancel a batch command. But when you cancel a batch command, DOS prompts you to confirm. To see this, create a short batch file named DIRS.BAT that first displays the entries in your \DOS directory (or on your DOS diskette) and then displays the entries in the current directory (\RUNNING).

If you're using a fixed disk, create the DIRS.BAT file shown below. (Replace *c:\dos* in the second line with the name of your DOS directory if your DOS command files are not in a directory named \DOS.) To create the batch file, type:

```
C>copy con dirs.bat
dir c:\dos
dir
^Z
        1 File(s) copied
```

If you're not using a fixed disk, type:

```
B>copy con dirs.bat
dir a:
dir
^Z
        1 File(s) copied
```

The directory displays should be long enough to give you time to press Ctrl-Break. Type the name of the Dirs batch command, then press Ctrl-Break as soon as DOS starts displaying the file names:

```
C>dirs

C>dir c:\dos

 Volume in drive C is FIXED DISK
 Volume Serial Number is 1608-5A30
 Directory of  C:\DOS
 .               <DIR>      10-10-89    6:05p
 ..              <DIR>      10-10-89    6:05p
DOSSHELL BAT       214 10-10-89    6:05p
COMMAND  COM     37637 06-17-88   12:00p
COUNTRY  SYS     12838 06-17-88   12:00p
DISKCOPY COM     10428 06-17-88^C

Terminate batch job (Y/N)?_
```

If you respond no, the command being carried out is canceled, but DOS continues with the next command in the batch file. Type *n*; DOS carries out the next command, which displays the current directory:

```
C>dir

 Volume in drive C is FIXED DISK
 Volume Serial Number is 1608-5A30
 Directory of  C:\RUNNING
```

```
     .              <DIR>        10-16-89    3:03p
     ..             <DIR>        10-16-89    3:03p
LETR1    DOC           26 10-16-89    3:13p
LETR2    DOC           26 10-16-89    3:13p
LETR3    DOC           26 10-16-89    3:13p
DIRLET   BAT           41 10-16-89    3:17p
PRNT     BAT           13 10-16-89    3:24p
DIRS     BAT           19 10-16-89    3:30p
              8 File(s)    13277184 bytes free
```

If you respond yes to the terminate question, DOS cancels the entire batch command and displays the system prompt. Type the Dirs batch command and cancel it
again, but this time respond *y*:

```
C>dirs

C>dir c:\dos

 Volume in drive C is FIXED DISK
 Volume Serial Number is 1608-5A30
 Directory of  C:\DOS

     .              <DIR>        10-10-89    6:05p
     ..             <DIR>        10-10-89    6:05p
DOSSHELL BAT          214 10-10-89    6:05p
COMMAND  COM        37637 06-17-88   12:00p
COUNTRY  SYS        12838 06-17-88   12:00p
DISKCOPY COM        10428 06-17-88   12:00p
DISPLAY  SYS        15741 06-17-88^C

Terminate batch job (Y/N)?y
```

DOS returns to the command level without completing the batch command.

Creating Your Own Startup Procedure

Each time you start or restart the system, DOS goes through a startup procedure that,
on some computers, includes prompting you for the current date and time and displaying the DOS version that you're using. If you want, you can substitute your own
startup procedure by creating a special batch file named AUTOEXEC.BAT in the root
directory of the disk from which you normally start DOS. Each time the system is
started, DOS carries out the commands in AUTOEXEC.BAT.

A Quick Safety Check

If you already have a file named AUTOEXEC.BAT in your root directory, the example
in the following procedure will replace it, whether or not you want it to. Even though
you might not have created an AUTOEXEC.BAT file, the dealer from whom you pur-
chased your computer or the person who set up your system might well may have created such a file—especially if you are using version 4 of DOS and your system has a
fixed disk. You'd be unhappy to lose a familiar startup procedure you're using now.

It's easy to guard against this; type the following Directory command:

```
C>dir \autoexec.bat
```

If DOS replies *File not found*, go on to the heading ''Creating AUTOEXEC.BAT.'' You don't have the file, so you won't hurt a thing by trying the example.

If, however, DOS displays a directory entry for a file named AUTOEXEC.BAT, you can protect it from inadvertent loss by renaming it before continuing with the example. Type the following:

```
C>ren \autoexec.bat autoexec.tmp
```

You'll restore your original AUTOEXEC.BAT at the end of the example.

Creating AUTOEXEC.BAT

Whenever DOS completes its diagnostic tests, it checks to see whether there is a file named AUTOEXEC.BAT in the root directory of the system disk. If there is not, DOS completes its startup and displays the system prompt. If there is an AUTOEXEC.BAT file, DOS carries out the commands in it before displaying the system prompt.

One useful entry in AUTOEXEC.BAT, especially if you keep DOS and your programs in subdirectories, is a Path command that tells DOS where to find its external command files and your programs. Another good command for AUTOEXEC.BAT— again, especially useful if you use subdirectories—is a Prompt command like the one introduced in Chapter 9, which has the system prompt display both the current drive and the current directory.

Then, too, you can use AUTOEXEC.BAT for more specialized tasks. For example, suppose that each time you start the system you change to a particular directory on your fixed disk and list its contents. Or, if you're not using a fixed disk, suppose you change the current drive to drive B and then display the directory. You can tell DOS to carry out these commands each time you start the system by putting them in AUTOEXEC.BAT.

To test all of this, create an AUTOEXEC.BAT file that includes Path and Prompt commands and also changes the current directory or drive and displays a directory listing. Create the file by copying from the console to the system disk.

If you're using a fixed disk, the Path command in this example uses the directory named \RUNNING that you created earlier and assumes that DOS is in a directory named \DOS. If you don't have a \DOS directory, substitute the name of the directory that contains your DOS files or just ignore that part of the Path command. Don't worry; you won't harm your system. Type the following:

```
C>copy con \autoexec.bat
rem NEW STARTUP PROCEDURE
path c:\;c:\dos;c:\running
prompt $p$g
```

```
cd \running
dir
^Z
        1 File(s) copied
```

If you're not using a fixed disk, type the following:

```
B>copy con a:autoexec.bat
rem NEW STARTUP PROCEDURE
path a:\
prompt $p$g
b:
dir
^Z
        1 File(s) copied
```

You created the file in the root directory of the system disk, because that's where DOS always looks for AUTOEXEC.BAT. To test your startup procedure, you must restart the system.

Note: If you're using a fixed disk, be sure to open the door latch on the diskette drive so that DOS restarts from the fixed disk.

Now restart the system by pressing Ctrl-Alt-Del. The startup screen differs from what you have seen before.

```
C>rem NEW STARTUP PROCEDURE

C>path c:\;c:\dos;c:\running

C>prompt $p$g

C:\>cd \running

C:\RUNNING>dir

 Volume in drive C is FIXED DISK
 Volume Serial Number is 1608-5A30
 Directory of  C:\RUNNING
.               <DIR>      10-16-89    3:03p
..              <DIR>      10-16-89    3:03p
LETR1    DOC        26 10-16-89    3:13p
LETR2    DOC        26 10-16-89    3:13p
LETR3    DOC        26 10-16-89    3:13p
DIRLET   BAT        41 10-16-89    3:17p
PRNT     BAT        13 10-16-89    3:24p
DIRS     BAT        19 10-16-89    3:30p
        8 File(s)   13275136 bytes free

C:\RUNNING>
```

Your new startup procedure not only tells DOS where to find the files it needs, it also changes the current directory or drive and tells you what it is, and then displays the entries in the current directory.

You can also use AUTOEXEC.BAT to handle special startup requirements. For example, if your system has equipment options that require special setup instructions with the Mode command, put the commands in AUTOEXEC.BAT so that you needn't type them each time you start or restart the system. Or, if your system has an electronic clock and calendar that require you to run a program to set the date and time, you can put the command in AUTOEXEC.BAT so that you don't have to enter the command each time you start the system.

If other people use the system to run an application program, such as a word processor or a spreadsheet, you can make a copy of the system diskette for them that includes an AUTOEXEC.BAT file ending with the command to start the application program automatically.

If you renamed your existing AUTOEXEC.BAT file at the beginning of this example, type the following to restore it:

```
C:\RUNNING>ren \autoexec.bat autoexec.run
```

```
C:\RUNNING>ren \autoexec.tmp autoexec.bat
```

Now your original AUTOEXEC.BAT will be executed the next time you start up your system; the version you created in the example is still in the root directory as AUTOEXEC.RUN, in case you want to experiment with it further.

If you didn't have an AUTOEXEC.BAT file to begin with, type the following to ensure that DOS will not carry out your example file the next time you start your system:

```
C:\RUNNING>ren autoexec.bat autoexec.run
```

Finally, to rid your system of a possibly invalid Path command, restart your computer by pressing Ctrl-Alt-Del. If you have a fixed disk, change the current directory to \RUNNING (type *cd \running*). If you don't have a fixed disk, change the current drive to B: (type *b:* at the system prompt). To simplify the system prompt, type *prompt*.

Making a Chain of Batch Files

You can use a batch command that defines another batch command in a batch file. The second batch file could contain still another batch command. This is called *chaining,* because each batch file is linked to the next one.

When DOS carries out the last command in a batch file, it returns to command level and displays the system prompt. If you put a chained batch command in another batch file, the chained batch command should be the last command in the first batch file, because any commands that follow it won't be carried out.

If you were to put a chained batch command in the middle of another batch file, DOS would carry out the commands in the first file, up to the chained batch command; then it would jump to the chained batch file, carry out the chained file's commands, and return to command level. Any commands that followed the chained batch command in the first batch file would not be carried out, because DOS does not return to a previous batch file.

For example, suppose you decide to create two batch commands:

- Dirprt, which displays the directory entry of a file, then prints the file.

- Disprt, which displays a file and then prints it.

Both batch commands end by printing the file. You have already entered a batch command named Prnt that prints a file; you can use it as a chained batch file in both the Dirprt and Disprt batch commands.

Type the following:

```
C>copy con dirprt.bat
dir  %1
prnt %1
^Z
        1 File(s) copied

C>copy con disprt.bat
type %1
prnt %1
^Z
        1 File(s) copied
```

Make sure the printer is on and use your AUTOEXEC.RUN file as a sample to test the Dirprt batch command. AUTOEXEC.RUN is in the root directory of your system disk, so if you're not using a fixed disk, type *a:autoexec.run* instead of *\autoexec.run* in the following examples.

Now test DIRPRT.BAT by typing:

```
C>dirprt \autoexec.run
```

First, DOS substitutes *\autoexec.run* for %1, displays the Directory command in DIRPRT.BAT, and carries it out; your display differs slightly from the following if you're not using a fixed disk:

```
C>dir \autoexec.run

 Volume in drive C is FIXED DISK
 Volume Serial Number is 1608-5A30
 Directory of  C:\

AUTOEXEC RUN          87 10-16-89    4:35p
        1 File(s)    13273088 bytes free
```

Next, DOS displays the Prnt batch command after again substituting *autoexec.run* for the replaceable parameter %1:

```
C>prnt \autoexec.run
```

Now DOS displays and carries out the Copy command (copy %1 prn) from PRNT.BAT, again substituting *autoexec.run* for %1:

```
C>copy \autoexec.run prn
        1 File(s) copied
```

The file is printed.

Test the Disprt batch command by typing:

```
C>disprt \autoexec.run
```

First, DOS displays the Type command in DISPRT.BAT and carries it out by listing the contents of AUTOEXEC.RUN:

```
C>type \autoexec.run
rem NEW STARTUP PROCEDURE
path c:\;c:\dos;c:\running
prompt $p$g
cd \running
dir
```

From here on, the Disprt batch command responds just as the Dirprt batch command did, because both batch files chain to PRNT.BAT:

```
C>prnt \autoexec.run

C>copy \autoexec.run prn
        1 File(s) copied
```

Again, the file is printed.

Chaining batch files is a good way to build powerful batch commands, because it lets you use one batch file in several different ways and reduces the chance of your batch files getting long and complicated.

Note: If you're using 3.3 or a later version, there's a way you can use a batch command anywhere in a batch file: It's the Call command, which is described in Chapter 15 under the heading ''Using a Batch Command in a Batch File.''

SOME USEFUL COMMANDS

This chapter concludes by describing a few batch commands you might find useful; they might also give you some ideas for other commands you could create. Each topic includes a description of what the command does, the contents of the batch file, and one or two examples of its use.

These examples are illustrative; they are not hands-on exercises because you might not have the necessary files or devices to use them. But remember that they're here; you'll probably find a situation in which they can be helpful.

Printing a File

Earlier in the chapter you created the Prnt batch command, which prints a file by copying it to the printer. PRNT.BAT contains *copy %1 prn*. To use it, you type the name of the batch file followed by the name of the file to be printed. (For example, to print a file named REPORT.DOC, you would type *prnt report.doc*.)

As the examples in Figure 12-1 on page 231 showed, you can make batch commands more specific by including common parts of a file name or extension in the batch file. For example, if you frequently print files that have the extension DOC, you could enter the command in the batch file as *copy %1.doc*; to print the file named REPORT.DOC, you would only have to type *prnt report*.

Printing a File in Small Type

If your printer is compatible with Epson or IBM dot-matrix printers, you can use the Mode command to change to smaller type so that 132 characters can be printed on a line. This type is handy for wide reports or spreadsheets, and putting the Mode and Copy commands in a batch file named SMALL.BAT makes them easy to use. SMALL.BAT contains:

```
mode lpt1: 132
copy %1 lpt1:
mode lpt1: 80
```

If your printer is attached to a different port, change *lpt1* to *lpt2* or *lpt3*, as necessary. The Small command takes one parameter, the name of the file to be printed in small type. To use the Small command to print the file REPORT.DOC, you would type:

```
C>small report.doc
```

DOS would display the Mode and Copy commands and print the file in small type:

```
C>mode lpt1: 132

LPT1: set for 132
```

```
C>copy report.doc lpt1:
        1 File(s) copied

C>mode lpt1: 80

LPT1: set for 80
```

The second Mode command resets the printer to normal type.

Eliminating Old BAK Files

Because Edlin and many word processors create a backup file with an extension of BAK each time you edit a file, your disks can get crowded with files you might not need. The CLEANUP.BAT batch file described here would erase all the files in the current directory whose extension is BAK. CLEANUP.BAT contains:

```
erase %1*.bak
```

The Cleanup command takes one parameter, the directory name followed by a backslash. If you omit the parameter, the command cleans up the current directory. You can clean up the disk in a different drive by preceding the path name with the drive letter and a colon. For example, to erase all files whose extension is BAK in the current directory, you would simply type *cleanup*. To erase all BAK files in the directory \MKT\WP, you would type *cleanup \mkt\wp*. Similarly, to erase all BAK files in the directory \LASTYEAR\RPT on the disk in drive A, you would type *cleanup a:\lastyear\rpt*. Finally, to erase all files whose extension is BAK in the current directory of the disk in drive B, you would type *C>cleanup b:*.

Batch files let you create your own commands to meet your needs. As you use DOS more, you'll probably find many uses for this capability. This chapter just introduces batch files. Chapters 13, 14, and 15 show you how to use several additional commands that make batch commands one of the most powerful features of DOS.

CHAPTER
13

TAKING CONTROL OF
YOUR SYSTEM

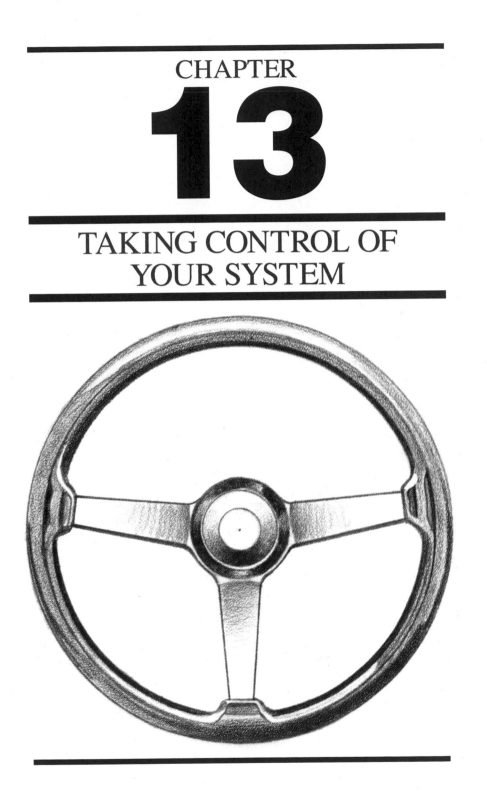

U p to now, you have used the DOS commands in their standard form. DOS, however, gives you a great deal of flexibility in controlling the way some commands do their work for you.

This chapter describes where commands get their input and what they do with their output. It shows you how to control some commands and describes some additional commands that give you the building blocks for creating your own set of customized commands.

It is easy to visualize what happens with command output, so even though it might seem odd to discuss results before discussing causes, the next section on command output gives you a foundation for understanding command input as well.

REDIRECTING COMMAND OUTPUT

The result, or output, of most commands is some action, such as copying a file (with the Copy command) or controlling the operation of a device (with the Mode command). The output of a few commands, however, such as Directory, Check Disk, and Tree, is a report. Up to now, you have used these reports primarily as displays—DOS has sent them to the *standard output* device, the console. (Recall from Chapter 7 that DOS uses the name CON, or console, for both the keyboard, which is input only, and the display, which is output only.)

As you'll see in this chapter, DOS lets you send reports and other output to a different device, such as a printer, or to a file. This is called *redirecting* the output of the command; you did it a few times in previous chapters with such commands as *dir > prn*. The technique is simple: To redirect the output of a command that normally sends its results to standard output (the display), you type the command name followed by > and the name of the device or file to which the output is to be sent. The > looks something like an arrowhead pointing toward the alternate output device or file.

Using redirection it's easy, for example, to print a copy of the directory as you did in Chapter 4. To repeat that example, but this time with an understanding of what happens, be sure the printer is turned on and type the following (if you're not using a fixed disk, the system prompt will be A>):

```
C:\DOS>dir > prn
```

The > tells DOS to redirect the output of the Directory command, and PRN tells DOS where to send it: to the printer. The directory should be printing now; if you want to cancel the printing, press Ctrl-Break.

REDIRECTING COMMAND INPUT

You've seen how quickly and easily you can redirect output to a device or a file. You can just as easily redirect input, in effect telling certain DOS commands to get their data from a source other than the one (often called *standard input*) they would normally use.

Together, redirected input and output are known as *redirection.* Although redirection sounds complicated, it is easy to understand, as the examples in this chapter show.

Three DOS commands, known collectively as *filter commands,* make particularly effective use of redirection.

FILTER COMMANDS

Filter commands take input from a device or a file, change the input in some way, and send the result to an output device or file. They are called filter commands because they work much like a filter in a water system, which takes incoming water, changes it in some way, and sends it along the system.

DOS includes three filter commands that allow you to:

- Arrange lines in ascending or descending order with the Sort command.

- Search for a string of characters with the Find command.

- Temporarily halt the display after one screenful of input lines (to give you a chance to read them) with the More command.

You can redirect both the input and the output of a filter command. The filter commands aren't really intended to be used with keyboard input. Rather, they are designed to get their input from a file or even from the output of another command. This chapter shows you how to use and combine the filter commands to create your own powerful, specialized commands.

PREPARING FOR THE EXAMPLES

Redirection and filter commands give you the elements of a simple file-management program. While they won't replace a file manager, they let you use DOS to search and sort simple lists without spending extra money or time on another program.

The examples in this chapter use a sample file that almost everyone needs: a list of names and telephone numbers. Too often, files of telephone numbers and business cards are out of date, incomplete, or in the other office. Questions arise: "Was that number in the telephone index or the business-card file?" Or "Did I file the number under Jones or under Accountants?" This example shows you how to let DOS keep track of your phone list and eliminate these questions.

If you're using a fixed disk, change the current directory to \RUNNING by typing the following:

```
C:\DOS>cd \running
```

If you want, change the system prompt to C>, as shown in the following examples, by typing *prompt*. Go on to the heading "Entering the Sample File."

If you don't have a fixed disk, put a formatted diskette that has room for a few small files in drive B. You also need the DOS diskette(s) containing, in order, the command files EDLIN.COM, FIND.EXE, SORT.EXE, and MORE.COM. Begin with the diskette containing EDLIN.COM in drive A. Now, type the following commands to change the current drive to B and to set the command path to the root directory of the system diskette in drive A:

```
A>b:

B>path a:\
```

Entering the Sample File

The sample file is named PH. You'll create the file with Edlin. (You can use your word processor instead if, like Microsoft Word, it lets you save a document without inserting its own formatting codes.)

Each line of the file contains six items of data: last name, first name, area code, telephone number, a key word that identifies a category, and a short description. The key words are: *cust* for customer, *cons* for consultant, and *vend* for vendor. You will enter the items in specific columns, so you can sort the list by any item.

To create the file PH, type the following:

```
C>edlin ph
New file
* i
        1:*_
```

Edlin is waiting for you to enter something.

To help you get the items in the correct columns, the following entry shows the first line with a period marking each space. Type the line as shown, but don't type the periods; press the spacebar once for each period:

```
1:*Jones.....Michele...(747).429-6360..cons.chemist
```

End the line by pressing the Enter key.

Now enter the remaining lines in the sample file, which is shown in Figure 13-1. Don't type the line numbers, and remember you already typed the first line.

When you have typed all the lines, press Ctrl-Break to end the Insert command and type *e* (End Edit) to save the file. When DOS has stored the file, it displays the system prompt.

```
 1:  Jones      Michele    (747)  429-6360   cons chemist
 2:  Smith      John       (747)  926-2945   vend furniture
 3:  White      Alice      (747)  425-7692   cust accountant
 4:  Green      Fred       (541)  926-4921   cust math teach
 5:  Black      John       (747)  426-3385   cons mech eng pkg
 6:  Smith      Ed         (541)  835-8747   vend caterer
 7:  Jones      Alison     (747)  429-5584   cons chem engineer
 8:  IBM        sales      (747)  463-2000   vend Dave Hill
 9:  Jones      James      (747)  636-3541   cust architect
10:  Black      Alice      (747)  426-7145   cust elec eng
```

Figure 13-1. Telephone and business-card list

Now you're ready to use the file. To see the entry for Alice White, type the following (notice the capital W):

```
C>find "Wh" ph

---------- PH
White      Alice      (747)  425-7692   cust accountant
```

That's fast, but it's just the beginning.

THE SORT FILTER COMMAND

The Sort filter command arranges, or sorts, lines of input and sends them to standard output (the display) unless you redirect the output—for example, to the printer. If you enter the command with no options, it sorts the lines of input in ascending order (alphabetically from A to Z, or numerically from lowest to highest number), starting the sort on the character in the first column.

The Sort command has two parameters:

sort /R /+<column>

/R (*Reverse*) sorts the lines in reverse order (Z to A, or highest to lowest number).

/+<column> sorts the lines starting at the specified column, rather than starting in the first column.

To sort a particular file, you can redirect the input of the Sort command by following the command name with < and the name of the file to be sorted; use a space both before and after the <. If you don't redirect the input, the Sort command sorts lines that you type at the keyboard (standard input).

Sort Command Examples

Figure 13-2 shows the column number of each of the six items in the telephone list: last name, first name, area code, telephone number, key word, and description. You'll use these column numbers to sort the file in different ways.

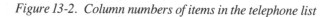

```
  1          11        21    27        37    42
  Jones      Michele   (747) 429-6360  cons  chemist
```

Figure 13-2. Column numbers of items in the telephone list

The simplest way to sort the file is in ascending order, starting in the first column (in the sample file, this sorts the entries by last name). Type:

```
C>sort < ph
```

DOS quickly displays the sorted result:

```
Black     Alice      (747) 426-7145   cust elec eng
Black     John       (747) 426-3385   cons mech eng pkg
Green     Fred       (541) 926-4921   cust math teach
IBM       sales      (747) 463-2000   vend Dave Hill
Jones     Alison     (747) 429-5584   cons chem engineer
Jones     James      (747) 636-3541   cust architect
Jones     Michele    (747) 429-6360   cons chemist
Smith     Ed         (541) 835-8747   vend caterer
Smith     John       (747) 926-2945   vend furniture
White     Alice      (747) 425-7692   cust accountant
```

The file itself isn't changed; what you see is simply the result of DOS reading, sorting, and displaying the lines of the file.

To sort the file in reverse order, use the /R option:

```
C>sort /r < ph
```

It doesn't take DOS any longer to sort backward:

```
White     Alice      (747) 425-7692   cust accountant
Smith     John       (747) 926-2945   vend furniture
Smith     Ed         (541) 835-8747   vend caterer
Jones     Michele    (747) 429-6360   cons chemist
Jones     James      (747) 636-3541   cust architect
Jones     Alison     (747) 429-5584   cons chem engineer
IBM       sales      (747) 463-2000   vend Dave Hill
```

```
Green      Fred       (541) 926-4921   cust math teach
Black      John       (747) 426-3385   cons mech eng pkg
Black      Alice      (747) 426-7145   cust elec eng
```

Suppose you wanted to arrange the list by the key word—first the consultants, then the customers, then the vendors. The first letter of the key word is in column 37, so use the column option:

```
C>sort /+37 < ph
```

Now it's easy to pick out the different categories:

```
Jones      Alison     (747) 429-5584   cons chem engineer
Jones      Michele    (747) 429-6360   cons chemist
Black      John       (747) 426-3385   cons mech eng pkg
White      Alice      (747) 425-7692   cust accountant
Jones      James      (747) 636-3541   cust architect
Black      Alice      (747) 426-7145   cust elec eng
Green      Fred       (541) 926-4921   cust math teach
Smith      Ed         (541) 835-8747   vend caterer
IBM        sales      (747) 463-2000   vend Dave Hill
Smith      John       (747) 926-2945   vend furniture
```

Sorting is fast, easy, and useful.

THE FIND FILTER COMMAND

The Find filter command searches lines of input for a string of characters you specify. If you enter the command with no parameters other than the string and the file name, the Find command displays all lines that contain the string.

The Find command has five parameters:

find /V /C /N <"string"> <filename>

/V displays all lines that do not contain the string.

/C (Count) displays just the number of lines found, not the lines themselves.

/N (Number) displays the input line number with each line found.

<"string"> is the string of characters you want to find; it must be enclosed in quotation marks. The Find command distinguishes between uppercase and lowercase letters, so ''cons'' and ''CONS'', for example, are different strings.

<filename> is the name of the file to be searched. If you omit <filename>, the Find command searches standard input. You can include several different file names in a single Find command simply by separating the file names with blanks. If some of the files are not on the disk in the current drive, precede their file names with the letter, followed by a colon, of the drive containing the disk they are on.

Find Command Examples

To display the entries for all consultants in the file named PH, type the following:

```
C>find "cons" ph
```

The first line of output identifies the input file, PH. Each line that contains the string *cons* is displayed immediately after:

```
---------- PH
Jones     Michele     (747) 429-6360   cons chemist
Black     John        (747) 426-3385   cons mech eng pkg
Jones     Alison      (747) 429-5584   cons chem engineer
```

To see how the Find command works with more than one file, type the following to make two duplicate copies of PH:

```
C>copy ph ph1

C>copy ph ph2
```

Now type the Find command you used in the preceding example, but this time include PH1 and PH2:

```
C>find "cons" ph ph1 ph2
```

DOS displays the name of each file as it finds "cons" in PH, PH1, and PH2:

```
---------- PH
Jones     Michelle    (747) 429-6360   cons chemist
Black     John        (747) 426-3385   cons mech eng pkg
Jones     Alison      (747) 429-5584   cons chem engineer

---------- PH1
Jones     Michelle    (747) 429-6360   cons chemist
Black     John        (747) 426-3385   cons mech eng pkg
Jones     Alison      (747) 429-5584   cons chem engineer

---------- PH2
Jones     Michelle    (747) 429-6360   cons chemist
Black     John        (747) 426-3385   cons mech eng pkg
Jones     Alison      (747) 429-5584   cons chem engineer
```

Obviously, using the Find command to search for a character string in several files is more productive when the contents of the files differ, but this example shows the method, if not the full capability, of the command.

Return now to the original phone list, PH. If you just want to know how many consultants are in the list, use the /C (Count) option:

```
C>find /c "cons" ph
```

This time, the line that identifies the input file also shows the number of lines that contain the string:

```
---------- PH: 3
```

Three lines in the file contain *cons*.

As often happens in a real telephone index, the sample file uses different words or abbreviations to mean the same thing. Both *engineer* and *eng* are used, for example, to describe an engineer. Both words contain *eng*, however, so you can find all the engineers by typing the following:

```
C>find "eng" ph

---------- PH
Black     John       (747) 426-3385  cons mech eng pkg
Jones     Alison     (747) 429-5584  cons chem engineer
Black     Alice      (747) 426-7145  cust elec eng
```

Finding Lines That *Don't* Contain the String

To display the entries *not* in the 747 area code, use the /V option:

```
C>find /v "(747" ph

---------- PH
Green     Fred       (541) 926-4921  cust math teach
Smith     Ed         (541) 835-8747  vend caterer
```

Including the left parenthesis with 747 distinguishes between entries with an area code of 747 and entries that might contain 747 in the phone number. Try the example without the left parenthesis:

```
C>find /v "747" ph

---------- PH
Green     Fred       (541) 926-4921  cust math teach
```

Ed Smith's telephone number is 835-8747, so his entry wasn't displayed even though his area code is 541. When you specify the characters to find, be sure to include enough to specify what you're looking for. In the sample file, for example, typing *"(7"* would be enough to specify the 747 area code; it wouldn't be enough, however, if the file contained another area code beginning with 7. And, as you saw, you must include the left parenthesis to distinguish an area code from some other set of numbers.

Including Line Numbers with the Output

To display the entries for people named Smith and to include the line numbers of the entries, use the /N option:

```
C>find /n "Smith" ph

---------- PH
[2]Smith      John        (747) 926-2945  vend furniture
[6]Smith      Ed          (541) 835-8747  vend caterer
```

The two entries displayed are the second and sixth lines of the sample file.

Combining Find Command Options

You can combine Find command options. For example, to display the entries not in the 747 area code and to include their line numbers, use both the /V and /N options:

```
C>find /v /n "(7" ph

---------- PH
[4]Green      Fred        (541) 926-4921  cust math teach
[6]Smith      Ed          (541) 835-8747  vend caterer
```

MORE ON REDIRECTING

Earlier in this chapter, you redirected input to the Sort command by specifying the file PH. You can also redirect the output of a filter command. To print the entries for all vendors (redirect output from the display to the printer), type the following:

```
C>find "vend" ph > prn
```

The entries are printed. If your phone list has two or three hundred entries, this technique of using options and redirecting output is a quick way to print a copy showing a selected group of entries.

Redirecting Both Input and Output

You can redirect both input and output by following the command name with < and the name of the input file or device and then > and the name of the output file or device. (Be sure to include blanks before and after both < and > if you don't have version 4 of DOS).

For example, to print the sorted version of PH, check that your printer is on and then type the command:

```
C>sort < ph > prn
```

The input for the Sort command comes from the file PH, and the output is redirected to the printer.

DOS allows you to redirect both the input and output of a single command from and to the same file. That is, DOS does not report any error if, for example, you type the command *sort < ph > ph*. Doing this, however, can make a large file unusable. If you want to sort a file and keep the same file name, use the following procedure:

- Redirect the output to a temporary file, such as PH-TMP. For example, to sort PH in reverse order, you would type *sort /r < ph > ph-tmp*.

- If you're certain you no longer need it, delete the original file (*erase ph*). If you want to keep the original, give it a different name, such as OLDPH, with the Rename command (*ren ph oldph*).

- Then use the Rename command to give the temporary file the original file name (*ren ph-tmp ph*).

- The new version of PH would contain the telephone list sorted in reverse order. You could verify the contents by displaying PH with the Type command.

Adding Redirected Output to a File

When you redirect output to an existing file, the redirected output replaces the original file. But you can also *add* redirected output to the end of an existing file by using >>, instead of >. If the file doesn't exist, it is created, just as when you use >.

CONNECTING COMMANDS WITH A PIPE

A powerful way of using a filter command is to redirect the output of some other command to the input of the filter command. In effect, the two commands are connected, with the output of the first command feeding directly into the filter command. Continuing the analogy to a water system, this connection is called a *pipe*.

You tell DOS to pipe the output of one command to the input of another by typing ¦ between the names of the two commands; the ¦ provides the connection between the two commands. The More filter command provides a simple example.

The More Filter Command

The More filter command displays one screenful (24 lines unless you've specified otherwise with the Mode command) followed by the line --*More*--, and then it pauses. When you press any key, More displays the next screenful and pauses again, continuing in the same way until all the input has been displayed.

For the following example, you need a disk or directory that contains more than one screenful of files. If you're using a fixed disk, your \DOS directory will do. If you're not using a fixed disk, try using your system (startup) disk.

If you have a fixed disk, type:

```
C>dir \dos ¦ more
```

If you don't have a fixed disk, place your system in drive A and type:

```
B>dir a: ¦ more
```

Either of these commands tells DOS to redirect the output of the Directory command to the input of the More command. The More command displays the first screenful of the directory and --*More*-- at the bottom of the screen. Press any key to see the rest of the directory, or press Ctrl-Break to cancel the More command and return to the system prompt. The More command lets you review a long output sequence or file without having to press Ctrl-Num Lock or Pause to start and stop the display.

Combining Filter Commands

You can pipe the output of one Find command to the input of another Find command to make a more specific search. A real-life list like the sample phone list, for example, might include several dozen customers. Suppose you want to display only the customers in the 747 area code. To do this, pipe the output of a Find command that searches for ''cust'' to another Find command that searches for "(7". If you don't have a fixed disk, check that the diskette in drive A contains the command file FIND.EXE.

Type:

```
C>find "cust" ph ¦ find "(7"
White     Alice      (747) 425-7692   cust accountant
Jones     James      (747) 636-3541   cust architect
Black     Alice      (747) 426-7145   cust elec eng
```

If you check an earlier list of the file, you'll see that Fred Green is a customer, but his area code is 541, so the second Find command eliminated the entry for his name. Notice that the line that identifies the file (----------*PH*) isn't displayed. The first Find command pipes ----------*PH* as part of its output to the second Find command, but because the line does not contain the string ''(7'', it is not included as part of the output of the second Find command.

You can also pipe the output of the Find command to the Sort command. To see all the consultants sorted by last name, type the following:

```
C>find "cons" ph ¦ sort

---------- ph
Black     John       (747) 426-3385   cons mech eng pkg
Jones     Alison     (747) 429-5584   cons chem engineer
Jones     Michele    (747) 429-6360   cons chemist
```

You can combine as many commands as you like. Suppose you want to print a list of all customers in the 747 area code, sorted by telephone number. You can search PH for ''cust'', pipe that output to a Find command that searches for ''(7'', pipe that output to a Sort command that sorts at column 27 (the telephone number), and redirect the output to the printer. Type the following:

```
C>find "cust" ph | find "(7" | sort /+27 > prn

White     Alice     (747) 425-7692  cust accountant
Black     Alice     (747) 426-7145  cust elec eng
Jones     James     (747) 636-3541  cust architect
```

If your list included several dozen customers, this could be a handy way to organize a calling campaign.

The Difference Between > and |

Sometimes the distinction between > and | isn't readily apparent, but the difference is easy to demonstrate. Sort is a filter command. To make the output of the Directory command the input to the Sort command, type the following:

```
C>dir | sort
```

As you would expect, DOS displays the directory sorted in alphabetic order. (If the directory includes two files whose names look like 072F2321 or %PIPE1.$$$ and whose lengths are 0, don't be alarmed. These are temporary files DOS creates in order to pipe the output of one command to the input of another; DOS deletes the files when the commands are completed.)

Now type:

```
C>dir > sort
```

This time you don't see anything on the screen because you told DOS to redirect the output of the Directory command to a file named SORT. Confirm this by displaying the file with the Type command:

```
C>type sort
```

The file contains the directory, which is not sorted. It's an ordinary directory. You created a file named SORT when you redirected the output of the Directory command.

CHAPTER SUMMARY

As you can see, redirection, filter commands, and pipes let you create powerful, specific commands. The next two chapters show you how to combine these capabilities with advanced batch commands to put the power of DOS to work for you.

CHAPTER
14

CREATING SMART COMMANDS

T he previous two chapters showed how batch files, redirection, pipes, and filter commands let you build your own commands and change the way that DOS commands work. This chapter shows how DOS gives you more control over the way it carries out the commands you build into a batch file. The techniques in this chapter help you create powerful commands tailored to your needs.

You can make your commands display their own instructions or warning messages. Or you can specify the circumstances under which DOS carries out one command—or a different sequence of commands altogether. You can even make the system pause until you tell it to proceed.

This chapter shows you how to develop a batch file that uses most of these capabilities. The next chapter extends the example, describes two additional batch commands, and shows several useful commands you can create. When you complete these two chapters, you'll be ready to apply the full power of DOS to your needs.

PREPARING FOR THE EXAMPLES

For these examples, you'll need one or two formatted diskettes and some sample files. If you completed the examples in Chapter 13, ''Taking Control of Your System,'' use the diskette on which you stored the phone-list file. If you're not using a fixed disk, you also have to copy some command files onto one of your practice diskettes. Follow the instructions under the heading that describes your system.

If You're Using a Fixed Disk

If you're using a fixed disk, you need one formatted diskette; put it in drive A. Change the current directory to \RUNNING by typing:

```
C:\DOS>cd \running
```

All the DOS commands you need are on the fixed disk. If you want, change the prompt to C>, as shown here, by typing *prompt*.

If You're Not Using a Fixed Disk

If you're not using a fixed disk, you need two formatted diskettes. Put the diskette with the phone list into drive B. You're going to take the DOS diskette out of drive A in a moment, so check the diskette in drive A for the command files FIND.EXE, SORT.EXE, and MORE.COM. Now enter the following commands to copy the Find, Sort, and More commands to the practice diskette:

```
A>copy find.exe b:
        1 File(s) copied
```

```
A>copy sort.exe b:
        1 File(s) copied

A>copy more.com b:
        1 File(s) copied
```

The examples in this chapter have you modify a batch file several times. You use Edlin commands to make the changes, so check the diskette in drive A for EDLIN.COM and then copy the Edlin program to drive B by typing the following:

```
A>copy edlin.com b:
        1 File(s) copied
```

Now remove the system diskette from drive A and replace it with the second formatted diskette. Change the current drive to B by typing:

```
A>b:
```

```
B>_
```

As you follow the examples, remember that your system prompt will be B>, not C>.

Creating the Sample Files

You will use six sample files in the next two chapters:

P.DOC	Q.DOC
P.BAK	Q.BAK
P.OLD	Q.OLD

Type the following to create the files (press F6 and Enter where you see ^Z):

```
C>copy con p.doc
This is a sample file.
^Z
        1 File(s) copied

C>copy p.doc p.bak
        1 File(s) copied

C>copy p.doc p.old
        1 File(s) copied

C>copy p.* q.*
P.DOC
P.BAK
P.OLD
        3 File(s) copied
```

If you're creating these files on a diskette, you'll need this diskette in the next chapter, so title it BATCH COMMANDS (if it's already labeled for the phone-list file, just add the new words). This completes the preparation for the examples.

CREATING AN ARCHIVE COMMAND

Disk files proliferate as you use your computer. You'll probably archive files from time to time, copying them to long-term storage diskettes and then erasing them from your working disks, just as you occasionally remove documents from your paper files and put them in long-term storage.

Although DOS includes the Backup and Restore commands to help you archive old files, this chapter shows you how to use the DOS batch commands to develop an Archive command that everyone can use, whether or not they're comfortable using DOS commands.

Starting with just a Copy command, you expand the batch file to display instructions, provide a safeguard against inadvertently erasing a previously archived file, and erase the file after it is archived.

The diskette in drive A represents the archive diskette, the one you store in a safe place. Your fixed disk or the diskette in drive B represents the working disk that contains files you want to archive.

Your Archive command will be a file named ARCHIVE.BAT. The initial version contains only a Copy command. To create the file, type the following:

```
C>copy con archive.bat
copy %1 a:%1
^Z
        1 File(s) copied
```

This file is the starting point for your Archive command. It requires only one parameter, the name of the file to be archived. The Copy command copies this file (%1 in the Copy command) to the diskette in drive A, giving it the same name (a:%1) as the original. To see how the batch file works, make certain the archive diskette is in drive A; archive P.DOC by typing:

```
C>archive p.doc
```

DOS responds by displaying and carrying out the Copy command in the batch file:

```
C>copy p.doc a:p.doc
        1 File(s) copied
```

This isn't much, but then it's only a starting point. You'll add significantly to this simple command as you go through the examples in this chapter.

MODIFYING THE SAMPLE BATCH FILE

This chapter describes four batch commands: Echo, Pause, If, and Goto. Each command description explains the purpose of the batch command, then adds it to ARCHIVE.BAT. The modified version of the batch file is shown with the changed or added lines shaded, then instructions are given for making the changes with Edlin.

CONTROLLING SYSTEM MESSAGES

The Echo command controls whether commands in a batch file are displayed, and it lets you display your own messages. It has three parameters:

echo on off <message>

on causes commands to be displayed as they are carried out (this is called "turning echo on"). Echo is on unless you turn it off.

off causes commands not to be displayed as they are carried out (this is called "turning echo off"). Eliminating the commands from the display can make a batch file easier to use by reducing clutter on the screen.

<message> is a string of characters, such as a reminder or a warning, that you want to display. <message> is displayed whether echo is turned on or off.

You can include only one parameter with an Echo command. If you omit all parameters (just type *echo*), DOS displays the status of echo (either *ECHO is on* or *ECHO is off*).

The first changes to your Archive command add an Echo command at the beginning to turn echo off and another Echo command after it to display a title message.

Here is the modified version of ARCHIVE.BAT (the Edlin line numbers are displayed only for reference):

```
1: echo off
2: echo Archive Procedure
3: copy %1 a:%1
```

Using Edlin, type these commands to make the change:

```
C>edlin archive.bat
End of input file
*i
        1:*echo off
        2:*echo Archive Procedure
        3:*<Ctrl-Break>
*e
```

To archive P.DOC with your new Archive command, type the name of the batch file and the name of the file to be archived:

```
C>archive p.doc
```

Because echo is always on when DOS starts carrying out the commands in a batch file, DOS displays the first Echo command, which turns echo off. Then it carries out the second Echo command, which displays the title *Archive Procedure*. Finally, it carries out the Copy command from the original ARCHIVE.BAT and copies the file:

```
C>echo off
Archive Procedure
       1 File(s) copied
```

Messages produced by a command itself (such as *1 File(s) copied* in the preceding example) are displayed whether echo is on or off.

Starting with version 3.3, you can prevent any command from being echoed by preceding it with the @ symbol. This means that you can eliminate even that first *echo off* message by changing the first line of ARCHIVE.BAT to *@echo off*. If you're using 3.3 or a later version, edit the file again to add the @ symbol at the beginning of line 1. From now on, all the examples will show the @ symbol; if you're not using 3.3 or a later version, simply ignore it.

Your Archive command is starting to take shape. It's time to add some instructions for the person who uses it.

MAKING THE SYSTEM PAUSE

Some DOS commands, such as Format and Diskcopy, display a message and wait for you to respond, giving you a chance to confirm your intention, or to complete preparation by inserting a diskette or by turning on the printer. You can have your batch files do the same; use the Pause command, which displays the message *Press any key to continue. . .* (*Strike a key when ready . . .* in versions prior to 4.0) and makes the system wait until you press any key.

The Pause command has one parameter:

pause <message>

<message> is a string of characters, such as a reminder or a warning, that you want the Pause command to display. <message> is displayed only if echo is on.

You'll add a Pause command to ARCHIVE.BAT now. You'll also add a message— a reminder to make certain the archive diskette is in drive A before the file is copied.

But wait: Any message you include as a parameter with the Pause command is displayed only if echo is on, and you have turned echo off in line 1 of ARCHIVE.BAT.

You can still use the Pause command, however. Instead of using the message capability of the Pause command, just use an Echo command to display the reminder, then add a Pause command without a message. This approach is a bit more work than simply adding a message after the Pause command, but the result is a command that's easier to use because you avoid cluttering the display with all the commands that DOS would display if you were to turn echo on.

The modified version of ARCHIVE.BAT is:

```
1: @echo off
2: echo Archive Procedure
3: echo Make sure archive diskette is in drive A
4: pause
5: copy %1 a:%1
```

Remember, if you're not using version 3.3 or later, ignore the @ in line 1.

The Edlin commands to make this change are:

```
C>edlin archive.bat
End of input file
*3i
        3:*echo Make sure archive diskette is in drive A
        4:*pause
        5:*<Ctrl-Break>
*e
```

Test this version by typing:

```
C>archive p.doc
Archive Procedure
Make sure archive diskette is in drive A
Press any key to continue . . .
```

—

The Echo command displays the reminder, then the Pause command displays its message telling you to strike a key and the system waits. Complete the command by pressing any key. DOS copies the file and acknowledges:

```
1 File(s) copied
```

CONTROLLING WHICH COMMANDS ARE CARRIED OUT

Besides carrying out DOS commands as though you had typed them individually, batch files let you specify that a command should be carried out only if some condition (such as whether a file exists) is true. This capability makes your batch files more flexible, letting you adapt them to a variety of situations.

The If command specifies the condition to be checked and the DOS command to be carried out. It has three parameters:

if not <condition> <command>

not qualifies the If command so that <command> is carried out only if <condition> is not true.

<condition> is the condition to check. It has two commonly used forms:

- *exist*<filename> checks whether the named file exists. You can include a path name, if necessary. If <filename> exists, the condition is true.

- <string1>==<string2> compares the two character strings you specify. If they are identical, the condition is true. Note that there are two equal signs.

<command> is any DOS command.

You'll add an If command to ARCHIVE.BAT to control when a warning message is displayed.

Adding Protection to Your Archive Command

When you copy a file with the Copy command, you tell DOS the name of the original and the name to be given to the new copy. DOS checks to see whether there is already a file with the same name as the copy on the target disk; if there is, DOS erases the existing file and replaces it with the copy. What if you didn't realize that a file with the same name existed on the disk? You might inadvertently lose a valuable file.

To protect yourself against such an oversight, you'll include two more commands in ARCHIVE.BAT. First, you'll add an If command that checks to see whether the file to be archived already exists on the archive diskette in drive A. If it does, an Echo command in the second part of the If command displays a warning message telling you that you can cancel the command by pressing Ctrl-Break.

Then you'll add a Pause command to give you time to read the warning message and, if necessary, cancel the Archive command by pressing Ctrl-Break. Here is the modified version of ARCHIVE.BAT:

```
1: @echo off
2: echo Archive Procedure
3: echo Make sure archive diskette is in drive A
4: pause
5: if exist a:%1 echo a:%1 exists. Press
   CTRL-BREAK to cancel, or
6: pause
7: copy %1 a:%1
```

Here are the Edlin commands to make this change. Type line 5 on one line, even though it is shown on two in the text:

```
C>edlin archive.bat
End of input file
*5i
        5:*if exist a:%1 echo a:%1 exists. Press
           CTRL-BREAK to cancel, or
        6:*pause
        7:*<Ctrl-Break>
*e
```

Test this version of your Archive command by typing:

```
C>archive p.doc
Archive Procedure
Make sure archive diskette is in drive A
Press any key to continue . . .
_
```

Press any key to continue the command:

```
a:p.doc exists. Press CTRL-BREAK to cancel, or
Press any key to continue . . .
_
```

Don't press any key yet.

You might not want to replace the copy of the file in drive A. Press Ctrl-Break to cancel the command. DOS asks whether you really mean it:

```
Terminate batch job (Y/N)?_
```

Type *y* to confirm. DOS cancels the rest of your Archive command and displays the system prompt without copying the file. If you had not pressed Ctrl-Break, the file would have been copied as before, erasing the previously archived version of P.DOC.

Smoothing a Rough Edge

Your Archive command is getting more useful; you've protected yourself from inadvertently erasing an existing file. But there's a problem now. See what happens if the name of the file to be archived isn't the name of a file already on the diskette in drive A. Erase P.DOC from drive A and archive it again:

```
C>erase a:p.doc

C>archive p.doc

Archive Procedure
Make sure archive diskette is in drive A
Press any key to continue . . .
_
```

Fine so far. Press the spacebar to continue:

```
Press any key to continue . . .
_
```

That's not too good. The system comes right back and pauses again, even though everything is OK, because the Pause command that follows the If command is always carried out. Press the spacebar again:

```
1 File(s) copied
```

DOS copies the file as it should. Your Archive command is working properly, but the two pauses could be confusing, especially if someone else uses your batch command. How can you fix this?

You could delete the first Pause command, but if you did, you wouldn't have a chance to make certain that the correct diskette has been placed in drive A. That's not a very good solution.

Or you could delete the second Pause command and change the If command, making the "file exists" warning a Pause message instead of an Echo message, as it is now. But then, recall that you would have to delete the command *echo off* at the beginning of the batch file so that the message following the new Pause command would be displayed. And that would mean all your commands in the file would be displayed. This solution would make the response to your Archive command somewhat cluttered and confusing, so it isn't very good either.

There is, however, a way to change your Archive command so that the second Pause command is carried out only if the file to be archived is on the diskette in drive A. This solution requires using another command for batch files, the Goto command.

CHANGING THE SEQUENCE OF COMMANDS

The batch files you have created up to now carry out the DOS commands they contain in the order in which the commands appear. Your batch commands would be more flexible if you could control the order in which the commands are carried out. The Goto command gives you this control by telling DOS to go to a specific line in the command file, rather than to the next command in the sequence.

You tell DOS where to go in the batch file by specifying a *label*. A label identifies a line in a batch file; it consists of a colon (:) immediately followed by a string of characters (such as *start*). A label is not a command. It merely identifies a location in a batch file. When DOS goes to a label, it carries out whatever commands follow the line on which the label appears.

The Goto command has one parameter:

goto <label>

<label> is the label that identifies the line in the batch file where DOS is to go.

The Goto command is often used as part of an If command. For example, the If command checks some condition. If the condition is not true, DOS carries out the next command; if the condition is true, DOS carries out the Goto command and moves to some other part of the batch file.

Remember the problem with your Archive command? If the file to be archived is already on the diskette in drive A, you want to display a warning message and pause; otherwise, you just want to copy the file. This situation is tailor-made for an If command that includes a Goto command.

The modified version of ARCHIVE.BAT is:

```
1: @echo off
2: echo Archive Procedure
3: echo Make sure archive diskette is in drive A
4: pause
5: if not exist a:%1 goto safe
6: echo a:%1 exists. Press CTRL-BREAK to cancel, or
7: pause
8: :safe
9: copy %1 a:%1
```

These changes warrant a bit more explanation:

- The If command still checks whether the name of the file to be archived exists on the diskette in drive A. Now, however, the command includes the parameter *not*, which means that the command in the second part of the If command is carried out only if the reverse of the condition is true (that is, if the file does *not* exist on the diskette in drive A).

- The second part of the If command—the command to be carried out if the condition is true—is changed to a Goto command that tells DOS to skip to a label called *:safe*.

- If the file to be archived doesn't exist on the diskette in drive A, the Goto command is carried out and DOS jumps to the label *:safe*, skipping the Echo and Pause commands. The Copy command following *:safe* copies the file.

- If the file to be archived does exist on the diskette in drive A, the Goto command is not carried out and DOS continues on to the Echo and Pause commands. If you don't cancel by pressing Ctrl-Break, DOS carries out the Copy command. In this instance, DOS ignores the line that contains the label *:safe* because the only purpose of the label is to identify a location in a batch file.

Use the following Edlin commands to make these changes. The symbol → means press the right arrow key; <Ins> means press the Insert key; <F2> means press the F2 function key; <F4> means press the F4 function key. Although lines 5 and 6 are shown on two lines, Edlin displays them on one line:

```
C>edlin archive.bat
End of input file
*5,5,6c
*5
        5:*if exist a:%1 echo a:%1 exists. Press CTRL-BREAK
           to cancel, or
        5:*→→→<Ins>not <F2>egoto safe
*6
        6:*if exist a:%1 echo a:%1 exists. Press CTRL-BREAK
           to cancel, or
        6:*<F4>e<F4>e<F3>
```

```
*8i
        8:*:safe
        9:*<Ctrl-Break>
*e
```

P.DOC is on the diskette in drive A (you archived it a bit earlier), so first see if this
version of your Archive command warns you that the file exists. Type the following:

```
C>archive p.doc
Archive Procedure
Make sure archive diskette is in drive A
Press any key to continue . . .
_
```

Press any key to continue the command:

```
a:p.doc exists. Press CTRL-BREAK to cancel, or
Press any key to continue . . .
_
```

There's the warning. Press any key to complete the command:

```
1 File(s) copied
```

But the problem came up when the file wasn't on the archive diskette: You got the
second pause anyway. Test your revised Archive command in this situation by archiving P.BAK, which hasn't yet been archived:

```
C>archive p.bak
Archive Procedure
Make sure archive diskette is in drive A
Press any key to continue . . .
_
```

Press a key:

```
1 File(s) copied
```

Problem solved. Because P.BAK wasn't on the archive diskette in drive A, the Goto
command was carried out; it caused DOS to skip over the intervening Echo and Pause
commands and to copy the file.

Your Archive command works properly. You had to do a little more work to
avoid the double pause, but now the command is less confusing and easier to use.
You'll probably encounter this kind of circumstance fairly often as you create batch
commands. Just remember: It takes a little more time to make a command easy to use,
but the investment is usually worthwhile, especially if someone other than you will
use the command.

Using Wildcard Characters with a Batch File

You can use wildcard characters to archive a series of files with your Archive command. Type the following command to archive all the files named P:

```
C>archive p.*
Archive Procedure
Make sure archive diskette is in drive A
Press any key to continue . . .
_
```

Press any key:

```
a:p.* exists. Press CTRL-BREAK to cancel, or
Press any key to continue . . .
_
```

You archived P.DOC and P.BAK in earlier examples, so they're on the archive diskette. The Archive command doesn't identify the specific file that exists, but it does give you a chance to cancel if you don't want to erase the file.

Press Ctrl-Break to cancel the rest of the command, and respond to the DOS prompt for confirmation with *y*:

```
Terminate batch job (Y/N)?y
```

If you had pressed any key other than Ctrl-Break, all the files named P would have been copied to the diskette in drive A, replacing any that were already there.

Erasing the Original of an Archived File

Archiving not only involves copying a file to an archive diskette, it also means deleting the original. Your Archive command only copies; now it's time to make it delete too. But just as it's prudent to check whether the file exists on the archive diskette before you make the copy, it's also prudent to check again before erasing the original, just to be sure the file was copied to the archive diskette.

You need only one additional If command to check whether the file to be archived is on the archive diskette and, if it is, to erase the original from the working disk. Here is this modified version of ARCHIVE.BAT:

```
 1: @echo off
 2: echo Archive Procedure
 3: echo Make sure archive diskette is in drive A
 4: pause
 5: if not exist a:%1 goto safe
 6: echo a:%1 exists. Press CTRL-BREAK to cancel, or
 7: pause
 8: :safe
 9: copy %1 a:%1
10: if exist a:%1 erase %1
```

The Edlin commands to make this change are:

```
    edlin archive.bat
End of input file
*10i
        10:*if exist a:%1 erase %1
        11:*<Ctrl-Break>
*e
```

The screen responses of this version of your Archive command are the same as in the previous version, but the new command erases the original file after copying it. Test it by archiving P.DOC again:

```
C>archive p.doc
Archive Procedure
Make sure archive diskette is in drive A
Press any key to continue . . .
_
```

Press any key:

```
a:p.doc exists. Press CTRL-BREAK to cancel, or
Press any key to continue . . .
_
```

You want to copy the file to the archive diskette, so press any key:

```
        1 File(s) copied
```

See if the original version of P.DOC still exists by typing:

```
C>dir p.doc

 Volume in drive C is FIXED DISK
 Volume Serial Number is 1608-5A30
 Directory of  C:\RUNNING

File not found
```

The original is gone. Your Archive command does copy the specified file to the archive diskette and then deletes the original.

Functionally, the command is complete.

DRESSING UP YOUR ARCHIVE COMMAND

The value of your batch files depends not only on what they do, but also on how easy it is to use them correctly. This ease of use is particularly important if you use a batch file only occasionally, or if someone else uses it; it's vital if the batch file erases other files, as your Archive command does.

That's why, for example, your Archive command starts by turning echo off: An uncluttered screen helps to make the responses less confusing. You can also do some other things to make a batch file easy to use:

- Clear the screen.

- Use the Echo command to display messages that report on progress or results.

- Use spaces or insert tabs so you can position messages displayed by the Echo command where they are prominent on the screen.

- Use the Echo command to include blank lines that further improve the readability of the screen.

You can also use the Remark command to put notes to yourself in the batch file. As long as echo is off, these remarks aren't displayed. Remarks can help you remember how a batch file works, in case you have to change it or you want to create a similar command using the same technique. Remarks are especially useful if the batch file is long or if it's one you may not look at very often.

Echoing a Blank Line

Up to now, you have used the Echo command either to turn echo off or to display a message. You can also use the Echo command to display a blank line—something you'll probably want to do fairly often to improve the appearance of the display.

You've seen that you turn echo on or off by following *echo* with either *on* or *off*. If you follow *echo* with some other words, they are displayed as a message, and if you simply type *echo*, DOS tells you whether echo is on or off. How do you tell DOS to echo a blank line? You type *echo*, press the spacebar once, hold down the key labeled Alt, type the number 255 on the numeric keypad (*not* the numbers in the top row of the keyboard), and then release the Alt key. The cursor moves over one column, but you shouldn't see any new characters displayed. This action is represented by <Alt-255> in the examples. Whenever you see <Alt-255>, hold down the Alt key, press the 2 key on the numeric keypad, press the 5 key on the numeric keypad twice, and then release the Alt key.

The following changes don't add any capability to your Archive command, but they do make it easier for someone to understand what's happening. The changes are described in more detail in a moment. The modified version of ARCHIVE.BAT appears at the top of the next page.

```
 1: @echo off
 2: cls
 3: REM THREE TABS IN FOLLOWING ECHO COMMAND
 4: echo<tab><tab><tab>***ARCHIVE PROCEDURE***
 5: echo <Alt-255>
 6: echo Make sure archive diskette is in drive A
 7: pause
 8: REM BRANCH AROUND WARNING IF FILE NOT ARCHIVED
 9: if not exist a:%1 goto safe
10: echo <Alt-255>
11: REM CTRL-G SOUNDS A BEEP
12: echo ^Ga:%1 exists. Press CTRL-BREAK to cancel, or
13: pause
14: :safe
15: copy %1 a:%1
16: if exist a:%1 erase %1
17: echo <Alt-255>
18: echo %1 archived
```

The purpose of each change is as follows:

- In line 2, the Clear Screen command starts your Archive command off with a blank screen, giving you complete control over what is displayed.

- In line 3, the Remark command reminds you that the space at the beginning of the Echo command in line 4 is created by pressing the tab key three times.

- In line 4, the title (* * *ARCHIVE PROCEDURE* * *) is made more prominent and is displayed in the center of the screen by the insertion of three tabs.

- In line 5, an Echo command displays a blank line below the title. The <Alt-255> represents holding down the key labeled Alt, typing the number 255 on the numeric keypad, and then releasing the Alt key.

- In line 8, the Remark command explains the purpose of the Goto command included in line 9.

- In line 10, another Echo command displays a blank line to make the warning message in line 12 more visible.

- In line 11, the Remark command explains how the beep is sounded by the Echo command in line 12.

- In line 12, the ^G (sometimes displayed as G^ in version 3.1 of DOS) in the message displayed by the Echo command represents a character called Ctrl-G, which causes the system to beep and calls attention to the warning. To enter Ctrl-G, hold down the Ctrl key and press G.

- In line 17, the Echo command displays another blank line, to make the message in line 18 more visible.

- In line 18, the Echo command's message tells which file has been archived.

Here are the Edlin commands to make these changes. Type line 4 as a single line:

```
C>edlin archive.bat
End of input file
*2i
        2:*cls
        3:REM THREE TABS IN FOLLOWING ECHO COMMAND
        4:*<Ctrl-Break>

*4
        4:*echo Archive Procedure
        4:*→→→→<space><tab><tab><tab>***ARCHIVE
           PROCEDURE***
*5i
        5:*echo<space><Alt-255>
        6:*<Ctrl-Break>
*8i
        8:*REM BRANCH AROUND WARNING IF FILE NOT ARCHIVED
        9:*<Ctrl-Break>

*10i
       10:*echo<space><Alt-255>
       11:*REM CTRL-G SOUNDS A BEEP
       12:*<Ctrl-Break>

*12
       12:*echo a:%1 exists. Press CTRL-BREAK to cancel, or
       12:*→→→→→<Ins><Ctrl-G><F3>
*#i
       17:*echo<space><Alt-255>
       18:*echo %1 archived
       19:*<Ctrl-Break>

*1l
```

The final command displays the entire file. Compare your display with the modified form of ARCHIVE.BAT shown earlier. If there are any differences, correct them before saving the revised version. (If you have trouble with any of the special keys used in line 12, simply type the entire new line.) When the file is correct, save it by typing *e*.

Although you haven't changed anything your Archive command does, its screen responses are quite different now. Test the new version by archiving P.OLD (which isn't on the archive diskette):

```
C>archive p.old
```

Because ARCHIVE.BAT now starts by clearing the screen, everything you see from this point on is displayed by your Archive command. When the command prompts you to check the diskette in drive A, press any key to continue.

The screen now looks like this:

```
                    ***ARCHIVE PROCEDURE***

    Make sure archive diskette is in drive A
    Press any key to continue . . .

            1 File(s) copied

    p.old archived
```

Test ARCHIVE.BAT again to see how it responds when the file already exists on the archive diskette. P.DOC and P.OLD are no longer on the disk in drive C (you archived them after making the change that erases the file), so archive P.BAK. Type the following, pressing any key to continue the command after each pause:

```
    C>archive p.bak
```

The screen looks like this:

```
                            ***ARCHIVE PROCEDURE***
    Make sure archive diskette is in drive A
    Press any key to continue . . .

    a:p.bak exists. Press CTRL-BREAK to cancel, or
    Press any key to continue . . .

             1 File(s) copied

    p.bak archived
```

ARCHIVE.BAT is quite a bit longer than when you began, but your Archive command doesn't look much like a homemade command any more. Although you needn't always go to such lengths when you create a command, it's nice to know that a little extra effort can make your work look professional. If others will use the batch files you create, the investment of your effort can quickly pay off in shorter training time, more efficient use of the system, and fewer mistakes.

CHAPTER SUMMARY

This chapter covered a lot of ground. Experimenting is the best way to put what you learned here into practice. Just be certain to use diskettes that don't contain files you need until you're sure your batch commands are working properly.

The next chapter describes two additional batch commands that let you create even more flexible batch files, and it shows you several useful batch commands you can use to start your personal collection. You need the archive diskette in drive A. Remove this diskette and label it ARCHIVED FILES.

CHAPTER
15
CREATING MORE SMART COMMANDS

The previous chapter showed you how to use the advanced capability of batch files. Knowing how to create batch files is only half the job, however; the other half is finding uses for them. This chapter shows you how to create some commands to search through the phone-list file you created in Chapter 13; it also describes two advanced batch commands and shows several useful batch files to give you some ideas for your own use.

PREPARING FOR THE EXAMPLES

For the first examples in this chapter, you need the phone-list file (PH) that you created in Chapter 13, "Taking Control of Your System." If you haven't gone through the examples in Chapters 13 and 14, you should do so before proceeding.

If you're using a fixed disk, PH should already be in the directory named \RUNNING. Change the current directory to \RUNNING by typing:

```
C:\DOS>cd \running
```

If your system prompt shows the current directory, type *prompt* if you want to change it to C>, as in the following examples.

If you're using diskettes, make sure the diskette that contains the PH file also contains the command files FIND.EXE, SORT.EXE, and MORE.COM. Put the diskette in drive B and change the current drive to B. The system prompt will be B>, not C>, as shown in the examples.

COMMANDS TO SEARCH THROUGH A FILE

In Chapter 13, you created a file of names, addresses, and telephone numbers, and you used the Find and Sort commands to display entries. You can also put the Find and Sort commands in batch files to create your own search commands and achieve some of the capabilities of a simple record-management program.

For example, the simplest search uses the Find command to display all records that contain a particular string. Create a batch file named SHOW.BAT by typing the following (ignore the @ symbol at the beginning of the Echo command if you're not using 3.3 or a later version):

```
C>copy con show.bat
@echo off
find "%1" ph
^Z
        1 File(s) copied
```

This batch file gives you a Show command that displays all records from PH that contain the string you specify as the parameter to your Show command. To search the phone list, type *show* followed by the string. For example, to display the entries for all consultants (entries that contain the string *cons*), type:

```
C>show cons
```

DOS displays all entries for consultants:

```
---------- PH
Jones     Michele    (747) 429-6360  cons chemist
Black     John       (747) 426-3385  cons mech eng pkg
Jones     Alison     (747) 429-5584  cons chem engineer
```

(If you're not using 3.3 or a later version, DOS displays *C>echo off* before displaying the list of entries.)

This is easier than typing *find "cons" ph.* Read on; you'll find that you can use batch files to make more powerful searches just as easily.

Compound Searches

As the examples in Chapter 13 showed, you can also combine Find commands to search for records that contain various combinations of character strings, such as all consultants named Jones or all entries that are outside the 747 area code. Putting these Find commands in a batch file saves even more typing than the Show command you just created.

For example, suppose you want to create a command to show all entries that contain both one string and another. As you saw in Chapter 14, this requires two Find commands, with the output of the first piped to the second. You could call such a command Showand; create a file named SHOWAND.BAT by typing:

```
C>copy con showand.bat
@echo off
find "%1" ph : find "%2"
^Z
        1 File(s) copied
```

This batch command takes two parameters: the two strings the Find command searches for. Now you can search the phone list for entries that contain two strings as easily as you can search it for entries containing one string; just type *showand* followed by the two strings. For example, to display all consultants named Jones, type:

```
C>showand cons Jones
```

DOS displays the records that contain both strings:

```
Jones     Michele    (747) 429-6360  cons chemist
Jones     Alison     (747) 429-5584  cons chem engineer
```

This is definitely easier than typing *find "cons" ph : find "Jones"*.

What if you want to create a command that shows all entries except those that contain a particular string? Use a Find command with the /V parameter. You could call this command Showxcpt; create SHOWXCPT.BAT by typing the following:

```
C>copy con showxcpt.bat
@echo off
find /v "%1" ph
^Z
        1 File(s) copied
```

This batch command requires one parameter, the string you don't want to see. For example, to display all entries not in the 747 area code, type the following:

```
C>showxcpt (7
```

DOS displays all lines from PH that don't contain *(7:*

```
---------- PH
Green      Fred      (541) 926-4921   cust math teach
Smith      Ed        (541) 835-8747   vend caterer
```

These three batch files—SHOW, SHOWAND, and SHOWXCPT—let you search a file quickly in several ways. You can combine all three searches into a single command just by changing SHOW.BAT.

Chaining Batch Files
To Create Powerful Commands

As Chapter 12, ''Creating Your Own Commands,'' described, you can chain batch files, using the name of one batch file as a command in another batch file. When you do this, DOS carries out the commands in the second batch file as if you had typed its name; if the second batch file contains the name of a third batch file, DOS carries out its commands, and so on.

You can modify SHOW.BAT to cover all three types of searches you just performed by chaining it to either SHOWAND.BAT or SHOWXCPT.BAT. When you do this, the parameters you type with the revised Show command must specify the type of search as well as the string or strings to search for.

You're creating your own Show command with the following parameters:

show xcpt and <string1> <string2>

xcpt searches for entries that don't contain a string.

and searches for entries that contain two strings.

<string1> and <string2> are the strings to search for. If you include *and*, you must include both <string1> and <string2>; otherwise just include <string1>.

If you don't specify either *xcpt* or *and*, your Show command searches for all entries that contain string1.

This more powerful version of SHOW.BAT is still fairly short; type the following:

```
C>copy con show.bat
@echo off
if %1==xcpt showxcpt %2
if %1==and showand %2 %3
find "%1" ph
^Z
        1 File(s) copied
```

The first If command checks whether the first parameter (%1) typed with the Show command is *xcpt* (recall that the == compares two strings to see if they are identical). If %1 is the same as *xcpt*, SHOWXCPT.BAT is carried out. The second parameter (%2) you type with the Show command is the string to search for; it is the single parameter that SHOWXCPT.BAT requires.

The second If command checks whether the first parameter typed with the Show command is *and*. If it is, SHOWAND.BAT is carried out. The second and third parameters (%2 and %3) typed with the Show command are the two strings to search for; they are the two parameters that SHOWAND.BAT requires.

If the first parameter (%1) typed with the Show command is neither *xcpt* nor *and*, the Find command is carried out to perform a simple search.

Except for the Echo command, only one of the commands in SHOW.BAT is carried out in any particular search. Figure 15-1 on the following page shows the contents of SHOW.BAT and an example of each type of search you can make. For each example, the figure lists the Show command as you would type it, and substitutes values for the replaceable parameters in SHOW.BAT. The command in SHOW.BAT that is carried out is not shaded. An arrow to the right represents chaining to SHOWXCPT or SHOWAND; the contents of each chained batch file, with values substituted for its replaceable parameters, are shown below the chained batch file.

Now you can make any of the three types of searches with the Show command. The simple search works as it did in the earlier Show command. For example, to display all entries that contain *Jones*, type:

```
C>show Jones

---------- PH
Jones     Michele    (747) 429-6360   cons chemist
Jones     Alison     (747) 429-5584   cons chem engineer
Jones     James      (747) 636-3541   cust architect
```

To display all entries that don't contain a particular string, type *xcpt* as the first parameter. For example, to display all entries outside the 747 area code, type:

```
C>show xcpt (7

---------- PH
Green     Fred       (541) 926-4921   cust math teach
Smith     Ed         (541) 835-8747   vend caterer
```

Or, to search for two strings, type *and* as the first parameter. For example, to display all entries that contain both *Jones* and *eng*, type:

```
C>show and Jones eng
Jones      Alison      (747) 429-5584   cons chem engineer
```

If you put your telephone numbers and business cards in a text file like this, these three batch files put the contents of the file at your fingertips. Not only can you search for an entry quickly, you can easily display groups of related entries.

You can use this same technique with other data files that might not justify a full database program, but whose contents are a constant part of your work; some more examples are shown in Chapter 16, "Tailoring Your System." This application, like the use of Edlin, is another example of how DOS can make your computer more valuable without the use of any additional software.

```
                    Contents of SHOW.BAT:


                    @echo off
                    if %1==xcpt showxcpt %2
                    if %1==and showand %2 %3
                    find "%1" ph

C>show cust

@echo off
if cust==xcpt showxcpt
if cust==and showand
find "cust" ph

C>show xcpt cust

@echo off
if xcpt==xcpt showxcpt cust  ----->  showxcpt cust
if xcpt==and showand cust
find "xcpt" ph                        @echo off
                                      find /v "cust" ph

C>show and cust Jones

@echo off
if and==xcpt showxcpt cust
if and==and showand cust Jones  -->  showand cust Jones
find "and" ph
                                      @echo off
                                      find "cust" ph | find "Jones"
```

Figure 15-1. Chaining batch files

SOME USEFUL BATCH FILES

To give you some ideas about the sort of batch commands that might help you from day to day, several useful batch files are shown here. These are not step-by-step examples; each description gives the purpose of the batch file, shows its contents, explains how it works, and describes how you would use it.

An effective way to become familiar with batch commands is to experiment. You could enter the following batch files, for example, then experiment with them, making changes and seeing the effects of the changes. Just be sure to use disks that don't contain irreplaceable copies of files you need.

You can create the batch files by copying from the console to a file or by using Edlin. Where line numbers are shown, they're just for reference; don't enter them. Most of the batch files include one or more Echo commands to add a blank line to the display (for readability); they appear as *echo <Alt-255>*. To make them work properly, hold down the Alt key, press 255 on the numeric keypad, release the Alt key, and then press Enter; if this doesn't work, type *echo*, press the spacebar, and press Enter.

Viewing a Long Directory Listing

Even though you back up old files and clear out unneeded ones regularly, a directory can soon contain more files than DOS can list on one screen. And some often-used directories—word-processing directories, for example, or collections of spreadsheets and charts—can become quite large.

If you have version 4 of DOS and an EGA or VGA display, you can use the LONGDIR.BAT file described here to change the display to 43 lines per screen, display a long directory one screenful at a time, and then change the display back to 25 lines.

LONGDIR.BAT contains:

```
1: @echo off
2: cls
3: mode con lines=43
4: dir %1 | more
5: pause
6: mode con lines=25
```

The Mode command in line 3 switches the display to 43 lines. The Dir command in line 4 finds the listings for the directory (%1) you specify as a parameter with the Longdir command and pipes the output to the More command, which displays the entries 43 lines at a time and waits for you to press a key. The Pause command in line 5 displays *Press any key to continue* when the directory listing is complete, and the Mode command in line 6 returns the screen display to 25 lines. (If you have good eyes and a VGA display, you could display 50 lines at a time by changing the 43 in line 3 to 50.)

To use the command, you type *longdir*, followed by the directory listing you want to see. You can include a drive letter, followed by a colon, a path name, and a file name including wildcard characters. For example, you can type the command as *longdir a:, longdir \clients\wp*, or *longdir \clients\wp\ *.doc*. If you don't include a drive, path, or file name (type just *longdir*), the command displays the current directory.

Cleaning Up Disk Storage

Because Edlin and many word processors create a backup file with the extension BAK each time you edit a file, your disks can get crowded with backup files you don't need. The CLEANUP.BAT batch file described here replaces one you created earlier; it displays the directory entries of all files with an extension of BAK and then pauses. At that point, you can cancel the command by pressing Ctrl-Break; if you press any key to proceed, the command erases the files.

CLEANUP.BAT contains:

```
1: @echo off
2: cls
3: echo ***Will erase the following files:***
4: dir %1*.bak
5: echo <Alt-255>
6: echo ^GPress Ctrl-Break to cancel, or
7: pause
8: erase %1*.bak
```

Notice that there is no blank between *%1* and *.bak* in lines 4 and 8; this lets you specify a drive letter or a path name as a parameter with the file name, but be sure to end a path name with a backslash (\ ).

The *^G* in line 6 (displayed as G^ in some versions of DOS) is Ctrl-G, which sounds a beep. To enter it, hold down the Control key and press G.

To erase all BAK files from the current directory on the disk in the current drive, type *cleanup* and press any key when the Pause command prompts you.

To erase all BAK files from another directory, type the path name followed by \ as a parameter; you can also precede the path name with a drive letter and colon (for example, *cleanup a:* or *cleanup \mkt\wp*).

Directory of Subdirectories

The Directory command displays *<DIR>* instead of the file size to identify a subdirectory. If a directory contains many files, picking out the subdirectories can be a bit difficult. The DIRSUB batch file described here lets you display only the entries for subdirectories.

DIRSUB.BAT contains:

```
1: @echo off
2: echo ***Subdirectories in %1***
3: echo <Alt-255>
4: dir %1 | find "<"
```

In this file, the output of the Directory command is piped to a Find command that displays all directory lines that contain a less-than sign (<).

You can type one parameter (%1) with the Dirsub command to specify the directory whose entries are to be displayed. The parameter can include a drive letter and colon, a path name, or both. If you don't include a parameter, this Dirsub command displays the subdirectories in the current directory.

To see the subdirectories in the current directory, you would type *dirsub*. To see the subdirectories in the current directory of drive B, you would type *dirsub b:*. To see the subdirectories in \MKT\WP, you would type *dirsub \mkt\wp*.

The special entries **.** and **..** are in all directories except the root. You can modify DIRSUB.BAT so that it doesn't display these entries by changing line 4 of the batch file to the following:

```
dir %1 ¦ find "<" ¦ find /v "."
```

Now the output of the Find command is piped to a second Find command that uses the /V parameter to eliminate all lines that contain a period. You would use this version of the Dirsub command just as you would use the earlier version.

Moving Files from One Directory To Another

In a tree-structured file system, you'll sometimes want to move files from one directory to another. You can do this by copying the file to the new directory with the Copy command, then erasing the original with the Erase command. MOVE.BAT combines these into one command.

MOVE.BAT contains:

```
 1: @echo off
 2: copy %1 %2
 3: cls
 4: echo Files in target directory:
 5: echo <Alt-255>
 6: dir %2
 7: echo <Alt-255>
 8: echo If files to be moved are not in directory,
 9: echo press Ctrl-Break to cancel. Otherwise
10: pause
11: erase %1
```

Here is how the batch file works, line by line:

- In line 1, the Echo command turns echo off.

- In line 2, the Copy command copies the files to the target directory.

- In line 3, the Clear Screen command clears the screen.

- In lines 4 and 5, Echo commands display a message and a blank line.

- In line 6, the Directory command displays the contents of the target directory.

- In lines 7 through 9, Echo commands display a blank line and a warning message.

- In line 10, the Pause command makes the system pause to let you cancel the Erase command in line 11 if the files you moved are not displayed in the listing of the target directory.

You have created a command with two parameters:

move   <source>   <target>

<source> is the name of the file to be moved (copied and then deleted). You can include a drive letter and path name. If you use wildcard characters in the file name, DOS displays the name of each file it copies.

<target> is the name of the directory to which the <source> files are to be copied. If you omit <target>, the files are copied to the current directory.

For example, assume that the current directory is \MKT\WP. To move the file REPORT.DOC to the directory \ENG\WP, you would type *move report.doc \eng\wp*. To move the file BUDGET.JAN from \ENG\WP to \MKT\WP, you type the command *move \eng\wp\budget.jan*. To move all files from \MKT\WP to \WORD\MKT, you would type *move *.* \word\mkt*.

THREE ADVANCED BATCH COMMANDS

Note: The batch commands you have worked with up to this point are sufficient for you to create useful batch files, like the search commands for the phone-list file that are tailored to your own needs. Rather than continue with the rest of this chapter right now, you might want to put the book aside for a while and experiment, and then return to learn the last three batch commands this book discusses.

The three remaining batch commands, Shift, For, and Call, give you even more control over how your batch files work. They're somewhat more complicated than the other batch commands, but the examples should make their use clear.

Preparing for the Advanced Examples

The remaining examples in the chapter require the P files you archived in Chapter 14. Put the diskette you labeled ARCHIVED FILES in drive A.

Shifting the List of Parameters

The Shift command moves the list of parameters you type with a batch command one position to the left. For example, suppose you type a Shift command with three parameters. After the Shift command is carried out once, what was %3 becomes %2 and what was %2 becomes %1; what was %1 is gone. After a second Shift command, what started out as %3 is %1; what started as %2 and %1 are both gone.

This command lets a short batch file handle any number of parameters; the following sample batch file illustrates the technique. ARCH1.BAT archives any number of files. Here are its contents; remember, the line numbers are just for reference:

```
1: @echo off
2: :start
3: if "%1"=="" goto done
4: echo ***Archiving %1***
5: if not exist a:%1 copy %1 a:
6: shift
7: goto start
8: :done
```

Here's a line-by-line description of how it works:

- As usual, the first line is an Echo command to turn echo off.

- In line 2, the label *:start* marks the beginning of the commands that will be repeated for each parameter.

- In line 3, the If command checks to see whether a parameter was entered for %1. It does this by comparing %1 with two quotation marks enclosing nothing at all (" "). You're telling DOS to compare the first parameter (if one was typed) with nothing, or no parameter. When the comparison is true, meaning that there are no more parameters, the Goto command sends DOS to the label *:done* in line 8.

- In line 4, the Echo command displays the name of the file that is being archived.

- In line 5, the If command checks whether the file to be archived exists on drive A; if it doesn't, the Copy command copies the file from the current drive to drive A. (The batch file assumes drive C or drive B is the current drive.)

- In line 6, the Shift command moves the list of parameters one position left.

- In line 7, the Goto command sends DOS back to the label *:start*.

- In line 8, the label *:done* marks the end of the command file.

To use this batch file you type *arch1* followed by the names of the files to be archived. The command stops when %1 equals " "—in other words, when there are no more file names to be substituted for %1.

To test the command, copy the file named P.OLD, which you archived in Chapter 14, from the diskette in drive A to the current drive by typing:

```
C>copy a:p.old
```

Now archive P.OLD, Q.DOC, and Q.OLD by typing:

```
C>arch1 p.old q.doc q.old

***Archiving p.old***
***Archiving q.doc***
     1 File(s) copied
***Archiving q.old***
     1 File(s) copied
```

The confirming messages show that DOS did not copy the file that was already on the diskette in drive A (P.OLD), but that it did copy the files that weren't on the diskette (both Q.DOC and Q.OLD).

This short Archive command doesn't display instructions or warnings like the batch file you created in Chapter 14, but it does show how you can use the Shift command to write a batch file that handles any number of parameters. The technique is simple: Do something with %1, shift the parameters, then use a Goto command to send DOS back to the beginning to do it all over again. Just make sure you define a way to stop the process, or DOS will carry out the command forever.

Carrying Out a Command More than Once

Sometimes you might want DOS to carry out a command more than once in a batch file, for instance once for each file that matches a file name with wildcard characters. The For command does just that. Like the If command, the For command has two parts: The first part defines how often a command is to be carried out, and the second part is the command to be carried out.

The For command is somewhat more complex than the other batch commands. If you don't fully understand the description of its parameters, read on and try the examples. As with many other aspects of using a computer, it's easier to use the For command than it is to read about it.

The For command has three parameters:

for %%p in (<set>) do <command>

The words *in* and *do* are required in the command; they are not parameters.

%%p is a replaceable parameter used inside the For command. DOS assigns to it, in turn, each value included in (<set>).

(<set>) is the list of possible values that can be given to %%p. You separate the values with blanks, and must enclose the entire list in parentheses—for example, *(1 2 3)*. You can also specify a set of values with a file name that includes wildcard characters—for example, *b: *.DOC*.

<command> is any DOS command other than another For command. You can use both batch-command parameters (such as %1) and the For command replaceable parameter (%%p) in <command>.

It's all less complicated than it sounds. When DOS carries out a For command, it assigns to %%p, in turn, each value that you specify in (<set>), then it carries out <command>. Each time it carries out <command>, DOS first substitutes for %%p the current value taken from (<set>).

A brief example shows how the For command works. The following batch command carries out an Echo command three times, displaying each of the three words enclosed in parentheses. Create FOR1.BAT by typing:

```
C>copy con for1.bat
for %%p in (able baker charlie) do echo %%p
^Z
        1 File(s) copied
```

In this For command, *(able baker charlie)* is (<set>) and *echo %%p* is <command>. The For command tells DOS to carry out the Echo command once for each word in parentheses, substituting, in turn, *able*, *baker*, and *charlie* for %%p. Test it by typing:

```
C>for1
```

For a change, this batch file doesn't begin by turning echo off, so DOS displays each command it carries out, starting with the For command:

```
C>for %p in (able baker charlie) do echo %p
```

DOS then displays and carries out the Echo command once for each value in the set, each time substituting the next value from the set for the replaceable parameter in the Echo command:

```
C>echo able
able

C>echo baker
baker

C>echo charlie
charlie
```

Instead of specifying actual values in the set, you can use replaceable parameters, such as %1. This technique works just like any other batch command, but can be confusing because now you can have %1 and %%p in the same command. Here's the difference: %1 refers to the first parameter typed with the batch command, %2 refers to the second parameter typed with the batch command, and so forth; %%p refers to the value selected from the set enclosed in parentheses within the For command.

The next example shows you the difference. Here, the words to be displayed are typed as parameters of the batch command, instead of being included as part of the For command. Create FOR2.BAT by typing:

```
C>copy con for2.bat
for %%p in (%1 %2 %3) do echo %%p
^Z
        1 File(s) copied
```

This For command tells DOS to carry out the Echo command (*echo %%p*) once for each value in parentheses, substituting for %%p the first, then the second, and finally the third parameter you type with the For2 command. Test it by typing:

```
C>for2 dog easy fox
```

DOS displays each command it carries out. First it displays the For command:

```
C>for %p in (dog easy fox) do echo %p
```

Note that DOS has substituted values for all replaceable parameters. The set in parentheses is now *(dog easy fox)* because those are the three parameters you typed; they have replaced *(%1 %2 %3)*. As you may have noticed in the preceding display, DOS has also dropped one of the percent signs from %%p. DOS removes the first percent sign when it substitutes the parameters you type with the command for %1, %2, and so forth. It does, however, leave one percent sign to show that a value must still be substituted for %p.

DOS then displays and carries out three Echo commands, each time substituting one value from the set in parentheses for %p:

```
C>echo dog
dog

C>echo easy
easy

C>echo fox
fox
```

If you wish, you can specify the set in a For command with a file name and wildcard characters. DOS then assigns to %%p, in turn, each file name that matches the wildcard characters. You can use this technique to create a simple Archive batch file using only a For command. The following command doesn't display instructions and warnings, but it does show you how much can be done with a single batch command.

Create a batch file named ARCH2.BAT by typing the following:

```
C>copy con arch2.bat
for %%p in (%1) do if not exist a:%%p copy %%p a:
^Z
        1 File(s) copied
```

Q.DOC and Q.OLD are on the diskette in drive A (you copied them in the example of the Shift command). Use them to test ARCH2.BAT by archiving all Q files:

```
C>arch2 q.*
```

DOS displays each command it carries out, starting with the For command (remember, you have not turned echo off):

```
C>for %p in (q.*) do if not exist a:%p copy %p a:
```

DOS then displays and carries out three If commands, each time substituting a file name that matches the set enclosed in parentheses for the replaceable parameter in the If command:

```
C>if not exist a:Q.DOC copy Q.DOC a:
```

```
C>if not exist a:Q.BAK copy Q.BAK a:
        1 File(s) copied
```

```
C>if not exist a:Q.OLD copy Q.OLD a:
```

The messages displayed by the Copy command confirm that DOS didn't copy either Q.DOC or Q.OLD because they were already on the archive diskette, but did copy Q.BAK, which hadn't been archived.

The For command gives you a quick way to carry out a DOS command several times. As shown in some of the sample batch files that conclude this chapter, the For command makes it possible to create powerful batch commands.

Using a Batch Command in a Batch File

Earlier in this chapter, in the final version of SHOW.BAT, you used batch commands (Showand and Showxcpt) in a batch file. DOS returned to the system prompt after carrying out these batch commands, even though neither was actually the last command in SHOW.BAT; the last command was Find. You can use this capability, called *chaining,* with any version of DOS.

If you're using 3.3 or a later version, however, you can also use the Call command in a batch file to tell DOS to carry out the commands in another batch file and then come back to continue with the next command in the original batch file instead of returning to the system prompt. This lets you use a batch command of your own making in a batch file, just as you would use a DOS command.

The Call command has two parameters:

call \<batchfile> \<parameters>

\<batchfile> is the name of a batch command that you want DOS to carry out from within the calling batch file.

\<parameters> represents any parameters that \<batchfile> requires.

Two short batch files demonstrate the usefulness of the Call command. First, create a batch file named ECHOIT.BAT by typing the following:

```
C>copy con echoit.bat
@echo off
echo %1
^Z
        1 File(s) copied
```

ECHOIT.BAT simply echoes the parameter you enter with it. For example, to echo *fred*, type the following:

```
C>echoit fred
fred
C>_
```

Now create another batch file named ECHOALL.BAT that uses a For command to carry out ECHOIT.BAT for each of up to three parameters:

```
C>copy con echoall.bat
@echo off
for %%p in (%1 %2 %3) do call echoit %%p
^Z
        1 File(s) copied
```

The For command carries out the Call command for each of up to three parameters that can be entered with the Echoall batch command. The Call command carries out the batch command ECHOIT.BAT, specifying, in turn, each parameter entered with the Echoall batch command.

Now type the following to echo the words *xray*, *yankee*, and *zulu*:

```
C>echoall xray yankee zulu
xray
yankee
zulu
C>_
```

If you hadn't included the Call command, DOS would have carried out ECHOIT.BAT once to display the first parameter (*xray*), then returned to the system prompt.

SOME MORE USEFUL BATCH FILES

The following batch files use the advanced batch commands. Again, they aren't step-by-step examples; they're working samples to give you an idea of what can be done with the full set of batch commands. You can enter the batch files by copying from the console or by using Edlin. The line numbers shown are for reference only.

Displaying a Series of Small Text Files

If you work with many small text files, such as batch files or boilerplate paragraphs for word-processed documents, it's handy to be able to review several files with one command, rather than having to print or display them one at a time. The batch file shown here, REVIEW.BAT, uses the Shift, Type, and Pause commands to display any number of files one at a time. As before, recall that <Alt-255> echoes a blank line. REVIEW.BAT contains:

```
 1: @echo off
 2: :start
 3: if "%1"=="" goto done
 4: cls
 5: echo<spacebar><tab><tab>***FILENAME: %1***
 6: echo <Alt-255>
 7: type %1
 8: echo <Alt-255>
 9: echo <Alt-255>
10: pause
11: shift
12: goto start
13: :done
```

This batch file uses the same technique as the earlier examples of the Shift command. The Echo command in line 5 displays the file name (moved toward the center of the screen with two tabs), so that you'll know what file is displayed. Lines 8 and 9 display two blank lines to separate the file from the Pause command message.

With this Review command, you type the names of the files as parameters. To display several files with the extension DOC, for example, you type *review 1.doc 2.doc 3.doc*. DOS clears the screen and displays the first file, then displays the Pause command message and waits for you to press any key before clearing the screen and displaying the next file. When the If command in line 3 finds the first null parameter (" "), DOS returns to command level.

Searching Files for a String of Characters

Have you ever searched through your paper files to find a specific letter or reference? Or wondered how many letters you wrote about a particular subject or how often you use a particular word? These three short batch files give you several ways to scan a file or set of files for lines that contain a string of characters.

Displaying All Lines That Contain a String

To help you find all lines that contain a particular string, SCAN.BAT lets you specify the file to be searched and one string to search for. It displays each line in the file that contains the string. You can also use wildcard characters to search a set of files. Here are the contents of SCAN.BAT:

```
1: @echo off
2: cls
3: echo<space><tab><tab>***LINES IN %1 THAT CONTAIN %2***
4: echo <Alt-255>
5: for %%p in (%1) do find " %2 " %%p
```

All the work here is done in the last line of the batch file. The earlier lines clear the screen and display a title. The For command in line 5 actually carries out the Find command for each file name that matches the first parameter you type with the Scan command; the Find command is the one that searches for the string that you type as the second parameter.

To display each line that contained the word *sales* in all files with an extension of DOC, you would type *scan *.doc sales*. DOS would clear the screen and display each line that contained the word *sales* preceded and followed by a blank (" %2 ").

Displaying the Number of Lines Containing The String

COUNT.BAT is a slightly modified version of SCAN.BAT that displays the number of lines in the file that contain the string, but doesn't display the lines themselves.

Here are the contents of COUNT.BAT (changes from SCAN.BAT are shaded):

```
1: @echo off
2: cls
3: echo<space><tab><tab>***NUMBER OF LINES IN %1 THAT CONTAIN %2***
4: echo <Alt-255>
5: for %%p in (%1) do find /c " %2 " %%p
```

The only two changes are in the title displayed by the Echo command (line 3) and the addition of the /C parameter to the Find command (line 5).

As an example, to see how many lines in all files with an extension of DOC in the current directory contained the word *night*, you would type *count *.doc night*. The Count command would clear the screen and display the number of lines in each file that contained the word *night*.

Searching for Several Strings

Another batch file, SCANALL.BAT, again gives a count of lines, but it uses a different approach. The file or set of files to be searched is named in the batch file, but you can type however many strings you want as parameters to search for. This approach is particularly useful if you frequently search the same set of files, such as your word-processing files. SCANALL.BAT contains:

```
 1: @echo off
 2: :start
 3: if "%1"=="" goto done
 4: cls
 5: echo<space><tab><tab>***LINES IN *.DOC THAT CONTAIN %1***
 6: echo <Alt-255>
 7: for %%p in (*.doc) do find /c " %1 " %%p
 8: echo <Alt-255>
 9: pause
10: shift
11: goto start
12: :done
```

This batch file uses both the For and Shift commands to search several files for several strings. A line-by-line description is in order:

- Line 1 turns echo off.

- The label :*start* identifies the beginning of the commands to be repeated (it is the destination of the Goto command in line 11).

- The If command checks whether the parameter is null. If it is, the Goto command sends DOS to the end of the batch file (line 12).

- Line 4 clears the screen.

- The Echo commands in lines 5 and 6 display a title and a blank line.

- The For command in line 7 searches each file with an extension of DOC and displays the number of lines that contain the string (" %1 ") specified in the first parameter you type when you use the Scanall command.

- Like line 6, line 8 displays a blank line.

- The Pause command displays its message and waits for a key to be pressed.

- Line 10 shifts the parameters one position to the left.

- The Goto command sends DOS to the label :*start*.

- The label :*done* identifies the end of the batch file (the destination of the Goto command in line 3).

To use the Scanall command, type the words to be searched for as parameters. Remember, the Find command distinguishes between uppercase and lowercase letters. If, for example, you wanted to search for the words *sales*, *January*, and *region*, you would type *scanall sales January region*.

The Scanall command would clear the screen, search all the files whose extension is DOC for the word *sales*, display the number of lines, and then pause. When you pressed any key, it would scan all the files for the word *January*, would again display the results, and so on for each word you specified. Try it with your own words and several dozen word-processing files; you'll be surprised at how quickly this command searches all the files, particularly if you're using a fixed disk.

If you wanted to display the lines containing the strings, rather than just the count, you could simply omit the /C parameter from the Find command in the batch file. This command could produce a lot of output. To print a record of it, you could press Ctrl-PrtSc after you entered the command, but before you pressed the Enter key, to start simultaneously printing and displaying the results.

Displaying a Sorted Directory

In Chapter 4 you displayed the directory sorted by file name. Because the items in a directory entry always begin in the same column, you can sort the directory entries four ways; all but one use the column parameter (/+<number>) of the Sort command to sort starting at the column where the information begins:

- Name—starts in column 1, so does not require the column parameter.
- Extension—starts in column 10.
- Size—starts in column 16.
- Time—starts in column 34.

Although the directory entry includes the date, you can't sort by date unless the date is shown as year-month-day, because January of one year would appear in the list before December of the preceding year (that is, 1-1-1988 would *precede* 12-31-1987). Most of the world (Japan excepted) shows either the day or the month first, so these examples don't sort by date.

The benefits of sorting a directory alphabetically by file name or by extension are obvious. In addition, if you need to delete some files to make space on a disk, or you're just interested in the relative sizes of files, sorting by size is useful. Even sorting by time can be helpful if you've updated a group of files and want to check on which you revised last.

You can create a command to display a directory sorted any of these ways with five short batch files: Four actually sort and display the directory, and one (the command that you type) chains to the correct one of the other four.

First, copy from the console, as you have done before, to create the following one-line batch files; their names tell how they sort the directory:

DIRNAME.BAT:

```
dir %1 | sort | find "-" | more
```

DIREXT.BAT:

```
dir %1 | sort /+10 | find "-" | more
```

DIRSIZE.BAT

```
dir %1 | sort /+16 | find "-" | more
```

DIRTIME.BAT

```
dir %1 | sort /+34 | find "-" | more
```

Each of these batch files sorts and displays the directory specified in the parameter %1 and pipes the output of the Sort command to a Find command that selects only the lines that contain a hyphen (file entries only). The output of the Find command is then piped to the More command to handle directories more than one screen long. If no parameter is specified, the batch command sorts and displays the current directory. The only difference among the batch files is the column in which sorting begins.

You now need the batch file that chains to the correct one of the previous four. Name the file DIRSORT.BAT; it contains:

```
1: @echo off
2: for %%p in (name ext size time) do if "%1"=="%%p" dir%%p %2
3: echo First parameter must be name, ext, size, or time
```

Be sure *not* to put a blank between *dir* and *%%p* in line 2, or the result won't be a valid file name for any of the chained batch files. The quotation marks around *%1* and *%%p* prevent DOS from displaying an error message if no parameter is typed with the command.

In the DIRSORT batch file, the For command sets %%p to each of the words, in turn, in the set in parentheses, then carries out the If command, which compares %%p to the first parameter typed with the Dirsort command. If there is a match, the If command adds the value of %%p to *dir* to produce the name of one of the four sort batch files, and chains to that batch file (for example, *dir + name* would become *dirname*). The second parameter (%2), if any, typed with the Dirsort command is the %1 parameter (the directory name) for the chained batch file.

If the first parameter you type with the Dirsort command isn't one of the four words in the set in parentheses, the condition in the If command is not true. Then the Echo command in the next line is carried out, displaying a message that lists the correct parameters, and the Dirsort batch command ends without chaining to one of the files that displays a sorted directory.

To display a sorted directory, you would type the Dirsort command with one or two parameters: The first, which is required, would specify how to sort and could be only *name*, *ext*, *size*, or *time*; the second parameter, which is optional, would be the drive letter, path name, or name of the directory to be displayed. If you didn't include the second parameter, the command would display the current directory of the disk in the current drive.

For example, to display the current directory, sorted by size, of the disk in the current drive, you would type *dirsort size*. To display the root directory, sorted by name, of the disk in drive A, you would type *dirsort name a:\ *.

CHAPTER SUMMARY

These batch files should give you a good start on a collection of special-purpose commands, as well as some ideas for creating more of your own. This is where the flexibility of DOS really becomes apparent: The wide range of DOS commands and capabilities is only the starting point for putting DOS to work. With redirection, filter commands, and batch files, you can combine all the other DOS commands into a set of custom-tailored commands, to make your personal computer truly personal.

16

I f you have tried the examples in the book, you have used all the major features of DOS. Although it may seem that DOS sometimes offers more options than you need, those options give you flexibility in tailoring DOS; they let you adapt the computer to yourself rather than adapt yourself to the computer.

This chapter shows several ways you can tailor DOS to your needs or preferences. Not only does this tailoring make DOS fit your work needs better, but some of the techniques described here can also make your system immediately useful without your having to buy application programs. Some of these techniques can also make the system more accessible to people who may need to use the computer but who don't have your experience with DOS. And tailoring can also make it easier to achieve consistency in such procedures as backing up a fixed disk when several people use the computer.

This chapter describes:

- Ways to set up a filing system that matches the way the computer is used.
- Batch commands that simplify using a multilevel filing system.
- Batch commands that automate backing up a fixed disk.
- Several simple record-management schemes similar to the telephone index described in Chapters 13 and 15.
- Commands that help you tailor your system hardware with the DOS file named CONFIG.SYS.
- Some less frequently used DOS commands.

Examples are included, but they are not step-by-step exercises. The intent of this chapter is to give you some ideas about how to tailor DOS by applying what you have learned in previous chapters.

SETTING UP A FILING SYSTEM

The multilevel file system described in Chapter 8, ''A Tree of Files,'' lets you organize your files to match your work. A file structure is affected by such factors as the application programs that are used, how many people use the computer, and how many departments are involved. This section shows several different file structures, each organized to focus on a different approach to using the computer. Because every real-life situation is different, these are guides, not exact models.

It doesn't take long to set up a file system—all you need are a few Make Directory commands—but changing a file structure after dozens or hundreds of files have been created can be time-consuming. A few minutes' thought ahead of time can result in a file structure that suits the way the computer will be used.

In the following examples, the computer system is assumed to have a fixed disk, on which a directory named DOS contains the DOS command files. The root directory is assumed to contain an AUTOEXEC.BAT file with a Path command that sets the command path at startup to \DOS and all other program directories in the file structure. General-purpose batch files and any other files that are needed by anyone using the system regardless of the current directory are also assumed to be in the root directory, though they, too, could be in directories of their own, with appropriate command paths added to AUTOEXEC.BAT.

An Application-based File System

If a computer is used for several applications—as it would be by an independent professional or a small business—a natural way to organize the file structure is by application program. Figure 16-1 shows how such a file system might be set up by an independent professional who uses the machine with a word processor, a spreadsheet program, and a database manager.

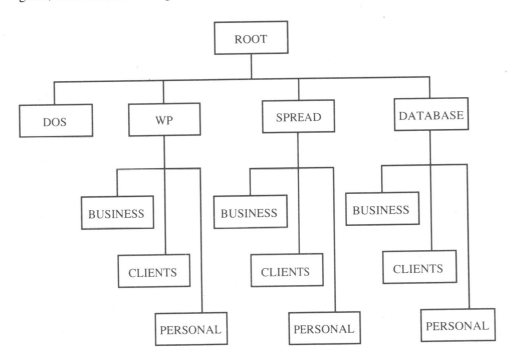

Figure 16-1. Application-based file structure for an independent professional

The first level of directories contains the DOS directory and three others (WP, SPREAD, and DATABASE) for the application programs. The next level (BUSINESS, CLIENTS, and PERSONAL) holds the data files for the applications.

With this file structure, when someone does some word processing, for example, the current directory is set to the directory that contains the document files (such as \WP\BUSINESS or \WP\PERSONAL) so that a path name does not have to be typed each time the person wants to start work on a different file. The Path command in AUTOEXEC.BAT provides access to the root directory (for general-purpose batch files), \DOS (for DOS commands), and \WP (for the word-processing program).

On the other hand, the file system for a computer used in a small business might define the second and subsequent directory levels to correspond to departments, rather than to data files for the applications. Figure 16-2 shows how such a file system might be set up.

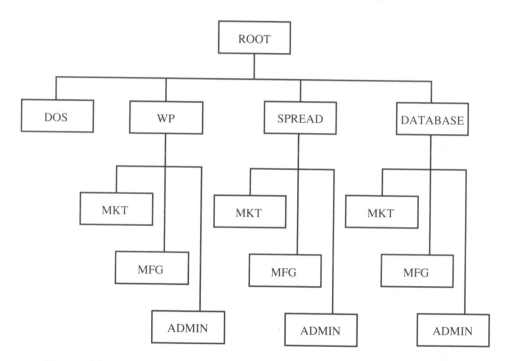

Figure 16-2. Application-based file structure for a small business

A Department-based File System

Rather than beginning with the application program, as the preceding examples do, you can also organize files to emphasize the departments for which files are created. Figure 16-3 shows a file system for a machine used to do work for the Marketing, Manufacturing, and Administration departments of a company. The application programs are the same as in the previous examples, but stored in subdirectories under \PROGRAMS. They are used for all three departments. Because each program is in a subdirectory of its own, and the Path command in AUTOEXEC.BAT sets the command path to the \PROGRAMS directory, work for any department can use any program.

Figure 16-3. Department-based file structure

As much as anything else, the choice of how to organize files depends on how you view your work. If you think primarily in terms of what you do ("I do mostly word processing"), the application-based structure might be the most comfortable. If you think in terms of whom you do it for ("I do most of my work for the Marketing department"), a department-based structure might be more appropriate. Neither structure is more efficient than the other; each simply reflects a different way of looking at the file system.

A User-based File System

If several people use the computer (share one, perhaps, or use the main computer on a network), a file structure that emphasizes the users might be most appropriate, especially if the people use the machine for different applications. Figure 16-4, shown on the following page, outlines a directory structure for a system used by three people.

Again, directories are defined for the same application programs used in the other sample file structures. If the computer is used by people with varying degrees of familiarity with DOS, and if not all users need each application, this type of file structure can make use of the system seem more natural, especially if some batch commands simplify using the directories.

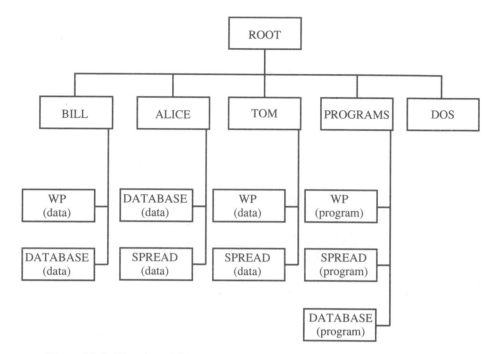

Figure 16-4. User-based file structure

Batch Files to Use Directories

Batch files designed for using directories can be simple or elaborate, depending on who will use them and how much time you want to invest in creating them. Creating separate directories for the people who use the system, for departments, and for application programs simplifies the appearance of the system and makes it easier to keep track of files. Separate directories, however, can also mean that you have to change directories more often. You can automate the use of directories with batch files; this technique makes it simple for all users to work with a structured filing system, even if they are not familiar with DOS. If you make certain the command search path always includes the directory in which they're stored, the batch files for using directories can be accessible from any directory or subdirectory. Switching from one directory and application program to another is always just a matter of typing a single command.

In its simplest form, a batch file to use a directory simply changes the current directory. For example, suppose you have the file structure shown in Figure 16-3, and you want a batch file called WORDMKT.BAT in the root directory to help manage word processing for the Marketing department.

A basic, but functional, version of WORDMKT.BAT could look like the following example (line numbers here and throughout the chapter are for reference only):

```
1: @echo off
2: cd \mkt\wp
```

The Change Directory command sets the current directory to \MKT\WP, which contains the Marketing word-processing files. To use your word-processing program with the Marketing data files, you would just type *wordmkt.*

You could create a similar batch file for each directory that contains data files, and then use any directory just by typing the name of the appropriate batch file. Figure 16-5 shows the directories in Figure 16-3 that contain data files and indicates how the corresponding batch files might be named.

Directory That Contains Data Files	Directory That Contains Program	Name of Batch File
\MKT\WP	\PROGRAMS\WP	WORDMKT.BAT
\MKT\SPREAD	\PROGRAMS\SPREAD	SPMKT.BAT
\MKT\DATABASE	\PROGRAMS\DATABASE	DBMKT.BAT
\MFG\WP	\PROGRAMS\WP	WORDMFG.BAT
\MFG\SPREAD	\PROGRAMS\SPREAD	SPMFG.BAT
\MFG\DATABASE	\PROGRAMS\DATABASE	DBMFG.BAT
\ADMIN\WP	\PROGRAMS\WP	WORDADM.BAT
\ADMIN\SPREAD	\PROGRAMS\SPREAD	SPADM.BAT
\ADMIN\DATABASE	\PROGRAMS\DATABASE	DBADM.BAT

Figure 16-5. Directories and batch files for a department-based file structure

To produce the other batch files, you simply change the Change Directory command to point to the corresponding directories that contain the data files. For example, the batch file (SPMFG.BAT) to do spreadsheets for the Manufacturing department could contain:

```
1: @echo off
2: cd \mfg\spread
```

With these batch files, anyone could then type *wordmkt* and edit a few Marketing documents, type *spadm* and work on some spreadsheets for the Administration department, then type *dbmfg* and update the Manufacturing inventory database, all without worrying about—or even knowing about—the correct directory.

A set of batch files like these makes the multilevel filing system not only more flexible, but also easier to use.

Improving the Appearance of the Batch Files

To dress up the appearance of your batch files for using directories, you could clear the screen and display the directory one screenful at a time. The Change Directory command would be unchanged; this modified version of WORDMKT.BAT would look like the following:

```
1: @echo off
2: cd \mkt\wp
3: cls
4: dir /w ¦ more
```

The /W parameter of the Directory command is used here in case the directory is long; the More command is used in case the directory is *very* long.

Creating Your Own Menu System

If someone unfamiliar with DOS will be using the system, you can use batch files to create a menu system that quickly moves the less-experienced user to the correct directory. For example, suppose you have the file structure shown in Figure 16-3; the batch files described here let someone turn on the system and, by typing *mkt*, see the following display:

```
                    * * *  MARKETING  * * *


Applications: Word processing
              Spreadsheet
              Database

Enter W, S, or D


_
```

If the user types *w*, the following type of directory format screen is displayed (the entries are hypothetical):

```
                 * * *  MARKETING--WORD PROCESSING  * * *
Document files:

 Volume in drive C is FIXED DISK
 Volume Serial Number is 1608-5A30
 Directory of  C:\MKT\WP


 .                    ..            TAXMEMO   DOC...
THP0315   DOC     BUDGET    DOC     INVEN01   DOC...
SLSLTR    DOC     THP0311   DOC     CONFNOT   DOC...
LETR04    DOC     SLSMEMO   DOC     LETR07    DOC...
INVEN04   DOC     INVEN02   DOC     SVCREC    DOC...
LETR06    DOC
        26 File(s)   17162384 bytes free

C>_
```

Displays of this kind would require four batch files for each department: For the Marketing department, there would be one (MKT.BAT) in the root directory and three (W.BAT, S.BAT, and D.BAT) in \MKT. First, here are the contents of MKT.BAT:

```
 1: @echo off
 2: cd \mkt
 3: cls
 4: REM THREE TABS AT BEGINNING OF FOLLOWING ECHO COMMAND
 5: echo <tab><tab><tab>*** MARKETING ***
 6: echo <Alt-255>
 7: echo Applications: Word processing
 8: echo                Spreadsheet
 9: echo                Database
10: echo <Alt-255>
11: echo Enter W, S, or D
12: prompt $a
```

As you can see, most of the commands are Echo commands. The batch file is straightforward: It turns off echo, changes the directory to \MKT, clears the screen, and displays the menu and choices. Then the Prompt command (described later in this chapter) makes the system prompt invisible, so the user sees only the cursor, and the system returns to command level. MKT.BAT has ended even though, as the sample screen showed, it appears to be waiting for a reply to the prompt *Enter W, S, or D*.

If the user types *w* (for word processing), DOS carries out the batch file W.BAT in \MKT. Its contents are:

```
 1: @echo off
 2: cls
 3: cd wp
 4: REM TWO TABS IN FOLLOWING ECHO COMMAND
 5: echo <tab><tab>*** MARKETING--WORD PROCESSING ***
 6: echo Document files:
 7: prompt
 8: dir *.doc /w | more
```

This batch file produces the second sample display (the response to the menu selection). It, too, is straightforward. It turns echo off, clears the screen, changes the directory to \MKT\WP, displays the titles, resets the system prompt to C>, and displays in wide format the directory entries of all files with an extension of DOC.

To complete the menu system in \MKT, you need two batch files similar to W.BAT, one for your spreadsheet and one for your database program. The contents of S.BAT for the spreadsheet are:

```
 1: @echo off
 2: cls
 3: cd spread
 4: REM TWO TABS IN FOLLOWING ECHO COMMAND
 5: echo <tab><tab>*** MARKETING--SPREADSHEET ***
 6: echo Spreadsheet files:
 7: prompt
 8: dir *.pln /w | more
```

In the preceding and following lists, the changes from W.BAT are shaded. You can see that the format is the same. In this example, spreadsheet files are given the extension PLN. To complete the menu system, here are the contents of D.BAT:

```
1: @echo off
2: cls
3: cd database
4: REM TWO TABS IN FOLLOWING ECHO COMMAND
5: echo <tab><tab>*** MARKETING--DATABASE ***
6: echo Database files:
7: prompt
8: dir *.dat /w | more
```

By clearing the screen, displaying your own titles, displaying directory entries, and otherwise controlling the appearance of the system, you can use batch files like these to make the system appear custom-tailored for your own company or department, or even for an individual user. One person who understands how to use the flexibility and power of DOS can make the system easier to use and more productive for everyone else. Batch commands are the key.

AUTOMATING BACKUP OF A FIXED DISK

Chapter 9, ''Managing Your Fixed Disk,'' described how to decide which files need backing up, and when, in order to reduce the number of backup diskettes you need. You can also reduce the amount of time required to back up files.

Suppose you have the file structure shown in Figure 16-3. You decide that each month you should back up all the Marketing and Manufacturing files (all files in \MKT and \MFG and their subdirectories), and each week you should back up all Marketing word-processing documents (files with an extension of DOC) and Manufacturing spreadsheets (files with an extension of PLN) that have changed since the previous week. You can create two batch files—MNTHBKUP.BAT and WEEKBKUP.BAT—that contain the required Backup commands.

The contents of MNTHBKUP.BAT are:

```
1: @echo off
2: cls
3: echo *** MONTHLY FILE BACKUP ***
4: echo <Alt-255>
5: echo Put a formatted diskette in drive A
6: pause
7: backup \mkt a: /s
8: backup \mfg a: /s /a
9: echo LABEL DISKETTE "BACKUP" AND THE MONTH
```

The batch file starts by clearing the screen, displaying a title, and instructing the user to put the backup diskette in drive A. The first Backup command backs up all files from \MKT and all its subdirectories. Any previously existing files on the backup diskette are erased. The second Backup command backs up all files from \MFG and all its subdirectories, adding them to the files backed up from \MKT.

The form of WEEKBKUP.BAT is similar:

```
1: @echo off
2: cls
3: echo ***WEEKLY DOCUMENT BACKUP***
4: echo <Alt-255>
5: echo Put a formatted diskette in drive A
6: pause
7: backup \mkt\wp\*.doc a: /m
8: backup \mfg\spread\*.pln a: /m /a
9: echo LABEL DISKETTE "BACKUP" AND MONDAY'S DATE
```

Like MNTHBKUP.BAT, WEEKBKUP.BAT starts by clearing the screen, displaying a title, and making sure the correct diskette goes in drive A. The first Backup command backs up all files with the extension DOC from \MKT\WP that have been modified since the last backup. Any previously existing files on the backup diskette are erased. The second Backup command backs up all files with the extension PLN from \MFG\SPREAD.

Unless your system is heavily used, only one or two high-capacity backup diskettes per week are likely to be required to back up the changed files of both departments. Because the monthly backup backs up all files, you can reuse the weekly backup diskettes in the following month.

With batch files like these, anyone who uses the system can back up files without knowing how to use the Backup command. All they have to do is type *weekbkup* once a week and *mnthbkup* once a month and follow the instructions on the screen. If your AUTOEXEC.BAT file sets the command search path to the directory containing the batch files, you or anyone else can use these batch files no matter what the current directory is.

RENAMING THE FORMAT COMMAND IN EARLY VERSIONS OF DOS

If you're not using version 3 or later, it's possible to erase all files on the fixed disk by inadvertently formatting it. The scenario goes like this: The fixed disk (drive C) is the current drive; you want to format a diskette, so you put it in drive A and type *format*, but you forget to add *a:* to the command. You have told DOS to format the disk in the current drive (the fixed disk). DOS displays its message warning you that formatting the disk erases all files. Believing that the disk to be formatted is the diskette in drive A, you press the Enter key. DOS dutifully formats the fixed disk, removing everything stored on it.

Although it's not likely you would make both these errors (forget to type *a:* and tell DOS to go ahead without checking), and even though versions 3 and 4 of DOS give an explicit warning if the disk to be formatted is a fixed disk, the consequences are severe enough in earlier versions that you should consider protecting yourself against the possibility. The technique is fairly simple: Rename the Format command file and create a batch file named FORMAT that always formats the diskette in drive A. The following commands do it (assuming the current directory is the directory on the fixed disk that contains the DOS files):

```
C>ren format.com xformat.com
C>copy con format.bat
xformat a: %1 %2 %3
^Z
        1 File(s) copied
```

To format a diskette in drive A with this batch file, you just type *format*; there's no chance of formatting the disk in the current drive.

To use any parameters of the Format command other than the drive letter, include them with your new Format command. To format a system diskette in drive A, for example, you would type *format /s*.

If you want to format a diskette in a drive other than A, just enter the Format command with the usual parameters, but remember to type the command as *xformat*, because you renamed the command file.

USING DOS AS A RECORD-MANAGEMENT PROGRAM

Chapters 13 and 15 showed you how to use filter commands and batch files to search a telephone list. This procedure can also be used to keep track of any small to medium-sized file—say, from 50 to 200 entries. Although this technique doesn't replace a record-management or file-management program, it's simple and quick, and the price is right: You don't need anything except DOS.

The following topics describe other types of information you can keep track of in the same way. Using the same sort of batch files you created in Chapter 15, you can quickly locate any entry or group of entries in your record files.

The descriptions here don't include examples; they simply describe the information included in each line and the columns in which the items of information begin (so that you can sort them). As with any batch files, the best way to get comfortable with this technique and apply it to your own needs is to experiment. These examples give you a starting point.

Keeping Track of Your Computer Files

As you use the computer, your collection of computer files will grow and grow. If you use a word processor, for example, keeping track of all the letters and other documents you create can be a problem. Using wildcard characters with the Directory command makes a particular file easier to find, but you still might have to do some searching to answer such questions as "How many letters did I write in October to the regional sales office?" or "When did we respond to that request from the National Science Foundation?"

You can solve this problem by creating an index file that describes all your word-processing files. You could use the same technique to keep track of any large collection of files.

Figure 16-6 shows the items of information and the columns in which they begin, to give you the format for an index file that keeps track of word-processing files.

Columns 1 through 3 contain the initials of the originator of the document (THP).

Columns 5 through 12 contain the file name (MFGLET31). All files are assumed to have the same extension.

Columns 14 through 21 contain the date the document was created (10/16/88).

Columns 23 through 79 contain a brief description of the document.

```
            Column
     5         14        23
     |         |         |
 THP MFGLET31 10/16/88 Letter to Don Smith about shielding
```

Figure 16-6. Word-processing index file

Keep this index file up to date as you create word-processing files, and you can quickly find files and answer questions with batch files like SHOW.BAT, SHOWAND.BAT, and SHOWXCPT.BAT, which you created in Chapter 15.

To Answer:	Type:
When did we respond to that request from the National Science Foundation?	show NSF
What letters did I write to the regional sales office in October?	show and sales 10/

Want a list of all the documents about the new inventory system, or a list of all letters sent in March? If you keep your index up to date, the answers are just a command away.

Simple Bibliographic Index

If your work requires a lot of reading, you're probably frustrated at times by how easy it is to forget where you saw something. If research is important to your job, but it is not significant enough to justify purchasing and learning to use a database manager or a bibliographic retrieval program, this simple technique might be the answer.

Again, the answer is to create an index file and search it with batch commands. Figure 16-7 shows the items of information and the columns in which they begin, to give you the format for an index file that keeps track of magazine articles, books, and other sources of reference material.

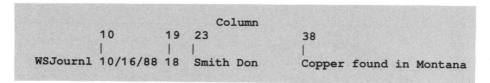

```
                              Column
            10        19  23              38
            |         |   |               |
   WSJournl 10/16/88 18   Smith Don       Copper found in Montana
```

Figure 16-7. Bibliographic index file

Columns 1 through 8 contain the abbreviated title of the journal, book, or other reference source.

Columns 10 through 17 contain the date of the reference.

Columns 19 through 21 contain the page number.

Columns 23 through 36 contain the author's name.

Columns 38 through 79 contain the title or description of the reference.

Again, with batch files like the ones you created in Chapter 15, you can find bibliographic references with one command:

To Answer:	Type:
Where did I see that article on kinesthesia?	show kine
I remember an article last June about laser surgery.	show and 6/ laser

The time it takes to keep this index up to date pays off in the ability to find valuable information much more quickly.

Capital Inventory

If you're an independent professional or you operate a small business, you could easily have a much larger investment in capital goods than you realize. Your accountant and your insurance agent probably emphasize the importance of keeping an up-to-date inventory of capital goods, but it's easy to put off this sort of record keeping.

Figure 16-8 shows a simple index file that lets you keep track of your capital goods. It's no substitute for a complete inventory system, but it's a start, and one that lets you quickly search and sort your inventory.

```
                              Column
              10        19        30          43
              |         |         |           |
   10/16/88 499.95    Ailanthus  H78449002-1  VHS video recorder
```

Figure 16-8. Capital inventory index file

Columns 1 through 8 contain the date of the acquisition.
Columns 10 through 17 contain the cost of acquisition.
Columns 19 through 28 contain the manufacturer's name.
Columns 30 through 41 contain the serial number.
Columns 43 through 79 contain the description.

Here, too, with batch files like the ones you created in Chapter 15, you can keep track of your inventory with one command:

To Answer:	Type:
When did we get the copy machine?	show copy
What did we buy before 1988?	show xcpt /88

This technique can also be used to keep track of your personal inventory for insurance purposes; with a bit of modification, it could also be used for collections, such as coins, stamps, or first editions.

CHANGING YOUR SYSTEM CONFIGURATION

Unlike the other DOS commands, which tell DOS *what* to do, the configuration commands tell DOS *how* to do something, such as use a device or communicate with a disk drive. These commands are required infrequently, usually only when you add a device to your computer system (thereby changing its setup, or *configuration*).

You don't type the configuration commands at the keyboard as you do with other DOS commands; you put them in a special file called CONFIG.SYS, which must be in the root directory of your DOS disk. DOS carries out these commands only when it is started; if you change a command in CONFIG.SYS, you must restart DOS for the command to take effect.

Some application programs or accessory devices require certain commands in CONFIG.SYS. The documentation of the application program or device usually includes step-by-step instructions.

The installation program that comes with version 4 of DOS creates a file of configuration commands for you. The file is named CONFIG.SYS if you install DOS on diskettes or on a fixed disk without an existing CONFIG.SYS file; it is initially named CONFIG.400 if you install DOS on a fixed disk that contains a CONFIG.SYS file (to avoid damaging the existing file). If you're using a fixed disk, you or the person who installed DOS should, if necessary, have renamed CONFIG.400 to CONFIG.SYS after the installation procedure was completed, editing the file to include any needed commands from an old CONFIG.SYS file.

If you need a configuration command and your DOS disk already has a file named CONFIG.SYS in the root directory, use Edlin or some other text editor to add the configuration command to the file. If your DOS disk doesn't have a CONFIG.SYS file in the root directory, use a text editor to create the file and put the configuration command in it; if you need only one or two configuration commands, however, you can use the Copy command to copy from the console to CONFIG.SYS, just as you created the sample files in earlier chapters.

The Device Command and Device Drivers

The Device configuration command specifies a program (a command file with an extension of SYS) that tells DOS how to use a particular device. Such a program is called a *device driver*. The form of the Device command is:

device=<device>

If you have a Microsoft Mouse, for example, the file named MOUSE.SYS is the device driver that tells DOS how to interpret the mouse movements. To tell DOS to use MOUSE.SYS, you would insert a line with the Device command *device=mouse.sys* in your CONFIG.SYS file, preceding *mouse.sys* with a path name if necessary.

Simulating a Disk Drive
In Memory with VDISK.SYS

Note: The ability to simulate a disk drive in memory is made possible by a file named VDISK.SYS in IBM's releases of DOS beginning with version 3.0. This capability was introduced in version 3.2 of MS-DOS, in a file named RAMDRIVE.SYS. Check your documentation if you are uncertain whether your version of DOS includes either VDISK.SYS or RAMDRIVE.SYS.

DOS reads from and writes to diskettes quickly, and it uses a fixed disk even more quickly; both devices are mechanical, however, and quite slow compared to the computer's electronic memory. Starting with some versions numbered 3.0, DOS lets you set aside a portion of the computer's memory for use as a simulated disk, making it possible for disk operations to be performed at memory speeds.

This simulated disk is called a *virtual* disk, because it's virtually the same as having another disk drive. It's also often called a *RAM disk* or *RAM drive*, because the ''disk'' exists in your computer's memory (RAM), rather than as a solid piece of hardware. VDISK.SYS or RAMDRIVE.SYS is the device driver that defines a virtual disk drive.

A virtual disk behaves like any other disk: It has a drive letter and a directory, and you can specify it in any command that uses a disk. It is much faster than a real disk drive, however, and the difference is especially noticeable when you use commands, such as Copy, that work with disk drives, or when you use application programs that access the disk frequently, as many word processors and database programs do. To use a virtual disk drive, you copy the files you need from a physical disk to the virtual drive after DOS has started, then copy them back to the disk after you have completed the work. Copying them back is particularly important, because any changes you make to the files are recorded only in memory when you are using a virtual disk, and the contents of memory disappear whenever you turn off your computer.

DOS assigns the next available drive letter to the virtual disk drive. On a two-drive system, the next available letter is usually C; on a system with one diskette drive and a fixed disk, the next available letter is usually D.

Although a real disk drive has a fixed capacity, such as 360 K or 1.44 MB, a virtual disk can have whatever capacity you want, within certain limits: It must be at least 1 K if you're using VDISK.SYS or 16 K if you're using RAMDRIVE.SYS, and there must be at least 64 K of memory remaining for program use after the virtual disk is defined. If your computer has enough memory, you can define more than one virtual disk by including more than one virtual-disk Device command in CONFIG.SYS.

If your computer is equipped with extended memory (above 1 MB, as in the IBM PC/AT or IBM PS/2 models 50 and 60 or compatible computers) or if it contains an expanded-memory board that increases the amount of available memory according to the Lotus/Intel/Microsoft Expanded Memory Specification, you can tell DOS to use this additional memory for your virtual disk, while leaving your computer's more conventional memory space for programs to use.

As fast and efficient as it is, the remarkable speedup offered by virtual disks can have some drawbacks. If your computer doesn't have extended memory or an expanded-memory board (or if you don't tell DOS to use it) the memory used for a virtual disk reduces the amount of memory available to programs. Furthermore, the contents of a virtual disk are lost each time you turn the computer off.

Make certain that your virtual disk leaves enough memory for the programs you use, and be sure to copy the files you want to keep onto a real disk before you turn the computer off. When you work with an application program, you can automate this process by using a batch file to copy your working files to the virtual disk, start the application program, and then copy the revised working files back to the real disk after you leave the application program.

The Device command to define a virtual disk has the following parameters. For IBM versions 3.0 and later:

device=vdisk.sys <size> <sector> <directory> /E /X

For MS-DOS versions 3.2 and later:

device=ramdrive.sys <size> <sector> <directory> /E /A

VDISK.SYS or RAMDRIVE.SYS is the name of the device-driver program. If it isn't in the root directory of the DOS disk, you must include the drive letter and path name of its directory—for example, *c:\dos\vdisk.sys.*

<size> is the size, in kilobytes, of the virtual disk. The minimum is 1 K if your device driver is named VDISK.SYS and 16 K if it is named RAMDRIVE.SYS. The maximum is the total available memory on your computer. If you omit <size> or specify an incorrect value, DOS sets <size> to 64.

<sector> is the size, in bytes, of each sector on the virtual disk. You can specify 128, 256, or 512 with either VDISK.SYS or RAMDRIVE.SYS; you can also specify 1024 with RAMDRIVE.SYS. If you omit <sector> or specify an incorrect value, DOS sets <sector> to 128.

<directory> is the number of directory entries allowed in the root directory of the virtual disk. For device=VDISK.SYS, you can specify any value from 2 to 512; for device=RAMDRIVE.SYS, you can specify 4 to 1024. Each directory entry takes up 32 bytes of the virtual disk. If you omit <directory> or specify an incorrect value, DOS sets <directory> to 64.

/E tells either VDISK.SYS or RAMDISK.SYS to put the virtual disk in extended memory. It is valid only if the computer contains extended memory. Using extended memory for a virtual disk leaves the maximum amount of memory for programs. If you use /E, you cannot use /X (with VDISK.SYS) or /A (with RAMDISK.SYS).

/A tells RAMDISK.SYS to put the virtual disk in expanded memory. It is valid only if the computer contains an expanded-memory board that meets the Lotus-Intel-Microsoft Expanded Memory Specification. Like the /E option, it leaves the maximum amount of memory available for programs. If you use /A, you cannot use /E.

/X tells VDISK.SYS to put the virtual disk in expanded memory. It is valid only if the computer contains an expanded-memory board that meets the Lotus-Intel-Microsoft Expanded Memory Specification. Like the /E option, it leaves the maximum amount of memory available for programs. If you use /X, you cannot use /E. The /X parameter is in IBM releases of DOS beginning with 4.0. It might, however, not be able to work with some hardware.

DOS may adjust some of the numbers you specify. If the <size> you specify doesn't leave at least 64 K of memory available, DOS reduces <size> so that 64 K to 100 K of memory is available for programs.

If the number of directory entries you specify, times 32 bytes per entry, leaves a partial sector remaining, DOS adjusts the number of directory entries upward to fill that final sector completely.

If there isn't enough memory to create the virtual disk as you specify it, DOS doesn't create the virtual disk.

Example of Simulating a Disk Drive in Memory

Suppose your computer has a fixed disk, one diskette drive, and 640 K of memory, and your word processor is Microsoft Word. You want to use a virtual disk to speed your word-processing sessions, and you also want to be sure not to forget to copy the edited files back from the virtual disk after you finish your work. You decide that you can afford to use 100 K of memory for the virtual disk, that each sector should be 512 bytes, and that you need only 32 entries in the root directory of the virtual disk.

First, using Edlin or another text editor, you would put one of the following Device configuration commands in CONFIG.SYS (which one depends on the name of your virtual-disk device driver):

```
device=vdisk.sys 100 512 32
```

or

```
device=ramdrive.sys 100 512 32
```

Because DOS treats the diskette drive as both A and B and the fixed disk as drive C, the virtual drive would be drive D. (If the system had two diskette drives and no fixed disk, the virtual drive would be C.)

Then you would create the following batch file named WP.BAT in the root directory of your system disk:

```
1: @echo off
2: cd \wp
3: copy %1 d:
4: d:
5: word
6: c:
7: copy d:%1
8: erase d:%1
9: cd \dos
```

Now suppose you start your system and want to edit a file named REPORT.DOC. You type:

```
C:\DOS>wp report.doc
```

The batch file does the following:

- In line 1, it turns echo off.

- In line 2, it changes the current directory to the word-processing directory.

- In line 3, it copies REPORT.DOC to the virtual disk drive.

- In line 4, it changes the current drive to the virtual drive.

- In line 5, it starts the word-processing program.

- In line 6, after you quit the word-processing program, it changes the current drive back to drive C.

- In line 7, it copies REPORT.DOC (which you edited and saved in the word-processing program) to the fixed disk.

- In line 8, it deletes REPORT.DOC from the virtual disk.

- In line 9, it changes the directory back to the DOS directory on the fixed disk, leaving you just where you were when you entered the batch command.

You could use this same batch file to edit a set of files with similar file names or extensions by using a wildcard character. For example, to work with all the files whose file name starts with LET and whose extension is DOC, you would type:

```
C:\DOS>wp let*.doc
```

Notice, however, that this would copy all the files that match the file name (*let*.doc) to the virtual disk and then back to the real one, whether or not you had changed them.

You could also copy program files to a virtual disk to reduce the time required to load and start executing a program. This is usually helpful only if you use a very large program that must periodically return to the program disk to load additional portions, or if you routinely use several different programs and switch back and forth.

How you use a virtual disk depends to a great extent on how much memory your computer has and what sort of work you do with it. As with many other DOS commands, you may need to do a bit of experimenting before you find the most useful way for you.

Controlling the Display with ANSI.SYS

DOS includes a device driver called ANSI.SYS. ANSI is an acronym for American National Standards Institute. ANSI.SYS defines a standard set of methods for managing a display, including how to display and erase characters, move the cursor, and select colors. Some programs require your system disk to have a CONFIG.SYS file that contains the command *device=ansi.sys*.

Some Other Configuration Commands

Several other configuration commands control internal operating characteristics of your system, and usually deal with how DOS handles files or reads disks. Some application programs or devices include detailed instructions for adding or changing configuration commands. These configuration commands are described in more detail in Appendix F.

Buffers

The Buffers configuration command defines the number of work areas in memory (*buffers*) that DOS uses to handle reading from and writing to a disk. The effect of this configuration command on system performance depends on the type of disk drive you use and the types of programs that you use. The form of the Buffers command is:

buffers=<number> /X

The /X parameter, new in version 4, tells DOS to create the buffers in expanded memory.

Unless otherwise instructed, versions of DOS through 3.2 use two or three buffers, depending on your system and the amount of memory it has. If you're using version 3.3, DOS might use more buffers. If you're using version 4, the installation program sets the number of buffers according to the amount of memory in your system. You can, of course, override these values by including or changing the Buffers configuration command in CONFIG.SYS. For optimum performance, some programs require you to set buffers to a higher number than DOS assumes. Fastback, for example, needs 40. For a list of the values that DOS uses, see the description of the Buffers command in Appendix F.

Files

The Files configuration command tells DOS how many files it can use at one time. Unless otherwise instructed, DOS can use a maximum of eight files at a time. The form of the Files command is:

files=<number>

Note: If you're using version 4, the installation program added a Files command to the configuration file it created. The number of files depends on the amount of memory in your system.

Lastdrive

The Lastdrive configuration command specifies the highest drive letter that DOS recognizes as valid. If you are using version 4, the installation program added a *lastdrive=e* command to your configuration file, meaning you have five drive letters available. With earlier versions, if CONFIG.SYS doesn't contain a Lastdrive command, the highest drive letter DOS recognizes is, again, E. This command is usually used to specify a higher letter (up to Z) if DOS needs more than five drive letters. This might happen because the computer is part of a network, because it uses many virtual disk drives, or because a large fixed disk is divided into sections, each of which is referred to by a different drive letter. The form of the Lastdrive command is:

lastdrive=<letter>

Blocking Enhanced Keyboard Functions

Beginning with version 4, IBM's release includes the Switches command, which prevents DOS from using the additional keys on the enhanced keyboard. You would most likely need the Switches command only if pressing one of the additional keys on the enhanced keyboard caused problems with one of your application programs. The form of the Switches command is:

switches=/k

COMMANDS FOR OCCASIONAL USE

This book has described all the commands you routinely use to operate DOS. There are a few remaining commands you might occasionally need, and there are several commands that you won't need unless you plan to do some programming or to use some of the advanced capabilities of DOS. The less commonly used commands are described briefly here, and in more detail in Appendix F.

Displaying the DOS Version Number

The Version command displays the number of the version of DOS you're using. If you use more than one version, or if you are using someone else's machine, this gives you a quick way to check the version.

The Version command has no parameters:

ver

If you're using IBM's version 4, for example, DOS replies *IBM DOS Version 4.00* in response to the command.

Changing the System Prompt

As shown in examples in earlier chapters, you can change the system prompt with the Prompt command to display much more than just the current drive letter. The change takes effect as soon as you enter the command.

The Prompt command has one parameter:

prompt <string>

<string> is a string of characters that defines the new system prompt. You can use any characters you want. You can also cause the new prompt to include one or more items of useful information by including a dollar sign and one of the following characters, to specify what you want the prompt to contain.

Character	Produces
d	The current date
p	The current directory
n	The current drive
t	The current time
v	The DOS version number
g	A greater-than sign (>)
l	A less-than sign (<)
b	A vertical bar (¦)
q	An equal sign (=)
e	An Escape character
h	A backspace
$	A dollar sign ($)
_	A signal to end the current line and start a new one. (The character is an underscore, not a hyphen.)

You can include as many combinations of $, followed by a character, as you wish. DOS ignores any combination of $ followed by a character that is not in the preceding list. You saw an example of this earlier in this chapter: In the batch file MKT.BAT, the system prompt was set to nothing (made invisible) with the command *prompt $a*.

If you enter the Prompt command with no parameter (just type *prompt*), DOS restores the prompt to the standard DOS version: the letter of the current drive followed by a greater-than sign (for example, C>).

The Prompt command takes effect immediately, so it's easy to experiment. You saw how to change the system prompt to a courteous request (*May I help you?*) in Chapter 3, and you've changed it to suit your needs in other chapters. Don't be afraid to experiment, because all you need do to restore the system prompt to its standard form is type *prompt*.

Several examples follow. Notice how the system prompt changes each time to show the effect of the previous Prompt command. Press the spacebar before pressing the Enter key to end each command, to leave a blank space between the end of the system prompt and the beginning of the command that you type next.

To define the system prompt as the current drive and directory, type:

```
C:\DOS>prompt $p
```

```
C:\MKT\WP _
```

The example assumes that the current drive is C and that the directory is \MKT\WP. To define the system prompt as two lines that show the date and time, type:

```
C:\MKT\WP prompt $d$_$t

Mon 10-16-1989
14:57:10.11 _
```

The time and date will vary, depending on how you have set them in your system. Press the Enter key several times to see that DOS keeps the time current.

Finally, combining several of the options shows just how much you can include in a prompt:

```
Mon 10-16-1989
15:02:10.11 prompt $v$_$d $t$_Current directory $q $p$_Command:

IBM DOS Version  4.00
Mon 10-16-1989 15:02:57.68
Current directory = C:\MKT\WP
Command:_
```

The Prompt command lets you easily tailor the system prompt to the balance of brevity and information that you prefer. When you design a system prompt that you like, put it in AUTOEXEC.BAT and you'll never have to type it again; DOS will carry out the command every time you start the system.

Speeding Up File Access

Note: The Fastopen command described here was introduced in version 3.3 of DOS. If you have an earlier version of DOS, skip to the next section, "Altering the Way DOS Interprets Drive Letters."

Each time you (or an application program) need a file, DOS might first need to search for the subdirectory that contains the file, then search the directory entries for the file itself. On a fixed disk with hundreds or thousands of files, all this searching can take some time.

The Fastopen command tells DOS to keep track (in memory) of the locations of subdirectories and files as it uses them; the next time it's asked for a file or subdirectory, DOS checks in memory before it searches the disk. If the location of the file or subdirectory is in memory, DOS can go directly to it on the disk instead of searching for it.

If you or your application programs tend to use the same files or directories over and over, the Fastopen command can make DOS visibly faster. The Fastopen command works only with fixed disks. It has two main parameters:

fastopen <drive>=<files>

<drive> is the drive letter, followed by a colon, of the fixed disk whose files and subdirectories you want DOS to keep track of (for example, *c:*).

<files> is the number of files and subdirectories whose location DOS is to keep in memory; it must be preceded by an equal sign. You can specify a value for <files> from 10 to 999. For example, if you had one fixed disk, drive C, and wanted DOS to keep track of the last 75 files and subdirectories used, you would type *fastopen c:=75*.

If you're using version 4 from a fixed disk, the installation program might have set up a Fastopen command telling DOS to keep track of the last *x* files and subdirectories you used. This command was placed in your configuration file in a form like this: *install=c:\dos\fastopen.exe c:=(50,25)*. Although the command looks a bit more complicated than *fastopen c:=50*, its purpose is the same. The *install* part of the command (described in Appendix F) simply tells DOS to use your computer's memory as efficiently as it can. If you want to change the number of files, change the command in CONFIG.SYS. For example, to keep track of the last 75 files and subdirectories, change the command to *install=c:\dos\fastopen.exe c:=(75,25)*.

Altering the Way DOS Interprets Drive Letters

Warning: The following three commands (Assign, Substitute, and Join) let you change the way DOS interprets drive letters. These commands restrict your use of other DOS commands, such as Backup, Restore, and Print, that deal with disks and files. Use the next three commands sparingly, and check the descriptions of the other disk and file commands in your DOS manual to make certain you understand the restrictions. The Substitute and Join commands must not be used on a network.

Assigning a Drive Letter to a Different Drive

Some application programs require that you put the diskettes with your data files in one particular drive. This can be inconvenient if you're using a fixed disk and prefer to use it for your data files. The Assign command gives you a solution: It lets you tell DOS to make a drive letter refer to a different drive (for example, to tell DOS to use the fixed disk, drive C, whenever it receives a request for drive B).

Because the Assign command affects all requests for a drive, you should use it with caution—especially if you are using a fixed disk. Always bear in mind that some DOS commands, such as Erase, delete existing files from the disk in the specified drive. If you use one of these commands after you have used Assign, you could inadvertently lose valuable programs or data files. Only three commands, Format, Diskcopy, and Diskcomp, ignore drive reassignments specified with Assign.

The Assign command has two parameters:

assign <drive1>=<drive2>

<drive1> is the letter of the drive to be assigned to a different drive.
<drive2> is the letter of the drive that is to be used in place of <drive1>.
If you omit both <drive1> and <drive2>, DOS cancels any assignments.

For example, suppose you have a graphics program that requires all data files to be on drive B, but you want to use your fixed disk (drive C) for data files. To tell DOS to assign all requests for drive B to drive C instead, you would type *assign b=c*.

The assignment affects all requests for the drive, including any commands you enter other than Format, Diskcopy, and Diskcomp. If you assign drive B to drive C as in the previous example, and then type *dir b:*, DOS displays the directory of the fixed disk. The assignment remains in effect until you restart DOS or cancel the assignment by typing *assign*.

Treating a Directory as if It Were a Disk

The Substitute (subst) command lets you treat a directory as if it were a separate disk. If your directory structure includes long path names, or if you use application programs that accept a drive letter but not a path name, you can use the Substitute command to tell DOS to treat all future references to a particular drive as references to a directory on the disk in a different drive.

After naming a drive letter in a Substitute command or in a Join command (described next), you cannot refer to that drive letter in any other command, so you will probably want to use a drive letter that doesn't refer to an existing drive. In order to do this, you must tell DOS to accept more drive letters than there are disk drives. You do this by putting a Lastdrive command in the CONFIG.SYS file in the root directory of your DOS system disk. The Substitute command has two parameters:

subst <drive> <pathname> /D

<drive> is the letter, followed by a colon, to be used to refer to <pathname>.
<pathname> is the path name of the directory to be referred to by <drive>.
/D deletes any substitutions that involve <drive>. If you include /D, you cannot include <pathname>.

If you omit all parameters (just type *subst*), DOS displays a list of any substitutions in effect.

For example, suppose you find yourself frequently referring to a directory whose path name is C:\MPLAN\SALES\FORECAST, and you would like to use a shorter synonym. To substitute *x:* for the path name, you would make certain that your CONFIG.SYS file contained a Lastdrive command that specified the letter x, then type *subst x: c:\mplan\sales\forecast*. The substitution would remain in effect until you restarted DOS or canceled the substitution by typing *subst x: /d*.

Treating a Disk as if It Were a Directory

The Join command lets you treat a disk drive as a directory on the disk in a different drive. If you use an application program that stores its data files on the program disk, you can use the Join command to tell DOS to treat another drive as if it were a directory on the program disk. The Join command has three parameters:

join <drive> <pathname> /D

<drive> is the letter, followed by a colon, of the drive to be connected to the directory specified by <pathname>. It cannot be the current drive.

<pathname> is the path name of the directory to which <drive> is to be joined. It must be an empty subdirectory in the root directory of the disk to which <drive> is to be joined.

/D deletes any joins that involve <drive>. If you include /D, you cannot include <pathname>.

If you omit all parameters (just type *join*), DOS displays a list of any joins in effect. Once you specify a drive letter as <drive> in a Join command, you cannot use that letter to refer to a drive.

For example, suppose you have an application program that takes up most of a diskette and you need a lot of disk space for data files. If you put the application program diskette in drive A and a blank diskette in drive B, you could tell DOS to treat the blank diskette in drive B as a directory named \DATA on the diskette in drive A by typing *join b: a:\data*. The join would remain in effect until you restarted DOS or canceled the join by typing *join b: /d*.

CHAPTER
17
THE DOS SHELL

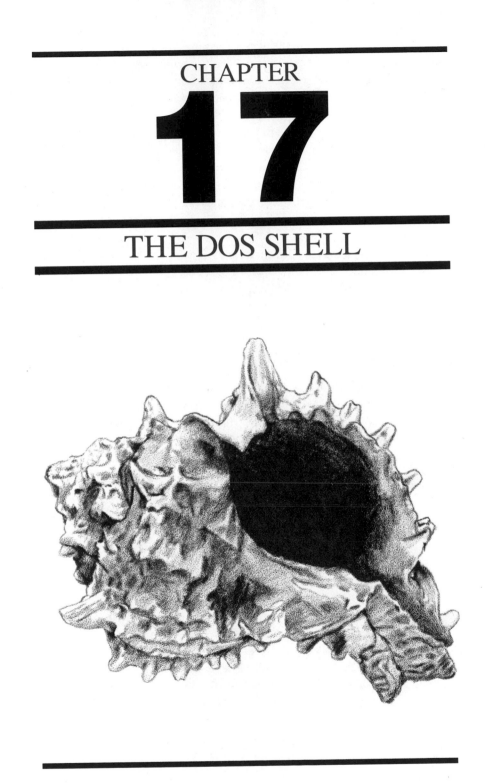

V ersion 4 of DOS includes a program called the DOS Shell. (If you installed version 4, chances are the Shell's opening screen came up when you restarted the computer after completing installation.) The Shell is a program that lets you manage your files and disks without typing DOS commands or file names; you can navigate through your directory structure without typing path names, and you can run application programs simply by selecting choices from a menu and occasionally typing a brief response to a prompt.

This program is called a *shell* because it surrounds DOS; when you use it, you see the Shell and its menus rather than DOS itself, or its system prompt. The Shell even adds some capabilities that DOS commands don't offer. For example, you can rename a directory, move one or more files without having to copy and erase them, or find a file anywhere on the disk.

This chapter gives you a quick tour of the Shell. It shows you how to use the Shell's major capabilities with either the keyboard or the mouse. It also shows you how to add your own application programs to the Shell.

If you haven't yet installed DOS, turn to Appendix B and follow the instructions there, then return to this chapter.

STARTING THE SHELL

When version 4 of DOS is installed with the Shell on a fixed disk, it can be set up either to run the Shell whenever you start or restart your computer or to wait until you give the command to run the Shell. If DOS runs the Shell automatically, the first thing you see when DOS starts is a screen similar to the one in Figure 17-1. If DOS does not run the Shell automatically, you see some startup messages, followed by the system prompt (probably C:\DOS>). In this case, you start the Shell by typing the file name part of its batch file (DOSSHELL.BAT):

```
C:\DOS>dosshell
```

Note: If you're using DOS from diskettes, you start or restart your computer with your Startup diskette. If the capacity of your diskette drive is less than 1.44 MB, replace the Startup diskette with the Shell diskette, and then type dosshell *at the system prompt (A>).*

The Shell program loads in a few moments, then displays its opening screen. Unless someone has changed the contents of DOSSHELL.BAT, your screen should look like Figure 17-1 (if you see a diagram of directory names on the left and a list of files on the right, skip to the heading ''The File System''). This is the *Start Programs* screen, one of the two major parts of the Shell. You'll switch to the other major part—the *File System*—in a moment.

```
 10-16-89                     Start Programs                        1:12 pm
  Program  Group  Exit                                             F1=Help
                               Main Group
                To select an item, use the up and down arrows.
              To start a program or display a new group, press Enter.

Command Prompt
 File System
 Change Colors
 DOS Utilities...




                                        ⍦




 F10=Actions               Shift+F9=Command Prompt
```

Figure 17-1. DOS Shell Start Programs screen

Parts of the Start Programs Screen

The Start Programs screen is divided into four areas:

- The top line identifies which part of the Shell is active. It shows the date, the name of the screen (*Start Programs*), and the time.

- The second line displays the names of the menus on the left—*Program*, *Group*, and *Exit*—and *F1=Help* on the right.

- The middle of the screen displays a list of programs or groups of programs.

- The bottom line of the screen displays some of the keys that have special meaning. *F10=Actions* on the left tells you that the F10 key activates the menus in the second line, and *Shift+F9=Command Prompt* means that holding down a Shift key and pressing F9 lets you temporarily leave the Shell and work at the DOS system prompt.

Help Is Always There

The Shell includes enough on-screen help information to guide you through most of the Shell's features. You can always press F1 to display a window of Help information. When the Help window is displayed, you can press F11 (or Alt-F1) to display an index of all the Help information that is available and, if you wish, you can display information about any item listed in the index.

Before trying out the menus, press F1 to see what help is available. The Shell displays a window of Help information in the lower middle of the screen, as shown in Figure 17-2.

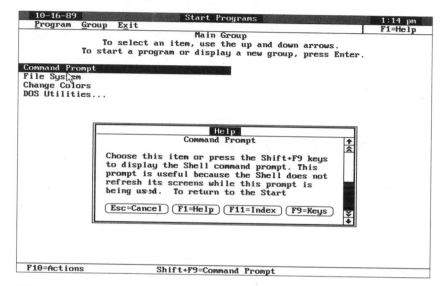

Figure 17-2. DOS Help display

The main part of the Help window describes what you can (or must) do; the bottom line of the Help window—no matter what Help information is displayed—offers you four choices:

- Esc cancels Help, removing the Help window and returning you to whatever you were doing when you pressed F1.

- F1 displays help about Help.

- F11 or Alt-F1 displays an index of all the Help screens. You can scroll through this list of topics and display information about the highlighted topic by pressing Enter.

- F9 displays a list of all the function keys you can use with the Shell.

Cancel Help by pressing Esc; the window disappears and the screen looks just as it did when you pressed F1.

Using the Keyboard and Mouse

Before you begin to explore the Shell, it's useful to know roughly how to get around in it with the keyboard or a mouse. Figure 17-3 describes the basic mouse techniques and tells how to perform the most common Shell operations using the keyboard or a mouse. The lengths of the descriptions are an accurate reflection of the difference between using the keyboard and using a mouse: Operating the Shell with a mouse is much quicker.

If you're a keyboard user, don't be concerned if the techniques don't have much meaning as yet; they soon will. If you're a mouse user, you're probably already familiar with pointing, clicking, double-clicking, and dragging, so the mouse techniques will give you a quick overview of what to do. In either case, the hands-on examples in this chapter help you along when necessary.

Mouse Techniques

Click:	Move the mouse pointer to the item and press the left mouse button once.
Double-click:	Move the mouse pointer to the item and press the left mouse button twice in rapid succession.
Drag:	Move the mouse pointer to the item, press and hold the left mouse button, move the mouse pointer to the new location, then release the left mouse button.

Keyboard	*Mouse*
To select a menu:	
If necessary, activate the area of the screen that contains the menu by pressing F10 or the Tab key. Now either press the key letter of the menu name (underlined in graphics mode, highlighted in text mode), or use the arrow keys to highlight the menu name, and then press Enter.	Click on the menu name.
To select a menu item:	
Select the menu, then either press the key letter of the item (underlined in graphics mode, highlighted in text mode), or use the arrow keys to highlight the item you want and then press Enter.	Click on the item.
To select a file:	
Highlight the file name with the arrow keys, then press the spacebar.	Click on the file name.
To select a command:	
Highlight the command with the arrow keys, then press the Enter key.	Double-click on the command name.

Figure 17-3. Keyboard and mouse techniques

THE FILE SYSTEM

To explore one of the most important areas of the Shell, use the Down Arrow key when the items in *Main Group* (the opening screen) are displayed. Highlight *File System* and press Enter or double-click on *File System* with the mouse. DOS should display the opening screen of the File System, then overlay it with a window that says *Reading disk information* while it reads the names of the directories and files on the current disk. When it has finished reading the disk information, it fills in the directory and file names on the display.

The Shell operates either in *text mode,* which uses only text characters in its displays, or in *graphics mode,* which uses both text characters and some graphic symbols. Unless the commands in DOSSHELL.BAT specify otherwise, DOS starts the Shell in graphics mode if your display can show graphics. Figure 17-4 shows the opening display of the File System in graphics mode, and Figure 17-5 shows the same screen in text mode. (For simplicity, these illustrations show only the three files most likely to be on any fixed-disk system. You might see others.)

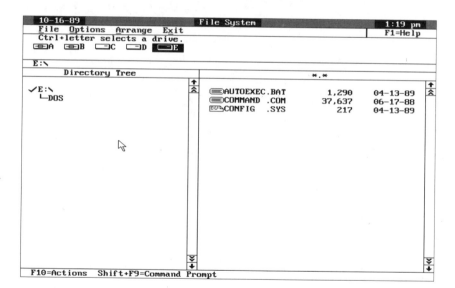

Figure 17-4. DOS Shell File System display (graphics mode)

```
 10-16-89                     File System                    1:45 pm
   File  Options  Arrange  Exit                           | F1=Help

 A  B  C  D  E

 E:\

        Directory Tree    More:  ↓        *.*              More:  ↓
► E:\                            AUTOEXEC.BAT     1,290    04-13-89
   └─DOS                         COMMAND .COM    37,637    06-17-88
                                 CONFIG  .SYS       217    04-13-88




            ▓




 F10=Actions  Shift+F9=Command Prompt
```

Figure 17-5. DOS Shell File System display (text mode)

Graphics Mode Versus Text Mode

The quickest way to tell whether the Shell is in graphics mode or text mode is to look
at the list of disk drives displayed in the third line. If the drives are represented by a
drawing of a disk drive, the Shell is in graphics mode; if they're represented by just
the drive letter, the Shell is in text mode.

The other major differences between graphics and text mode:

- If you're using a mouse, the pointer is an arrow when the Shell is in graphics
  mode, a small rectangle when the Shell is in text mode.

- A symbol is displayed to the left of each file name when the Shell is in
  graphics mode.

- The key letters—usually the first letter—of menu names and menu choices
  are underlined in graphics mode, but highlighted in text mode.

The remainder of this chapter shows screens in graphics mode.

*Note: The illustrations in this chapter show five drives, A through E. Your system probably
shows fewer, and drive A or C instead of E is probably highlighted. This difference is of no
importance.*

Parts of the File System Screen

The File System screen consists of several areas that show you which drive is selected and where you are in the file system:

- The top line still identifies which part of the Shell is active. It shows the date, the name of the screen (which now reads *File System*), and the time.

- The second line now displays the names of the File System menus: *File, Options, Arrange,* and *Exit. F1=Help* is still displayed on the right.

- The next line displays the list of disk drives attached to your system (including any RAM disks you may have defined).

- The left side of the middle portion of the screen shows all the directories on the current disk, arranged with subdirectories indented to the right and connected with lines to show the structure. This display is like the output of the version 4 Tree command.

- The right side of the middle portion of the screen lists all the files in the selected directory. In graphics mode, the file names are preceded by a symbol that roughly identifies the type of file. The symbol for a command file—a file whose extension is COM, EXE, or BAT—is a round-cornered rectangle with several lines inside it; it represents a display screen. The symbol for all other types of files is a rectangle filled with broken lines and with one corner folded over; it represents a piece of paper.

- The bottom line of the screen still displays the messages *F10=Action* and *Shift+F9=Command Prompt,* both of which mean the same as in the Start Programs screen.

If you're using the keyboard to operate the Shell, you must use the Tab key to select the portion of the screen you want to work in before selecting a menu, disk drive, directory, or file. If you're using a mouse, you can select any item in any part of the screen by moving the mouse pointer to it and clicking the left mouse button.

Selecting a Directory

The selected directory is marked with a check mark (a right-facing triangle in text mode) to the left of the directory name. When the File System starts, the root directory is selected. Select the \DOS directory with the mouse or with the arrow keys. Depending on how many directories are in your root directory, you might have to scroll down the list to find *DOS*; if so, just press the Down Arrow key until *DOS* (or the name of your DOS directory) is highlighted, then press Enter. The screen should look like Figure 17-6.

```
┌─10-16-89───────────────────File System─────────────────1:47 pm─┐
│ File  Options  Arrange  Exit                          │F1=Help │
│ Ctrl+letter selects a drive.                                   │
│ ▄▄A   ▄▄B   ▄▄C   ▄▄D   ▄▄E                                     │
│                                                                │
│ E:\DOS                                                         │
│     Directory Tree                              *.*           │
│                                 ┌─┐                        ┌─┐ │
│                                 │↑│                        │↑│ │
│  E:\                            │⊼│ 4201    .CPI   6,404   │⊼│ │
│  └─DOS                          │ │ 4208    .CPI     641   │ │ │
│  ✓  ▒▒▒                         │ │ 5202    .CPI     402   │ │ │
│                                 │ │ ANSI    .SYS   9,148   │ │ │
│                                 │ │ APPEND  .EXE  11,170   │ │ │
│                                 │ │ ASSIGN  .COM   5,785   │ │ │
│                                 │ │ ATTRIB  .EXE  18,247   │ │ │
│                                 │ │ BACKUP  .COM  33,754   │ │ │
│                                 │ │ BASIC   .COM   1,065   │ │ │
│                                 │ │ BASICA  .COM  36,285   │ │ │
│                                 │ │ CHKDSK  .COM  17,771   │ │ │
│                                 │ │ COMMAND .COM  37,637   │ │ │
│                                 │ │ COMP    .COM   9,491   │ │ │
│                                 │ │ COUNTRY .SYS  12,838   │ │ │
│                                 │ │ DEBUG   .COM  21,606   │ │ │
│                                 │ │ DISKCOMP.COM   9,889   │ │ │
│                                 │ │ DISKCOPY.COM  10,428   │ │ │
│                                 │ │ DISPLAY .SYS  15,741   │ │ │
│                                 │ │ DOSSHELL.BAT     184   │ │ │
│                                 │⊻│ DOSUTIL .MEU   6,660   │⊻│ │
│                                 │↓│ DRIVER  .SYS   5,274   │↓│ │
│ F10=Actions   Shift+F9=Command Prompt                          │
└────────────────────────────────────────────────────────────────┘
```

Figure 17-6. Files in \ DOS

Scrolling Through the Directories

On a fixed disk, the list of files in \DOS is too long to fit on the screen. You can scroll through this list—or any other list that won't fit on the screen—by pressing the Down Arrow key to move a line at a time or the PgDn key to move a screen at a time. As you're scrolling through the list, you can also use the Up Arrow key to move back up a line and the PgUp key to move back up a screenful. But the Shell includes a mechanism that makes scrolling easier if you're using a mouse: the *scroll bar*.

In text mode, the scroll bar is simply the word *More* followed by a down arrow, an up arrow, or both. Clicking on one of these arrows moves the highlight one line in the direction of the arrow, scrolling the list if you're at the top or bottom of the window.

In graphics mode, the scroll bar is a more detailed structure at the right margin of each window, as shown in Figure 17-6. Clicking on the single arrow at the top or bottom of the scroll bar moves the list one line in the direction of the arrow; clicking on the double arrows moves a screenful. You can scroll any distance by dragging the light-colored box in the scroll bar to any position between the top and bottom.

You can use these techniques to scroll through any list that the Shell displays: directories, lists of files, or help text.

Managing Your Files with the File Menu

The Shell menus show you what items you can choose and whether the Shell will ask for more information when you make a choice. To see this, select the File menu; the screen should look like Figure 17-7.

```
┌─────────────┬──────────────────────────────────────────────┬────────────┐
│ 10-16-89    │              File System                     │   1:48 pm  │
├─────────────┴────────────────────────────────────┬─────────┴────────────┤
│ File│ Options  Arrange   Exit                     │          F1=Help     │
├──────────────────────┐drive.                      └──────────────────────┤
│ Open (start)...      │ ═╗E                                               │
│ Print...             │                                                    │
│ Associate...         │                                                    │
│                      │                    *.*                             │
│ Move...          ┌┐  │                                               ┌┐  │
│ Copy...          │▲  │ ═╗4201    .CPI      6,404     06-17-88        │▲  │
│ Delete...        │▲  │ ═╗4208    .CPI        641     06-17-88        │▲  │
│ Rename...           ▒│ ═╗5202    .CPI        402     06-17-88          ▒│
│ Change attribute...  │ ═╗ANSI    .SYS      9,148     06-17-88           │
│ View                 │ ▤APPEND   .EXE     11,170     06-17-88           │
│                      │ ▤ASSIGN   .COM      5,785     06-17-88           │
│ Create directory...  │ ▤ATTRIB   .EXE     18,247     06-17-88           │
│ Select all           │ ▤BACKUP   .COM     33,754     06-17-88           │
│ Deselect all         │ ▤BASIC    .COM      1,065     06-17-88           │
└──────────────────────┘ ▤BASICA   .COM     36,285     06-17-88           │
│                        ▤CHKDSK   .COM     17,771     06-17-88           │
│                        ▤COMMAND  .COM     37,637     06-17-88           │
│                        ▤COMP     .COM      9,491     06-17-88           │
│                        ═╗COUNTRY .SYS     12,838     06-17-88           │
│                        ▤DEBUG    .COM     21,606     06-17-88           │
│                        ▤DISKCOMP.COM       9,889     06-17-88           │
│                        ▤DISKCOPY.COM      10,428     06-17-88           │
│                        ═╗DISPLAY .SYS     15,741     06-17-88           │
│                        ▤DOSSHELL.BAT         184     04-13-89           │
│                      ▼ ═╗DOSUTIL .MEU      6,660     06-17-88        ▼  │
│                      ↓ ═╗DRIVER  .SYS      5,274     06-17-88        ↓  │
├────────────────────────────────────────────────────────────────────────┤
│ F10=Actions   Shift+F9=Command Prompt                                    │
└────────────────────────────────────────────────────────────────────────┘
```

Figure 17-7. The File menu

So that you can quickly pick out the available menu items, in graphics mode the Shell displays unavailable choices in broken gray letters, as shown in Figure 17-7; in text mode the Shell replaces the key letters of unavailable choices with an asterisk.

Because no file is selected right now, the only available choices are *Delete*, *Rename*, *Create directory*, and *Select all*. The ellipsis (...) following *Delete*, *Rename*, and *Create directory* means that the Shell will prompt you for more information before carrying out those choices. *Delete* and *Rename* are available because the Shell lets you delete and rename directories as well as files.

This topic shows you a few of the File menu items; you can explore the rest. Most of the items are self-explanatory, but a few might not seem obvious. *Associate* lets you tell the Shell to run an application program when you select a file with a particular file extension. You might associate your word-processing program, for example, with files whose extension is DOC. *Select all* means select all the files in the selected directory, so that you can, for example, copy or move them all; *Deselect all* means select none of the files in the selected directory, even if you have selected some.

Copying a File

To see how the Shell prompts you for additional information, press Esc and the Tab key to move the highlight to the list of files. Scroll through the list of files on the right side of the screen until you see DOSSHELL.BAT, and then select the file by highlighting it and pressing the spacebar. Now select *Copy* from the File menu; the screen should look like Figure 17-8.

```
 10-16-89                    File System                    1:49 pm
  File   Options   Arrange   Exit                          F1=Help
  Ctrl+letter selects a drive.
 ▭A   ▭B   ▭C   ▭D   ▭E

 E:\DOS
       Directory Tree                          *.*
                         ┌──────── Copy File ────────┐      06-17-88  ↑
    E:\                  │                           │      06-17-88  ≈
   ✓└─DOS                │                           │      06-17-88
                         │  From:  ┌DOSSHELL.BAT    ─→│      06-17-88
                         │         └                 │      06-17-88
                         │  To:    ┌E:\DOS          ─→│      06-17-88
                         │         └                 │      06-17-88
                         │                           │      06-17-88
                         │                           │      06-17-88
                         │                           │      06-17-88
                         │  ┌←─┘=Enter┐┌Esc=Cancel┐┌F1=Help┐  06-17-88
                         │  └         ┘└          ┘└       ┘  06-17-88
                         └───────────────────────────┘
                              COUNTRY .SYS    12,838  06-17-88
                           ▭DEBUG    .COM    21,606  06-17-88
                           ▭DISKCOMP .COM     9,889  06-17-88
                           ▭DISKCOPY .COM    10,428  06-17-88
                           ▭DISPLAY  .SYS    15,741  06-17-88
                           ▭DOSSHELL .BAT       184  04-13-89
                        ≈  ▭DOSUTIL  .MEU     6,660  06-17-88  ≈
                        ↓  ▭DRIVER   .SYS     5,274  06-17-88  ↓
 F10=Actions  Shift+F9=Command Prompt
```

Figure 17-8. Copying a file

The Shell displays a window in the middle of the screen titled *Copy File*. The window, called a *dialog box,* is what the Shell uses to ask for any additional information it needs in order to carry out a menu choice. The *From* field is already filled in with *DOSSHELL.BAT*, the file you selected to copy, and the cursor is in the *To* field. Notice that it already contains the name of the current directory, C:\DOS, with the cursor under the C. You must include a path name when you copy files; the path here is correct, so press the End key to move the cursor to the end of the directory name, and then type \ *fred.bat* (don't forget the backslash). Press Enter.

The dialog box disappears, and FRED.BAT is added to the list of files in \DOS (again, you can scroll to find the file). It's just as if you had typed the command *copy dosshell.bat fred.bat* at the system prompt.

Moving a file works just like copying a file, but the Shell deletes the original file after making the new copy. If you used the Shell to move DOSSHELL.BAT from \DOS to the root directory, for example, it would be as if you typed *copy dosshell.bat* \ and *erase dosshell.bat.*

Viewing a File

Viewing a file is a quick way to see what's in it; you can't change the file—you can only look at it. Select DOSSHELL.BAT again, then select *View* from the File menu. The screen should look like Figure 17-9.

```
 10-16-89                      File System                      1:51 pm
                                                               F1=Help
 ┌──────────────────────────────────────────────────────────────────┐
 │                           File View                                │
 │                                                                    │
 │    To view a file's content press  PgUp  or  PgDn .                │
 │                                                                    │
 │    Viewing file:   E:\DOS\DOSSHELL.BAT                             │
 └──────────────────────────────────────────────────────────────────┘

 @C:
 @CD C:\DOS
 @SHELLB DOSSHELL
 @IF ERRORLEVEL 255 GOTO END
 :COMMON
 @BREAK=OFF
 @SHELLC /MOS:PCIBMDRV.MOS/TRAN/COLOR/DOS/MENU/MUL/SND/MEU:SHELL.MEU/CLR:SHELL.CL
 R/PROMPT/MAINT/EXIT/SWAP/DATE
 :END
 @BREAK=ON

                                    ▷

 <─┘=Enter   Esc=Cancel   F9=Hex/ASCII
```

Figure 17-9. Viewing a file in ASCII

The top few lines identify the screen (*File View*) and the name of the file, and tell you that you can press the PgUp and PgDn keys to scroll through the file. If you're using a mouse, you can also click on the PgUp and PgDn symbols to scroll.

You can view the file either as you see it now—in *ASCII mode,* so called because you're looking at the file translated into characters according to the American Standard Code for Information Interchange, or ASCII—or in the hexadecimal representation of the characters in the file. To see the hexadecimal view, press F9. (If you're using a mouse, you can click on the *F9* at the bottom of the screen.) Now the screen should look like Figure 17-10.

Each line of the hexadecimal view shows 16 characters. The first column of numbers at the left margin is the address—in hexadecimal, of course—of the beginning of each line, starting at 0 at the beginning of the file. Each of the middle four columns of numbers is the hexadecimal representation of four characters, two digits per character. The 16 columns at the right show the ASCII characters that correspond to the hexadecimal digits in the line.

```
 10-16-89                        File System                        1:51 pm
                                                                 F1=Help

                                   File View

        To view a file's content press PgUp or PgDn .

        Viewing file:   E:\DOS\DOSSHELL.BAT


      000000    40433A0D  0A404344  20433A5C  444F530D    .C....CD.C..DOS.
      000010    0A405348  454C4C42  20444F53  5348454C    ..SHELLB.DOSSHEL
      000020    4C0D0A40  49462045  52524F52  4C455645    L...IF.ERRORLEVE
      000030    4C203235  3520474F  544F2045  4E440D0A    L.255.GOTO.END..
      000040    3A434F4D  4D4F4E0D  0A404252  45414B3D    :.COMMON...BREAK.
      000050    4F46460D  0A405348  454C4C43  202F4D4F    OFF...SHELLC..MO
      000060    533A5043  49424D44  52562E4D  4F532F54    S.PCIBMDRV.MOS.T
      000070    52414E2F  434F4C4F  522F444F  532F4D45    RAN.COLOR.DOS.ME
      000080    4E552F4D  554C2F53  4E442F4D  45552E53    NU.MUL.SND.MEU.S
      000090    48454C4C  2E4D4555  2F434C52  3A534845    HELL.MEU.CLR.SHE
      0000A0    4C4C2E43  4C522F50  524F4D50  542F4D41    LL.CLR.PROMPT.MA
      0000B0    494E542F  45584954  2F535741  502F4441    INT.EXIT.SWAP.DA
      0000C0    54450D0A  3A454E44  0D0A4042  5245414B    TE...END...BREAK
      0000D0    3D4F4E0D  0A                              .ON..




 <─┘=Enter    Esc=Cancel   F9=Hex\ASCII
```

Figure 17-10. Viewing a file in hexadecimal

This way of looking at a file is normally used by programmers who must often work with files of program code that have no human-readable representation, but you might sometimes find it useful if you want to know exactly what characters are in a file, including those that don't represent normal characters.

Press (or click) F9 again, and the display returns to the ASCII view. Press Esc (if you're using a mouse, you can click the *Esc* at the bottom of the screen) to return to the File System display.

Deleting a File

Using the Shell, you can delete one file, several files, or even all files in a directory (or the directory itself) simply by selecting the file, files, or (empty) directory you want to delete, then selecting *Delete* from the File menu. Because it's so easy to change directories and select files in the Shell, using the Shell to erase files you no longer need from many different directories is a snap compared to typing Change Directory and Erase commands at the DOS system prompt.

You can tell the DOS Erase command to prompt you for confirmation before deleting a file, but the Shell goes DOS one better: You can protect yourself not only against inadvertently deleting a file with the Erase command, but also against inadvertently replacing a file by copying another file in its place.

Simply because the Shell makes it so quick and easy to delete files, it's a good idea to make sure that the Shell will ask you to confirm each deletion.

Protecting Yourself

To protect yourself against inadvertently deleting a file, select the Options menu, then select *File Options*. The Shell displays the dialog box shown in Figure 17-11.

```
┌─────────────────────────────────────────────────────────────────┐
│ 10-16-89                    File System                  1:52 pm  │
│  File  Options  Arrange  Exit                            F1=Help  │
│  Ctrl+letter selects a drive.                                     │
│  ⊜A  ⊜B  ⊐C  ⊐D  ⊐E                                               │
│ E:╔═══════════════ File Options ═══════════════╗                  │
│   ║                                            ║        *.*        │
│  E║   ⊠  Confirm on delete          │ .CPI       6,404  06-17-88  │
│ ✓└║   ⊠  Confirm on replace         │ .CPI         641  06-17-88  │
│   ║   ☐  Select across directories  │ .CPI         402  06-17-88  │
│   ║                                 │ .SYS       9,148  06-17-88  │
│   ║                                ID .EXE      11,170  06-17-88  │
│   ║                                :N .COM       5,785  06-17-88  │
│   ║  (◄┘=Enter) (Esc=Cancel) (F1=Help) B .EXE   18,247  06-17-88  │
│   ╚══════════════════════════════════╝P .COM    33,754  06-17-88  │
│                               ⊜BASIC    .COM     1,065  06-17-88  │
│                               ⊜BASICA   .COM    36,285  06-17-88  │
│                               ⊜CHKDSK   .COM    17,771  06-17-88  │
│                               ⊜COMMAND  .COM    37,637  06-17-88  │
│                               ⊜COMP     .COM     9,491  06-17-88  │
│                               ⊡COUNTRY  .SYS    12,838  06-17-88  │
│                               ⊜DEBUG    .COM    21,606  06-17-88  │
│                               ⊜DISKCOMP.COM      9,889  06-17-88  │
│                               ⊜DISKCOPY.COM     10,428  06-17-88  │
│                               ⊡DISPLAY .SYS     15,741  06-17-88  │
│                               ⊜DOSSHELL.BAT        184  04-13-89  │
│                               ⊡DOSUTIL .MEU      6,660  06-17-88  │
│                               ⊡DRIVER  .SYS      5,274  06-17-88  │
│  F10=Actions   Shift+F9=Command Prompt                            │
└─────────────────────────────────────────────────────────────────┘
```

Figure 17-11. File Options dialog box

The box to the left of each option contains an X if the option is active (in text mode, a right-pointing triangle is displayed to the left of an active option). Selecting an active option turns it off; selecting an inactive option turns it on.

Confirm on delete means the Shell should prompt you for confirmation before deleting a file. *Confirm on replace* protects you against a less-obvious way of losing a file: It means the Shell should prompt you for confirmation before copying over an existing file.

It's not quite so obvious what *Select across directories* means; take this opportunity to check out the Shell's Help feature. Highlight *Select across directories* (with the arrow keys or the mouse) and press F1. The Shell should display the Help window shown in Figure 17-12.

As the Help window explains, this option controls whether the Shell remembers which files you selected when you change directories, or whether it starts over each time you change directories. Press Esc to get rid of the Help window, make sure that both *Confirm on delete* and *Confirm on replace* are active, and press Enter.

Now to delete a file. A while ago you created a file named FRED.BAT by copying DOSSHELL.BAT. You don't need FRED.BAT, so select it, then select *Delete* from the File menu. The Shell displays the Delete File dialog box, which simply shows the name of the file to be deleted; press Enter (or click on *Enter* at the bottom of the dialog box). Now the Shell displays the confirming dialog box shown in Figure 17-13.

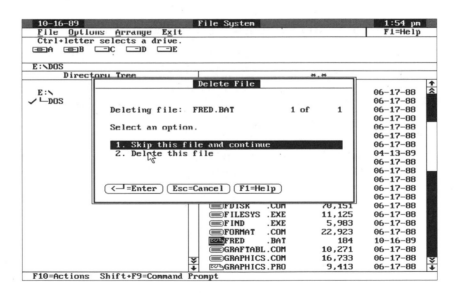

Figure 17-12. Select across directories *Help window*

Figure 17-13. *Delete File dialog box*

This is how the Shell gives you a second chance. The first line shows the name of the file to be deleted and a count of how many files are to be deleted. You selected only one file, so FRED.BAT is 1 of 1. The first numbered option tells the Shell not to delete the file named in the first line, but to go on to confirm the next file to be deleted (if you selected more than one); the second numbered option deletes the file named in the first line and continues if you selected more than one file.

The first option is highlighted. If you pressed Enter now (or clicked on this item), the Delete operation would be canceled because you selected only one file. Select the second option (either use the Down Arrow key and press Enter, or click on the second option) to delete FRED.BAT and return to the File System display.

You can delete an entire directory and its contents in two quick steps with the Shell. Because it's so easy, first make sure you do, indeed, want to eliminate both the directory and everything in it (one or a few valuable files might be hidden in a welter of unnecessary ones). If you decide to delete the directory and its contents, select the directory and then select all files in it with the *Select all* option on the File menu. Choose the File menu again, select *Delete*, and press Enter to begin deleting the files as already described. When that's done, select *Delete* a second time and press Enter.

If you have not set *Confirm on delete*, the directory's gone. If you have set *Confirm on delete*, the Shell prompts you to confirm before deleting the directory. Notice, however, that you must, in either case, first delete all files in the directory. Just as when you use the Remove Directory command at the DOS system prompt, the Shell (or DOS) refuses to remove a directory that contains any files. Likewise, you cannot delete any directory that contains subdirectories. Nor can you delete (or rename) the root directory, because each disk must contain this directory.

Using the Options and Arrange Menus

You just used File Options from the Options menu to protect against inadvertently deleting or copying over a file. Other choices on the Options and Arrange menus let you specify the order in which file names are listed; display information about the selected file, directory, and disk; display the files in two directories at once; and display all the files on the selected disk.

Controlling the Order in Which
File Names Are Displayed

When you first start the Shell, the File System displays the file names in alphabetic order. You can change this order to display the files arranged by extension, date, size, or even the order in which they are stored on the disk. To display the files arranged by extension, select *Display options* from the Options menu. The Shell displays the Display Options dialog box, as shown in Figure 17-14.

The options are in the list at the right side of the dialog box. Only one of the options can be active; it's indicated by a dot inside the circle (a right-facing triangle in text mode). Select *Extension* (if you're not using a mouse, you must first use the Tab key to select the option list within the dialog box) and press Enter. Now the files are listed alphabetically by extension—BAT files, then COM files, and so forth.

```
┌─────────────────────────────────────────────────────────────────────────────┐
│ 10-16-89                        File System                        1:58 pm    │
│  File  Options  Arrange  Exit                                 F1=Help         │
│  Ctrl+letter selects a drive.                                                 │
│  ⊞A   ⊞B ▷C  □D   □E                                                          │
├─────────────────────────────────────────────────────────────────────────────┤
│ E:\DOS                                                                         │
│      Directory Tree                                    *.*                     │
│                       ┌──── Display Options ────┐           06-17-88      ▲    │
│    E:\                │                          │           06-17-88      ▲    │
│    └─DOS              │   Name:  *.*             │           06-17-88           │
│  ✓                    │                          │           06-17-88           │
│                       │              Sort by:    │           06-17-88           │
│                       │                          │           06-17-88           │
│                       │          ⦿  Name         │           06-17-88           │
│                       │          ○  Extension    │           06-17-88           │
│                       │          ○  Date         │           06-17-88           │
│                       │          ○  Size         │           06-17-88           │
│                       │          ○  Disk order   │           06-17-88           │
│                       │                          │           06-17-88           │
│                       │ ⎣←┘=Enter⎦ ⎣Esc=Cancel⎦ ⎣F1=Help⎦    06-17-88           │
│                       └──────────────────────────┘           06-17-88           │
│                        COUNTRY .SYS       12,838   06-17-88                     │
│                        DEBUG   .COM       21,606   06-17-88                     │
│                        DISKCOMP.COM        9,889   06-17-88                     │
│                        DISKCOPY.COM       10,428   06-17-88                     │
│                        DISPLAY .SYS       15,741   06-17-88                     │
│                        DOSSHELL.BAT          184   04-13-89                     │
│                        DOSUTIL .MEU        6,660   06-17-88      ▼              │
│                        DRIVER  .SYS        5,274   06-17-88      ▼              │
├─────────────────────────────────────────────────────────────────────────────┤
│ F10=Actions   Shift+F9=Command Prompt                                          │
└─────────────────────────────────────────────────────────────────────────────┘
```

Figure 17-14. The Display Options window

Displaying File, Directory, and Disk Information

The *Show information* choice of the Options menu displays a window that contains information about the selected file, directory, and disk. Select FORMAT.COM, then select *Show information* from the Options menu. The screen should look like the one in Figure 17-15.

```
┌─────────────────────────────────────────────────────────────────────────────┐
│ 10-16-89                        File System                        1:59 pm    │
│  File  Options  Arrange  Exit                                 F1=Help         │
│  Ctr ┌──── Show Information ────┐                                              │
│  ⊞A  │                          │                                             │
│      │  File                    │                                             │
│ E:\D │    Name  : FORMAT.COM    │                                   *.*        │
│      │    Attr  : ...a          │                                             │
│      │  Selected        E       │  DOSSHELL.BAT       214   04-13-89     ▲     │
│    E:│    Number:        1       │  SHELL   .CLR     4,438   06-17-88     ▲     │
│  ✓ └─│    Size  :   22,923      │  COMMAND .COM    37,637   06-17-88           │
│      │  Directory               │  DISKCOPY.COM    10,428   06-17-88           │
│      │    Name  : DOS           │  FDISK   .COM    70,151   06-17-88           │
│      │    Size  : 1,107,634     │  FORMAT  .COM    22,923   06-17-88           │
│      │    Files :       64      │  KEYB    .COM    14,759   06-17-88           │
│      │  Disk                    │  SYS     .COM    11,472   06-17-88           │
│      │    Name  : SMALL_ONE     │  ASSIGN  .COM     5,785   06-17-88           │
│      │    Size  : 6,250,496     │  BASIC   .COM     1,065   06-17-88           │
│      │    Avail : 5,025,792     │  BASICA  .COM    36,285   06-17-88           │
│      │    Files :       73      │  COMP    .COM     9,491   06-17-88           │
│      │    Dirs  :        2      │  DEBUG   .COM    21,606   06-17-88           │
│      │                          │  DISKCOMP.COM     9,889   06-17-88           │
│      │ ⎣Esc=Cancel⎦ ⎣F1=Help⎦   │  EDLIN   .COM    14,294   06-17-88           │
│      └──────────────────────────┘  LABEL   .COM     4,490   06-17-88           │
│                                    MODE    .COM    23,056   08-03-88           │
│                                    MORE    .COM     2,166   06-17-88           │
│                                    TREE    .COM     6,334   06-17-88           │
│                                    CHKDSK  .COM    17,771   06-17-88     ▼     │
│                                    PRINT   .COM    14,024   08-03-88     ▼     │
├─────────────────────────────────────────────────────────────────────────────┤
│ F10=Actions   Shift+F9=Command Prompt                                          │
└─────────────────────────────────────────────────────────────────────────────┘
```

Figure 17-15. The Show Information window

There's nothing in this window for you to type or select; it simply shows you the following information:

- *File* shows the name and attributes of the selected file (the last file selected if you've chosen more than one).

- *Selected* shows the letter of the selected disk and the number and total size of all selected files; if you're displaying directories from two disks, it shows both disk letters and the number and total size of all selected files on both disks.

- *Directory* shows the name of the directory containing the file named under *File*, the number of bytes taken up by all the files in the directory, and the number of files. (Knowing the size of a directory can be extremely useful in certain operations, such as copying a directory and its contents from a fixed disk to a diskette.)

- *Disk* shows the name (volume label), total capacity, available space, number of files, and number of directories on the disk containing the file named at the top of the window under *File*.

Press or click on Esc to remove the Show Information window from the screen.

Displaying Two Directories at Once

The Shell lets you display the files in two directories, on the same or different drives. First, select *Multiple file list* from the Arrange (not Options) menu. The Shell divides the middle portion of the screen horizontally into two windows, one above the other. The windows are nearly identical: Each includes the disk-drive list, diagram of the directory structure, and files in the selected directory. The only difference is that the name of the current directory appears above the top window border.

In this example, the top file window lists the names of the files in the directory \DOS on the system disk (usually drive C), and the bottom file window lists the names of the files in the root directory, as shown in Figure 17-16.

You can use either window to select files to copy, delete, or view, or to use any other Shell function. You can even view directories on two disks by selecting a different drive in one of the windows.

Return the display to one directory again by selecting *Single file list* from the Arrange menu.

```
┌──────────────────────────────────────────────────────────────────┬──────────┐
│ 10-16-89                         File System                      │ 1:59 pm  │
├──────────────────────────────────────────────────────────────────┼──────────┤
│  File  Options  Arrange  Exit                                     │ F1=Help  │
├───────────────────────────────────────────────────────────────────┴──────────┤
│ Ctrl+letter selects a drive.                                                 │
│  ▭A   ▭B   ▭C   ▭D   ▭E          ⇲                                           │
├──────────────────────────────────────────────────────────────────────────────┤
│ E:\DOS                                                                        │
├───────────────────────────────────┬──────────────────────────────────────────┤
│          Directory Tree           │                *.*                       │
├───────────────────────────────────┼──────────────────────────────────────────┤
│ E:\                            ▲  │ ▭DOSSHELL.BAT        214   04-13-89    ▲  │
│ ✓└─DOS                         ⏶  │ ▣SHELL   .CLR      4,438   06-17-88       │
│                                   │ ▭COMMAND .COM     37,637   06-17-88       │
│                                   │ ▭DISKCOPY.COM     10,428   06-17-88    ⏷  │
│                                ⏷  │ ▭FDISK   .COM     70,151   06-17-88    ▼  │
│                                ▼  │                                          │
├───────────────────────────────────┴──────────────────────────────────────────┤
│  ▭A   ▭B   ▭C   ▭D   ▭E                                                      │
├───────────────────────────────────┬──────────────────────────────────────────┤
│          Directory Tree           │                *.*                       │
├───────────────────────────────────┼──────────────────────────────────────────┤
│ ✓E:\                           ▲  │ ▭AUTOEXEC.BAT      1,290   04-13-89    ▲  │
│   └─DOS                        ⏶  │ ▭COMMAND .COM     37,637   06-17-88       │
│                                   │ ▣CONFIG  .SYS        217   04-13-89       │
│                                   │                                          │
│                                   │                                          │
│                                ⏷  │                                       ⏷  │
│                                ▼  │                                       ▼  │
├──────────────────────────────────────────────────────────────────────────────┤
│  F10=Actions   Shift+F9=Command Prompt                                       │
└──────────────────────────────────────────────────────────────────────────────┘
```

Figure 17-16. Displaying two directories

Displaying All the File Names on a Disk

Sometimes you can't remember just where you stored a file. Rather than search
through each directory, you can tell the Shell to list the name of each file on the disk.
Searching through one list—even if it's a long one—is much quicker than selecting a
directory and searching its file list, then selecting another directory and searching its
file list, and so forth, especially if you know the file's name, extension, or date of
creation and you use *Display options* on the Options menu to sort the files in that particular order.

To display information about the files in all directories, select *System file list* from
the Arrange menu. Nothing might appear for a few seconds, but soon the Shell displays a list of files. The order in which the files are displayed is the same as the order
in which files were displayed in the single file list.

This completes a quick tour of the File System. You didn't use all its capabilities,
but you should have a good feeling for what it can do for you. Although the Shell isn't
suited for everything you'll do with DOS, it makes many routine file-management
tasks much simpler and quicker.

Leaving the File System and the Shell

The Exit menu simply lets you leave the File System (or continue operating the File
System if you change your mind). To return to the Start Programs part of the Shell,
either select *Exit File System* from the Exit menu or press F3. (To leave the Shell, just
press F3 again or select *Exit Shell* from the Start Programs Exit menu.)

START PROGRAMS

The Shell once again displays the Start Programs screen, shown earlier in Figure 17-1. Rather than displaying a list of directories and files in the middle of the screen, as the File System does, Start Programs displays four choices: *Command Prompt*, *File System*, *Change Colors*, and *DOS Utilities*.

These four choices represent the upper level of Start Programs' two-level structure. As you become adept at using the Shell, you can tailor this list of choices, adding either individual programs or groups of programs to it—a group named *word processing,* perhaps, that contains your word processor and associated programs, or a group named *financial* that contains your spreadsheet or accounting programs. The second level would then contain the programs themselves—Microsoft Word, dBASE III, Microsoft Excel, or whatever other programs you use, grouped according to the preferences you used in setting up your Start Programs screen.

On the original Start Programs screen, selecting *File System*, as you saw earlier, starts the File System. *Command Prompt* temporarily stops the Shell and displays the DOS system prompt so that you can type DOS commands; you return to the Shell by typing *exit*. *Change Colors* lets you choose one of several color combinations the Shell offers. These three choices are all programs.

The ellipsis after *DOS Utilities* tells you that this choice represents a group, which means that the Shell changes the screen to show new choices instead of starting a program. The choices in the utilities group let you perform some routine DOS operations on disks and files.

Like the File System, Start Programs displays the names of additional menus on the second line. You use the choices in the main part of the window to start a program or display a group of related choices you add to the Shell; the *Program* and *Group* menus named on the second line contain choices that let you manage or add to the choices on the main screen. The *Exit* menu lets you leave the Shell and return to DOS.

The Program Menu

The Program menu lets you add a program to the Start Programs screen, change the definition of one of the existing program choices, delete an added program from the list of choices, or copy a program to a different group of choices. (*Start* simply starts a program; it has the same effect as selecting the highlighted choice by pressing Enter or double-clicking on the item.)

You can't change the File System, Change Colors, or Command Prompt items on the Start Programs screen. If you select the Program menu with one of these items highlighted, the only available options are *Start* and *Add*. You can modify the DOS Utilities group and the individual programs it contains.

Adding a Program

Adding a program can be fairly simple. Suppose you wanted to add an entry to the Start Programs screen. The entry would be called *Memory Check* and would carry out the DOS Mem command. (No, you wouldn't be apt to do this, but it provides a simple, universal example.) Select *Add* from the Program menu. The Shell displays the Add Program dialog box, shown in Figure 17-17.

```
┌──────────────────────────────────────────────────────────────────────┐
│ 10-16-89                    Start Programs                    2:01 pm  │
│  Program  Group  Exit                                        F1=Help   │
│                            Main Group                                  │
│              To select an item, use the up and down arrows.            │
│            To start a program or display a new group, press Enter.     │
│                                                                        │
│ Command Prompt                                                         │
│ File System    ┌───────────────── Add Program ─────────────────┐       │
│ Change Colors  │                                               │       │
│ DOS Utilities..│ Required                                      │       │
│                │                                               │       │
│                │  Title . . . .  [            ]          [→]   │       │
│                │                                               │       │
│                │  Commands  . .  [            ]          [→]   │       │
│                │                                               │       │
│                │ Optional                                      │       │
│                │                                               │       │
│                │  Help text . .  [            ]          [→]   │       │
│                │                                               │       │
│                │  Password  . .  [         ]                   │       │
│                │                                               │       │
│                │   (Esc=Cancel)  (F1=Help)  (F2=Save)          │       │
│                │                                               │       │
│                └───────────────────────────────────────────────┘       │
│                                                                        │
│                                                                        │
│ F10=Actions              Shift+F9=Command Prompt                       │
└──────────────────────────────────────────────────────────────────────┘
```

Figure 17-17. Adding a program to the main group

For this simple example, you need to fill in only the *Title* and *Commands* fields to define the new entry. The *Title* field specifies how the Start Programs item will read; type *Memory Check* and press Enter or the Tab key. The cursor moves to the *Commands* field, which specifies the command to be carried out; type *mem*. To end the definition and add the entry to the Start Program screen, press F2.

The Add Program dialog box disappears, and now the last item in the menu should read *Memory Check*. Select it and press Enter; but watch closely. The screen clears and DOS briefly displays the report of the Mem command, but before you really have time to read it, DOS displays the Shell screen again. You can fix that because the Shell lets one entry carry out more than one command. The Pause command tells DOS to display the message *Press any key to continue . . .*, then waits for you to press a key. If you tell the Shell to carry out a Pause command after the Mem command, you can read the report, then press any key to return to the Shell.

Changing a Program's Definition

Memory Check should still be highlighted; if it isn't, highlight it with the arrow keys or by clicking on it with the mouse, then select *Change* from the Program menu. The Shell displays the Change Program dialog box, shown in Figure 17-18.

```
┌──────────────────────────────────────────────────────────────────────┐
│ 10-16-89              Start Programs                     2:03 pm       │
│  Program  Group  Exit                                   F1=Help        │
│                         Main Group                                     │
│              To select an item, use the up and down arrows.            │
│         To start a program or display a new group, press Enter.        │
│                                                                        │
│ Command Prompt                                                         │
│ File System        ┌──────────────────────────────────────────┐       │
│ Change Colors      │             Change Program                │       │
│ DOS Utilities..    │                                           │       │
│ Memory Check       │ Required                                  │       │
│                    │                                           │       │
│                    │   Title . . . .  [Memory Check        ]→  │       │
│                    │                                           │       │
│                    │   Commands  . .  [mem                 ]→  │       │
│                    │                                           │       │
│                    │ Optional                                  │       │
│                    │                                           │       │
│                    │   Help text . .  [                    ]→  │       │
│                    │                                           │       │
│                    │   Password  . .  [            ]           │       │
│                    │                                           │       │
│                    │   ( Esc=Cancel ) ( F1=Help ) ( F2=Save )  │       │
│                    └──────────────────────────────────────────┘       │
│                                                                        │
│ F10=Actions              Shift+F9=Command Prompt                       │
└──────────────────────────────────────────────────────────────────────┘
```

Figure 17-18. Changing a program definition

Because you're changing the definition of an existing item, the *Title* and *Commands* fields are filled in. You want to add to the *Commands* field, so move the cursor to that field by clicking on it with the mouse or by pressing the Tab key. Now press the End key to move the cursor to the end of *mem*.

To carry out more than one command, you separate the commands by pressing the F4 key, which displays a double vertical bar. Press F4, then type *pause*. The same dialog box also lets you specify what the Shell displays if someone should press F1 for Help when the item is selected; for good measure, tab to the *Help text* field and type *This carries out the DOS Mem command*. Now the screen should look like Figure 17-19.

This version tells DOS to carry out the Mem command, then the Pause command. Press F2 to save the new definition, then press Enter to select your menu item (which should still be highlighted). DOS displays the report of the Mem command, followed by the Pause command message, and waits for you to press any key. Now you can read how much memory is installed and available. Press a key to return to the Shell.

To check out the Help message, press F1. The Shell displays the Help window, which now contains the text you typed in the *Help text* field.

```
┌─10-16-89───────────────── Start Programs ────────────── 2:05 pm─┐
│ Program  Group  Exit                                   F1=Help  │
│                          Main Group                             │
│           To select an item, use the up and down arrows.        │
│       To start a program or display a new group, press Enter.   │
│                                                                 │
│ Command Prompt                                                  │
│ File System      ┌──────────── Change Program ────────────┐     │
│ Change Colors    │                                         │     │
│ DOS Utilities..  │ Required                                │     │
│ Memory Check     │                                         │     │
│                  │   Title . . . .  ┌Memory Check      ─┬►┐ │     │
│                  │                  └──────────────────┴──┘ │     │
│                  │   Commands  . .  ┌mem│pause         ─┬►┐ │     │
│                  │                  └──────────────────┴──┘ │     │
│                  │ Optional                                │     │
│                  │                                         │     │
│                  │   Help text . .  ┌◄DOS Mem command.│─┬►┐ │     │
│                  │                  └──────────────────┴──┘ │     │
│                  │   Password  . .  ┌──────────┐             │     │
│                  │                  └──────────┘             │     │
│                  │   ┌Esc=Cancel┐ ┌F1=Help┐ ┌F2=Save┐      │     │
│                  │   └──────────┘ └───────┘ └───────┘      │     │
│                  └─────────────────────────────────────────┘     │
│                                                                 │
│                                                                 │
│                                                                 │
│ F10=Actions          Shift+F9=Command Prompt                    │
└─────────────────────────────────────────────────────────────────┘
```

Figure 17-19. Specifying multiple commands for a Start Programs item

Deleting a Program

That's about as much as you can do with the Mem command. The example has served its purpose, so you'll delete the menu item you added. Make sure that *Memory Check* is still highlighted and select *Delete* from the Program menu. The Shell displays the Delete Item dialog box, shown in Figure 17-20.

```
┌─10-16-89───────────────── Start Programs ────────────── 2:06 pm─┐
│ Program  Group  Exit                                   F1=Help  │
│                          Main Group                             │
│           To select an item, use the up and down arrows.        │
│       To start a program or display a new group, press Enter.   │
│                                                                 │
│ Command Prompt                                                  │
│ File Sys┌──────────────── Delete Item ─────────────────┐        │
│ Change C│                                               │        │
│ DOS Util│                                               │        │
│ Memory C│  1. Delete this item                          │        │
│         │  2. Do not delete this item                   │        │
│         │                                               │        │
│         │  ┌◄─┘=Enter┐ ┌Esc=Cancel┐ ┌F1=Help┐          │        │
│         │  └─────────┘ └──────────┘ └───────┘          │        │
│         └───────────────────────────────────────────────┘        │
│                                                                 │
│                                                                 │
│                                                                 │
│                                                                 │
│                                                                 │
│                                                                 │
│                                                                 │
│ F10=Actions          Shift+F9=Command Prompt                    │
└─────────────────────────────────────────────────────────────────┘
```

Figure 17-20. Deleting a Start Programs item

Like the Delete File dialog box, the Delete Item dialog box offers two numbered choices that delete or leave the item. Choice 1, which deletes the selected Start Programs item, is highlighted; select it by pressing Enter or by clicking on it with the mouse. The Shell continues to display the Start Programs screen, but now *Memory Check* is gone.

Running an Application Program From the Shell

You could follow the steps of the preceding simple example to add one of your application programs, such as a word processor or a spreadsheet, to the Start Programs screen. But with a bit more effort, you can both add a program and create a dialog box of your own that prompts you to enter one or more parameters before DOS carries out the command and starts the program. This lets you specify a particular file name, for example, or type other parameters when you run an application program.

You can also specify: the name of the dialog box that the Shell displays, the wording of the prompt, the wording of the instructions that the Shell displays before each parameter field, and a value for the Shell to assume if you don't specify a parameter, all in the *Commands* field of the Add or Change Program dialog box. You'll use a few of these in the next example to see how they work.

Adding a Group of Programs

Suppose you wanted to run Edlin from the Shell (again, you probably wouldn't want to do this, but it's a program that everyone has, so it serves as a universal example of adding a program with more complex parameters), and suppose you wanted to create a separate program group named *Text Files* that would contain Edlin.

First, select *Add* from the Group menu. The Shell displays the Add Group dialog box shown in Figure 17-21.

As the dialog box shows, you must enter a title for the group (this will be the wording of the item on the Start Programs screen) and a file name (this will contain the program-group definition). The Shell creates the file and provides the extension MEU; all you have to type is a name for the file. If you wish, you can also specify the Help text that the Shell displays if F1 is pressed when the group name is highlighted, and you can add a password that must be entered in order to use the group. You'll enter all of these except the password in this example.

First, type *Text Files* in the *Title* field. Tab to the *Filename* field and type *textfile*, then tab to the *Help text* field and type *Programs for working with text files*. Press F2 to save these entries; the Shell creates the file TEXTFILE.MEU that contains these entries and displays the full Start Programs screen again, this time with the added item *Text Files*.

```
 ▓10-16-89▓                    Start Programs                     2:07 pm
  Program   Group   Exit                                          F1=Help
                                Main Group
         ↖ To select an item, use the up and down arrows.
        To start a program or display a new group, press Enter.

 Command Prompt
 File System              ┌──────────── Add Group ────────────┐
 Change Colors            │                                   │
 ▓DOS Utilities..▓        │  Required                         │
                          │                                   │
                          │    Title . . . . ┌──────────┐→│  │
                          │                                   │
                          │    Filename  . . ┌──────────┐     │
                          │                                   │
                          │  Optional                         │
                          │                                   │
                          │    Help text . . ┌──────────┐→│  │
                          │                                   │
                          │    Password  . . ┌──────────┐     │
                          │                                   │
                          │   ( Esc=Cancel ) ( F1=Help ) ( F2=Save )  │
                          └───────────────────────────────────┘



  F10=Actions              Shift+F9=Command Prompt
```

Figure 17-21. Adding a program group

Select the new item and press Enter. The title line in the main portion of the display changes from *Main Group* to *Text Files*, but instead of a list of program choices, you see the message *Group is empty.* You just created the group, so of course there aren't any programs in it. As you add programs to the Text Files group, the Shell adds the entries that define the programs to TEXTFILE.MEU.

Adding a Program with Style

Except in the simplest case (the earlier Memory Check example), adding a program with the *Add* option of the Program menu can also include typing parameters in the *Commands* field. These parameters define one or more prompts that the Shell displays in a dialog box. You can specify for each prompt the title and text for the dialog box, any Help text, and a value that the Shell assumes if you just press Enter in response to the prompt (the default value). When you fill in the *Commands* field, you enclose the parameters that define each prompt in a pair of square brackets ([ ]). If you don't specify any title, instructions, or prompt text for a prompt, the Shell supplies generic wording for these text elements.

When you select a program and respond to the prompts, the Shell creates a temporary batch file that contains the DOS commands required to perform the tasks according to your responses. (Batch files are described in Chapters 12, 14, and 15.) After you respond to the final prompt and press Enter to start the program, the Shell tells DOS to carry out the temporary batch file. In addition to the parameters you use to define the prompts for a command, you can include any command in the *Commands* field that you would use in a batch file.

Shell Program Definition Parameters

Figure 17-22 describes the parameters you can enter in the *Commands* entry field to define the prompts of a program you've added to the Shell. Unless the description specifies otherwise, the parameters must be enclosed in the pair of square brackets that define a prompt.

Parameter	Effect
`/T"<text>"`	Specifies the title for the dialog box. Maximum length is 40 characters.
`/I"<text>"`	Specifies the instruction to be displayed above the entry field in the dialog box. Maximum length is 40 characters.
`/P"<text>"`	Specifies the text of the prompt to be displayed to the left of the entry field. Maximum length is 20 characters.
`%<n>`	If you enter this as the first parameter inside the pair of brackets that defines a prompt, the Shell remembers whatever is typed in response to the prompt. `<n>` can be any number from 1 through 10. You can use this saved value later in the program definition by including %n outside a pair of brackets. If the prompt calls for a file name, for example, and this parameter is specified as %1, then you could cause the file to be printed by including *print %1* outside a pair of brackets later in the program definition.
`/D"<text>"`	Specifies a default value that is to be displayed in the entry field.
`/D"%<n>"`	Specifies that the value saved for %n be displayed as the default value that the Shell will assume if nothing is typed in response to the prompt. `<n>` can be a number from 1 through 10. When the prompt is displayed, you can override this default by typing a new value over it and deleting any remaining characters (with the Del key).
`/R`	Specifies that the default value displayed in a prompt should be erased if any key other than Enter is pressed in response to the prompt.
`/L"<n>"`	Sets the maximum length of the prompt response. `<n>` can be a number from 1 through 127. If you don't specify this parameter, the Shell assumes a maximum length of 127.
`/M"e"`	Specifies that only the name of an existing file can be entered in response to the prompt.
`/C"%<n>"`	If the definition of the preceding prompt included a %n parameter, specifies that the saved value is to be the value for this prompt.
`/F"<file>"`	Tells the Shell to make sure that the file named by `<file>` exists before the command is carried out. The Shell doesn't carry out the command if `<file>` doesn't exist. If you include a drive letter with `<file>`, you can use this parameter to guarantee that the correct diskette is in the drive before the command is carried out.

Figure 17-22. Add Program command field parameters   (continued)

Figure 17-22. (Continued)

Parameter	Effect
/#	Inserts the drive letter, followed by a colon, from which the Shell was started. Don't enclose this parameter in square brackets.
/@	Inserts the path (string of directory names) from the root directory to the directory from which the Shell was started. Don't enclose this parameter in square brackets.

You're going to add the Edlin program to the Text Files group. The parameters you type in the *Commands* field will do the following:

1. Name the dialog box *Edlin Text Editor*. This requires the /T parameter: /T"Edlin Text Editor".

2. Display the instructions *Default file name is FRED.DOC* at the top of the dialog box. This requires the /I parameter: /I"Default file name is FRED.DOC".

3. Display the prompt *File name:* to the left of the entry field. This requires the /P parameter: /P"File name: ".

4. Display the default file name *FRED.DOC*. This requires the /D parameter: /D"fred.doc".

5. Clear the default file name if any key other than Enter is pressed in response to the prompt. This requires the /R parameter: /R.

Select *Add* from the Program menu. The Shell displays the Add Program dialog box, just as it did when you added *Memory Check* in the earlier example. The cursor is in the *Title* entry field, which specified the wording of the menu item; type *DOS Edlin Program* and press the Tab key or the Enter key to move to the *Commands* field.

For the Memory Check, all you entered in the *Commands* field was *mem‖ pause*; this time the entry will be quite a bit longer. Because this program issues only one prompt, you'll enclose the entire string of parameters in one pair of square brackets. Type the following as a single line; you're typing the Edlin command itself, followed by the parameters described in items 1 through 5 above:

```
edlin [/T"Edlin Text Editor" /I"Default file name is
FRED.DOC" /P"File name: " /D"fred.doc" /R]
```

When you have typed this line, press Tab or Enter to move to the Help text field and type the following:

```
Because you must specify a file name when you start the
Edlin program, this selection edits a file named FRED.DOC
(or creates the file if it doesn't exist) if you don't
specify a file name in response to the prompt.
```

Testing the Program You Added

Press F2 to save this definition, then press Enter to select DOS Edlin Program. The Shell should display the Edlin Text Editor dialog box shown in Figure 17-23.

```
┌─────────────────────────────────────────────────────────────────┐
│ 10-16-89                    Start Programs              2:11 pm   │
├─────────────────────────────────────────────────────┬───────────┤
│  Program  Group  Exit                                │  F1=Help  │
│                          Text Files...                           │
│              To select an item, use the up and down arrows.      │
│           To start a program or display a new group, press Enter.│
│ ┌─────────────────────────────────────────────────────┐         │
│ │ DOS Edlin Program                                     │         │
│ └─────────────────────────────────────────────────────┘         │
│                                                                  │
│                  ┌──────────────────────────────────┐            │
│                  │         Edlin Text Editor         │            │
│                  │                                    │           │
│                  │   Default file name is FRED.DOC    │           │
│                  │                                    │           │
│                  │   File name:  ┌Fred.doc      ┐ →   │           │
│                  │                                    │           │
│                  │  ┌<─┘=Enter┐ ┌Esc=Cancel┐ ┌F1=Help┐│           │
│                  └──────────────────────────────────┘            │
│                                                                  │
│ F10=Actions   Esc=Cancel   Shift+F9=Command Prompt               │
└──────────────────────────────────────────────────────────────────┘
```

Figure 17-23. The Edlin Text Editor dialog box

Check the title of the dialog box, the instruction line at the top, and the prompt to the left of the entry field. They should match the text that you typed with the /T, /I, and /P parameters. Now press F1; the Shell should display the Help window with the text you typed in the *Help text* field. Press Esc to get rid of the Help window.

The entry field contains *fred.doc*, the default file name you specified with the /D parameter. If you pressed Enter now, the Shell would tell DOS to run the command *edlin fred.doc*. Because there is no file named FRED.DOC, Edlin would create it and wait for you to enter some lines. Instead, you'll request the DOSSHELL.BAT file that comes with version 4 of DOS. First, type the letter *d*; because you specified the /R parameter, the Shell erases all of the default file name and displays *d*. Finish typing the file name:

```
dosshell.bat
```

Now press Enter. The screen should clear, then Edlin should display the message *End of input file*. To make sure you've got the right file, type *p* (the Edlin Page command). Edlin should display something like the following (your equivalent of line 7 might break at a different place):

```
1: @C:
2: @CD C:\DOS
3: @SHELLB DOSSHELL
4: @IF ERRORLEVEL 255 GOTO END
5: :COMMON
6: @BREAK=OFF
7: @SHELLC /MOS:PCIBMDRV.MOS/TRAN/COLOR/DOS/MENU/MUL/SND/
MEU:SHELL.MEU/CLR:SHELL.CLR/PROMPT/MAINT/EXIT/SWAP/DATE
8: :END
9: @BREAK=ON
*
_
```

You just wanted to verify that the Edlin command worked, so type *q* to quit Edlin without changing the file. When Edlin displays *Abort edit (Y/N)?*, type *y*. The Shell screen returns, showing your Text Files group and its only choice, *DOS Edlin Program*.

If the Shell doesn't respond as described, or if a window labeled *Warning* appears, telling you there is a problem with your Program Startup command, make sure *DOS Edlin Program* is highlighted, select *Change* from the Program menu, and compare the entries in the Title, Commands, and Help fields to the example instructions. Correct any differences, and try again.

The DOS Utilities Group

This section relies on several of the Shell's program-definition parameters to explain the DOS Utilities group, which you choose from the Start Programs screen. Figure 17-24 on the following page shows the definitions of each program in the DOS Utilities group that comes with the Shell. You can learn more about defining programs by selecting an item from this group and comparing how the program operates with its definition in Figure 17-24. (You can look at the definition itself too. Highlight the item and choose *Change* from the *Program* menu. Just don't change anything.)

Although the definitions are printed on several lines, they are entered in the *Commands* field as a continuous string. Blanks have been added to the definitions to make them more readable; the Shell ignores blanks between parameters, so you can enter these blanks—as you did in the Edlin example—to make your command definitions easier to read.

Item	Program Definition Parameters
Set Date and Time	`date [ /T"Set Date and Time Utility" /I "Enter new date ??-??-??" /L"8"] || time [ /T "Set Date and Time Utility" /I"Enter new time hh:mm" /L"5" ] || pause`
Disk Copy	`diskcopy [ /T"Diskcopy Utility" /I "Enter source and destination drives." /P "Drives . . " /D"a: b:" /R ] || pause`
Disk Compare	`diskcomp [ /T"Diskcomp Utility" /I "Enter drive for comparison." /P "Parameters . . " /D"a: b:" /R ] || pause`
Backup Fixed Disk	`backup [ /T"Backup Utility" /I"Enter source and destination drives." /P "Parameters . . " /D"c:\*.* a: /s" /R ] || pause`
Restore Fixed Disk	`restore [ /T"Restore Utility"/I"Enter source and destination drive." /P "Parameters . . " /D"a: c:\*.* /s" /R ] || pause`
Format	`format [ /T"Format Utility" /I "Enter drive to Format." / P"Parameters . . " /D"a: " /R ] || pause`

Figure 17-24. DOS Utilities group program definitions

Another way to learn how the program definition parameters work is to experiment: Change the parameters in one of the DOS Utilities program definitions with the Change Program function, then select the program to see the effect of the change. Before you do this, make a copy of the file DOSUTIL.MEU called DOSUTIL.SAV. DOSUTIL.MEU is in your DOS directory; select it and use the *Copy* command on the File menu to copy DOSUTIL.MEU to C:\DOS\DOSUTIL.SAV. To restore the original form of the DOS Utilities group later on, just erase the changed DOSUTIL.MEU from the \DOS directory and change the name of DOSUTIL.SAV back to DOSUTIL.MEU with the *Rename* command on the File menu.

The Edlin example showed the degree to which you can tailor the Shell to your own use. Although the example prepared only one command for DOS to carry out (the Edlin command with a file name as a parameter), you can prepare several commands, if necessary, by separating the commands with a double vertical bar (the F4 key) as you did in the Memory Check example. Each of the commands can have its own dialog box, with separate instructions, prompts, and default values. This should let you add any application program to the Shell menus and provide all the parameters you need to start the application program.

You added only one program to the Text Files group, but you could add several more using the same method you used to add Edlin. If you add your own application programs to the Shell, you might want to put them in a group titled Application Programs; if you had several related application programs, such as a series of programs related to desktop publishing or financial management, you might want to create a separate group for those programs. Just as you can structure your file system to match your work, so can you structure the program choices of the Shell.

Deleting a Group of Programs

When you're through experimenting with the Edlin program, you can delete either the DOS Edlin Program item from the Text Files group, or the Text Files group itself. You saw earlier how to delete an individual program; deleting a group is just as easy. Press Escape, if necessary, to return to the Start Programs main menu, highlight Text Files, then select Delete from the Group menu. The Shell displays the Delete Item dialog box, shown in Figure 17-25.

```
┌─────────────────────────────────────────────────────────────────────┐
│ 10-16-89              Start Programs                        2:12 pm   │
│                                                            F1=Help    │
│  Program  Group  Exit                                                 │
│                          Main Group                                   │
│           To select an item, use the up and down arrows.              │
│         To start a program or display a new group, press Enter.       │
│                                                                       │
│ Command Prompt                                                        │
│ File Syst┌──────────────── Delete Item ────────────────┐              │
│ Change C │                                             │              │
│ DOS Util │ ┌─────────────────────────────────────────┐ │             │
│ Text Fil │ │ 1. Delete this item                     │ │             │
│          │   2. Do not delete this item                │              │
│          │                                             │              │
│          │ (<─┘=Enter) (Esc=Cancel) (F1=Help)          │              │
│          └─────────────────────────────────────────────┘              │
│                                                                       │
│                                                                       │
│ F10=Actions              Shift+F9=Command Prompt                      │
└─────────────────────────────────────────────────────────────────────┘
```

Figure 17-25. Deleting a program group

Select the first (highlighted) choice to delete the group. The Shell deletes the file TEXTFILE.MEU and displays the Start Programs list again, this time without the *Text Files* item.

TAILORING THE SHELL
STARTUP OPTIONS

The Shell must be started with the batch file named DOSSHELL.BAT, provided with version 4 of DOS. Although the contents of the file may vary, it looks something like this, as you've already seen:

```
@C:
@CD C:\DOS
@SHELLB DOSSHELL
@IF ERRORLEVEL 255 GOTO END
:COMMON
@BREAK=OFF
@SHELLC /TRAN/DOS/MENU/SND/MEU:SHELL.MEU/CLR:SHELL.CLR/
PROMPT/MAINT/EXIT/DATE
:END
@BREAK=ON
```

DOSSHELL.BAT must contain at least the following:

- A command called *Shellb*, which makes sure that the Shell can run on your system. It doesn't actually run the Shell, but is necessary to start the Shell.

- An If command that checks the result of the Shellb command and ends the batch file without starting the Shell if your system isn't set up properly to run the Shell.

- A command called *Shellc* that starts the Shell.

- The label END that allows the Shellb command to prevent the Shellc command from being carried out.

The Shellc command has a host of parameters—called *startup parameters*—that control how the Shell operates. Many of the features of the Shell, such as Start Programs, the File System, and the ability to change screen colors, are available only if their corresponding startup parameters are specified in DOSSHELL.BAT.

Figure 17-26 describes all the Shell startup parameters.

/B:<n>KB	Specifies the amount of memory (in kilobytes) available for the File System buffer. You might want to use this parameter to limit the amount of memory the Shell uses if you run it as a resident program (one that stays in memory). (IBM releases)
/CLR:<file>	Specifies the name of the file that defines the colors that the Shell is to use. The file provided with version 4 of DOS is named SHELL.CLR. This file must be in the directory from which you start the Shell.
/CO1	Displays the Shell in 16-color 640-by-350 graphics.
/CO2	Displays the Shell in two-color (black and white) 640-by-480 graphics.
/CO3	Displays the Shell in 16-color, 640-by-480 graphics.
/COLOR	Includes the *Change Colors* choice on the Start Programs screen.
/COM2	Tells the Shell to look for a serial mouse on COM2, not COM1.
/DATE	Displays the date and the time in the top line.
/DOS	Includes the File System part of the Shell.
/EXIT	Includes the Exit menu. If you don't specify this parameter, once you start the Shell you can't stop it.
/LF	Reverses the meaning of the mouse buttons for left-handed users.
/MAINT	Lets you add and change programs and groups in Start Programs.
/MENU	Includes the Start Programs part of the Shell.
/MEU:<file>	Specifies the name of the file that contains the Start Programs list of choices. If you're using a network, you can use this parameter to specify a different list for each connected system, but still have only a single copy of the Shell program on the main computer, or server. The menu file provided with version 4 of DOS is named SHELL.MEU.
/MOS:<file>	Specifies the name of the file that contains the mouse device driver program. Version 4 of DOS includes the following files:
PCIBMDRV.MOS	IBM PS/2 mouse
PCMSPDRV.MOS	Microsoft parallel mouse (IBM releases)
PCMSDRV.MOS	Microsoft serial mouse (IBM releases)
/MUL	Reserves enough memory for multiple File System directory and file buffers, which can make the Shell operate more quickly.
/PROMPT	Includes the *Command Prompt* choice (which lets you temporarily leave the Shell to type commands at the DOS system prompt) on the Start Programs screen.
/SND	Turns sound (beep) on.

Figure 17-26. The Shell startup parameters (continued)

Figure 17-26. (Continued)

/SWAP	Lets the File System save (or *swap*) its directory and file information to a disk file when you are using the Shell commands or running a program. If you have several hundred files on your fixed disk, include this parameter to reduce the number of times the Shell reads directory and file information from the disk.
/TEXT	Displays the Shell in text (non-graphics) mode.
/TRAN	Runs the Shell as a transient (non-resident) program. To save memory, you should include this parameter unless you're willing to give up the memory to run the Shell as a resident (always in memory) program.

    The Shell can either operate as a transient program (which means that DOS loads it into memory each time you run it and makes the memory available to other programs when you end the Shell) or run as a resident program (which means that DOS loads it into memory the first time you run it and leaves it there when you leave the Shell, making the memory used by the Shell permanently unavailable to other programs). Because this can cause other programs to run more slowly—and keep some programs from being able to run at all—it's best to run the Shell as a transient program. You must include the /TRAN parameter to run the Shell as a transient program, so if you decide to modify the Shell startup parameters, don't delete the /TRAN parameter in DOSSHELL.BAT unless you want to run it as a resident program.

    If you don't include any of the startup parameters that control how the Shell is displayed (/CO1, /CO2, /CO3, or /TEXT), the Shell determines what type of display you have and uses the display's highest resolution and color capability.

    If you have a mouse installed, you might be able to use your existing driver and not include the /MOS:<filename> parameter.

    Because the Shell needs several data files to operate—such as SHELL.MEU, SHELL.HLP, and, if you're using color, SHELL.CLR—it's best to start the Shell from the disk or directory that contains all the Shell files (probably \DOS). If you must start the Shell from another directory, you can use the Append command to tell DOS where to look for files that aren't in the current directory.

    As delivered by IBM, DOS includes all the capabilities of the Shell. If you're satisfied with the way the Shell operates, or if you use it only occasionally, you should probably leave DOSSHELL.BAT unchanged. In any case, use the Shell for a while before deciding whether to change the startup parameters.

The Shell Function Keys

You can use many of the cursor-movement and function keys to control the Shell. The effect of some of these keys depends on what you're doing at the time you press the key. Figure 17-27 describes the effect of these keys in each context in which they can be used.

Key	Effect
Down Arrow	If you have highlighted a menu name, displays the menu. If you have selected a menu, highlights the next menu item. If you're in the File System, highlights the next directory or file name. If you're reading Help information that won't fit on the screen, scrolls to the next line.
End	If you're typing an entry in a dialog box, moves the cursor to the end of the entry.
Enter	If you're typing something in the entry field of a dialog box, moves to the next entry field. If a menu or menu item is highlighted, selects the menu or menu item. If a command file's name is highlighted, runs the program. If a non-command file's name is highlighted, runs the program that uses the file if you have associated a program with the file extension.
Esc	Cancels the current operation and usually returns to the previous operation.
F1	Displays the Help window.
F2	If you're typing an entry in a Start Programs dialog box, saves what you typed. If you're copying a program in Start Programs, completes the copy.
F3	If you're in the File System, leaves the File System and displays the Start Programs screen. If you're in Start Programs, leaves the Shell and displays the DOS system prompt.
F4	If you're adding or changing a program in Start Programs, separates multiple commands on the command line.
F9	If a Help window is displayed, shows the list of function key actions. If you're viewing a file, switches the display back and forth between ASCII and hexadecimal. If you're typing an entry in a dialog box, returns the entry to its original value.
F10	If you're in Start Programs, switches back and forth between the menu line and the main area of the screen. If you're in the File System, switches back and forth between the menu line and whichever part of the rest of the screen was last active.
F11 or Alt-F1	If a Help window is displayed, shows the index of Help topics.

Figure 17-27. The DOS Shell function keys   *(continued)*

Figure 17-27. (Continued)

Key	Effect
Home	If you're typing an entry in a dialog box, moves the cursor to the beginning of the entry.
Left Arrow	If you're typing an entry in a dialog box, moves the cursor toward the beginning of the entry. If you're in the File System and have selected the disk-drive line, selects the previous drive. If you're using the menu line, moves the highlight to the left.
PgDn	Scrolls to the next screenful of a list that won't fit on the screen.
PgUp	Scrolls to the previous screenful of a list that won't fit on the screen.
Right Arrow	If you're typing an entry in a dialog box, moves the cursor toward the end of the entry. If you're in the File System and have selected the disk-drive line, selects the next drive. If you're using the menu line, moves the highlight to the right.
Shift-F9	Temporarily leaves the Shell and displays the DOS system prompt (type *exit* to return to the Shell).
Shift-Tab	If you're in the File System, selects the previous area of the screen. If you're filling in a dialog box, moves to the previous entry.
Spacebar	If you're in the File System, alternately selects and deselects a filename.
Tab	If you're in the File System, selects the next area of the screen. If you're filling in a dialog box, moves to the next entry.
Up Arrow	If you have selected a menu, highlights the previous menu item. If you're in the File System, highlights the previous directory or file name. If you're reading Help information that won't fit in a single screen, scrolls to the previous line.

This chapter hasn't covered all the features of the Shell, but it has shown you the most common ones. Because the operating techniques are fairly consistent throughout the Shell and because the Help information is quite thorough, you should be able to learn what isn't covered by selecting the menu items and using the Help feature to guide you.

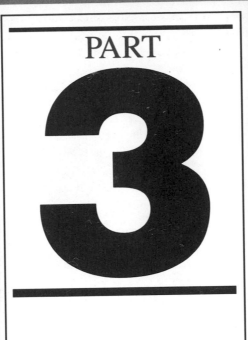

PART

3

APPENDIXES

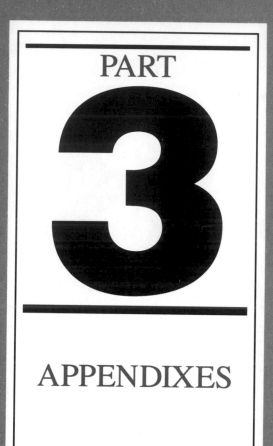

PART

3

APPENDIXES

Six appendixes are included in Part 3. Appendixes A through E provide material you need only occasionally or for background information. For example, Appendix A, "Preparing Your Fixed Disk," might be needed only once or twice in the lifetime of your computer; Appendix E, the Glossary, defines commonly used terms and those presented in the main portions of the book.

Appendix F serves a very different purpose. A comprehensive reference to DOS and Edlin commands, it provides easy-to-find answers to questions about the form or use of a command. Cross-references to Part 2 guide you to the discussions in Chapters 5 through 17.

APPENDIX

A

PREPARING YOUR FIXED DISK

If your computer has a fixed disk, the disk was most likely prepared for use before you picked it up, and the computer might well have been delivered with DOS already installed. If your fixed disk was not prepared, however, DOS includes the Fdisk command, which starts a program that guides you through the fixed-disk preparation process.

Starting with version 4, the DOS installation program (started by the Select command) can prepare the fixed disk for you without requiring you to start and use the Fdisk program beforehand. If you're using an earlier version of DOS, you prepare the fixed disk with the Fdisk program, and then you format the fixed disk with the Format command and copy the DOS files from the DOS diskettes to the fixed disk.

These steps are covered thoroughly in the documentation that comes with DOS. Both the version 4 installation program and the Fdisk program in all versions use menus of options that lead you through the process of preparing your fixed disk.

Note: If you use Fdisk to prepare a fixed disk that already contains information, be sure to back up any of the information you want to save before using Fdisk. Otherwise, you'll lose it all and will not be able to recover it.

A FEW NEW TERMS

Fdisk is called a *menu-driven program* because it displays a series of screens from which you choose, much as you choose from a restaurant menu. Each menu choice you make causes Fdisk to display another menu, and so the procedure continues until you finish setting up (*configuring*) or changing the configuration of your fixed disk. The Fdisk displays use a few terms you don't encounter in your everyday use of DOS. Before you start Fdisk, you might want to familiarize yourself with these terms:

- Partition: a portion of the fixed disk. You can divide your fixed disk into either one or two partitions devoted to DOS. One, called the *primary DOS partition,* is the one from which you start DOS. Beginning with version 4, the primary DOS partition can be any size, up to the full capacity of your fixed disk. In earlier versions, the primary DOS partition could be no larger than 32 megabytes. The second type of partition, called an *extended DOS partition,* is available only in versions 3.3 and later. It enables you to create a secondary partition and thus divide the storage space on a large fixed disk into two smaller units.

- Active partition: the partition from which you start DOS. If you want DOS to start from your fixed disk, the primary DOS partition must also be the active partition. You use Fdisk to set the active partition.

- Logical drive: a portion of an extended DOS partition that you use as if it were a separate drive. It's called a *logical* drive because DOS sets aside part of your fixed disk and treats it as a separate drive. When you create a logical drive with the Fdisk program, you (or DOS) assign it a drive letter (such as drive D:) and a size (such as 10 MB). Each logical drive you create behaves—and can be treated—as if it were a real (physical) disk drive.

- Cylinder: a way of measuring storage space on a fixed disk. You see this term if you're using Fdisk with version 3.3. The program tells you how large your fixed disk is (in cylinders) and, if you're creating an extended DOS partition, asks you how large the partition should be—again, in cylinders. You can estimate roughly how many cylinders equal a given percentage of your fixed disk by using simple arithmetic: decide on a percentage, and then multiply the total number of cylinders by that amount.

APPENDIX

INSTALLING VERSION 4
OF DOS

S tarting with version 4.0, setting up DOS to work on your computer is easier than with earlier versions because the DOS Select command now starts a program that guides you through the installation process. If you start your system with the version 4 Install disk in drive A, DOS starts the installation process.

The program prompts you through each step required to install DOS on a fixed disk or on diskettes. Installing the system on diskettes is new with version 4, and on the face of it might seem unnecessary—after all, with previous versions you simply copied the DOS diskettes, then stored the originals in a safe place and operated the system with the copies. But because of the large number of files and options included in version 4 and because the type of display, printer, and printer connection varies from one computer to another, the installation program lets you select the options you want, tailors DOS to work with your system, and then prompts you to install diskettes and copies just the files you need.

The installation program is quite detailed and thorough in its prompts, and includes online help that explains most of the choices. The manual that comes with DOS also includes detailed instructions for using the installation program with different types of disk drives: fixed disk, 5.25-inch diskette, and 3.5-inch diskette.

Essentially, all you do is place the diskette labeled *Install* in drive A, start or restart your computer, and then press the Enter key to begin. From that point on, the Select program asks you questions about your computer system and tells you which of the original DOS diskettes it needs, and when. Before you start, however, there are a few things you should know or prepare for, to make the procedure as easy as possible.

YOUR COMPUTER

Find out (roughly) how much memory your system has. The Select program doesn't ask you for the exact amount, but during installation it asks you to choose how you want to balance the memory used by DOS and by your programs.

If your system contains less than 512 K of memory, choose the first option (*Minimum DOS function; maximum program workspace*) to give your programs as much working room as possible. If your system has 512 K of memory, choose the option Select proposes (*Balance DOS function with program workspace*). If your system has 640 K of memory, choose the third option (*Maximum DOS function; minimum program workspace*), so that both DOS and your programs have plenty of room to work in.

Check the make and model of printer you use. Also, find out whether it is a serial or a parallel printer, and find out the number of the port it is connected to (for example, LPT1: for a parallel printer or COM1: for a serial printer). The Select program will ask you to choose your printer from a list. It will also propose a printer port, so it is up to you to know whether Select is correct.

In most instances, Select finds out about your computer system by offering you a list of options to choose from, one of which is highlighted. If you already know about your computer's memory and your printer, you shouldn't have any problems. If, for some reason, you don't understand what to do, request help by pressing the F1 key.

PREPARING FOR INSTALLATION

Note: If you are using a fixed disk and are upgrading to version 4 from an earlier version of DOS, do not try to install IBM's release of DOS if your computer is currently running a version of DOS released by another manufacturer. There is a small but significant difference between IBM's release and others that prevents successful installation. You can install the IBM release, but to do so you must back up your fixed disk, reformat it, and then install DOS. If you are not sure of your version of DOS, start your computer; if the manufacturer name and version number are not displayed, type ver *to check.*

Whether you install DOS on a fixed disk or on diskettes, Select needs one or more blank diskettes for the installation. One of the first things Select does is display a list showing the number and capacity of diskettes it needs for installing DOS on various types of disk drives. You can find the diskettes during the installation, when Select provides a list or prompts for a blank diskette, but you'll probably be more comfortable having them on hand and labeled ahead of time. (This is especially important if you're installing DOS on diskettes.)

The diskettes don't have to be formatted; Select will do that for you. In fact, if your computer has a 1.2 MB 5.25-inch diskette drive, notice that Select requests 360 K diskettes; avoid using 1.2 MB diskettes, especially if they're preformatted by the manufacturer. Depending on what type of disk you're installing DOS on, you'll need the following number of blank diskettes:

Type of Disk Installing On	Diskette Capacity	Number of Blank Diskettes (IBM Release of DOS)	Number of Blank Diskettes (Microsoft Release of DOS)
360 K diskette	360 K	4	5
1.2 MB diskette	360 K	4	5
720 K diskette	720 K	2	3
1.44 MB diskette	1.44 MB	1	2
Fixed disk and 5.25-inch diskette drive	360 K	1	1
Fixed disk and 3.5-inch diskette drive	any capacity	1	1

Finally, if you're installing DOS on diskettes, make sure you label your blank diskettes *exactly* the way the program suggests. The instructions for inserting diskettes can be confusing, especially if you're installing on 360 K diskettes. The program asks for diskettes by name; it does not give you messages such as ''Insert the diskette you labeled Working 1.'' So keep your stack of DOS diskettes separate from your blank diskettes. The program asks for some diskettes more than once, and sometimes it asks for more than one DOS diskette before it asks for one of your blank diskettes. And don't be dismayed if your disk drive seems to continue working for quite some time. Select will tell you if it has any problems.

When you reach the end of the installation procedure, Select tells you how to restart your computer with version 4 of DOS. If you're using DOS from diskettes or from a fixed disk that did not contain an earlier version of DOS, you're done. If you're using a fixed disk you updated to version 4, continue with the following section.

FINISHING UP

When the Select program finishes putting DOS on a fixed disk that contains an earlier version of DOS, its final message might tell you that Select has saved information about your computer, printer, display, screen, and the DOS Shell in two files it named AUTOEXEC.400 and CONFIG.400. You'll want DOS to be able to find this information whenever you start or restart your computer, and in order for that to happen, you'll have to rename the files as AUTOEXEC.BAT and CONFIG.SYS. Only then will DOS automatically search for the information saved by the Select program.

The reason Select does not simply name these files AUTOEXEC.BAT and CONFIG.SYS to begin with is that you already have startup files by those names on your fixed disk. Select protects you (and your startup files) by giving the AUTOEXEC and CONFIG files the extension 400, but in return it expects you to merge any information you want to keep from your existing AUTOEXEC.BAT and CONFIG.SYS files with the files it has created. Such information might include a Path command in AUTOEXEC.BAT that guides DOS to your program files, or it might include a Device command in CONFIG.SYS that tells DOS you have a mouse attached to your system. You can quickly find out what's in either an AUTOEXEC.BAT or a CONFIG.SYS file.

If you see something like the screen at the top of the next page when you restart your computer at the end of the installation process, DOS has started by displaying the DOS Shell. Press the F3 key to leave the Shell and have DOS display the system prompt (C:\DOS>). Now type the following to be sure you're in the working area where DOS keeps your AUTOEXEC.BAT and CONFIG.SYS files (if any):

```
C:\DOS>cd \
```

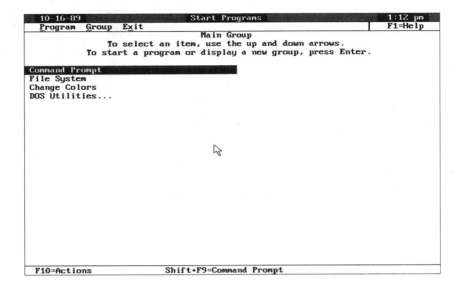

Check for AUTOEXEC.BAT and AUTOEXEC.400 by typing:

```
C:\>dir autoexec.*
```

If you see entries for both AUTOEXEC.BAT and AUTOEXEC.400, go on to the next section.

Now check for CONFIG.SYS and CONFIG.400 by typing:

```
C:\>dir config.*
```

If you see entries for both CONFIG.SYS and CONFIG.400, go on to the next section.

Changing AUTOEXEC.BAT And CONFIG.SYS

If you have both an AUTOEXEC.BAT and an AUTOEXEC.400 file or both a CONFIG.SYS and a CONFIG.400 file, you can see what they contain with the DOS Type command:

```
C:\>type autoexec.bat
```

```
C:\>type autoexec.400
```

and

```
C:\>type config.sys
```

```
C:\>type config.400
```

You can also print their contents by pressing Shift-PrtSc when they're displayed. (If you have a laser printer like the LaserJet+, you might have to press the ON LINE and FORM FEED buttons to get a copy.)

Once you know what your existing files contain, you can transfer any commands you want to keep to AUTOEXEC.400 or CONFIG.400 with the DOS editor, Edlin, or with a word processor that allows you to save files in *unformatted* form. This appendix unfortunately can't give you any further instructions because there's no way to tell what your AUTOEXEC.BAT and CONFIG.SYS files contain.

If you're new to DOS, however, there's a chance that you don't yet know what to keep and what to discard in your existing AUTOEXEC.BAT and CONFIG.SYS files. When in doubt, save. Type the following command to rename your existing AUTO-EXEC.BAT file and keep it safe until you know how or can find out how to merge its contents with AUTOEXEC.400:

```
C:\>ren autoexec.bat autoexec.sav
```

And type the following to rename your CONFIG.SYS file:

```
C:\>ren config.sys config.sav
```

Now you can safely change AUTOEXEC.400 to AUTOEXEC.BAT by typing:

```
C:\>ren autoexec.400 autoexec.bat
```

And you can change CONFIG.400 to CONFIG.SYS by typing:

```
C:\>ren config.400 config.sys
```

Start your computer again by pressing Ctrl-Alt-Del, and DOS will start up, tailored to the choices you made during the installation procedure. If you've saved an old AUTOEXEC.BAT or CONFIG.SYS file, Chapters 1 through 16 and Appendix F contain the information you need to understand and to edit the commands in these two files.

APPENDIX

C

COPYING THE DOS DISKETTES AND INSTALLING VERSION 3 ON A FIXED DISK

Note: This appendix describes how to make copies of your DOS diskettes and how to install version 3 of DOS on your fixed disk. If you're installing version 4, see Appendix B.

COPYING THE DOS DISKETTES

You've probably heard or read about the importance of copying valuable diskettes to protect yourself from loss in case of damage. If you have not made copies of your DOS diskettes, follow the step-by-step procedure given here under the heading that describes your system. Don't worry if you don't understand everything that is happening. It's important that you do this copying as soon as possible, so that you don't chance damaging the originals.

If you have already made copies of your DOS diskettes and are installing a new release of version 3 on your fixed disk, go on to the heading "Installing Version 3."

If You Have One Diskette Drive

During the procedure, DOS might prompt you to exchange the *source* and *target* diskettes in the drive several times. Follow the prompts, and remember that the DOS diskette is the *source* and the blank diskette is the *target*.

1. If you're using IBM's version 3.3 with a 5.25-inch diskette drive, place the diskette labeled *Operating* in your diskette drive. Otherwise, place your DOS system diskette (usually labeled *DOS* or *DOS Programs*) in the diskette drive. Make sure the latch is closed.

2. If you have a fixed disk, type:

   `C>a:`

   to tell DOS to use your diskette drive.

3. Type the following (but not the A>, and don't forget to press Enter):

   `A>diskcopy`

   This command tells DOS to copy everything on the source diskette to the target diskette. DOS responds:

   `Insert SOURCE diskette in drive A:`

   `Press any key when ready . . .`

   `—`

   The correct diskette is already in drive A, so press the spacebar or any other key. DOS responds:

   ```
   Copying 40 tracks
   9 Sectors/Track, 2 Side(s)
   ```

This message may vary, depending on the version of DOS you're using and the type of diskette drive you have. Regardless, DOS reads as much of the diskette as it can, then asks you to exchange diskettes:

```
Insert TARGET diskette in drive A:

Press any key when ready . . .
_
```

4. Remove the DOS diskette, put in a blank new diskette, and press the spacebar or any other key. DOS writes the data it read from the system diskette onto the blank diskette. It might then request that you put the DOS diskette back in the drive:

```
Insert SOURCE diskette in drive A:

Press any key when ready . . .
_
```

5. Continue exchanging diskettes as DOS prompts you. After the last exchange, DOS tells you it has finished:

```
Copy another diskette (Y/N)?_
```

6. Remove the diskette to which you copied DOS and label it with the name on the original DOS diskette—OPERATING, for example, or DOS. Use a felt-tip pen, not a ballpoint pen, to avoid damaging the surface of the diskette.

7. Remove the original DOS diskette and put it in its plastic sleeve in the manual binder (or some other safe place).

8. Unless you're using 3.5-inch diskettes, you have another diskette to copy, so type *y* in answer to the *Copy another diskette* question. DOS replies with the message to put the source diskette in drive A, as in step 3. If you are using 3.5-inch diskettes, there is only one DOS diskette, so go on to the heading "Installing Version 3" if you need to install DOS on your fixed disk. If you don't, you're done.

9. If you're using IBM's version 3.3 of DOS, insert the diskette labeled *Startup* in the diskette drive. Otherwise, put your second DOS diskette (usually labeled *Supplemental* or *Supplemental Programs*) in the diskette drive.

10. Press the spacebar or any other key. DOS responds as in step 3. When DOS prompts you to exchange diskettes, remove the original DOS diskette, put in a blank new diskette, and press the spacebar or any other key.

11. If necessary, continue to exchange the diskettes as you did before. When the copy is complete and DOS asks if you want to make another copy, remove the diskette to which you copied the DOS programs, label it with the name on the original DOS diskette, and put it with your other working diskettes.

12. Remove the original DOS diskette and put it in its plastic sleeve in the manual binder (or some other safe place).

13. If you don't have a fixed disk, put your new copy of the DOS system diskette in your diskette drive (Operating diskette if you're using IBM's version 3.3).

14. Type *n* to answer the *Copy another diskette* question. DOS responds by displaying the system prompt.

If You Have Two Diskette Drives

These instructions assume that your DOS system diskette is in drive A, that you have performed the startup steps of entering the date and time, and that you have the DOS system prompt, A>, on the screen. During the procedure, DOS prompts for the *source* and *target* diskettes. Remember that the DOS diskette is the *source* and the blank diskette is the *target*.

1. If you're using IBM's version 3.3 of DOS with 5.25-inch diskette drives, place the diskette labeled *Operating* in drive A.

2. Put a blank new diskette in drive B.

3. Type the following (but not the A>, and don't forget to press Enter):

   `A>diskcopy a: b:`

   This command tells DOS to copy everything on the diskette in drive A to the diskette in drive B. DOS responds:

   `Insert SOURCE diskette in drive A:`

   `Insert TARGET diskette in drive B:`

   `Press any key when ready . . .`
   —

4. Your source (DOS) and target (blank) diskettes are in the correct drives, so press the spacebar or any other key. DOS responds:

   `Copying 40 tracks`
   `9 Sectors/Track, 2 Side(s)`

   A short while later, DOS displays:

   `Formatting while copying`

   The message may vary, depending on the version of DOS you're using and the type of diskette drives you have. It takes about a minute to copy the diskette. When the diskette is copied, DOS responds:

   `Copy another diskette (Y/N)?_`

5. Remove the diskette from drive B and label it with the name on the original DOS diskette—OPERATING, for example, or DOS. Use a felt-tip pen, not a ballpoint pen, to avoid damaging the surface of the diskette.

6. Remove the original DOS diskette from drive A and put it in its plastic sleeve in the manual binder (or some other safe place).

7. Unless you're using 3.5-inch diskettes, you have another diskette to copy, so type *y* to answer the *Copy another diskette* question. DOS replies with the messages to put the source and target diskettes in drives A and B as in step 3. If you're using 3.5-inch diskettes, there is only one DOS diskette, so go on to the heading ''Installing Version 3'' if you also have a fixed disk. Otherwise, you're done.

8. If you're using IBM's version 3.3 of DOS, put the diskette labeled *Startup* in drive A. Otherwise, put your second DOS diskette (usually labeled *Supplemental* or *Supplemental Programs*) in drive A.

9. Put a blank new diskette in drive B.

10. Press the spacebar, or any other key. DOS responds as in step 4.

11. When the copy is complete and DOS asks if you want to make another copy, remove the copy from drive B, label it with the name on the original DOS diskette, and put it with your other working diskettes.

12. Remove the original DOS diskette from drive A and put it in its plastic sleeve in the manual binder (or some other safe place).

13. If you don't have a fixed disk, put your copy of the system diskette in drive A.

14. Type *n* to answer the *Copy another diskette* question. DOS responds by displaying the system prompt.

Installing Version 3

If DOS is installed on your fixed disk and you want to install a newer release of version 3, you must replace not only all the DOS command and data files, but also two hidden files that DOS requires. The System (sys) command transfers these two hidden files from the diskette in the drive from which you started DOS to the fixed disk drive.

After you have copied the two hidden files with the System command, you must copy all the DOS files from both DOS diskettes to the fixed disk. COMMAND.COM must be stored in the root directory of the fixed disk, but the other DOS files can be stored in any directory. The example that follows shows you a complete procedure for installing a new version of DOS.

Example of Installing a New Version of DOS

This example shows you how to install version 3.3 of DOS on your fixed disk by copying the two hidden files, then copying the DOS files to either the root directory of the fixed disk or to a directory named \DOS (remember, COMMAND.COM must always be stored in the root directory). If you're installing an earlier version, the procedure is the same; just remember that references to the version 3.3 system diskette mean the system diskette for the new version you're installing.

Note: If your DOS files are in the root directory, but you want to put them in a directory named \DOS (or any directory other than the root), the topic ''Moving the DOS Files from the Root Directory to \DOS'' in Chapter 9 gives instructions.

Installing a new version of DOS takes only a few commands:

1. Put the version 3.3 Startup diskette in drive A (if you're installing 3.2 or an earlier version, put in the diskette labeled DOS). Turn the computer on or, if it's already running, press Ctrl-Alt-Del to restart it.

2. Enter the date and time if DOS prompts for them. When DOS displays the system prompt, type the System command to copy the two hidden files:

```
A>sys c:
```

DOS responds *System transferred.* If you're installing version 3.3 on a system on which version 3.1 or an earlier version is installed, DOS might display the message *Insufficient memory for system transfer.* This means that there isn't room to store the hidden files in their proper location on the fixed disk. You must back up all the files on your fixed disk, format it with the Format command (which erases all the files, so be sure to back up the fixed disk first), then start again with step 1.

3. Now you must copy the DOS command and data files to the fixed disk. To put all the DOS files in the root directory of the fixed disk, type the following Copy command (the number of files copied varies with different versions of DOS):

```
A>copy *.* c:\
        22 File(s) copied
```

To put COMMAND.COM in the root directory of the fixed disk and to put the other DOS files in a separate directory (\DOS, in this example), type the following commands, substituting the name of your DOS directory, if it differs from \DOS:

```
A>copy command.com c:\
        1 File(s) copied

A>copy *.* c:\dos
        22 File(s) copied

A>erase c:\dos\command.com
```

You deleted COMMAND.COM from C:\DOS because the second Copy command copied it, along with the other DOS files, to C:\DOS, and you don't need it there. It's quicker to copy all the files and then delete COMMAND.COM than it is to use several Copy commands to avoid copying COMMAND.COM.

4. If you're using 3.5-inch diskettes, you're through; go on to step 5. If you're using 5.25-inch diskettes, copy the remaining DOS files from the second (supplemental) DOS diskette to the directory named \DOS on the fixed disk. Take out the Startup diskette and put in the Operating diskette. (If you're installing 3.2 or an earlier version, take out the diskette labeled DOS and put in the diskette labeled Supplemental Programs.)

   If you're putting all the DOS files in the root directory of the fixed disk, type:

```
A>copy *.* c:\
       31 File(s) copied
```

   If you're putting the DOS files in a directory of their own, such as \DOS, type the following, substituting your directory name for \DOS if necessary:

```
A>copy *.* c:\dos
       31 files copied
```

5. That's it. Now open the latch on drive A so that DOS will start from the fixed disk, and press Ctrl-Alt-Del. You should see the sign-on message of the new version you just installed.

APPENDIX

DOS IS AN INTERNATIONAL SYSTEM

Many languages share the basic Latin alphabet, but some add different characters, including both accented Latin characters, such as é, è, ë, or ê, and some use characters that are altogether different, such as ¿ or £ . Other languages, such as Arabic, Chinese, Hebrew, Japanese, and Korean, don't use the Latin alphabet at all.

Different countries, regardless of language, also represent the numeric form of a date in different ways. In most North American and European countries, the numeric form of a date is shown in a day-month-year sequence (for example, 16-10-89 for October 16, 1989). In the United States, however, the sequence is month-day-year (10-16-89), and in Japan it is year-month-day (89-10-16). Different countries with different traditions also use different currency symbols and ways of separating large numbers or decimal fractions.

Depending on the country for which your computer was manufactured, DOS assumes a keyboard arrangement and country code that determine how the date, currency symbols, and decimals are handled. Beginning with version 3.0, DOS lets you change these characteristics. The language that DOS itself uses—its command names and the messages it displays—remains unchanged, but you can tailor many of its operating qualities to the linguistic and monetary traditions of a particular country. This capability can be particularly useful if you use your computer for work with different languages or currencies, or if persons with different language requirements use the same computer.

Starting with version 3.3, the ability of DOS to handle many different languages was expanded. These changes, in fact—referred to as *national language support*—made up the most extensive changes from version 3.2 to version 3.3.

Because of these differences, this appendix presents the international side of DOS in two parts. The first part describes multiple-language support available in versions 3.0 through 3.3, with examples tailored for users of versions 3.0 through 3.2; the second part, starting with the heading "National Language Support," describes the enhancements, including changes in some commands available in earlier versions. Altogether, this appendix shows you how to:

- Choose a keyboard layout with one of the Keyboard commands.

- Set the country code with the Country configuration command.

- Create a DOS system diskette tailored to a particular country with the Select command.

- Use national language support, including the Keyboard (keyb), Change Code Page (chcp), National Language Support Function (nlsfunc), Mode, and Device commands.

If you use your computer only in the language of the country for which it was manufactured, you don't need national language support, and you can safely skip this entire appendix.

If you're using version 3.3 or version 4, and you want to learn what the new commands are for and how they are used to set up national language support, read the first part of the appendix to see how earlier versions handled multiple languages, then read the description of national language support (beginning with the heading "National Language Support").

If you're using version 3.3 or version 4, and you want to set up your system so you can use it with United States or Canadian English and most European languages, but you don't need to learn what each command does, turn to the end of this appendix and follow the instructions under the heading "Setting Up Code-page Switching for an EGA-only System" or "Setting Up Code-page Switching for an IBM PS/2 and Printer," whichever better describes your system.

CHOOSING A KEYBOARD LAYOUT

Keyboards used in different countries must accommodate different characters and often use a different arrangement of common keys. The Keyboard commands, Keyb*xx* in versions 3.0 through 3.2 and Keyb starting with version 3.3, change the keyboard layout to match the conventions of a specific country.

In versions through 3.2, the Keyboard command for each country loads a small program that combines with the part of DOS kept in memory and decreases the amount of available memory by about 2000 bytes. The actual size of the program depends on the number of changes the new layout requires. If you enter a Keyboard command, then enter another Keyboard command without restarting DOS, the second keyboard program is loaded to reconfigure the keyboard. The program loaded by the first Keyboard command remains in memory, but you cannot return to it, so issuing a series of Keyboard commands reduces the amount of available memory.

Starting with version 3.3, the first time the Keyboard command is carried out, it increases the size of DOS in memory by about 5000 bytes. Subsequent Keyboard commands then tell DOS to load different sets of specifications, called *translation tables,* that accommodate different country-specific keyboard layouts.

Switching Keyboards While DOS Is Running

If your computer was manufactured for use in the United States, the configuration of the United States keyboard is stored in the computer's permanent memory. After changing the keyboard layout with a Keyboard command, you can switch back and forth between the United States configuration and the new one: Press Ctrl-Alt-F1 (hold down both the Ctrl and Alt keys and press the F1 function key) for the United States layout, and Ctrl-Alt-F2 for the other layout. If your word processor or spreadsheet program accepts characters other than standard keyboard characters—you'll have to try it to see—this lets you switch back and forth while editing a document to include information for either country and to use the more familiar keyboard layout to operate the application.

If your computer was manufactured for multilingual operation, you may be able to switch among several keyboard configurations without using a Keyboard command. See your computer's documentation (the *Guide to Operations* if the computer was manufactured by IBM) for a description of how to switch among different keyboard layouts.

Note: Not all printers can print accented or other characters not in the standard set. Check your printer's documentation to see if it can print the characters you need.

Typing Accented Characters With Dead Keys

Many languages use *accented characters* that combine an accent mark and a common character (such as Å or ñ). Some of these accented characters are assigned locations on the keyboard; on the French keyboard, for example, you type *è* by pressing the 7 key in the top row of the keyboard (to type the number 7, you press Shift-7).

Often, there aren't enough available keys to provide all the accented characters, however, so DOS also uses *dead keys* to combine accent marks and characters. Some typewriters use this same technique, so using dead keys might be a familiar procedure for you.

A dead key is one that represents just an accent mark. Pressing a dead key doesn't produce any apparent result, but it tells DOS to combine the accent mark with the next key you press. On the French keyboard, for example, you type *ô* by pressing the dead key for the circumflex (ˆ), then pressing the key labeled O.

If you press a dead key, then press a character that cannot be combined with the accent mark represented by the dead key, DOS does one of the following:

- In most cases, it beeps and displays the accent mark, followed by the key you pressed, to show you it can't combine them as an accented character.

- If the dead key represents the diaeresis (¨), DOS displays a small, filled-in square (■) followed by the second key you pressed.

To correct the error, backspace to erase the two characters and type the correct dead-key sequence.

Keyboard Layouts

If you're using a version of DOS prior to 3.3, each language DOS supports has its own Keyboard command. The Keyboard commands have no parameters (the country names in the right column of the following table are for information only):

Keyboard Command	Country
keybuk	United Kingdom
keybgr	Germany
keybfr	France
keybit	Italy
keybsp	Spain

Because entering a Keyboard command changes the location of common keys (especially punctuation marks), the character that results from pressing a key doesn't always match the United States label on the key. You may want to chart the keyboard layout and keep a paper copy handy, mark the keys, or even move the key caps to the new location.

Figures D-1 and D-2 show the French keyboard layout for the IBM PC (and PC/XT) keyboard and for the enhanced IBM PC/AT keyboard. The figures show the shifted and unshifted characters produced by each key in the main typewriter portion of the keyboard, and also identify the dead keys.

Figure D-1. IBM PC and PC/XT French keyboard layout (keybfr)

Figure D-2. Enhanced IBM PC/AT French keyboard layout (keybfr)

Example of Using the Keyboard Command

Note: If you're using version 3.3 or version 4, your Keyboard command is described later in this appendix, after you've been introduced to the basics of national language support. Read the following example to see how to use the French keyboard. If you want, you can return to try the example once you've learned how to select the keyboard in your version of DOS.

To change the keyboard arrangement to French, type the following if you're using a version of DOS between 3.0 and 3.2:

```
C>keybfr
```

If you are accustomed to the United States layout, here are the most obvious changes with the French layout: You must hold down the Shift key to type a number; the locations of two pairs of letter keys are reversed (Q-A and W-Z); M is to the right of L; and most symbols and punctuation marks are in different places.

Now that you have switched keyboards, you must follow the new layout. For example, the command to display a directory in wide format is *dir /w*. If you don't follow the French keyboard layout, you'll type *dir =z*, because the equal sign is where the forward slash used to be, and the W and Z have changed places.

Suppose you wanted to type the sentence *L'hôtel célèbre est grand* (The famous hotel is big). Both the é and the è are on the keyboard, but the ô is not, so you must use the dead key for the circumflex. And remember, the Q and the A keys have changed places. Here, step-by-step, is how you would type the phrase:

```
C>L
```

For the apostrophe, press the 4 key in the top row. After the apostrophe, type *h*:

    `C>L'h`

Now, you have to use the circumflex dead key, which is to the right of the French p. Press the circumflex dead key. Nothing happens yet. Now type *o*; DOS displays *ô*. Continue by typing *tel c*:

    `C>L'hôtel c`

For é, press the 2 key in the top row; then type *l*:

    `C>L'hôtel cél`

For è, press the 7 key in the top row; then type *bre est gr*:

    `C>L'hôtel célèbre est gr`

And finally, press Q to get the French a, and type *nd*:

    `C>L'hôtel célèbre est grand`

Although that's a painfully long list of instructions just to type a simple sentence, in fact it goes quite quickly after a bit of practice. Press Esc to clear the line, and press Ctrl-Alt-F1 to return to the United States keyboard layout.

Changing the Country Code with the Country Configuration Command

The country code is a number that DOS uses to control the way the date and time are displayed. Application programs also have access to this code, and they can use it to control other format characteristics, such as currency symbols and the characters, such as commas and decimal points, used to separate thousands and decimal fractions in numbers.

The Country configuration command lets you set the country code. As with other configuration commands, you don't type the Country command at the system prompt; you put it in the file named CONFIG.SYS in the root directory of the system disk. DOS then carries out the command each time you start it.

In versions prior to 3.3, the Country configuration command has one parameter:

country=<country-code>

<country-code> is one of the three-digit codes shown in Figure D-3 on the next page; it's usually the same as the country's international long-distance dialing prefix. You must include all three digits, including any zeros at the beginning.

For example, suppose your computer was built for use in the United States, but someone also uses it for writing in French. To tell DOS to follow French conventions for date, currency, and decimals, you could create or modify a DOS system diskette for that person, including the command *country=033* in CONFIG.SYS. (If there were no CONFIG.SYS file in the root directory, you would create it and put the Country command in it.) Once the CONFIG.SYS file was saved, each time DOS was started from the French disk it would adopt the French conventions.

When DOS displayed the current date and asked for the new date, for example, it would display the date in the sequence day-month-year, and ask the user to *Enter new date (dd-mm-yy).*

To change the country code, you would edit CONFIG.SYS again. For the United States, you could either delete the Country command or change *country=033* to *country=001* (001 is the code for the United States).

Country or Language	Country Code	Valid Code Pages
Arabic	785	864[1], 850
Australia	061	437, 850
Belgium	032	850, 437
Canada (French)	002	863, 850
Chinese (simplified)	086	936[2], 437
Chinese (traditional)	088	938[2], 437
Denmark	045	850, 865
Finland	358	850, 437
France	033	437, 850
Germany	049	437, 850
Hebrew	972	862[1], 850
Italy	039	437, 850
Japan	081	932[2], 437
Korea	082	934[2], 437
Latin America	003	437, 850
Netherlands	031	437, 850
Norway	047	850, 865
Portugal	351	850, 860
Spain	034	437, 850
Switzerland	041	850, 437
United Kingdom	044	437, 850
United States	001	437, 850

1. Valid only with version 4 installed with a country-specific supplement.
2. Valid only with the Asian edition of version 4 running on a computer manufactured for use in Asia.

Figure D-3. Country codes and their code pages

Creating a Language-specific DOS System Diskette

Note: This section describes the use of the Select command in version 3 of DOS. If you're using version 4, the Select command starts the installation program, which asks you which countries and languages you want to use and creates a set of DOS diskettes that support the countries and languages you chose; go on to the heading "National Language Support."

If you use more than one language, or if several users with different languages share the computer, DOS offers a simple way to handle multilingual operation: the Select command, which creates a system diskette tailored to the language and conventions of a particular country.

The Select command makes a copy of the DOS system disk that contains files that configure DOS for a specific country, including CONFIG.SYS and AUTOEXEC.BAT files. If you create several country-specific diskettes, you can change languages simply by restarting DOS after putting the appropriate system diskette in drive A.

The Select command has four parameters:

select <source> <target> <country> <keyboard>

<source> is the letter, followed by a colon, of the drive that contains the DOS system diskette. You can specify either *a:* or *b:*. If you don't specify <source>, DOS assumes drive A.

<target> is the drive letter, followed by a colon, and the path name of the directory on the diskette to which the DOS files are to be copied. If you omit the drive letter, DOS assumes drive B; if you omit the path name, DOS assumes the root directory. <target> and <source> must specify different drives. If you specify only one drive letter, DOS assumes it is <target>.

<country> is the three-digit country code you want set on the new DOS diskette. You must include all three digits of the country code, including any zeros at the beginning. <country> corresponds to the country's long-distance telephone prefix.

<keyboard> is the two-letter abbreviation of the country whose keyboard layout is to be selected for the new DOS diskette (these are the last two letters of the corresponding Keyboard command).

Warning: The Select command formats the target disk, erasing all files on it, so either use a new diskette or make sure that the diskette or fixed disk you use as the target contains no files that you must keep.

Figure D-4 on the following page shows the country code and keyboard values allowed with the Select command in version 3 of DOS. Only those countries marked with an asterisk (*) are available in versions 3.0 through 3.2; the others are available starting with version 3.3. You can enter the keyboard code in either uppercase or lowercase.

Country	Country Code	Keyboard Code
Australia	061	US
Belgium	032	BE
Canada (English)	001	US
Canada (French)	002	CF
Denmark	045	DK
Finland	358	SU
France *	033	FR
Germany *	049	GR
Israel	972	—
Italy *	039	IT
Latin America	003	LA
Middle East (Arabic)	785	—
Netherlands	031	NL
Norway	047	NO
Portugal	351	PO
Spain *	034	SP
Sweden	046	SV
Switzerland (French)	041	SF
Switzerland (German)	041	SG
United Kingdom *	044	UK
United States *	001	US

Figure D-4. Country and keyboard codes for the Select command

Example of Creating a Language-specific System Diskette

The Select command uses the Diskcopy command to make the copy of the system diskette and then compares the two diskettes with the Diskcomp command to make sure the copy was accurate. The prompts and sequence of steps are the same as if you had entered a Diskcopy command, then a Diskcomp command.

If you're using a computer with a fixed disk, you must start DOS with the system diskette in the diskette drive, even if you normally start DOS from the fixed disk. If you have only one diskette drive, DOS may prompt you to switch diskettes; the number of times you must switch diskettes depends on the amount of memory available in your computer.

Throughout the Select procedure, DOS refers to the original system diskette as the first or source diskette and refers to the language-specific system diskette you're creating as the second or target diskette.

To create a French system diskette on a computer with one diskette drive, you perform the following steps:

1. Start DOS with the system diskette in drive A, even if you normally start DOS from a fixed disk.

2. Type *select 033 fr* (*033* is the country code for France, and *fr* is the keyboard code). DOS prompts you to insert the source diskette in drive A and press any key.

3. The source diskette is in drive A, so press any key. DOS reads from the system diskette, then prompts you to put the target diskette in drive A.

4. Put a blank diskette, formatted or unformatted, in drive A and press any key. If the new diskette isn't formatted, DOS formats it, then notifies you how many tracks, sectors, and sides it's copying and starts to copy the system to the new diskette. After copying the system diskette, DOS asks *Copy another diskette (Y/N)?* Type *n*.

5. Now DOS compares the two diskettes to make sure the copy was accurate. It prompts you to *Insert FIRST diskette in drive A:* and press any key.

6. Leave the new (French) diskette in drive A and press a key. DOS tells you how many tracks, sectors, and sides it's comparing, reads the files from the diskette, and prompts you to *Insert SECOND diskette in drive A:* and press any key.

7. Put the original DOS system diskette in drive A and press a key. After comparing the diskettes, DOS displays *Compare OK* and asks *Compare another diskette (Y/N)?* (If it displays a different message, start again at step 2.) Type *n*.

8. Now DOS prompts you to *Insert TARGET diskette in drive A* and press a key. Put the new French-specific system diskette in drive A and press a key. To make sure it is correct, restart DOS by pressing Ctrl-Alt-Del, check whether the date is displayed in the day-month-year (not month-day-year) sequence, and see if the keyboard follows the French layout (press the Q and A keys to see if they are interchanged from the United States layout).

That's it. You have a system diskette configured for France.

National Language Support

The national language support introduced in version 3.3 replaces the methods used in previous versions to change the keyboard layout and the character sets used by the display and printer. The changes include four new or changed system files, three new commands, three new options for the Mode command, a new parameter for the Graftabl command, and a new parameter for the Country and Device configuration commands.

Some New Terms: Code Page and Code-page Switching

The key element of national language support is called a *code page*—a table of 256 codes for different characters. DOS recognizes two types of code pages. A *hardware code page* is the character table built into a device and is determined by the country for which the device is manufactured. The hardware code page is the code page used by a device unless you specify otherwise.

A *prepared code page* is an alternate character table available through DOS. A prepared code page can replace the hardware code page of a device.

A code page can be any of the following:

437	United States
850	Multilingual
860	Portuguese
863	French Canadian
865	Nordic

The identifying numbers bear no relationship to the country code used by the Country configuration command.

Code page 437 is the character table used in previous versions of DOS; its character set supports United States English and includes many accented characters used in other languages, as well as symbols and straight lines, corners, and other characters that can be used to draw boxes on the screen. Code page 437 is the hardware code page for all but a few countries.

Code page 850 replaces two of the four box-drawing sets and some of the mathematical symbols in code page 437 with additional accented characters; it includes enough characters to cover United States and Canadian English, and Latin American and most European languages.

The three remaining code pages cover a few additional languages: Code page 860 is for Portuguese, code page 863 is for Canadian French, and code page 865 is for Norwegian. These are also the hardware code pages for these countries; code page 865 is also the hardware code page for Denmark.

You select prepared code pages from the five included with 3.3 and later versions with the *cp prepare* option of the Mode command. The *current code page* is the code page most recently selected.

National language support is often referred to as *code-page switching* because, once you have defined the devices and code pages required by your system, the only commands you deal with simply switch from one code page to another.

Setting Up Your System for Code-page Switching

Although several commands are required to manage national language support, the process is straightforward. Setting up a system requires the following commands:

- A Device configuration command in CONFIG.SYS.

- A National Language Support Function (nlsfunc) command in AUTOEXEC.BAT.

- A Mode command in AUTOEXEC.BAT to prepare code pages for each device that supports code-page switching.

- A Mode or Change Code Page (chcp) command in AUTOEXEC.BAT to select the initial code page.

- A Keyboard (keyb) command in AUTOEXEC.BAT to select the initial keyboard layout.

With these commands in CONFIG.SYS and AUTOEXEC.BAT, it takes only one or two commands after you start your system to change to a different language during a DOS session.

If you're using version 3.3, you still use the Select command to create a country-specific system disk and the Country configuration command to control country-specific characteristics such as the date format and currency symbol; an added parameter on the Country command lets you also specify a code page. If you're using version 4, the installation program asks you for which country your system should be configured and copies the appropriate files for you.

The next few topics describe the new and changed commands in detail, including examples of their use. A complete example of how to set up a system follows the command descriptions.

National Language Support Commands

National language support can require the use of up to six commands—National Language Support (nlsfunc), Change Code Page (chcp), Keyboard (keyb), Mode, Load Graphics Table (graftabl), and Country—and two system files, DISPLAY.SYS and PRINTER.SYS.

National Language Support Function Command—NLSFUNC

If there is no Country configuration command in CONFIG.SYS, the National Language Support Function (nlsfunc) command names the file that contains country-specific information such as date format and currency symbol. You must enter the

Nlsfunc command before you can use the Change Code Page (chcp) command. If you use national language support every time you use the system, you can put the Nlsfunc command in AUTOEXEC.BAT.

The Nlsfunc command has one parameter:

nlsfunc <country-file>

<country-file> is the name of the country information file; in most versions of DOS, this file is named COUNTRY.SYS. If you omit <country-file>, DOS assumes the file is the one specified in the Country configuration command in CONFIG.SYS. If there is no Country configuration command in CONFIG.SYS, DOS looks for a file named COUNTRY.SYS in the root directory of the current drive.

For example, the following command specifies C:\DOS\COUNTRY.SYS as the country information file:

```
C>nlsfunc c:\dos\country.sys
```

Loading the country information in COUNTRY.SYS with the Nlsfunc command increases the size of DOS in memory by about 2500 bytes.

Keyboard Command—KEYB

The Keyboard (keyb) command selects a keyboard layout. It replaces the Keyb*xx* commands used in earlier versions of DOS to select keyboard layouts.

The Keyb command has four parameters:

keyb <country>,<code-page>,<kbdfile> /ID:<kbdid>

<country> is one of the following two-character keyboard codes:

Country	Keyboard Code	Valid Code Pages	Keyboard ID
Belgium	BE	850, 437	120
Canada (French)	CF	863, 850	058
Denmark	DK	850, 865	159
Finland	SU	850, 437	153
France	FR	437, 850	120, 189
Germany	GR	437, 850	129
Italy	IT	437, 850	141, 142
Latin America	LA	437, 850	171
Netherlands	NL	437, 850	143
Norway	NO	850, 865	155
Portugal	PO	850, 860	163

(continued)

Country	Keyboard Code	Valid Code Pages	Keyboard ID
Spain	SP	437, 850	172
Switzerland (French)	SF	850, 437	150
Switzerland (German)	SG	850, 437	000
United Kingdom	UK	437, 850	168, 166
United States	US	437, 850	103

<code-page> is a three-digit number that specifies the code page that DOS is to use. <code-page> can be 437 (United States), 850 (Multilingual), 860 (Portuguese), 863 (French Canadian), or 865 (Nordic).

<kbdfile> is the name of the system file that contains the keyboard layouts; this file is KEYBOARD.SYS in most versions of DOS. If you don't specify <kbdfile>, DOS assumes that the file is named KEYBOARD.SYS and is stored in the root directory of the system disk.

/ID:<kbdid> is a three-digit code that specifies a keyboard layout to be used when a country has more than one keyboard ID as listed in the preceding table. If you don't specify /ID:<kbdid> and more than one keyboard ID is listed for the country specified, DOS assumes the first keyboard ID listed. (Version 4)

For example, the following command would select the French keyboard layout, code page 850, the keyboard definition file named C:\DOS\KEYBOARD.SYS, and (in version 4) the keyboard ID 120.

```
C>keyb fr,850,c:\dos\keyboard.sys /id:120
```

If you omit all parameters (just type *keyb*), DOS displays the currently active keyboard country code, keyboard code page, and console device (display) code page. If you have selected the French keyboard and code page 850 for both the keyboard and the console, for example, DOS responds to the command *keyb* with the message:

```
Current keyboard code: FR    code page: 850
Current keyboard ID  : 120
Current CON code page: 437
```

If DOS includes more than one keyboard layout for the country and you don't want DOS to choose the default layout, you must specify the keyboard ID in the Keyboard command. For example, the following command specifies the French keyboard, as the previous example does, but also, in version 4, specifies keyboard ID 189 so that DOS won't choose the default keyboard ID of 120:

```
C>keyb fr,850,c:\dos\keyboard.sys /id:189
```

Change Code Page Command—CHCP

The Change Code Page (chcp) command tells DOS which code page to use for all devices that support code-page switching. You use it to change code pages when you want to change character sets.

You must execute the National Language Support Function (nlsfunc) command before you can use the Change Code Page command. Change Code Page is a system-wide command: It specifies the code page to be used by DOS and by each device attached to the system that supports code-page switching. The *cp select* option of the Mode command (described later) specifies the code page for a single device.

If the code page you specify with Change Code Page isn't compatible with a device, DOS responds *Code page* nnn *not prepared for all devices.* If you specify a code page with Change Code Page that you didn't first identify with the *cp prepare* option of the Mode command, DOS responds *Code page* nnn *not prepared for system.*

The Change Code Page command has one parameter:

chcp <code-page>

<code-page> is the three-digit number that specifies the code page that DOS is to use. As listed earlier, they are 437 (United States), 850 (Multilingual), 860 (Portuguese), 863 (French Canadian), or 865 (Nordic). If you omit <code-page>, Change Code Page displays the current DOS code page.

For example, the following command would change the system code page to 850:

```
C>chcp 850
```

If the current code page were 850 and you typed *chcp*, DOS would respond by displaying *Active code page: 850.*

Mode Command

National language support uses four Mode command options:

- *codepage prepare* defines the code pages that you want to use.

- *codepage select* selects a code page for a particular device.

- *codepage status* displays the code pages that are available and active.

- *codepage refresh* restores a code page that was erased from memory after you selected it.

When you enter the Mode command, you can abbreviate *codepage* to *cp.*

Preparing a Code Page

When used to define the code page or code pages to be used with a device, the Mode command has three parameters:

mode <device> cp prepare=((<code-page>) <font-file>)

<device> is the name of the device for which the code page or code pages are to be prepared. It can be CON, PRN, LPT1, LPT2, or LPT3.

<code-page> is the three-digit code-page number, enclosed in parentheses, that specifies the code page to be used with <device>. If you specify more than one code-page number, separate them with blanks. Valid code pages are listed earlier, under the heading ''Some New Terms: Code Page and Code-page Switching.''

<font-file> is the name of the code-page information file that contains the font information for <device>. DOS includes four files for IBM devices. Your version of DOS may include others; the code-page information files have the extension CPI:

EGA.CPI	Enhanced graphics adapter (EGA) or IBM PS/2
4201.CPI	IBM Proprinter and Proprinter XL
4208.CPI	IBM Proprinter X24 and Proprinter XL24 (version 4)
5202.CPI	IBM Quietwriter III printer
LCD.CPI	IBM Convertible liquid crystal display (LCD)

For example, assume your display is attached to an EGA; the following command would prepare code pages 437 and 850 for the console, specifying C:\DOS\EGA.CPI as the code-page information file:

```
C>mode con cp prepare=((437 850) c:\dos\ega.cpi)
```

Selecting a Code Page

When used to select a code page for a device, the Mode command has two parameters:

mode <device> cp select=<code-page>

<device> is the name of the device for which the code page is to be selected. You can specify CON, PRN, LPT1, LPT2, or LPT3.

<code-page> is the three-digit number that specifies the code page to be used with <device>. The code page you specify must be one that has already been prepared with the *codepage prepare* option of the Mode command.

For example, the following command would select code page 850 for the console:

```
C>mode con cp select=850
```

Displaying the Code-Page Status

When used to display the status of the code pages, the Mode command has one parameter:

mode <device> cp

<device> is the name of the device whose code-page status is to be displayed. It can be CON, PRN, LPT1, LPT2, or LPT3.

For example, the following command would display the status of the console device:

```
C>mode con cp
```

Restoring a Code Page That Was Lost

Some circumstances can cause a code page to be erased from memory. For example, if you prepare and select a code page for the printer, then turn the printer off and turn it back on again, the code page in the printer's memory may be different from the one you selected. The *codepage refresh* option of the Mode command restores the code page you selected without your having to specify the code-page number.

mode <device> cp refresh

<device> is the name of the device whose most recently selected code page is to be restored. It can be CON, PRN, LPT1, LPT2, or LPT3.

For example, the following command would restore the most recently selected code page for the printer attached to the LPT2 port:

```
C>mode lpt2 cp refresh
```

Graftabl Command

The Load Graphics Table (graftabl) command includes a parameter that loads a code page for the color/graphics adapter (CGA) so that its character set matches the code page used by DOS and other devices when displaying accented and other special characters in graphics mode.

The first time a Graftabl command is executed, the size of DOS in memory is increased by about 1500 bytes.

The Graftabl command has two parameters:

graftabl <code-page> /status

<code-page> is the three-digit number that specifies the code page that Graftabl is to use; it can be 437, 850, 860, 863, or 865.

/status displays the name of the graphic character set table that Graftabl is using.

Country Configuration Command

The Country configuration command includes a parameter that specifies the code page to be used by DOS. The Country command isn't required; if you don't include a Country command in CONFIG.SYS, DOS assumes country 001 (US), code page 437, and country information file \COUNTRY.SYS on the disk in the current drive.

The Country configuration command has three parameters:

country=<country-code>,<code-page>,<country-file>

<country-code> is one of the three-digit country codes shown in Figure D-3 on page 388.

<code-page> specifies the code page that DOS is to use.

<country-file> is the name of the file that contains the country-specific information; in most versions of DOS, this is COUNTRY.SYS. If you omit <country-file>, DOS assumes that the file is named COUNTRY.SYS and that it is stored in the root directory of the current drive.

For example, the following configuration command in CONFIG.SYS would specify the French country code, code page 850, and C:\DOS\COUNTRY.SYS as the country information file:

```
country=033,850,c:\dos\country.sys
```

National Language Support System Files

DOS includes four system files for national language support functions:

- PRINTER.SYS handles code-page switching for the IBM Proprinter and Quietwriter printers.

- DISPLAY.SYS takes care of the EGA, IBM PC Convertible LCD, and IBM PS/2 displays. All displays compatible with the EGA and PS/2 are also supported.

- COUNTRY.SYS contains data such as date formats and currency symbols.

- KEYBOARD.SYS defines the keyboard layouts for different countries.

Specifying the Display Driver — DISPLAY.SYS

The file that controls code-page switching for the display is DISPLAY.SYS. It supports the IBM Enhanced Graphics Adapter (EGA), the IBM Personal System/2 display adapter, the liquid crystal display (LCD) of the IBM PC Convertible, and all display adapters compatible with those IBM devices. Code-page switching cannot be used with the monochrome display/printer adapter (MDA) or the color/graphics adapter (CGA). If you also use the ANSI.SYS display driver, the Device command that defines it must precede the Device command that defines DISPLAY.SYS.

When used to specify a code-page switching file for the display, the Device configuration command has five parameters:

device=<filename> con=(<type>,<hwcp>,<prepcp>,<sub-fonts>)

<filename> is the name of the code-page switching file for the display. If you omit <filename>, DOS assumes that the file is named DISPLAY.SYS and that it is in the root directory of the current drive.

<type> defines the type of display adapter attached to the system. If you don't specify >type>, DOS determines what type of display is attached to your system. <type> must be one of the following:

mono	Monochrome display/printer adapter
cga	Color/graphics adapter
ega	Enhanced graphics adapter or IBM Personal System/2
lcd	IBM PC Convertible liquid crystal display

<hwcp> is a three-digit number that specifies the hardware code page built into the display adapter. Valid code pages are listed earlier, under the heading ''Some New Terms: Code Page and Code-page Switching.''

<prepcp> is the number of additional code pages that the display can support. These are referred to as *prepared code pages,* and must be defined by the *cp prepare* option of the Mode command. If <type> is either *mono* or *cga,* <prepcp> must be 0; DOS assumes 0. If <type> is *ega* or *lcd,* <prepcp> can be from 1 through 12; DOS assumes 1. If <hwcp> is 437, let DOS assume 1; if <hwcp> is not 437, specify 2.

<sub-fonts> is the number of sub-fonts supported for each code page. If <type> is either *mono* or *cga,* <sub-fonts> must be 0; DOS assumes 0. If <type> is *ega,* <sub-fonts> can be 1 or 2; DOS assumes 2. If <type> is *lcd,* <sub-fonts> can be 1 or 2; DOS assumes 1. Unless you have unusual requirements, you needn't specify a value for <sub-fonts>; the value that DOS assumes covers all normal systems.

For example, the following configuration command in CONFIG.SYS would specify C:\DOS\DISPLAY.SYS as the code-page switching file for an EGA whose hardware code page is 437; DOS is allowed to assume values of 1 and 2 for <prepcp> and <sub-fonts> respectively:

```
device=c:\dos\display.sys con=(ega,437)
```

Specifying the Printer Driver—PRINTER.SYS

The file that controls code-page switching for dot-matrix printers is PRINTER.SYS. It supports the IBM Proprinter, the IBM Quietwriter III Printer, and all printers compatible with either of these IBM devices.

When used to specify the code-page switching file for the printer, the Device configuration command has five parameters:

device=<filename> <printer>=(<type>,<hwcp>,<prepcp>)

<filename> is the name of the code-page switching file for the printer. If you omit <filename>, DOS assumes that the file is named PRINTER.SYS and that it is in the root directory of the current drive.

<printer> is the DOS device name for the printer port being defined. It can be LPT1 (or PRN), LPT2, or LPT3. You can specify a different set of parameters for each of the three printer ports in one command.

<type> defines the type of printer attached to the system. It must be either *4201* for the IBM 4201 Proprinter Family or IBM 4202 Proprinter XL; *4208* for the IBM 4207 Proprinter X24 or IBM Proprinter XL24; or *5202* for the IBM 5202 Quietwriter III (or a printer compatible with one of these IBM models).

<hwcp> is a three-digit number that specifies the hardware code page built into the adapter. Valid code pages are listed earlier, under the heading ''Some New Terms: Code Page and Code-Page Switching.'' If <type> is *5202*, you can specify two hardware code-page numbers, enclosed in parentheses and separated by a comma. If you do specify two hardware code pages, you must specify <prepcp> as 0. If you don't specify <hwcp>, DOS assumes 437.

<prepcp> is the number of additional code pages, referred to as *prepared code pages,* DOS should be prepared to use. These code pages must be defined by the *cp prepare* option of the Mode command. <prepcp> can be from 0 through 12. If <hwcp> is 437, specify 1; if <hwcp> is not 437, specify 2.

For example, the following configuration command in CONFIG.SYS would define C:\DOS\PRINTER.SYS as the code-page switching file for the device named PRN. The printer is an IBM Proprinter Model 4201 whose hardware code page is 437; DOS is instructed to allow for one prepared code page:

```
device=c:\dos\printer.sys prn=(4201,437,1)
```

The following configuration command in CONFIG.SYS would define the code-page switching file as C:\DOS\PRINTER.SYS for the devices named LPT1 and LPT2. The printer attached to LPT1 is the same (4201) as in the previous command. The printer attached to LPT2 is an IBM Quietwriter III Printer Model 5202 with two hardware code pages (437 and 850); DOS is instructed to allow for no prepared code pages:

```
device=c:\dos\printer.sys lpt1=(4201,437,1) lpt2=
(5202,(437,850),0)
```

Setting Up Code-page Switching
For an EGA-only System

Figure D-5 on the following page shows the commands that are needed to set up national language support for a system whose only code-page switching device is a display attached to an EGA or EGA-compatible adapter. The hardware code page of the EGA is 437 (United States English), and the system is set up to handle code pages 437 and 850.

All DOS files are assumed to be in the directory C:\DOS. If you don't use the ANSI.SYS device driver, omit the configuration command *device=c:\dos\ansi.sys* from CONFIG.SYS; if you do use ANSI.SYS, however, be sure that its Device configuration command precedes the Device configuration command that defines DISPLAY.SYS, as in Figure D-5.

Put these commands in CONFIG.SYS:

```
country=001,437,c:\dos\country.sys
device=c:\dos\ansi.sys
device=c:\dos\display.sys con=(ega,437)
```

Put these commands in AUTOEXEC.BAT:

```
nlsfunc c:\dos\country.sys
mode con cp prepare=((437 850) c:\dos\ega.cpi)
mode con cp select=437
keyb us,437,c:\dos\keyboard.sys
```

Figure D-5. Setup commands for a system with EGA only

When you start the system, code page 437 is selected for DOS, the display, and the keyboard. To change to code page 850, type *chcp 850*.

Setting Up Code-page Switching For an IBM PS/2 and Printer

Figure D-6 shows the commands required to set up national language support for an IBM PS/2 or compatible system that includes both a VGA (or compatible) display and an IBM Proprinter Model 4201 printer. The hardware code page of both devices is 437 (United States English), and the system is set up to handle code pages 437 and 850. (Note that the *ega* in the Device configuration command that specifies DISPLAY.SYS means both EGA and PS/2.)

Again, all DOS files are assumed to be in the directory C:\DOS. If you don't use the ANSI.SYS driver, omit the configuration command *device=c:\dos\ansi.sys* from CONFIG.SYS; if you do use ANSI.SYS, however, be sure that its Device configuration command precedes the Device configuration command that defines DISPLAY.SYS, as shown in Figure D-6.

When you start the system, code page 437 is selected for DOS, the display, the keyboard, and the printer. To change to code page 850 during the session, type *chcp 850*. To switch back to code page 437, type *chcp 437*.

Put these commands in CONFIG.SYS:

```
country=001,437,c:\dos\country.sys
device=c:\dos\ansi.sys
device=c:\dos\display.sys con=(ega,437)
device=c:\dos\printer.sys prn=(4201,437,1)
```

Put these commands in AUTOEXEC.BAT:

```
nlsfunc c:\dos\country.sys
mode con cp prepare=((437 850) c:\dos\ega.cpi)
mode prn cp prepare=((437 850) c:\dos\4201.cpi)
mode con cp select=437
mode prn cp select=437
keyb us,437,c:\dos\keyboard.sys
```

Figure D-6. Setup commands for a PS/2 with display and printer

APPENDIX

E

GLOSSARY

A

Adapter: A term sometimes used to refer to printed-circuit cards that plug into a computer and control a device, such as a display or a printer.

Application program: A program, such as a word processor or spreadsheet, that performs a specific task; an application of the computer to a particular type of work.

Archive: To duplicate files on a separate disk or on a backup tape for safekeeping. The Backup command helps archive files; the Restore command can, if necessary, be used to return archived files to the disk from which they were backed up.

ASCII: A standardized coding scheme that uses numeric values to represent letters, numbers, symbols, and so on. ASCII is an acronym for American Standard Code for Information Interchange and is widely used in coding information for computers.

AUTOEXEC.BAT: A name reserved for a batch file that contains commands that are carried out by DOS each time the system is started. An AUTOEXEC.BAT file can be used to perform a desired set of startup procedures without having to type the commands each time.

AUX: Short for *auxiliary*. The communications port DOS uses unless instructed otherwise. AUX can be either COM1 or COM2 in versions of DOS through 3.2; it can be COM1, COM2, COM3, or COM4 in version 3.3.

B

Backspace key: The key labeled with a single, left-pointing arrow; erases characters you have typed, one at a time.

Back up: To copy one or more files to diskettes or tapes for safekeeping.

BAK: An extension assigned, by Edlin and by many word processors, to the next-most-recent (penultimate) version of a text file. If the working copy of a file is damaged, the BAK file can be used to salvage a near-current version of the document.

BASIC: A programming language included with versions of DOS; BASIC is an acronym for Beginner's All-purpose Symbolic Instruction Code.

Batch file: A text file whose extension is BAT; contains DOS commands. When you type the name of the batch file while DOS is at the command level, DOS carries out the commands in the file.

Baud: The rate at which data is transmitted over a communications link. One character per second equals approximately 10 baud.

Binary: The base-2 numbering system whose only digits are 0 and 1. The binary system is particularly well suited to use with computers because the two digits can be represented by the presence (1) or absence (0) of a voltage.

Bit: The smallest unit of information used with computers; corresponds to a binary digit (either 0 or 1). Eight bits make up one byte.

Boot: To start up a computer; derived from "pull yourself up by your own bootstraps."

Byte: The unit of measure used for computer memory and data storage. One byte contains eight bits and can store one character (a letter, number, or punctuation mark, or other symbol).

C

Character string: A group of characters that you tell DOS to treat as a set of letters or numbers, rather than as a command. The Find filter command searches for character strings enclosed in quotation marks (" "). In other commands, such as the Edlin Search and Replace commands, the quotation marks are not needed.

Chip: *See* Integrated circuit.

Color/Graphics Adapter (CGA): A printed-circuit card in the system unit of a computer that controls the display. Shows both text and graphics at low resolution in up to sixteen colors.

COM1, COM2, COM3, COM4: Short for *communications*. The names of the serial communications ports. All versions of DOS recognize COM1 and COM2; version 3.3 also recognizes COM3 and COM4.

Command: An instruction you use to control a computer program, such as DOS or an application program.

Command file: A file that contains the program or instructions required to carry out a command. If the file's extension is COM or EXE, the command file contains machine instructions; if its extension is BAT, the command file is a batch file and contains DOS commands.

Communications: The transmission of data between computers; also called telecommunications.

Communications port: *See* Port.

CON: Short for *console*. The name by which DOS refers to the keyboard (input) and the display (output).

Control key: The key labeled Ctrl; use it, as you do the Shift key, by holding it down while pressing another key. The Control key usually causes something to happen, rather than displaying a character on the screen. If displayed, it is shown as ^, as in the end-of-file marker, ^Z (Ctrl-Z).

CPU: Acronym for *central processing unit*. The part of a computer that performs calculations and processes information. In most microcomputers that use DOS, for example, the CPU is the 8086/8088, 80286, or 80386 chip.

Ctrl: *See* Control key.

Ctrl-Break: The key combination that cancels a command; entered by holding down the Ctrl key and pressing the Break key.

Ctrl-C: Same as Ctrl-Break.

Ctrl-Num Lock: The key combination that stops DOS until you press any other key. Usually used to freeze the display so you can view long displays. Entered by holding down the Ctrl key and pressing the Num Lock key.

Ctrl-P: Same as Ctrl-PrtSc.

Ctrl-PrtSc: The key combination that controls simultaneous printing and displaying. Pressing Ctrl-PrtSc once causes DOS to print everything that is displayed; pressing Ctrl-PrtSc again causes DOS to stop printing everything that is displayed. Entered by holding down the Ctrl key and pressing the PrtSc key.

Ctrl-S: Same as Ctrl-Num Lock.

Ctrl-Z: The key combination that creates the special character (displayed as ^Z) that DOS uses to mark the end of a file. Created by holding down the Ctrl key and pressing Z, or by pressing the function key labeled F6.

Current directory: The directory in which DOS looks for files unless otherwise instructed.

Current drive: The drive containing the disk on which DOS looks for a directory or file unless otherwise instructed.

D

Data: The numbers and text processed by a computer in doing its work.

Data bit: A signal used in serial communications to represent the transmission of a character; seven or eight data bits can be used to represent one character.

Data file: A file that contains the data needed by a program; can be numbers, text, or a combination of the two.

Device: A piece of computer equipment, such as a display or a printer, that performs a specific task; the program that controls a device is called a device driver.

Device name: The name by which DOS refers to a device (for example, PRN, LPT1, LPT2, or LPT3 for a printer). Device names are treated like file names by DOS.

Directory: The index of files that DOS maintains on a disk. The directory entry for each file includes the file's name, extension, size, date and time it was created or last changed, and the location of the beginning of the file. All but the last item are displayed by the Directory command.

Disk: A magnetically coated disk used to store information. The term is used when no distinction need be made between a diskette and a fixed disk.

Disk drive: The device that rotates a disk in order to read (retrieve) and write (store) information.

Diskette: A disk for storing files, made of thin plastic and enclosed in a protective jacket.

Diskette drive: A disk drive used for diskettes.

Display: The screen on which the computer shows both what you type at the keyboard and the result of its work; assumed by DOS to be the standard output device unless a different device is specified.

Drive letter: The letter that identifies a disk drive.

E

Edit: To change the contents of a file, usually with a word processor or an editing program such as Edlin.

Editor: A program used to create or change text files; also called a *text editor.*

Edlin: The DOS text editor.

Enhanced Graphics Adapter (EGA): A printed-circuit card in the system unit of a computer that controls the display. Shows both text and graphics at medium resolution in up to 64 colors.

Enter key: The key you press to tell DOS that you have finished typing a line. Labeled *Return* on some keyboards.

Esc: *See* Escape key.

Escape key: The key labeled Esc; cancels a line you have typed but have not yet entered by pressing the Enter key.

Expanded memory: Additional memory that can be installed on any IBM PC or compatible computer. A special program called an Expanded Memory Manager is required to use this memory; programs must be written specifically to use such memory. Use of expanded memory is governed by the Lotus-Intel-Microsoft (LIM) specification. Up to eight megabytes of expanded memory can be installed.

Extended memory: Additional memory that can be installed on an IBM PC/AT, IBM PS/2 Models 50, 60, 70, or 80, or any computer compatible with those models that has an 80286 or 80386 microprocessor. Up to 15 megabytes of extended memory can be installed.

Extension: A suffix of up to three characters that can be added to a file name to identify the contents of the file more precisely.

F

File: A named collection of information stored on a disk; usually contains either data or a program.

File name: A name of up to eight characters that you assign and that DOS uses to find a file on a disk; can be followed by a period and three additional characters called the file name extension.

Filespec: The complete specification of a file; can include a drive letter, path name, file name, and extension.

Filter command: A DOS command that reads standard input, processes it in some way (for example, sorts it in alphabetic order), and writes the result to standard output.

Fixed disk: A disk of large capacity (10 MB or more) that cannot be removed from its drive. Also called a *hard disk.*

Floppy disk: *See* Diskette.

Format: To prepare a disk for use.

Function key: One of several keys, usually labeled F1, F2, and so on, that cause DOS (or an application program) to perform a certain function, such as copying characters in a line of text.

H

Hard disk: *See* Fixed disk.

Hardware: The equipment that makes up a computer system, as opposed to the programs, or software.

Hexadecimal: The base-16 numbering system whose digits are 0 through F (the letters A through F represent the decimal numbers 10 through 15); often used in computer programming because it is easily converted to and from binary, the base-2 numbering system the computer itself uses.

Hidden file: A file, usually used only by DOS, that is not listed when you display the directory. Hidden files cannot be erased, copied, or otherwise affected by DOS commands.

Hierarchical filing system: *See* Multilevel filing system.

I

Initialize: *See* Format.

Input: The data that a program reads.

Input/output: A term that refers to the devices and processes involved in the computer's reading (input) and writing (output) data.

Integrated circuit: An electronic device that combines thousands of transistors on a small sliver, or chip, of silicon. Such devices are the building blocks of computers. Also referred to as a *chip*.

Interface: The boundary between two systems or entities, such as a disk drive and the computer, or the user and a program.

I/O: Abbreviation for *input/output*.

I/O redirection: *See* Redirection.

K

Keyboard: The device consisting of alphabetic and other keys where instructions and data are typed into the computer; assumed by DOS to be the standard input device unless a different device is specified.

L

LPT1, LPT2, LPT3: Short for *line printer*. The names that DOS uses to refer to the three ports to which parallel printers can be attached.

M

Memory: A type of electronic circuitry that the computer uses to store programs and data. Unlike disk storage, which is permanent, memory is temporary—its contents are lost when power is removed from the computer. Memory is usually measured in units of 1024 bytes, called a kilobyte and abbreviated K or KB; a megabyte is 1000 kilobytes, or 1,024,000 bytes.

Microcomputer: A small computer system, usually used by only one person.

Microprocessor: An integrated circuit, or chip, that contains the circuits the computer needs to calculate and to communicate with the other parts of the system.

Modem: A device that permits the transmission of computer data over telephone lines. Contraction of *modulator-demodulator*.

Monitor: A device that displays computer input and output; usually used synonymously with *display*.

Monochrome: A term used to describe a computer display capable of displaying one color (usually white, green, or amber).

Monochrome Display Adapter (MDA): A printed-circuit card in the system unit of a computer that controls the display. Shows text only at medium resolution in one color.

Multicolor Graphics Array (MCGA): A printed-circuit card in the system unit of a computer that controls the display. Shows both text and graphics at low to medium resolution in up to 256 colors; used in IBM PS/2 model computers.

Multilevel filing system: A computer filing system that lets you define directories within other directories, creating a structure with many levels. Also called a *tree-structured* or *hierarchical* filing system.

N

Network: A group of computers, linked by printed-circuit cards, cables, and network software, that share resources, such as disk drives and printers.

O

Operating system: A program that coordinates the operation of all parts of a computer system.

Output: The result of a program's processing its input data.

P

Parallel communications: A communications technique that uses multiple interconnecting wires to send eight bits of a byte at once (in parallel).

Parallel port: The port to which the printer is usually attached.

Parameter: A qualifier that you include with a command to define more specifically what you want DOS to do; also called an *argument* or an *option*.

Parity: An error-detection technique used for accuracy in data communications.

Path: The list of directory names that defines the location of a directory.

Path name: The portion of a file specification that defines the path to the file; can include a drive letter followed by a colon.

Pipe: To direct the output of one command to be used as the input of another command. The pipe symbol DOS uses is the broken vertical bar (¦).

Port: The electrical connection through which the computer sends and receives data to and from devices or other computers.

Print queue: The list of files to be printed by DOS; you create, examine, and modify the print queue with the Print command.

Printed-circuit card: A thin, rectangular card or board, usually made of fiberglass or epoxy and coated with copper. A circuit is etched into the copper, and electronic devices, such as integrated circuits, are soldered to the circuit. Computer systems are made up of these cards.

Printer: A device that produces images of text and graphics on paper.

PRN: Short for *printer*. The printer DOS uses unless instructed otherwise. Can refer to LPT1, LPT2, or LPT3.

Program: A set of instructions for a computer.

Prompt: A request displayed by the computer for you to provide some information or perform an action.

Q

Queue: *See* Print queue.

R

RAM: Short for *random access memory*. The memory that DOS uses for programs and data; RAM content changes often while you use the computer, and is lost when the computer is turned off.

RAM disk: *See* Virtual disk.

Read-only file: A file whose read-only attribute is set so that its contents can be displayed and read, but not changed.

Redirection: The process of causing a command or program to take its input from a file or device other than the keyboard (standard input), or of causing the output of a command or program to be sent to a file or device other than the display (standard output). The DOS redirection symbols are the greater-than (>) and less-than (<) signs.

Replaceable parameter: A symbolic reference, consisting of a percent sign followed by a one-digit number (such as %1), that can be included with commands in a batch file to refer to the parameters entered with the batch command.

Return key: The Enter key.

ROM: Short for *read-only memory*. A type of computer memory that is permanently recorded in hardware; contains instructions that help a computer carry out routine tasks, such as starting itself up. The contents of ROM cannot be changed and are not lost when the computer is turned off.

Root directory: The main directory that DOS creates on each disk; the top directory in a multilevel filing system.

S

Serial communications: A communications technique that uses as few as two interconnecting wires to transmit bits serially, one after the other.

Serial port: The communications port (COM1, COM2, COM3, or COM4) to which devices, such as a modem or a serial printer, can be attached.

Shell: A program that shows itself to the person using the computer, then passes commands to a different program to be carried out. It's called a shell because it effectively surrounds the other program, hiding it from view. Version 4 of DOS introduced such a Shell program that lets you use many DOS commands without having to type commands or file names at the system prompt. Other DOS shell programs are also available.

Software: The programs that are used with a computer system, as opposed to the equipment, or hardware.

Standard input: The device from which a program reads its input unless the input is redirected; in normal DOS operation, standard input is the keyboard.

Standard output: The device to which a program sends its output unless the output is redirected; in normal DOS operation, standard output is the display.

Stop bit: A signal used in serial communications that marks the end of a character.

Subdirectory: A file that contains directory entries; sometimes also used to refer to the group of files whose directory entries are in the same file.

System program: A program whose purpose is to control the operation of all or part of the computer system, such as managing the printer or interpreting commands.

System prompt: The characters DOS displays when it is at the command level (ready to accept a command); unless you specify otherwise, the system prompt consists of the letter of the current drive followed by a greater-than sign (for example, C>).

T

Telecommunications: *See* Communications.

Temporary file: A file that DOS may create when told to redirect command input or output; deleted by DOS when the command is completed.

Text: Ordinary, readable characters, including the uppercase and lowercase letters of the alphabet, the numerals 0 through 9, and punctuation marks.

Text editor: A program that you use to create or change text files. Also called simply an *editor*.

Text file: A file that you can read (contains ordinary letters, numbers, and punctuation marks).

U

Update: To change a file, creating a new (or updated) version.

V

Video Graphics Array (VGA): A printed-circuit card in the system unit of a computer that controls the display. Shows both text and graphics at medium to high resolution in up to 256 colors; used in IBM PS/2 model computers.

Virtual disk: A portion of the computer's random access memory reserved for use as a simulated disk drive. Also called an *electronic* or *RAM* (for random access memory) *disk*. Unless saved on a physical disk, the contents of a virtual disk are lost when the computer is turned off.

Volume label: An 11-character identifying name you can assign to a disk.

W

Wildcard character: A special character that, like the wild card in a poker game, can be used to represent any other character. DOS recognizes two wildcard characters: the question mark (?), which can represent any single character, and the asterisk (*), which can represent more than one character.

Write-protect: To cover the small notch or opening on a diskette so that new or changed information cannot be written onto the diskette.

APPENDIX

F

DOS COMMAND REFERENCE

ANSI.SYS
Control Program for Screen and Keyboard
Versions 2.0 and later

Page 314

ANSI.SYS is a program that lets you control the console device. With it, you can manipulate the characters assigned to keys on the keyboard, and the color, position, and other attributes of the display. A program that controls a device is called a *device driver;* ANSI.SYS is a device driver that follows the conventions adopted by the American National Standards Institute (ANSI) for screen and keyboard control.

ANSI.SYS is widely used and offers many ways to extend your control over the console, but it is not required in your everyday use of DOS. A full description is beyond the scope of this book; for details, refer to the explanations and examples in *Supercharging MS-DOS* (Microsoft Press, 1989) or the DOS *Technical Reference.*

APPEND
Define a Data Path
Versions 3.2 and later

Page 151

The Append command specifies one or more directories that DOS searches for a data file that isn't in the current directory. Starting with version 4, you can specify that the Append command search for command files—files whose extension is COM, EXE, or BAT—as well as data files; this means you can use the Append command as an adjunct to the Path command. You can use the Append command on a network.

append /E /X or /x:off /path:on(off) <path> ;

/E makes the data path part of the DOS environment. You can specify /E only the first time you enter an Append command after starting DOS. If you specify /E, you cannot specify any path names; you must enter another Append command to define the data path. (If you're using version 4, the installation program added an Append /E command to the AUTOEXEC file it created; if you already had an AUTOEXEC.BAT file on your fixed disk, your earlier AUTOEXEC.BAT file might contain the same command.)

/X has different meanings, depending on the version of DOS you're using:

- Starting with version 4, /X tells DOS to search for command files (files with the extensions COM, EXE, and BAT) as well as data files in the appended directories.

- In version 3.3, /X makes the data path available to additional DOS commands. You can specify /X only the first time you enter an Append command after starting DOS. If you specify /X, you cannot specify any path names; you must enter another Append command to define the data path.

/X:off tells DOS not to search the appended directories for command files. It has the reverse effect of /X, which can, in fact, also be entered as /X:*on* in version 4.

/path:on(off) tells DOS whether or not to search the appended directories for a file if the file name is not preceded by a drive letter or a path name. /path:*on* tells DOS to include the drive letter or path name; *path:off* tells DOS not to include them. If you don't specify otherwise, DOS assumes /path:on. (Version 4)

<path> is the name of the directory to be added to the path. You can specify a directory on the same or a different drive, or you can specify just a drive letter (such as a:). If you specify more than one drive or directory, separate the path names with a semicolon (;).

Note: Use the Append command with care, especially if you are not using version 4 of DOS. If you define a data path consisting of several directories, DOS doesn't tell you where it found a file you requested. Nor does DOS necessarily save a revised file in its original directory, if the directory is part of the data path; it might instead save the file in the current directory. In version 4, using the /path:off parameter helps to avoid this problem.

Examples

To tell DOS to search for data files in \MKT\WP and \ENG\WP on drive C:

```
C:\>append \mkt\wp;\eng\wp
```

To tell DOS to search the data path for command files as well as data files (version 4 only):

```
C:\>append /x:on
```

To display appended directories:

```
C:\>append
```

If you type *append* when no data path is defined, DOS displays *No Append*.

To limit searches to the current directory (remove all directories from the data path):

```
C:\>append ;
```

ASSIGN
Route Disk Operations to a Different Drive
Versions 3.0 and later, IBM releases 2.0 and later

Page 319

The Assign command routes requests for disk operations on one drive to a different drive. Its primary use is with application programs that look for files on a specific drive (such as B) and don't let you specify a different drive (such as C).

assign **<drive1>=<drive2>**

<drive1> is the letter (without a colon in versions prior to 4.0) of the drive to be assigned.

<drive2> is the letter (without a colon in versions prior to 4.0) of the drive that is to be used instead of <drive1>.

Both <drive1> and <drive2> must refer to existing disk drives (including fixed disks and virtual drives). You can assign more than one drive in a single Assign command by separating the <drive1>=<drive2> pairs with blanks.

If you omit all parameters (just type *assign*), DOS deletes all drive assignments, so that all drive letters refer to their original drives.

Note: The Assign command masks the actual type of disk drive from DOS, so use it only when necessary, and don't enter a Backup, Restore, Label, Join, Substitute, or Print command that uses an assigned drive. Four DOS commands—Format, Diskcopy, Diskcomp, and System—ignore any drive assignments made with the Assign command. If you have version 3.1 or later, use the Substitute command instead of the Assign command; for example, type subst b: c:<path> *instead of* assign b=c.

Examples

To assign drive B to drive C:

```
C:\>assign b=c
```

To assign drives A and B to drive D:

```
C:\>assign a=d b=d
```

To reset all drive letters to their original drives:

```
C:\>assign
```

ATTRIBUTE
Display or Change File Attributes
Versions 3.0 and later

Pages 75, 160

The Attribute command (attrib) displays or changes the read-only status and the archive status of a file. If a file is read-only, you cannot change or delete the file. A file's archive status can be used by the Backup, Restore, and Xcopy commands to determine whether the file should be copied to another disk.

attrib +R −R +A −A <filename> /S

+R makes the file read-only.

−R removes the read-only attribute.

+A assigns the archive attribute. (Versions 3.2 and later)

−A removes the archive attribute. (Versions 3.2 and later)

<filename> specifies the name of the file whose read-only or archive attribute is to be changed or displayed. The file name can include a drive letter, followed by a colon, and a path name.

/S applies the Attribute command to all subdirectories contained in <filename>. (Versions 3.3 and later)

If you specify only *attrib <filename>*, DOS displays an R to the left of the file name if the file is read-only. In versions 3.2 and later, DOS also displays an A to the left of the file name if the file has changed since it was last archived (in other words, the archive attribute is on).

Examples

To make the file named REPORT.DOC in the current directory on the disk in the current drive a read-only file:

```
C:\>attrib +r report.doc
```

To remove the read-only attribute from the file named REPORT.DOC in the directory named \WORD\MKT on the disk in drive D:

```
C:\>attrib -r d:\word\mkt\report.doc
```

To display the read-only and archive attributes of all files in the directory named \WORD\MKT on the disk in the current drive:

```
C:\>attrib \word\mkt\*.*
```

DOS responds:

```
      C:\WORD\MKT\REPORT.DOC
A     C:\WORD\MKT\FORECAST.DOC
   R  C:\WORD\MKT\SALESREP.DOC
A  R  C:\WORD\MKT\FCST-APR.DOC
      C:\WORD\MKT\FCST-MAY.DOC
   R  C:\WORD\MKT\FCST-MAR.DOC
   R  C:\WORD\MKT\BUDGET.DOC
A  R  C:\WORD\MKT\FCST-JUN.DOC
```

BACKUP
Make a Backup Copy of Files
Versions 2.0 and later

Page 169

The Backup command makes a backup copy of files so you can safeguard data against damage or other loss. Files can be backed up from and to any type of source and target disk. Rather than making an exact copy of the file, as the Copy command does, the Backup command records the directory from which each file was backed up. The Restore command uses this data to reinstate files in the correct locations.

Although the Backup command is present in versions 2.0 and later, not all the parameters described here are in every release of DOS; refer to your DOS manual to find out which parameters are available to you.

backup <path><filename> <drive> /A /S /M /F /D:<date> /T:<time> /L:<logfile>

<path> and <filename> specify the file or files to be backed up. You must specify at least a drive letter, followed by a colon. You can include a path name or a file name, or both, and you can use wildcard characters. The following list shows what files DOS backs up if you specify:

- Drive letter: all files in the current directory of the disk in the specified drive.
- Drive letter and path name: all files in the specified directory on the disk in the specified drive.
- Drive letter and file name: the specified file from the current directory of the disk in the specified drive.

<drive> is the letter of the drive, followed by a colon (such as *a:*), that contains the backup disk.

/A adds the backup files to the backup disk. If you don't use /A, DOS displays a warning message and then erases any files on the target disk before copying the files. If you omit /A, be sure the backup diskette doesn't contain any files you want to keep.

/S backs up all files in all subdirectories contained in the current directory or the specified directory.

/M backs up only files that have been modified since they were last backed up.

/F formats the target disk if it isn't already formatted. If you specify /F, the current command path must include the directory containing the file FORMAT.COM (version 3.3). In version 4, the Backup command automatically formats the backup diskette if it isn't already formatted, so /F isn't required, although DOS must still be able to find FORMAT.COM. If Backup does the formatting for you, it's a good rule of thumb to match the capacity of your diskettes to the capacity of your diskette drive (that is, use 1.2 MB diskettes in a 1.2 MB drive, and so on).

/D:<date> backs up only files that have been modified since the date specified in <date>. Specify <date> just as you would for the Date command.

/T:<time> backs up all files that have changed since <time> on <date>. Specify <time> just as you would for the Time command. Not all releases of DOS include the /T:<time> option.

/L:<logfile> creates a log file on the source drive that contains the date and time of the backup, the path name and file name of each file that is backed up, and the backup number that DOS assigned to the diskette on which the file is backed up. If a log file already exists, the backup information is added at the end, creating a history of backups for the source drive. If you don't specify a name for the log file, DOS names it BACKUP.LOG and stores it in the root directory of the source drive. Not all releases of DOS include the /L:<logfile> parameter.

Unless you're using version 3.3 or later, the target disk must be formatted. If the files to be backed up require more than one diskette, DOS prompts you to insert another diskette; be sure to label these diskettes, because the Restore command asks for them by number. Files can't be backed up from a diskette with a write-protect tab.

DOS displays the name of each file as it is backed up. If the target disk is a diskette, the backup files are stored in its root directory. If the target disk is a fixed disk, the backup files are stored in a directory named \BACKUP.

When it finishes, the Backup command reports to DOS on the backup procedure by setting *errorlevel* to one of the following values:

- 0: Backup was completed successfully.

- 1: No files were found to back up.

- 2: Some files were not backed up because of conflicting file-sharing needs (networks only).

- 3: Ctrl-C was pressed to end the backup process before all files were backed up.

- 4: System problems stopped the backup process.

If you use batch files to help with your backup procedure, you can check this value with the *errorlevel* option of the If batch command and use the result to control what other commands are carried out in a batch file.

Because the Backup command varies among different versions of DOS, it's advisable to use the same version both to back up and to restore files. In particular, do not try to use version 3.3 or later to restore files backed up with version 3.2 or earlier.

Note: Do not back up files from a drive that is affected by an Assign, Substitute, or Join command; restoring the files with the Restore command can damage the directory structure of the disk to which the files are restored.

Examples

To back up all files with the extension DOC from the current directory on the disk in the current drive to the disk in drive A:

```
C:\>backup c:*.doc a:
```

To back up all files whose extension is DOC from the directory named \WORD\MKT on the disk in the current drive to the disk in drive A:

```
C:\>backup c:\word\mkt\*.doc a:
```

To back up to drive A all files in all subdirectories on drive C that have been modified since they were last backed up:

```
C:\>backup c:\ a: /s /m
```

(If the disk in drive A is filled before all the files are backed up, you are prompted to insert a new disk. If you're using a version earlier than 3.3 and you regularly back up large files from a fixed disk to diskettes, prepare an adequate supply of formatted diskettes before beginning a backup procedure. If you're using version 3.3 with unformatted diskettes, use the /F parameter.)

To back up all files whose extension is DOC from the current directory and all its subdirectories in drive D to the disk in drive A and add them to the backup disk:

```
C:\>backup d:*.doc a: /s /a
```

To back up all files whose extension is DOC that were changed on or after October 16, 1988, backing them up from the directory \WORD\MKT on the disk in drive C to the disk in drive A:

```
C:\>backup c:\word\mkt\*.doc a: /d:10-16-88
```

Many options can be used in one Backup command. For example, the following command backs up all files that were changed on or after October 16, 1988, and have not been archived since then, copying them from both the current directory and all its subdirectories from the disk in drive D, then adds them to the disk in drive A and creates the log file named BACKUP.LOG:

```
C:\>backup d: a: /a /s /d:10-16-88 /l
```

BATCH COMMANDS AND BATCH FILES
Executing a File of DOS Commands

In addition to typing DOS commands at command level, you can put one or more commands in a batch file—a file with the extension BAT—and carry out all the commands by typing the name of the file (with or without the extension). For example, assume the file named CDIR.BAT contains the following lines:

```
cls
dir
```

Typing *cdir* at the system prompt causes DOS to clear the screen and display the directory entries of the current directory. The effect is the same as typing the two commands separately. You can create a batch file with Edlin, with a word processor that lets you save a file without formatting, or by copying from the console (CON) to the file with the Copy command.

- The Rem command lets you include comments (remarks) in a batch file. *See* Rem.

- The Shift command moves a series of command-line parameters entered with a batch command one position to the left. The first parameter is lost, the second parameter becomes the first, and so on. *See* Shift.

BREAK
Controlling When DOS Checks for Ctrl-C
Versions 2.0 and later

The Break command lets you control how often DOS checks to find out whether you typed Ctrl-C (or Ctrl-Break on some machines) to end a program. Normally, DOS checks for Ctrl-C only when it reads or writes characters from or to a standard character device, such as the display, a printer, or a communications port.

break on off

on tells DOS to extend its Ctrl-C checking to include each time it reads from or writes to a disk drive.

off tells DOS to check for Ctrl-C only when it reads from or writes to a standard character device.

If you enter break with no parameters, DOS displays the current break status: either *BREAK is on* or *BREAK is off*.

If break is off, your system runs somewhat faster than when break is on, but you have fewer opportunities to stop a program that spends a lot of time doing computations without using an input or output character device.

DOS starts with break off unless you specify otherwise. You can use the Break command described here to set break to *on* any time after starting DOS, or you can tell DOS to start with break on by including the very similar Break configuration command in your CONFIG.SYS file. For information on the Break configuration command, see the following entry.

Examples

To turn break on:

    C:\>break on

To turn break off:

    C:\>break off

To display the break status:

    C:\>break

BREAK
(CONFIGURATION COMMAND)
Controlling When DOS Checks for Ctrl-C
Versions 2.0 and later

Like the DOS Break command, the Break configuration command controls how often DOS checks for Ctrl-C. DOS normally starts with break off, meaning that it checks for Ctrl-C whenever it reads from or writes to a character device, such as the keyboard or display. You can set the break status with the DOS Break command any time while you're using DOS. You can also start DOS with break on by placing a *break=on* configuration command in CONFIG.SYS.

If you're using version 4 of DOS, the installation program added the command *BREAK=ON* to your file of configuration commands. This file is called CONFIG.SYS if you installed DOS on diskettes or on a fixed disk without a CONFIG.SYS file. If you're using DOS from a fixed disk that already contained a CONFIG.SYS file, the configuration file was named CONFIG.400. You or the person who installed DOS should have renamed this file to CONFIG.SYS, editing the commands in it, if necessary, to include needed commands from your earlier CONFIG.SYS file.

If you need more information on this command, refer to the documentation that came with your version of DOS.

BUFFERS
(CONFIGURATION COMMAND)
Controlling the Number of Disk Buffers

Page 314

The Buffers configuration command specifies how many disk buffers DOS sets aside each time it starts. A disk buffer is an area of memory that DOS uses to hold data being read from or written to disk.

The optimum number of buffers depends on several factors, among them:

- The type of disk drives you use. A small increase in the number of buffers speeds fixed-disk operations.

- The amount of memory your computer has. Each buffer reduces available memory by more than 500 bytes, so a large number of buffers can cause your system to run more slowly or run out of memory faster.

- The type of programs you use. For example, increasing the number of buffers speeds up programs that perform a lot of sequential disk access. A database program or a word processor, for example, might benefit from 10 to 20 buffers.

■ The number and levels of subdirectories in your file structure. If you have a large, multilevel subdirectory structure, increasing the number of buffers to between 10 and 25 can significantly speed disk operations.

Increasing the number of buffers to more than about 30, however, can slow the system, because DOS might then be able to read a record from disk faster than it could search through all the buffers.

Unless you specify otherwise with a Buffers command in CONFIG.SYS, DOS uses the following number of buffers:

2	If the system has less than 128 K of memory and 360 K diskette drives.
3	If the system includes a diskette drive with a capacity greater than 360 K.
5	If the system has more than 128 K of memory. (Versions 3.3 and later)
10	If the system has more than 256 K of memory. (Versions 3.3 and later)
15	If the system has more than 512 K of memory. (Versions 3.3 and later)

Finding the right number of buffers for your system might require some experimentation. After changing the number of buffers, use your system for a while and note its performance, then change the number of buffers and repeat your observations. Some programs may suggest or require a minimum number of buffers.

Starting with version 4.0, DOS can "look ahead" by reading data from the sections of a file (called *sectors*) that follow the first sector read. If a program uses data sequentially, that is, it doesn't jump from place to place in a file, looking ahead like this can speed things up by further reducing the time that the program must wait for DOS to locate the data. Version 4.0 also adds a parameter that lets you tell DOS to put the buffers in expanded memory, thus saving the computer's regular memory for programs.

If you're using version 4 of DOS, the installation program added a Buffers command to your file of configuration commands. If you installed DOS on diskettes or on a fixed disk without an existing CONFIG.SYS file, this file was named CONFIG.SYS. If you installed DOS on a fixed disk that already contained a CONFIG.SYS file, the file was named CONFIG.400. You or the person who installed DOS should have renamed the file to CONFIG.SYS, editing it if necessary to include any needed commands from your earlier CONFIG.SYS file.

The Buffers command can have three parameters:

buffers=<number>,<advance>/X

<number> is the number of buffers to set aside. It can be from 1 through 99 in versions through 3.3, and 1 through 99 in version 4.0 if buffers are placed in regular memory. In version 4, if you include the /X parameter to place buffers in expanded memory, and if enough memory is available, <number> can be from 1 through 10,000. Each buffer takes about 530 bytes of memory.

<advance> is the number of sectors that DOS can read, beyond the sector currently being used. <advance> can be from 1 through 8. Each advance, or look-ahead, buffer takes up 512 bytes of memory. (Version 4)

/X tells DOS to put the disk buffers in expanded memory. You can specify /X only if your computer has expanded memory. (Version 4)

Examples

To allocate 25 buffers, put the following Buffers command in CONFIG.SYS:

```
buffers=25
```

The following Buffers command allocates 25 regular buffers and 4 buffers for looking ahead:

```
buffers=25,4
```

CALL (BATCH COMMAND)
Carry Out Another Batch File
Versions 3.3 and later

Page 287

You can use the Call batch command in a batch file to tell DOS to carry out the commands in a second batch file, then return to the original batch file and continue with the next command in it instead of returning to the system prompt. This lets you use a batch command of your own making in a batch file just as you would use any other DOS command.

call <batchfile> <parameters>

<batchfile> is the name of the file of commands you want DOS to carry out.

<parameters> represents any parameters that <batchfile> requires. You can enter the parameters themselves, or you can use replaceable parameters, so that parameters typed on the command line with the name of the first batch file are passed along to the batch file being called.

Example

Suppose you have two batch files. One, named SORTFILE.BAT, first uses the Sort command to sort the file whose name you type as a parameter with *sortfile,* then redirects the sorted output to the printer; the other, WEEKRPT.BAT, carries out several commands to print a series of sorted lists that make up a weekly report.

To use the SORTFILE batch command in WEEKRPT.BAT to print the sorted version of the file named REPORT.LST, include the following Call command in WEEKRPT.BAT:

```
call sortfile report.lst
```

DOS carries out the commands in SORTFILE.BAT—printing the sorted version of REPORT.LST—and continues with the command that follows the Call command in WEEKRPT.BAT.

CHANGE CODE PAGE (CHCP)
Display or Change System-Wide Code Page
Version 3.3

Page 396

The Change Code Page command (chcp) tells DOS which code page to use for all devices that support code-page switching. You use it to change code pages when you want to change the language or character set that DOS uses. The *codepage select* option of the Mode command changes the code page for individual devices.

> **chcp <code-page>**

<code-page> is the three-digit number from the list below that specifies the code page that DOS is to use.

Code-Page Number	Code Page
437	United States
850	Multilingual
860	Portuguese
863	French Canadian
865	Nordic

If you omit <code-page>, Change Code Page displays the current code page. If the code page you specify with Change Code Page isn't compatible with a device, DOS responds *Code page* nnn *not prepared for device* nnn. If you specify a code page with Change Code Page that you didn't first identify with the *codepage prepare* option of the Mode command, DOS responds *Code page* nnn *not prepared for system*.

You must execute the National Language Support Function (nlsfunc) command before you can use the Change Code Page command to change a code page.

Examples

To change the system code page to multilingual (850):

```
C:\>chcp 850
```

To display the current code page (assume that it's 850):

```
C:\>chcp
```

DOS responds *Active code page: 850*.

CHANGE DIRECTORY (CD)
Change Current Directory
Versions 2.0 and later

Page 139

The Change Directory command (cd or chdir) changes or displays the current directory.

cd <drive><path>

<drive> is the letter, followed by a colon, of the drive whose current directory is to be displayed or changed.

<path> is the path name of the directory that is to become the current directory.

If you omit <path>, DOS displays the current directory of the disk in <drive>. If you omit both <drive> and <path>, DOS displays the current directory of the disk in the current drive.

Examples

To change the current directory on the disk in the current drive to \MKT\WP:

```
C:\>cd \mkt\wp
```

To change the current directory on the disk in drive A to \MKT\WP:

```
C:\>cd a:\mkt\wp
```

To display the current directory of the disk in the current drive:

```
C:\>cd
```

To display the current directory of the disk in drive D:

```
C:\>cd d:
```

CHECK DISK (CHKDSK)
Check Disk Status
Versions 1.0 and later

Page 102

The Check Disk command (chkdsk) checks the allocation of storage on a disk and displays a report that shows the total amount of disk space, how much is used by directories and files, including hidden files, and how much is not available because of disk imperfections. Chkdsk also tells you how much memory is in the system and how much is free for use. Beginning with version 4, Chkdsk also reports on disk usage in terms of allocation units (storage units consisting of groups of bytes).

chkdsk <drive><filename> /V /F

<drive> is the letter, followed by a colon, of the drive that contains the disk to be checked (such as *a:*). If you omit <drive>, DOS checks the disk in the current drive.

<filename> specifies one or more files to be checked to see if they are stored in noncontiguous sectors. If you omit <filename>, Chkdsk doesn't check for noncontiguous sectors. If you don't specify a drive letter, Chkdsk checks for the file on the disk in the current drive.

/V displays the full path name and file name of each file and directory on the disk being checked. (Versions 2.0 and later)

/F tells Chkdsk to correct allocation errors, if it finds any and if you respond *y* when it notifies you of the errors and asks whether to correct them. Correcting allocation errors requires changing the information on the disk and may cause loss of some data, so this parameter safeguards against disk changes unless you approve them. (Versions 2.0 and later)

If Chkdsk finds errors in the allocation of disk space, it refers to this space as *clusters* and *chains* and asks whether you want to recover the space into a file. If you reply *y*, Chkdsk corrects the errors only if you included the /F parameter. The space is then recovered into a file named FILE*nnnn*.CHK in the root directory of the drive being checked (*nnnn* is a sequence number that starts with 0000).

If you specify a file name or a set of file names (by using wildcards) when you enter the Chkdsk command, the Chkdsk report tells you whether any of the files are fragmented (stored in noncontiguous sectors) and displays the names of those files. A badly fragmented disk can slow performance. If too many files on a diskette are fragmented, restore them to contiguous sectors by copying them all to another diskette with the Copy command (*copy *.* *). If too many files on a fixed disk are fragmented, you can restore them to contiguous sectors by backing up all the files, reformatting the fixed disk, and restoring the files to the fixed disk.

Note: Chkdsk cannot be used with a drive created or affected by a Join or Substitute command, nor with a network drive.

Examples

To check the disk in the current drive:

```
C:\>chkdsk
```

If there are no errors, Chkdsk displays its report:

```
Volume FIXED DISK  created 10-16-1989 3:12p
Volume Serial Number is 1608-5A30

  33280000 bytes total disk space
     71680 bytes in 3 hidden files
     90112 bytes in 38 directories
```

(continued)

```
19951616 bytes in 938 user files
13166592 bytes available on disk

    2048 bytes in each allocation unit
   16250 total allocation units on disk
    6429 available allocation units on disk

  655360 total bytes memory
  517776 bytes free
```

To check the disk in drive A, checking all files in the directory \MKT\WP to see if they are fragmented:

```
C:\>chkdsk a:\mkt\wp\*.*
```

CHKDSK displays its usual report, followed by a list of any fragmented files:

```
A:\MKT\WP\REPORT.DOC Contains 2 non-contiguous blocks
A:\MKT\WP\FORECAST.DOC Contains 5 non-contiguous blocks
A:\MKT\WP\SALESREP.DOC Contains 4 non-contiguous blocks
```

To check the disk in the current drive and tell CHKDSK you want to be able to recover any lost clusters:

```
C:\>chkdsk /f
```

CHKDSK displays its usual report. If there are allocation errors, it displays a message such as:

```
4 lost clusters found in 4 chains.
Convert lost chains to files (Y/N) ?
```

If you want to recover the clusters, reply *y*. When the command has completed, display the file named FILE*nnnn*.CHK; rename it if it contains data you want to keep, or delete it to make the disk space available to other files.

CLS
Clear the Screen
Versions 2.0 and later

Page 112

The Clear Screen command clears the screen and displays the system prompt in the top left-hand corner. Clear Screen has no parameters.

cls

Example

To clear the screen:

```
C:\>cls
```

COMMAND
Start a New Command Processor
Versions 1.0 and later

The Command command loads another copy of the DOS command processor (COMMAND.COM), the program that displays the system prompt and responds to the commands you type.

command /P /C <command>

/P makes the new copy of COMMAND.COM permanent. It displays the sign-on message and system prompt, and waits for a command. There is no way to return to the previous command processor. (Versions 2.0 and later)

/C <command> loads the new copy of COMMAND.COM, carries out the command specified by <command>, and returns control to the previous command processor. (Versions 2.0 and later)

If you enter a Command command with no parameters, the new copy of COMMAND.COM displays the sign-on message and system prompt and waits for a command. The new copy of COMMAND.COM remains in memory until you type *exit*. Control then returns to the previous command processor.

If you put a Command command with the /C parameter in a batch file and use it to carry out another batch file, DOS continues with the next statement in the first batch file when the second batch file completes. This allows a batch file to call another batch file, as well as to chain to another batch file. This technique is unnecessary in versions 3.3 and later, because they include the Call command.

Examples

To load a new copy of COMMAND.COM that remains in control until you type *exit*:

```
C:\>command
```

To load a permanent new copy of COMMAND.COM:

```
C:\>command /p
```

To cause a batch file (BATCH1.BAT) to load a new copy of COMMAND.COM, carry out the commands in a second batch file (BATCH2.BAT), finish carrying out the commands in the first batch file, and return to the previous command processor, put the following command in BATCH1.BAT:

```
command /c batch2.bat
```

COMPARE (COMP)
Compare Two Files
Version 3.3, IBM releases 1.0 and later

Page 77

The Compare command (comp) compares two files or sets of files byte by byte and reports up to 10 differences for each comparison. If it finds any differences, Compare displays the location (counting from the beginning of the file) and hexadecimal (base-16) value of the differing bytes in each file. While you probably don't want to interpret these values, Compare is useful, for example, in helping you determine whether two files with the same name in different directories are exact duplicates.

If the files are the same, DOS displays *Files compare OK*. If the files are different lengths, DOS displays *Files are different sizes*. If the files are the same length but their content differs, DOS displays the first 10 bytes it finds that are different; if more than 10 bytes are different, it displays *10 Mismatches - ending compare*. After completing the comparison, DOS asks if you want to compare any more files.

comp <file1> <file2>

<file1> is the name of the first file to be compared. You can include a drive and path, and you can use wildcard characters to specify a group of files with similar names or extensions.

<file2> is the name of the second file to be compared. You can include a drive and path and use wildcard characters to specify a group of files with similar names or extensions. If you specify only a drive letter or path name, DOS compares <file1> to the file with the same name in the drive or directory specified in <file2>; if you use wildcard characters in <file1>, DOS compares all files in the drive or directory that match <file1>.

If you omit <file2>, DOS prompts for it. If you omit both <file1> and <file2> (just type *comp*), DOS prompts you for both file names.

Examples

To compare two files in the current directory named REPORT.DOC and FEB.RPT:

```
C:\MKT\WP>comp report.doc feb.rpt
```

To compare the file in the current directory named REPORT.DOC to the file named FEB.RPT in the directory named \REPORTS on the disk in the current drive:

```
C:\MKT\WP>comp report.doc \reports\feb.rpt
```

To compare the file in the current directory named REPORT.DOC with the file with the same name in the directory named \REPORTS on the disk in drive A:

```
C:\MKT\WP>comp report.doc a:\reports
```

To compare all files in the current directory whose extension is DOC with all files with the same name and extension in the current directory of the disk in drive A:

```
C:\MKT\WP>comp *.doc a:
```

CONFIG.SYS
File of System Configuration Commands

Page 309

CONFIG.SYS is a file that contains configuration commands that define the hardware and software that make up your system. It must be in the root directory of the system disk. Each time DOS starts, it carries out the commands in CONFIG.SYS. If there is no file named CONFIG.SYS in the root directory of the system disk, DOS assumes certain configuration values.

The configuration commands include:

- Break, which controls how often DOS checks for Ctrl-C. *See* Break.

- Buffers, which specifies how many disk buffers DOS sets aside. *See* Buffers.

- Country, which specifies the country whose date and time format is to be used. *See* Country.

- Device, which identifies a file that contains a program to control a device (such a program is called a *device driver*). *See* Device.

- Drivparm, which defines the operating characteristics of a disk or a tape drive. *See* Drivparm.

- FCBS, which specifies the number of files controlled by File Control Blocks (FCBs) that can be open at the same time. *See* FCBS.

- Files, which specifies how many files controlled by handles can be open at the same time. *See* Files.

- Install, which loads a command file from CONFIG.SYS. *See* Install.

- Lastdrive, which sets the highest drive letter that DOS recognizes. *See* Lastdrive.

- Shell, which specifies the name of a command processor to be used instead of COMMAND.COM. *See* Shell.

- Stacks, which tells DOS how much memory to reserve for its temporary use. *See* Stacks.

- Switches, which blocks enhanced keyboard functions. *See* Switches.

CONFIG.SYS is a text file; you can create it with a text editor, such as Edlin, or a word processor that lets you store a file without formatting codes.

The Select command creates a CONFIG.SYS file that includes a Country configuration command. You can add more configuration commands to this CONFIG.SYS file with a text editor or word processor.

COPY
Copy a File or Device
Versions 1.0 and later

Pages 65, 122

Copy copies one or more files from a disk or a device to another file or device. File attributes are not copied; DOS won't copy a file to itself.

The Copy command has the following parameters. Some, such as /A and /B, are not often needed and thus are not described in the body of this book. Also, because the Copy command can be used with either files or devices, the following description refers to the *source* and *target* of a Copy command. In Chapter 5 and elsewhere, specific uses of the Copy command sometimes refer to *source* and *target* as either *file1* or *file2,* or as *device.*

copy <source> /A /B +<source> <target> /A /B /V

<source> is the file or device to be copied. You can use wildcard characters to copy a set of files with similar names or extensions. You can combine several source files into one target file by separating the source file names with plus signs (+)—if you don't specify <target>, the files are combined into the first source file in the series; otherwise, the files are combined into <target>.

<target> is the file or device to which <source> is to be copied. If <source> is to be copied to the same directory on the same disk, <target> must be different from <source>. If you specify a source file on a different drive or in a different directory and you omit <target>, the source file is copied to a file with the same name in the current directory. If you specify just a drive letter, a path name, or a file name as <target>, the source file is copied as described below:

Target:	Source file is copied to:
Drive letter	A file with the same name in the current directory of the specified drive.
Path name	A file with the same name in the specified directory.
File name	A file with the specified name in the current directory.

/A (for *ASCII*) treats the preceding file named in the Copy command as a text file. If /A is included in a Copy command, it affects the file preceding the /A and all subsequent file names listed in the command up to, but not including, a file name followed by the /B option.

If /A is specified with one or more source files, the files are copied up to the first Ctrl-Z character in each. The Ctrl-Z and any data that follows are not copied. If /A is specified with one or more target files, DOS adds a Ctrl-Z character at the end of each file. When DOS combines files or copies to or from a device, it uses the /A option.

/B (for *binary*) treats the files as non-text files. If /B is specified with one or more source files, the files are copied in their entirety (based on the file size recorded in the directory entry). If /B is specified with one or more target files, DOS does not add a Ctrl-Z character at the end of each.

/V verifies that the file was copied correctly. DOS turns verification on, copies the file, then turns verification off. You don't need this parameter if you've turned on the DOS verify option with the Verify command. Verification slows the copy process.

Examples

To copy the file named REPORT.TXT from the root directory of drive A to a file named FINAL.RPT in the directory named \MKT\WP on the disk in the current drive:

```
C:\>copy a:\report.txt \mkt\wp\final.rpt
```

To copy the file named FORECAST.DOC from the directory named \MKT\WP on the disk in drive A to the current directory on the disk in the current drive, giving the file the same name:

```
C:\MKT\BUDGET>copy a:\mkt\wp\forecast.doc
```

To copy all files with the extension TXT from the current directory of the disk in drive D to the current directory of the disk in the current drive, giving the copies the extension DOC:

```
C:\MKT\WP>copy d:*.txt *.doc
```

To combine the files named FCST-APR.DOC, FCST-MAY.DOC, and FCST-JUN.DOC in the current directory into a file named FCST-2Q.DOC in the current directory:

```
C:\MKT\WP>copy fcst-apr.doc+fcst-may.doc+fcst-
jun.doc fcst-2q.doc
```

To add the files named FCST-MAY.DOC and FCST-JUN.DOC to the file in the current directory named FCST-APR.DOC:

```
C:\MKT\WP>copy fcst-apr.doc+fcst-may.doc+fcst-jun.doc
```

To combine all the files in the current directory whose extension is DOC, in the order in which their directory entries appear, into another file, named TOTAL.DOC, which is also in the current directory:

```
C:\MKT\WP>copy *.doc total.doc
```

Note: When you use wildcard characters to combine one or more source files into a target file that already exists, the original contents of the target file are lost—replaced by the contents of the combined source file(s). DOS does not warn you that data will be lost, but does display the message Content of destination lost before copy *when the copy procedure is completed. If you want to add files to an existing file, but keep the original information intact, use the plus sign between the names of the source files, specifying the target file name first.*

To copy the file REPORT.DOC to the display (CON):

```
C:\MKT\WP>copy report.doc con
```

The file is displayed, just as if you had entered *type report.doc*.

To copy from the keyboard (CON) to a file named REPORT.DOC in the current directory:

```
C:\MKT\WP>copy con report.doc
```

Type the lines you want in the file. To end the copy, press Ctrl-Z, then press Enter.

To copy from the keyboard (CON) to the printer (PRN):

```
C:\>copy con prn
```

Type the lines to be printed. To print the lines, press Ctrl-Z, then press Enter.

COUNTRY
(CONFIGURATION COMMAND)
Set the International Date
And Currency Format
Versions 2.1 and later, IBM releases 3.0 and later

Pages 387, 399

The Country command tells DOS which conventions to follow when displaying the date, by specifying a country code for a particular country. If there is no Country command in CONFIG.SYS, DOS follows the conventions of the country for which it was manufactured.

DOS also uses the country code to choose the currency symbol and the character that separates the thousands and decimal fraction parts of a number. Although these characters aren't used in normal DOS operation, the country code is available to application programs so that they can use the proper conventions.

country=<country-code>,<code-page>,<country-file>

<country-code> is the three-digit country code that specifies the country whose date format is to be followed; it is the same as the international telephone dialing prefix. DOS can recognize the following country codes. You must include all three digits, including any zeros at the beginning.

Country or Language	Country Code	Valid Code Pages	DOS Version/Notes
Arabic	785	864, 850	Version 4 with country-specific supplement
Australia	061	437, 850	Versions 2.1 and later
Belgium	032	850, 437	Versions 2.1 and later
Canada (French)	002	863, 850	Versions 3.3 and later
Chinese (simplified)	086	936, 437	Asian edition of version 4 on a computer manufactured for use in Asia
Chinese (traditional)	088	938, 437	Asian edition of version 4 on a computer manufactured for use in Asia
Denmark	045	850, 865	Versions 2.1 and later
Finland	358	850, 437	Versions 2.1 and later
France	033	437, 850	Versions 2.1 and later
Germany	049	437, 850	Versions 2.1 and later
Hebrew	972	862, 850	Version 4 with country-specific supplement
Italy	039	437, 850	Versions 2.1 and later
Japan	081	932, 437	Asian edition of version 4 on a computer manufactured for use in Asia
Korea	082	934, 437	Asian edition of version 4 on a computer manufactured for use in Asia
Latin America	003	437, 850	Versions 3.3 and later
Netherlands	031	437, 850	Versions 2.1 and later
Norway	047	850, 865	Versions 2.1 and later
Portugal	351	850, 860	Versions 3.3 and later
Spain	034	437, 850	Versions 2.1 and later
Switzerland	041	850, 437	Versions 2.1 and later
United Kingdom	044	437, 850	Versions 2.1 and later
United States	001	437, 850	Versions 2.1 and later

<code-page> is a three-digit number that specifies the code page that DOS is to use. (Versions 3.3 and later)

<country-file> is the name of the DOS file that contains the country-specific information. If you omit <country-file>, DOS assumes the file is COUNTRY.SYS and is stored in the root directory of the current drive. (Versions 3.3 and later)

Example

In Belgium, the date is formatted as dd/mm/yyyy; for example, 16/10/1989 for October 16, 1989. To specify the Belgian format, put the following Country command in CONFIG.SYS:

```
country=032
```

CTTY
Change the Console Device
Versions 2.0 and later

The CTTY command specifies the device to be used for standard input and standard output. You can assign standard input and output to a communications port, for example, to permit remote operation of the computer, or assign them to special devices supported by custom control programs.

Not all programs recognize the assignment of standard input and standard output. The Microsoft BASIC interpreter, for example, does not, and so is unaffected by the Change Console command.

ctty <device>

<device> is the name of the device that is to be used for standard input and standard output; the device must be capable of both input and output. If <device> specifies a device other than CON, AUX, or COM*n*, CONFIG.SYS must include a Device command that names the file that contains the control program (device driver), and DOS must have access to that file.

Examples

To assign standard input and standard output to communications port COM1:

```
C:\>ctty com1
```

To reassign standard input and standard output to the keyboard and display:

```
C:\>ctty con
```

DATE
Change or Display the System Date
Versions 1.0 and later

Page 13

The Date command displays the date maintained by DOS and prompts you to enter a new date. The sequence of the day, month, and year depends on the country code set with the Country or Select commands. The sequence here is for the United States.

date <mm-dd-yy>

<mm-dd-yy> is the new date to be set. <mm> is the month (1 through 12), <dd> is the day (1 through 31), and <yy> is the year (1980 or later). You can separate the day, month, and year with hyphens, slashes, or periods: 10-16-89 or 10/16/89 or 10.16.89.

If you type just *date*, DOS displays the current date and prompts you to enter the new date. Type a new date or press the Enter key to leave the date unchanged.

Examples

To set the date to October 16, 1989:

```
C:\>date 10-16-89
```

To display the current system date and respond to the prompt for a new date:

```
C:\>date
```

DOS responds:

```
Current date is Mon 10-16-1989
Enter new date (mm-dd-yy): _
```

Type the new date, or press the Enter key to leave the current date unchanged.

DELETE (DEL)
Delete (Erase) a File

See Erase.

DEVICE
(CONFIGURATION COMMAND)
Define a Device-Control Program
Versions 2.0 and later

Page 310

The Device configuration command identifies a file that contains a program to control a device. DOS automatically recognizes and works with certain devices, such as the keyboard and the display. But other devices, such as a mouse, can be added to a computer system. If you add a device that DOS doesn't already know about, you must tell DOS the name of the device's controlling program. Such a control program, called a *device driver,* usually has the extension SYS and comes with the device. You can put more than one Device command in CONFIG.SYS.

device=<device>

<device> is the name of the file that contains the device driver.
The device drivers listed at the top of the next page are included with DOS.

Driver Name	DOS Version	Controls
ANSI.SYS	2.0 and later	Display and keyboard. This is an advanced use of DOS briefly described in the entry ANSI.SYS. Details are in the DOS *Technical Reference* manual and the book *Supercharging MS-DOS* (Van Wolverton, Microsoft Press, 1989).
VDISK.SYS	3.0 and later (IBM releases only)	Virtual disk drive; *see* VDISK.SYS.
RAMDRIVE.SYS	3.2 and later (Microsoft releases)	Virtual disk drive; *see* VDISK.SYS.
DISPLAY.SYS	3.3 and later	Display (code-page switching; *see* Appendix D).
PRINTER.SYS	3.3 and later	Printer (code-page switching; *see* Appendix D).
DRIVER.SYS*	3.2 and later	Diskette drives. This device driver enables you to assign a drive letter to an internal or external diskette drive.
XMAEM.SYS*	4.0 and later (IBM releases only)	Extended/expanded memory. This device driver enables use of extra memory in computers, such as the IBM PS/2 Model 80, based on an 80386 processor.
XMA2EMS.SYS	4.0 and later (IBM releases only)	Expanded memory. This device driver enables use of extra memory based on the Lotus-Intel-Microsoft Expanded Memory Specification.
SMARTDRV.SYS	4.0 and later (Microsoft releases)	Expanded/extended memory. This device driver enables a computer with a fixed disk and extra memory to use some or all of that memory as a temporary storage area (disk cache) for current information.

* Use of this device driver is beyond the scope of this book; for details, refer to your computer's manual(s) and to your DOS manual.

Example

To load the device driver (from the root directory) for the Microsoft mouse, put the following Device command in CONFIG.SYS:

```
device=mouse.sys
```

DIRECTORY (DIR)
Display Directory Entries
Versions 1.0 and later

Page 62

The Directory command (dir) displays the directory entry of one or more files. A Directory command display looks like the following:

```
Volume in drive C is FIXED DISK
Volume Serial Number is 1608-5A30
Directory of  C:\MKT\WP

.              <DIR>       09-02-89    5:24p
..             <DIR>       09-02-89    5:24p
REPORT   DOC     60780 08-15-89    1:09a
FORECAST DOC     18256 10-10-89    7:46p
SALESREP DOC     25728 10-13-89    8:42a
LETTERS        <DIR>
FCST-APR DOC      4328 10-12-89    9:07a
FCST-MAY DOC     20982 09-24-89   10:09p
STYLE          <DIR>
FCST-MAR DOC       996 10-12-89    5:36p
WKRPT    STY      2688 10-12-89    5:50p
BUDGET   DOC      5888 10-11-89    9:28a
        12 File(s)    23633152 bytes free
```

The first three lines show the volume label of the disk (FIXED DISK), the volume serial number (beginning with version 4), and the drive and path name of the directory whose entries are displayed (C:\MKT\WP). The last line shows the number of directory entries displayed (12) and the available space on the disk (23,633,152 bytes).

The directory entry for a file includes the file name and extension, size in bytes, and the date and time it was created or last changed. The directory entry for a subdirectory (LETTERS and STYLE in the preceding example) includes the file name and extension, followed by <DIR>.

The first two subdirectory entries in the preceding example are symbolic; the first (one period) represents the directory whose entries are displayed, and the second (two periods) represents the directory that contains the directory whose entries are displayed (sometimes referred to as the *parent* directory). The entries . and .. do not appear in the listing of the root directory of a disk.

dir <filename> /W /P

<filename> is the name of the file whose directory entry is to be displayed. You can use wildcard characters to display the entries of a set of files with similar names or extensions. If you omit <filename>, DOS displays the directory entry of each file in the specified or current directory. If you specify only a drive letter, DOS displays the directory entry of each file in the current directory of the specified drive. If you

specify a file name but no extension, DOS displays the directory entry for each file with that file name, regardless of extension.

/W (for *wide*) displays just the file name and extension of each directory entry in five columns across the screen.

/P (for *pause*) displays the directory one screenful at a time, displaying *Press any key to continue . . .* (*Strike a key when ready . . .* in versions prior to 4) at the bottom of the screen. Pressing any key displays the next screenful of entries.

Examples

To display the directory entry of each file with the extension DOC in the current directory on the disk in drive A:

```
C:\>dir a:*.doc
```

To display the directory entry of each file in the directory \MKT\WP on the disk in the current drive, in wide format:

```
C:\>dir \mkt\wp /w
```

To display the directory entry of each file in the parent (MKT) of the current directory on the disk in the current drive, pausing after each screenful:

```
C:\MKT>dir .. /p
```

To display the directory entry of each file without an extension in the current directory on the disk in the current drive:

```
C:\>dir *.
```

DISK COMPARE (DISKCOMP)
Compare Two Diskettes
Versions 3.2 and later, IBM releases 1.0 and later

Page 99

The Diskcomp command compares two diskettes of the same size and capacity track by track and reports the side and track of any sectors that differ; if the diskettes are identical, it reports *Compare OK*. Because it compares the sectors of the diskettes, Diskcomp does not necessarily report that two diskettes containing the same files are identical; the files could be stored in different locations.

The Diskcomp command automatically determines the number of sides and sectors per track from the disk in the first drive specified (which it calls the source). You cannot compare a diskette in a double-sided drive to a diskette in a single-sided drive, nor can you compare two diskettes with different numbers of sectors per track. You can, however, compare just one side of diskettes in double-sided drives, or just the first 8 sectors of each track on diskettes written with 9 sectors per track.

Note: The Diskcomp command cannot be used with a fixed disk, with a drive created or affected by an Assign, Join, or Substitute command, or with a network drive.

diskcomp <drive1> <drive2> /1 /8

<drive1> is the letter of the diskette drive, followed by a colon, that contains the first diskette to be compared (such as *a:*).

<drive2> is the letter of the diskette drive, followed by a colon, that contains the second diskette to be compared. If you omit <drive2> (type only one drive letter), DOS compares the diskette in <drive1> to the diskette in the current drive. If you omit both <drive1> and <drive2>, or if you omit <drive2> and specify the current drive as <drive1>, or if you specify the same drive for both <drive1> and <drive2>, DOS prompts you through a one-drive comparison. If you type the Diskcomp command when the current drive is a fixed disk, you must specify both <drive1> and <drive2> because Diskcomp is for diskettes only.

/1 compares only the first side of the diskettes, even if they are in double-sided diskette drives.

/8 compares only the first 8 sectors of each track, even if the diskettes have more sectors per track.

If you have only one diskette drive, or you specify a one-drive comparison, the Diskcomp command prompts you to swap diskettes.

After it has compared the diskettes, the Diskcomp command prompts *Compare more diskettes (Y/N)?* If you reply *y*, it again prompts you to insert the source and target diskettes in the specified drives.

Examples

To compare the diskette in drive A to the diskette in drive B:

```
C:\>diskcomp a: b:
```

If you have only one diskette drive, the Diskcomp command tells you when to swap diskettes.

To compare the first side of the diskette in drive A to the first side of the diskette in the current drive (B):

```
B>diskcomp a: /1
```

If drive A were the current drive, DOS would prompt you through a one-drive comparison.

To compare two diskettes using only the current drive (A):

```
A>diskcomp
```

DISKCOPY
Copy a Complete Diskette
Versions 2.0 and later

Page 97

The Diskcopy command makes a sector-by-sector copy of a diskette. If the target diskette isn't formatted to match the source diskette, the Diskcopy command in version 4 and in all earlier IBM releases of DOS formats the target diskette; in other releases numbered 2.0 through 3.1, the target diskette may need to be formatted before the Diskcopy command is entered.

Because the Diskcopy command makes an identical copy, it does not consolidate fragmented files; to consolidate fragmented files, use the Copy command and specify *.* to copy all files from the source diskette to the target diskette.

Note: The Diskcopy command cannot be used with a fixed disk, with a drive created or affected by an Assign, Join, or Substitute command, or with a network drive. You cannot use Diskcopy with dissimilar diskette types—for example, a 720 K diskette and a 1.2 MB diskette. Nor can you copy a diskette in a double-sided drive to a diskette in a single-sided drive, although you can use the /1 option to copy the first side of a diskette in a double-sided drive to a diskette in a single-sided drive.

diskcopy <source> <target> /1

<source> is the letter, followed by a colon, of the diskette drive that contains the diskette to be copied (such as *a:*). If you enter only one drive letter, DOS assumes it contains the source diskette.

<target> is the letter of the diskette drive, followed by a colon, that contains the diskette to which <source> is to be copied. If you omit <target> (enter only one drive letter), DOS copies the diskette in <source> to the diskette in the current drive. If you omit both <source> and <target>, or if you omit <target> and specify the current drive (which cannot be a fixed disk) as the <source>, or if you specify the same drive for both <source> and <target>, DOS prompts you through a one-drive copy. If you type the Diskcopy command when the current drive is a fixed disk, you must include both <source> and <target> because Diskcopy is for diskettes only.

/1 copies only the first side of <source>, even if <source> is a double-sided diskette.

If you have only one diskette drive, or specify a single diskette drive as both the source and the target, DOS prompts you to swap diskettes.

After it has copied the diskette, DOS prompts *Copy another (Y/N)?* If you reply *y*, DOS prompts you to insert the source and target diskettes. After ending the Diskcopy command by replying *n* to the concluding prompt, you can verify the copy with the Diskcomp command.

The Diskcopy command reports the side, track, and sector of any disk errors it encounters. If these sectors contain valid data, the copy may not be usable.

Examples

To copy the diskette in drive A to the diskette in drive B:

```
C:\>diskcopy a: b:
```

If you have only one diskette drive, DOS prompts you through a one-drive copy.

On a system with two diskette drives, to copy the first side of the diskette in drive B to the first side of the diskette in the current drive (A):

```
A>diskcopy b: /1
```

If drive B were the current drive, DOS would prompt you through a one-drive copy.

To copy a diskette using only the current drive (A):

```
A>diskcopy
```

DOSSHELL
Start the DOS Shell
Version 4.0 and later

Page 324

DOSSHELL.BAT is a batch file that starts the DOS Shell, which was introduced with version 4 of DOS. Use of the Shell, including startup parameters in DOSSHELL.BAT, is described in Chapter 17, ''The DOS Shell.''

DRIVE PARAMETERS—DRIVPARM
(CONFIGURATION COMMAND)
Define a Disk or Tape Drive
Versions 3.2 and later, non-IBM releases only

The Drive Parameters configuration command (drivparm) defines the operating characteristics of a disk or tape drive. If you don't specify device characteristics with Drivparm, DOS assumes standard characteristics for that type of device. In general, you need to use the Drivparm command only if you attach a nonstandard disk or tape drive to your system. If you need more information on this command, refer to the documentation that came with your version of DOS.

ECHO (BATCH COMMAND)
Display a Message
Versions 2.0 and later

Page 259

The Echo command sends a message to the standard output device (usually the display), controls whether DOS displays commands as it carries them out (echo on), or displays the status of echo (on or off). DOS turns echo on when it starts carrying out the commands in a batch file, unless the file is started by another batch file that turns echo off.

    echo on off <message>

on tells DOS to display each command as it is carried out.
off tells DOS not to display each command as it is carried out.
<message> is a message to be sent to standard output.
If you enter an Echo command with no parameters (just type *echo*), DOS displays the status of echo (either *ECHO is on* or *ECHO is off*).

Examples

To turn echo on:

    `echo on`

To turn echo off:

    `echo off`

To display the message *Put the backup diskette in drive A*:

    `echo Put the backup diskette in drive A`

To display the echo status:

    `C:\>echo`

EDLIN
Create or Modify a Text File
Versions 1.0 and later

Page 194

Edlin is a program for creating and changing files of text. It includes a variety of single-letter commands for inserting, deleting, changing, copying, and moving lines. Each line can be up to 253 characters long. In addition to the Edlin commands, you can use the DOS editing keys to edit individual lines.

Because Edlin is a line-oriented editor, it displays a line number at the beginning of each line; these numbers are for reference only and are not part of the file. Edlin renumbers lines after any command that changes the sequence or number of lines in the file, to maintain an unbroken sequence.

When you enter the Edlin command (type *edlin* followed by a file name) at the system prompt, Edlin loads the file to be edited (or creates it, if it's a new file), displays an asterisk (its prompt), and waits for a command. If the file to be edited would fill more than 75 percent of available memory, Edlin loads the file until the available memory is 75 percent full, then reserves the remaining 25 percent for additions. The Write and Append commands write edited lines to disk and read more unedited lines into memory, letting you edit a file larger than available memory.

Most Edlin commands consist of a single character preceded by one or more parameters. The command characters can be entered in either uppercase or lowercase; you end a command by pressing Enter. You can enter more than one command on a line, separating them with semicolons.

Just as DOS keeps track of a current drive and current directory, Edlin keeps track of the *current line,* which is the target for many commands if you don't specify a line number. Many of the Edlin commands operate on a range of lines, which you define by specifying the beginning and ending line numbers.

All Edlin commands that accept a line number or range of line numbers recognize the following symbolic references:

#	means the line after the last line in the file.
.	(a period) means the current line.
+ or −	specifies line numbers relative to the current line; for example, +3 means three lines past the current line.

When you end an editing session and write a revised file back to disk, Edlin renames the original version to give it the extension BAK, thus saving a backup copy of the original. If a file with the same name and the extension BAK exists on the same disk, Edlin deletes the existing file before renaming the original.

To start Edlin, you enter the Edlin command at the DOS system prompt.

edlin <filename>

<filename> is the name of the text file to be created or changed. If the file exists, Edlin copies it into memory. If the file doesn't exist, Edlin creates it. Except in version 3.3, Edlin won't edit a file whose extension is BAK. To edit a file whose extension is BAK, first change the extension with the DOS Rename command.

For quick reference, the table at the top of the next page lists the name and format of the Edlin commands.

Command	Format
Append	\<lines>a
Copy	\<from>,\<to>,\<target>,\<count>c
Delete	\<from>,\<to>d
Edit	\<line> or .
End	e
Insert	\<target>i
List	\<from>,\<to>l
Move	\<from>,\<to>,\<target>m
Page	\<from>,\<to>p
Quit	q
Replace	\<from>,\<to>?r\<string1>\<F6 or Ctrl-Z>\<string2>
Search	\<from>,\<to>?s\<string>
Transfer	\<target>t\<filename>
Write	\<lines>w

Individual command descriptions follow. The examples at the end of each description show representative uses of the command. Several examples use the symbolic references to show more than one way to accomplish the same editing task.

EDLIN: APPEND
Read Lines from Disk into Memory
Versions 1.0 and later

Page 223

The Edlin Append command reads additional lines of a file being edited from disk to the end of the file in memory. It is used when a file is larger than 75 percent of the available memory. If all available memory is full, you must use the Write command to write lines from memory to disk to make room for the appended lines.

\<lines>a

\<lines> specifies the number of lines to append. If you omit \<lines>, Edlin appends lines until 75 percent of the available memory is full. If that memory is already 75 percent full, Edlin ignores the Append command.

Examples

To append lines until available memory is 75 percent full:

   *a

To append 200 lines:

```
*200a
```

EDLIN: COPY
Copy Lines
Versions 2.0 and later

Page 221

The Edlin Copy command copies one or more lines from one place in a file to another. The first copied (target) line becomes the new current line.

<from>,<to>,<target>,<count>c

<from> is the number of the first line to be copied. If you don't specify <from>, Edlin starts with the current line. If you omit <from>, you must still enter the comma that follows, to show that you omitted it.

<to> is the number of the last line to be copied. The number in <to> must be equal to or greater than the number in <from>. If you don't specify <to>, Edlin stops with the current line. If you omit <to>, you must still enter the comma that follows, to show that you omitted it. To copy a single line, specify the same line number for both <to> and <from>. To copy the current line, omit both <from> and <to> and begin the command with two commas.

<target> is the number of the line *before* which the lines are to be copied. You must enter <target>.

<count> specifies how many times the lines are to be copied. If you don't specify <count>, Edlin copies the lines once.

Examples

The following examples assume that the current line is 20.
To copy lines 20 through 25 before line 5:

```
*20,25,5c
```

or

```
*,25,5c
```

To copy line 20 through the last line before line 5:

```
*20,#,5c
```

To copy line 20 before line 30:

```
*20,20,30c
```

or

```
*,,+10c
```

To copy lines 20 through 25 three times before line 1:

    `*20,25,1,3c`

or

    `*,+5,1,3c`

To copy line 20 fifteen times before line 10:

    `*,20,10,15c`

EDLIN: DELETE
Delete a Line
Versions 1.0 and later

Page 199

The Delete command deletes lines from the file. The line after the last line deleted becomes the new current line.

    <from>,<to>d

    <from> is the number of the first line to be deleted. If you don't specify <from>, Edlin starts with the current line. If you omit <from>, you must still enter the comma, to show that you omitted <from>.

    <to> is the number of the last line to be deleted. The number in <to> must be equal to or greater than <from>. If you don't specify <to>, Edlin deletes just the line specified by <from>. If you omit both <from> and <to> (just type *d*), Edlin deletes the current line.

Examples

The following examples assume that the current line is 20.

    To delete lines 20 through 25:

    `*20,25d`

or

    `*,+5d`

To delete line 20:

    `*20d`

or

    `*d`

To delete line 20 through the last line in the file:

    *20,#d

or

    *,#d

EDLIN: EDIT
Edit a Line
Versions 1.0 and later

Page 205

There is no Edit command character. To edit a line, simply type the line number and press Enter; Edlin displays the line, moves the cursor to the beginning of the next line, displays the line number and the following colon, then waits for you to edit the line. You can change the line by pressing the editing keys or by typing new text, or you can leave the line unchanged by pressing Enter when the cursor is at the beginning of the line. The line you are editing becomes the new current line.

You can edit the current line by typing a period and pressing Enter; you can edit the line that follows the current line just by pressing Enter.

<line> or .

<line> is the number of the line to be edited. If you specify <line> as a period, Edlin displays the current line for editing. If you omit <line>, Edlin displays the line following the current line.

Examples

The following examples assume that the current line is 20. Pressing the Enter key is represented by <Enter>.

To edit line 25:

    *25<Enter>

or

    *+5<Enter>

To edit line 20:

    *.<Enter>

To edit line 21:

    *<Enter>

To edit the last line in the file:

    *#;-1<Enter>

This example shows two commands on the same line. The # at the beginning of the command changes the current line to the line following the last line in the file. The *−1* specifies the line that precedes the current line. The semicolon (*;*) separates the two commands.

EDLIN: END EDIT
End the Editing Session
Versions 1.0 and later

Page 198

The End edit command writes the file currently being edited from memory to disk and ends the editing session. (To end the session without saving the file, use the Edlin Quit command, described later.)

If an existing file was being edited, Edlin changes the extension of the original file to BAK. If there isn't room on the disk to save the revised version of the file, Edlin writes as much of the file as it can on the disk, gives the file the same name with the extension $$$, and displays the message *Disk full. Edits lost*; the part of the file in memory is lost (in this case, Edlin does not change the extension of the original file to BAK).

If the last line of the file doesn't end with a carriage return when you enter the End command, Edlin adds a carriage return. If the last character of the file isn't a Ctrl-Z, Edlin adds a Ctrl-Z.

The End edit command has no parameters.

Example

To end an editing session and save the current file on disk:

        *e

EDLIN: INSERT
Insert Lines
Versions 1.0 and later

Page 195

The Insert command enters new lines into the file being edited. Edlin prompts with the number of the new line, and continues to prompt for a new line each time you press Enter, until you press Ctrl-C to stop inserting lines. The first line following the inserted line or lines becomes the new current line.

You can enter a control character (such as Ctrl-G, to cause the system to beep) into a file by first pressing Ctrl-V and then typing the uppercase letter that corresponds to the control character you want to enter. To include an Escape character, press Ctrl-V and then the left bracket key ([ ). This is a convenient way to create escape sequences to use with ANSI.SYS or with programs that require an Escape character in a text file.

<target>i

<target> is the line before which the new lines are to be inserted. If you don't specify <target>, Edlin inserts the new lines before the current line. If you specify <target> as # or as a number larger than the highest line number in the file, Edlin adds the lines at the end of the file.

Examples

The following examples assume that the current line is 20.

To insert lines after line 20:

```
*21i
```

To insert lines before line 17:

```
*17i
```

or

```
*-3i
```

To insert lines at the beginning of the file:

```
*1i
```

To insert lines at the end of the file:

```
*#i
```

EDLIN: LIST
Display Specified Lines
Versions 1.0 and later

Page 196

The List command displays one or more lines of the file being edited. It doesn't change the current line.

<from>,<to>l

<from> is the number of the first line to be displayed. If you don't specify <from>, Edlin starts the display with the line 11 lines before the current line. If you omit <from> but want to specify <to>, you must enter the comma, to show that you omitted <from>.

<to> is the number of the last line to be displayed. It must be equal to or greater than <from>. If you omit <to>, Edlin displays one screenful of lines starting with

<from>. If you omit both <from> and <to> (just type *l*), Edlin displays one screenful of lines centered around the current line; if the current line is less than 13, Edlin displays a total of one screenful of lines, starting at the beginning of the file.

Beginning with version 4, Edlin displays the message *Continue (Y/N)?* at the bottom of the screen if the file continues beyond the last line displayed. On a computer with a display running in normal 25-line mode, the List command shows 24 lines at a time. If you've used the Mode command to change the display to 43 or 50 lines, the List command shows more.

If your version of DOS is earlier than 4, the List command shows 23 lines at a time and does not display the *Continue (Y/N)?* message.

Examples

The following examples assume that the display is in 25-line mode and that the current line is 30.

To display lines 30 through 40:

```
*30,40l
```

To display lines 19 (11 lines before the current line) through 35:

```
*,35l
```

or

```
*,+5l
```

To display 24 lines centered around line 30 (lines 19 through 42):

```
*l
```

If the current line were 10, *l* would display lines 1 through 24.

To display only line 30:

```
*30,30l
```

EDLIN: MOVE
Move Lines
Versions 2.0 and later

Page 220

The Edlin Move command moves a line or lines from one place in the file to another, deleting them from the original location and renumbering the lines of the file. The first line moved becomes the new current line.

<from>,<to>,<target>m

<from> is the number of the first line to be moved. If you don't specify <from>, Edlin starts with the current line. If you omit <from>, you must enter the comma that follows, to show that you omitted it.

<to> is the number of the last line to be moved. It must be equal to or greater than <from>. If you don't specify <to>, Edlin stops with the current line. If you omit <to>, you must enter the comma that follows, to show that you omitted it. To move a single line, specify the same line number as both <from> and <to>. To move the current line, omit both <from> and <to> and begin the command with two commas.

<target> is the line before which the lines are to be moved. You must enter it.

Examples

The following examples assume that the current line is 20.

To move lines 20 through 25 before line 5:

```
*20,25,5m
```

or

```
*,+5,-15m
```

To move lines 20 through the last line in the file before line 5:

```
*20,#,5m
```

or

```
*,#,5m
```

To move line 20 before line 30:

```
*20,20,30m
```

or

```
*,,30m
```

To move the last 15 lines in the file before line 1:

```
*#;-15,#,1m
```

This example shows two commands on the same line. The # at the beginning of the command changes the current line to the line following the last line in the file. The *−15, #, 1m* moves the preceding 15 lines to the beginning of the file. The semicolon (;) separates the two commands.

EDLIN: PAGE
Display a Screenful of Lines
Versions 2.0 and later

Page 219

The Page command displays one or more lines of a file, up to one screenful at a time. Unlike the List command, the Page command changes the current line to the last line displayed; this lets you page through a file one screenful at a time by entering successive Page commands with no parameters.

> **<from>,<to>p**

<from> is the number of the first line to be displayed. If you don't specify <from>, Edlin starts with the line after the current line. If you omit <from> but include <to>, you must enter the comma, to show that you omitted <from>.

<to> is the number of the last line to be displayed. It must be equal to or greater than <from>. If you don't specify <to>, Edlin displays one screenful of lines starting with <from>. If you omit both <from> and <to> (just type *p*), Edlin displays one screenful of lines starting with the line after the current line. On a display running in normal 25-line mode, the Page command displays 23 lines.

Examples

The following examples assume that the display is in 25-line mode and the current line is 30.

To display lines 30 through 40 and change the current line to 40:

> `*30,40p`

To display 23 lines starting with the line after the current line (lines 31 through 53):

> `*P`

EDLIN: QUIT
Terminate the Editing Session
Versions 1.0 and later

Page 200

The Quit command ends an Edlin session without saving any changes to the file currently being edited. To reduce the chance of your inadvertently losing work, Edlin prompts for confirmation before quitting. The Quit command has no parameters.

> **q**

Example

To quit the editing session without saving the current file:

> `*q`

Edlin responds:

> `Abort edit (Y/N)?`

Reply *y* to return to DOS without saving the revised file; reply *n* to remain in Edlin.

EDLIN: REPLACE
Replace One Character String with Another
Versions 1.0 and later

Page 203

The Edlin Replace command replaces one character string with another, in one or more lines of the file. Edlin displays the line or lines that are changed. You can tell Edlin to prompt for confirmation before each replacement (rather than change all occurrences) with the question mark (?) parameter of the Replace command. The last line changed becomes the new current line.

<from>,<to>?r<string1><Ctrl-Z or F6><string2>

<from> is the number of the first line in which the string is to be replaced. If you don't specify <from>, you must still enter the comma, to show that you omitted <from>. Edlin then starts replacing with the line following the current line.

<to> is the number of the last line in which the string is to be replaced. It must be equal to or greater than <from>. If you don't specify <to>, Edlin stops with the last line in the file. To change one line, use the same line number for <from> and <to>.

? tells Edlin to prompt you for confirmation before each replacement. Edlin displays the line as it will be changed and asks *O.K.?* If you reply *y* or press Enter, Edlin makes the change; if you reply *n*, Edlin doesn't make the change.

<string1> is the string to be replaced. If you don't specify <string1>, Edlin uses the last <string1> you specified with a Search or Replace command; if there was no preceding <string1>, Edlin displays the message *Entry error*. If you omit <string1> but include <string2>, you must enter Ctrl-Z (by pressing Ctrl and Z or by pressing F6) before typing <string2>, to show that you omitted <string1>.

<string2> is the replacement string. If you enter both <string1> and <string2>, separate them with Ctrl-Z. If you omit <string2>, each occurrence of <string1> is replaced with the last replacement string you specified with a Replace command. If you omit <string2> but end <string1> with Ctrl-Z, each occurrence of <string1> is deleted (replaced with a null string). If another command follows the Replace command on the same line, end <string2> with Ctrl-Z.

Examples

The following examples assume that the current line is 20. <Ctrl-Z> means press either Ctrl-Z or F6.

To replace all occurrences of *company* with *corporation* in lines 21 through 30:

```
*21,30rcompany<Ctrl-Z>corporation
```

or

```
*,30rcompany<Ctrl-Z>corporation
```

To replace all occurrences of *March* with *April* from line 21 through the end of the file, instructing Edlin to prompt before each replacement:

```
*21,#?rMarch<Ctrl-Z>April
```

or

```
*,#?rMarch<Ctrl-Z>April
```

EDLIN: SEARCH
Find a String
Versions 1.0 and later

Page 201

The Edlin Search command searches for a character string. If Edlin finds the string, it displays the line, makes it the current line, and stops searching. You can also tell Edlin to prompt you for confirmation before stopping the search; this lets you continue the search beyond the first occurrence of the string.

If Edlin doesn't find the string, it displays *Not found* and leaves the current line unchanged.

<from>,<to>?s<string>

<from> is the number of the first line to be searched. If you don't specify <from>, you must still enter the comma, to show that you omitted <from>. Edlin then starts with the line following the current line.

<to> is the number of the last line to be searched. It must be equal to or greater than <from>. If you don't specify <to>, Edlin stops with the last line in the file.

? tells Edlin to prompt you for confirmation before ending the search. Edlin displays the line that contains the string, followed by *O.K.?* If you reply *y* or press Enter, Edlin makes the displayed line the current line and stops searching; if you reply *n*, Edlin searches for the next occurrence of <string>.

<string> is the string to search for. If another command follows the Search command on the same line, follow <string> with Ctrl-Z.

Examples

The following examples assume that the current line is 20.

To find the first occurrence of *value* in lines 21 through 30:

```
*21,30svalue
```

or

```
*,30svalue
```

To find a particular occurrence of *value*, searching the entire file and instructing Edlin to prompt before setting the current line and stopping the search:

```
*1,#?svalue
```

EDLIN: TRANSFER
Copy Another File into
The One Being Edited
Versions 2.0 and later

Page 222

The Transfer command merges the contents of another file into the file you're editing.

<target>t<filename>

<target> is the number of the line before which the contents of the file will be merged. If you don't specify <target>, Edlin assumes the current line.

<filename> is the name of the file whose contents are to be merged with the file you're editing. The file name can be preceded by a drive letter and, in versions 3 and later, a directory path.

Example

The following example assumes that the current line is 20.

To merge the contents of the file named REPORT.DOC before line 20:

```
*20treport.doc
```

or

```
*treport.doc
```

EDLIN: WRITE
Write Lines from Memory to Disk
Versions 1.0 and later

Page 223

The Edlin Write command writes lines from the beginning of the file being edited to the disk. It makes room for more lines to be read from disk into memory with the Append command.

<lines>w

<lines> specifies the number of lines to write. If you omit <lines>, Edlin writes lines until available memory is 25 percent full. If that memory is already no more than 25 percent full, Edlin ignores the Write command.

Examples

To write lines to disk until available memory is 25 percent full:

```
*w
```

To write 200 lines to disk:

```
*200w
```

ERASE
Erase a File
Versions 1.0 and later

Page 71

The Erase command (erase or del) erases a file or set of files.

erase <filename> /P

<filename> is the name of the file to be erased. You can use wildcard characters to erase a set of files with similar file names or extensions.

/P tells DOS to prompt you for verification before deleting a file. (Version 4)

Examples

To erase the file named REPORT.DOC in the current directory on the disk in the current drive:

```
C:\MKT\WP>erase report.doc
```

To erase all files with the extension BAK in the directory named \MKT\WP on the disk in drive A, telling DOS to prompt for verification:

```
C>erase a:\mkt\wp\*.bak /p
```

EXE2BIN
Convert an Executable (EXE) File
To COM Format
Versions 1.0 and later

The Exe2bin command converts a program command file from EXE format to COM format. Exe2bin is an advanced DOS command, usually used by programmers, and a description of its use is beyond the scope of this book; if you need details, refer to the DOS *Technical Reference* or the *Programmer's Reference* manual.

EXIT
End a Secondary Command Processor
Versions 2.0 and later

The Exit command stops a secondary copy of COMMAND.COM (the DOS command processor) and returns control of the system to the program or previous copy of COMMAND.COM that requested the copy. The Exit command has no effect if a secondary copy of COMMAND.COM hasn't been loaded, or if the secondary command processor was loaded by a Command command with the /P (for permanent) parameter. The Exit command has no parameters.

exit

Example

To terminate a secondary, nonpermanent copy of COMMAND.COM and return control to the original command processor:

`C:\>exit`

FASTOPEN
Speed Up File Access
Versions 3.3 and later

Page 318

The Fastopen command tells DOS to keep in memory a list of the fixed disk storage locations of subdirectories and files that have been used during the current session. When the Fastopen command is used, DOS checks in memory before searching the disk whenever it is told to find a file or a subdirectory. If the file or subdirectory has already been used, its disk location is in memory, and DOS can go directly to the storage location, instead of searching through each directory in the path. Fastopen cannot be used to keep track of files stored on a network drive.

fastopen <drive>=<files> /X

<drive> is the drive letter, followed by a colon, of the fixed disk whose files and subdirectories you want DOS to track. The drive letter must refer to a fixed disk.

<files> is the number of file and subdirectory locations DOS is to keep in memory. The number of files must be separated from <drive> by an equal sign. You can specify up to 999 files; each file requires about 50 bytes of memory. If you don't specify <files>, DOS keeps track of the last 34 files and subdirectories (the last 10 in non-IBM releases of DOS).

/X tells DOS to keep Fastopen information in expanded memory. (Version 4)

Note: You can enter the Fastopen command only once during a session with DOS. If you or your application programs tend to use the same files or directories over and over, the Fastopen command can make your system noticeably faster. If you are using a version of DOS earlier than 4, and you find that Fastopen does speed your system, consider putting a Fastopen command in AUTOEXEC.BAT.

Beginning with version 4 of DOS, the installation program might include, in your CONFIG.SYS file, an Install command that, in turn, starts Fastopen with <files> set to a value such as 50. To change the <files> setting, edit the command in CON-FIG.SYS. (If you installed DOS on a fixed disk that already contained a CONFIG.SYS file, this command was placed in a file named CONFIG.400. You or the person who installed DOS should have renamed the file to CONFIG.SYS, editing it as necessary to include needed commands from the earlier CONFIG.SYS file.)

Example

To keep track of the last 30 files and subdirectories used on the fixed disk in drive C:

```
C:\>fastopen c:=30
```

or (editing a version 4 CONFIG.SYS file if FASTOPEN.EXE is in the C:\DOS subdirectory):

```
INSTALL=C:\DOS\FASTOPEN.EXE C:=30
```

FC (FILE COMPARISON)
Compare Two Files
Versions 2.0 and later, non-IBM releases only

The File Comparison command (fc) compares two files and sends the differences to standard output—normally the display. By redirecting output, you can also send the results of a comparison to a file or to another device, such as a printer.

Note: Another way to compare files is with the Compare command, available in IBM versions of DOS and in Microsoft's versions 3.3 and later. It's described in the entry COMPARE.

You can use FC to compare either text files or command files (program files with such extensions as EXE, COM, and SYS). Depending on the parameters you specify, you can compare files either line by line or byte by byte.

In a line-by-line comparison, FC starts by reading as many lines from each file as will fit in the portion of memory it uses (enough to hold 100 lines, unless you specify otherwise). It then compares the lines of the first file against the lines of the second.

If it finds any differences, FC displays the name of the first file, the last line that matched, each subsequent mismatched line, and the first matching line that follows the mismatches. It then displays the same type of information for the second file. If the files contain more than one group of mismatched lines, FC reports on each group until it either reaches the last of the lines in memory or runs out of memory space.

When it finds mismatched lines, FC assumes that the lines of the two files are no longer synchronized—they don't correspond on a one-to-one basis. Unless you specify otherwise, FC looks for two sequential matching lines before it once again assumes the files are synchronized. If FC finds more mismatched lines than will fit into the amount of memory it has set aside for the comparison, the comparison stops and you see the message *Resynch failed. Files are too different* (∗ ∗ ∗*Files are different*∗ ∗ ∗ in some versions of DOS).

The other type of comparison (byte-by-byte) that FC performs is useful primarily for checking program files stored in machine-readable, rather than human-readable, form. In a byte-by-byte comparison, FC reads as much of the files as it can into memory and compares them, then continues loading more parts of the files until it has compared both files completely. It does not display mismatched lines, but tells you which bytes (counting from the beginning of the file) are different, and what their coded values are in the hexadecimal (base-16) numbering system.

For example, if FILE1 contains *This is file 1* and FILE2 contains *This is file 2*, the File Comparison command displays the following report when you do a byte-by-byte comparison of the two files:

0000000D: 31 32

telling you that byte 13 (D in hexadecimal, counting from 0) has the value 31 in FILE1 and 32 in FILE2. (If you're curious, the hexadecimal value 31 is the code the computer uses for the numeral 1; likewise, hexadecimal 32 is the code for 2.)

If all the lines in memory have been compared and one file is shorter than the other, you see a message at the end of the report. For example, if FILE1 has fewer lines than FILE2, FC reports on any mismatches and ends by displaying the message *fc: file2 longer than file1*.

The File Comparison command includes the following parameters (if you're using version 3.1 or earlier, note that some parameters are not available):

fc **/B** **/A** **/C** **/L** **/LB***n* **/N** **/***nnnn* **/T** **/W** **<filename1>** **<filename2>**

/B (for *binary*) specifies that the files are to be compared byte by byte. If you use /B, you cannot use any parameters other than <filename1> and <filename2>.

/A tells FC to abbreviate its report, displaying only the beginning and ending lines of each group of matched/mismatched lines. (Versions 3.2 and later)

/C tells FC to ignore differences between uppercase and lowercase.

/L tells FC you want a line-by-line comparison. It assumes this parameter for all text files (those without program-file extensions, such as EXE, COM, and SYS). (Versions 3.2 and later)

/LB*n*, where *n* is a number you supply, specifies how many lines FC reads into memory. If you don't specify a number (for example, */LB200*), FC assumes 100.

/N tells FC to display line numbers in its report of an ASCII comparison.

/nnnn, where *nnnn* is a number you supply, tells FC how many matching lines it must find after a mismatch to assume that the two files once again correspond on a line-by-line basis. If you don't specify *nnnn*, FC assumes 2 lines (3 lines in versions through 3.2).

/T tells FC to treat tabs as tabs, rather than as strings of blanks.

/W tells FC to ignore spaces and tabs at the beginning and end of a line, and to convert consecutive spaces and tabs within a line to a single space.

<filename1> is the name of the first file to be compared. It can include a drive letter and path, but not wildcard characters.

<filename2> is the name of the second file to be compared. It can include a drive letter and path, but not wildcard characters.

Examples

Suppose two text files named FILE1.DOC and FILE2.DOC in the current directory on the disk in the current drive contain the lines shown below (mismatched lines are in *italics*).

FILE1.DOC	FILE2.DOC
First line.	First line.
Second line.	Second line.
Third line.	Third line.
Fourth line.	*Seventh line.*
Fifth line.	*Eighth line.*
Sixth line.	*Ninth line.*
Seventh line.	*Tenth line.*
Eighth line.	*Fourth line.*
Ninth line.	*Fifth line.*
Tenth line.	*Sixth line.*
Eleventh line.	Eleventh line.
Twelfth line.	Twelfth line.
Thirteenth line.	Thirteenth line.
Fourteenth line.	Fourteenth line.
Fifteenth line.	Fifteenth line.

To compare the files line by line:

```
C:\>fc file1.doc file2.doc
```

FC displays the blocks of lines that differ, treating the files as matched after two consecutive matched lines following a mismatch (the comments to the right are descriptive and aren't part of the command output):

```
****** file1.doc        Name of first file
Third line.             Last match
Fourth line.
Fifth line.             Mismatched lines
Sixth line.
Seventh line.           First of two more matching lines
****** file2.doc        Name of second file
Third line.             Last match
Seventh line.           Next match (no intervening mismatches)
******                  Files synchronized at this point

****** file1.doc        Name of first file
Tenth line.             Last match
Eleventh line.          Next match (no intervening mismatches)
****** file2.doc        Name of second file
Tenth line.             Last match
Fourth line.
Fifth line.             More mismatched lines
Sixth line.
Eleventh line.          Next match
******                  Resynchronized ; no more mismatches
```

The following command and its resulting output show what happens when five lines, rather than two, are needed to synchronize the files (again, the comments to the right aren't part of the output):

```
C:\>fc /5 file1.doc file2.doc

****** file1.doc        Name of first file
Third line.             Last match
Fourth line.
Fifth line.
Sixth line.
Seventh line.           Mismatches
Eighth line.
Ninth line.
Tenth line.
Eleventh line.          First of five matching lines
****** file2.doc        Name of second file
Third line.             Last match
Seventh line.
Eighth line.
Ninth line.
Tenth line.             Mismatches
Fourth line.
Fifth line.
Sixth line.
Eleventh line.          First of five matching lines
******
```

To compare two text files named REPORT.DOC and REPORT.BAK in the current directory on the disk in the current drive, ignoring case and redirecting the output to the printer:

```
C:\MKT\WP>fc /c report.doc report.bak > prn
```

To compare the same files, ignoring leading spaces, trailing spaces, and tabs, compressing each internal space and tab to a single space, and redirecting the output to a file named REPORT.DIF:

```
C:\MKT\WP>fc /w report.doc report.bak > report.dif
```

To compare byte by byte two nontext files named PICTURE.MSP, the first in the current directory on the current drive and the second in the directory named \WIN on the disk in drive A:

```
C:\PAINT>fc /b picture.msp a:\win\picture.msp
```

FCBS (CONFIGURATION COMMAND)
Set Maximum Open File Control Blocks (FCBs)
Versions 3.0 and later, IBM releases 3.1 and later

One of the two ways DOS keeps track of file usage is by means of small blocks of information called File Control Blocks, or FCBs. The FCBS configuration command lets you specify the largest number of files controlled by File Control Blocks that can be open at the same time when file sharing is in effect. The FCBS command also lets you protect some or all of the open files from being automatically closed. Unless you specify otherwise, DOS assumes four FCB-controlled files, none of them protected from closure.

You're unlikely to need the FCBS configuration command in everyday use of your computer. If you need more information on this command, refer to the documentation that came with your version of DOS.

FDISK
Configure a Fixed Disk
Versions 3.2 and later, IBM releases 2.0 and later

The Fdisk command prepares a fixed disk for use by DOS. It creates on the disk one or more independent areas called *partitions*.

Computers are often delivered with the fixed disk already prepared—sometimes with DOS already installed and ready to start from the fixed disk. To check whether this has been done, try to start the system from the fixed disk. You can also start the system with a DOS diskette, then use the Fdisk command to try to create a partition for DOS; the Fdisk command tells you if the disk has already been configured.

fdisk

The Fdisk command has no parameters; when you type *fdisk*, you start a program that steps you through the procedure via a series of question-and-answer menus. For more details, see the documentation that came with your version of DOS.

FILES (CONFIGURATION COMMAND)
Set Maximum Open File Handles
Versions 2.0 and later

Page 315
One of the two ways DOS keeps track of file usage is by assigning a number called a *handle* to each open file. The Files configuration command sets the maximum number of files controlled by a file handle that can be open at the same time.

files=<number>

<number> is the number of files that can be open at the same time. It can be from 8 through 255; if you don't specify <number>, DOS assumes 8.

If you're using version 4 of DOS, the installation program included a Files command in your file of configuration commands. The file was named CONFIG.SYS if you installed DOS on diskettes or on a fixed disk that didn't have an existing CONFIG.SYS file, and it was named CONFIG.400 if you installed DOS on a fixed disk with an existing CONFIG.SYS file. If the latter is true of your system, you or the person who installed DOS should have renamed CONFIG.400 to CONFIG.SYS, editing the file as necessary to include any needed commands from the earlier CONFIG.SYS file.

Each additional open file above eight increases the memory used by DOS. If a program you're using requires more than eight open files, edit your CONFIG.SYS file or check the program's documentation for an appropriate Files command. If you need more information on this command, refer to the documentation that came with your version of DOS.

FIND
Search Files for a Character String
Versions 2.0 and later

Page 247
The Find filter command searches one or more files for a character string, and sends each line that contains the string to standard output (usually the display).

find /V /C /N <"string"> <filename>

/V finds lines that *don't* contain <string>.

/C sends the total number of lines, rather than the lines themselves, to standard output. If you specify both /C and /N, the Find command ignores /N.

/N includes the line number with each line of output.

<"string"> is the character string to search for. You must enclose the string in quotation marks. To include a quotation mark in <string>, type two quotation marks.

<filename> is the name of the file or files to be searched. You can specify more than one file name, separating them with spaces. If you omit <filename>, the Find command searches its standard input; you can either redirect standard input or pipe the output of another command to the Find command. You cannot use wildcards in <file name>.

Examples

To find all lines that contain the string *Sales* (note the capital *S*) in the file REPORT.DOC in the current directory:

```
C;\MKT\WP>find "Sales" report.doc
```

To find all lines that don't contain the string <DIR> in the output of a Directory command:

```
C:\>dir | find /v "<DIR>"
```

To find all lines that contain the string *April* in the file LETTERS.DOC in the current directory, include the line numbers, and redirect the output to the printer:

```
C:\MKT\WP>find /n "April" letters.doc > prn
```

To display just the number of lines that don't contain the string *Sales* in the files named FCST-APR.DOC and REPORT.DOC in the current directory:

```
C:\MKT\WP>find /c /v "Sales" fcst-apr.doc report.doc
```

FOR (BATCH COMMAND)
Carry Out a Batch Command
Several Times
Versions 2.0 and later

Page 284

The For batch command carries out a DOS command once for each member of a set of character strings.

for %%p in (<set>) **do** <command>

%%p is a replaceable parameter that is given the value of each member of <set> by DOS before <command> is carried out. It is represented by two percent signs (%%) followed by any character except one of the redirection symbols: <, >, or ¦.

<set> is a series of strings separated by blanks. <command> is carried out once for each member of <set>. If <set> is empty, <command> isn't carried out. <set> can contain character strings, path names, or file names. If one of the strings is a file name that includes wildcard characters, DOS sets %%p, in turn, to each file name that matches the wildcard character, then carries out <command>.

<command> is any DOS command except another For command. Through version 3.2, you can carry out another batch command without returning to the system prompt, by making <command> a Command command with the /C parameter and specifying the name of the batch file as the string that follows the /C parameter (see the second example below). If you're using version 3.3 or later, you can accomplish the same thing by using the Call command.

Note: You can type a For command at the system prompt, rather than enter it in a batch file. If you do, use %p instead of %%p. Everything else is the same.

Examples

To copy up to nine files named in the batch command line to the current directory of the disk in drive A:

```
for %%p in (%1 %2 %3 %4 %5 %6 %7 %8 %9) do copy %%p a:
```

To carry out the batch files named BAT1.BAT, BAT2.BAT, and BAT3.BAT:

```
for %%p in (1 2 3) do command /c bat%%p
```

If you specified the command to be carried out as *bat%%p* (omitting *command /c*), DOS would return to the system prompt after carrying out BAT1.BAT.

If you're using version 3.3 or later, you can use the Call command instead of Command:

```
for %%p in (1 2 3) do call bat%%p
```

FORMAT
Prepare a Disk
Versions 1.0 and later

Page 95

The Format command prepares a disk for use by DOS. Because formatting destroys any data written on the disk, DOS requests confirmation before formatting the disk. Be sure you know that the specified drive contains the disk to be formatted, especially if you're using 3.1 or an earlier version of DOS. With these versions, if you don't specify a drive letter with the Format command, DOS formats the disk in the current drive even if it's a system disk or a fixed disk.

Note: Don't use Format with a drive affected by a Join or Substitute command. Format can't be used with a network drive. The following description includes some parameters not mentioned in earlier chapters.

> **format <drive> /V:<label> /B /O /1 /4 /8 /N:<sectors> /T:<tracks> /F:<size> /S**

<drive> is the letter of the drive, followed by a colon, that contains the disk to be formatted. Although specifying a drive letter isn't mandatory through version 3.1, you should make a habit of typing the drive letter of the disk you want to format.

/V:<label>, in version 4, assigns <label> as a volume label to the formatted disk. In versions 3.3 and earlier, /V (without the colon and <label>) tells DOS to prompt you for a volume label when formatting was complete.

/B formats a diskette and reserves space for the DOS hidden files. The hidden files aren't copied to the disk but, because space is reserved for the system files, you can later copy any version of DOS to the disk with the System (sys) command.

/O prepares a diskette that is compatible with version 1 of the IBM releases of DOS. Don't use this parameter unless you need the compatibility, because it takes longer to format a disk this way, and disk operations on the resulting disk will be noticeably slower. This parameter may not be included in your version of DOS.

/1 formats only the first side of a 5.25-inch diskette, even if the drive is a double-sided drive.

/4 formats a single-sided (180 K) or double-sided (360 K) diskette in a 1.2 MB high-capacity drive. Diskettes formatted with this parameter in a high-capacity drive may not work reliably in a 180 K or 360 K diskette drive.

/8 formats a 5.25-inch diskette for 8 sectors per track.

/N:<sectors> specifies the number of sectors per track to format, if you want to format less than the maximum capacity of the diskette drive. If you specify /N:<sectors>, you must also specify /T:<tracks>. (Versions 3.2 and later)

/T:<tracks> specifies the number of tracks to format, if you want to format less than the maximum capacity of the diskette drive. If you specify /T:<tracks>, you must also specify /N:<sectors>. (Versions 3.2 and later)

/F:<size> specifies the capacity (in kilobytes) for which the diskette should be formatted. This is simpler than using /N:<sectors> and /T:<tracks> to format a diskette to hold less than its maximum capacity. Valid entries for /F:<size> are 160, 180, 320, 360, 720, 1200, and 1440 (or any of the variations shown in Chapter 6, Figure 6-5). (Version 4)

/S creates a system disk by copying DOS system files to the formatted disk. If you specify /B, you cannot specify /S.

Examples

To format the diskette in drive A:

```
C:\DOS>format a:
```

To format the diskette in drive A and assign it the volume label LETTERS (version 4):

```
C:\DOS>format a: /v:letters
```

To format a system disk in drive A and assign it a volume label:

```
C>format a: /v /s
```

After formatting the disk, DOS prompts you to enter a volume label of 11 characters or less. You can change or delete this volume label later with the Volume (vol) command.

The following Format commands all format a 360 K diskette in a 1.2 MB drive:

```
C:\DOS>format a: /f:360
C:\DOS>format a: /4
C:\DOS>format a: /n:9 /t:40
```

GOTO (BATCH COMMAND)
Jump to a Label
Versions 2.0 and later

Page 264

The Goto batch command tells DOS to jump to a specified label in a batch file and carry out the commands that follow. A label is a line that consists of a colon (:) followed by a character string up to eight characters long.

goto <label>

<label> is the label in the batch file you want DOS to jump to. Beginning with version 4, you can either include or omit the colon in the Goto command; for example, if the label in the batch file were *:end*, the Goto command could be *goto end* or *goto :end*. In earlier versions of DOS, omit the colon.

Example

The line numbers in the following batch file are included only for reference. The batch file includes two labels, *:start* in line 2 and *:end* in line 7. These two labels control the backup procedure performed by the Backup command in line 3.

The If command in line 4 includes a *goto end* command that sends DOS to the label *:end* and ends the backup if an error occurs. The *errorlevel* option of the If command detects errors by checking a special *errorlevel* value that Backup sets to report on each backup it performs (0 is success, 1 through 4 represent different reasons why a backup attempt was not completed). Thus, *goto end* is carried out and the batch file ends if the Backup command in line 3 reports an *errorlevel* of 1 or greater. Otherwise, the *goto start* command in line 6 sends DOS back to line 3, to back up another file, until an error occurs or no more files remain to be backed up.

```
1: @echo off
2: :start
3: backup %1 a:
4: if errorlevel 1 goto end
5: shift
6: goto start
7: :end
```

GRAFTABL
Enable Graphics Character Set
Versions 3.0 and later

Page 124

The Load Graphics Table command (graftabl) enables DOS to display special characters, such as accented letters, symbols, and line-drawing characters (character codes 128–255). When you use the Graftabl command, DOS can display the characters when the color/graphics adapter is in graphics mode. The command is unnecessary with an enhanced graphics adapter, and has no effect when the monochrome display adapter is used. You can use Graftabl only once during a session with DOS.

graftabl <code-page> /status ?

<code-page> is the three-digit number that specifies the code page that DOS is to use. You cannot specify <code-page> in versions prior to 3.3. Valid code pages are:

437	United States
850	Multilingual
860	Portuguese
863	Canada (French)
865	Nordic

/status displays the current code page. (Versions 3.3 and later)

? (typed as *graftabl ?*) displays the current code page, a description of the parameters you can use, and a list of the numbers and names of available code pages.

Examples

To enable DOS to display the graphics characters in graphics mode:

```
C:\DOS>graftabl
```

DOS reads the table of character definitions into memory and tells you it has done so. If you enter a Graftabl command again, DOS simply tells you the characters are already loaded and returns to the system prompt.

To enable DOS to display the Canadian French character set (code page 863) in graphics mode (versions 3.3 and later):

```
C:\DOS>graftabl 863
```

To display the current graphics code page (versions 3.3 and later):

```
C:\DOS>graftabl /status
```

GRAPHICS
Enable Printing of a Graphics Display
Versions 3.2 and later, IBM releases 2.0 and later

Page 123

The Graphics command loads a program that DOS keeps in memory to print the display produced by the Color/Graphics Adapter (CGA), Enhanced Graphics Adapter (EGA), or Video Graphics Array (VGA) used in a graphics mode. After you enter the Graphics command, pressing Shift-PrtSc enables DOS to print either a color/graphics screen or the text-based display produced by a monochrome adapter.

Note: Not all printers can reproduce graphics images. The Graphics command itself is not compatible with Hercules monochrome graphics adapters or with enhanced graphics adapters in enhanced display modes.

The Graphics command can include several parameters or none at all; to see which, if any, are available to you, check the documentation that came with your version of DOS.

graphics \<printer\> \<profile\> /R /B /LCD /C /F /P\<port\> /PB:\<id\>

\<printer\> specifies the type of printer supported; it can be one of the following:

color1	IBM Personal Computer Color Printer or compatible with a black ribbon.
color4	IBM Personal Computer Color Printer or compatible with a red-green-blue-black (RGB) ribbon.
color8	IBM Personal Computer Color Printer or compatible with a cyan-magenta-yellow-black (CMY) ribbon.
compact	IBM Personal Computer Compact Printer or compatible.
graphics	IBM Personal Computer Graphics Printer, IBM Quietwriter, IBM Proprinter, Pageprinter, or compatible.
graphicswide	IBM Quietwriter, Proprinter, or compatible with wide carriage.
thermal	IBM PC Convertible Printer or compatible (versions 3.3 and later).

<profile> specifies the name of the file that contains detailed information about the printers attached to your system. The file GRAPHICS.PRO, supplied with DOS, describes all the supported IBM printers. (Version 4)

If you don't specify <printer>, DOS assumes *graphics*.

/R prints the screen as you see it on the display: light images on a dark background.

/B prints the background in color. It is valid only if <printer> is *color4* or *color8*.

/LCD prints the image from the liquid crystal display (LCD) screen of the IBM PC Convertible. (Versions 3.3 and later)

/C centers the printed image on the paper. It works with an image resolution of 640 by 200 or with a 320-by-200 image printed with the /F parameter. (Versions prior to 4)

/F rotates a 320-by-200 image 90 degrees (prints it sideways). (Versions prior to 4)

/P <port> specifies the printer port. It can be *1* (LPT1), *2* (LPT2), or *3* (LPT3). (Versions prior to 4)

/PB:<id> tells DOS what aspect ratio (ratio of display width to display height) to use when printing a graphics image. Valid entries for <id> are STD, which specifies the aspect ratio of a standard display, and LCD, which specifies that the aspect ratio of an LCD display should be used. (Version 4)

On a non-color printer, the Graphics command prints the screen with up to four shades of gray. On a color printer, screen colors are reproduced with or without the background color, depending on the Graphics parameter you specify. If the display is in a 640-by-200 or a higher-resolution graphics mode, the printed image is rotated 90 degrees (printed sideways).

Examples

To enable printing a graphics display on an IBM Personal Computer Graphics printer:

```
C:\DOS>graphics
```

To enable printing a graphics display with a colored background on an IBM Personal Computer Color printer with an RGB ribbon:

```
C:\DOS>graphics color4 /b
```

To enable printing a graphics display on an IBM Personal Computer Graphics printer, reversing the image so that a reverse-video image (white on black) is printed :

```
C:\DOS>graphics /r
```

IF (BATCH COMMAND)
Deciding Whether to Carry Out
A Batch Command
Versions 2.0 and later

Page 261

The If batch command tests a condition and carries out another command if the condition is met.

if not <condition> <command>

not reverses the meaning of <condition>. That is, <command> is carried out only if <condition> is *not* true.

<condition> is the condition to be tested. Using <condition>, a batch file can be used to check on the outcome of a command, such as Backup or Restore (with the *errorlevel* option); check whether a file exists; or check whether two strings are identical. <condition> takes one of the following forms:

errorlevel <number>	True if *errorlevel* is equal to or greater than <number>. *Errorlevel* represents a special value that is set by some DOS commands to indicate whether they were carried out successfully or not.
exist <filename>	True if <filename> exists in the specified directory.
<string1> ==<string2>	True if <string1> and <string2> are identical; remember, uppercase and lowercase are different. Notice that two equal signs separate the strings. This form of the If command can be used to compare file names, replaceable parameters entered on the command line with the batch command, or character strings.

<command> is the command to be carried out. It can be any DOS command, including another If command.

Examples

To jump to the label *:end* if *errorlevel* is equal to or greater than 1:

```
if errorlevel 1 goto end
```

(For a sample batch file using this command, see the GOTO batch command.)

To copy the file named in the first replaceable parameter from the disk in the current drive to the disk in drive A if the file doesn't exist on the disk in drive A:

```
if not exist a:%1 copy %1 a:%1
```

INPUT/OUTPUT REDIRECTION
Redirecting Standard Input and Standard Output

Page 242

Unless instructed otherwise, DOS takes its input from standard input (usually the keyboard) and sends its output to standard output (usually the screen). You can redirect standard input and output, however, to a file or a device by using the symbols <, >, and >>. If a program writes to standard output, as the DOS commands do, its output can also be sent with the pipe symbol (¦) to the input of a program that reads standard input.

The < and > symbols redirect the input or output of a command or program.

The < symbol redirects input. For example, to tell the Sort filter command to read its input from the file named LIST.DOC, you would type *sort < list.doc*.

Similarly, you redirect output with the > symbol. For example, to send the output of a Directory command to a file named DIRFILE.DOC in the current directory, you would type *dir > dirfile.doc*. If there were no file named DIRFILE.DOC, DOS would create it. If a file named DIRFILE.DOC already existed, DOS would replace its contents with the output of the Directory command.

You can, however, tell DOS to *add* output to the end of an existing file by using the symbols >>. For example, to add the output of the Directory command to an existing file named DIRFILE.DOC, you would type *dir >> dirfile.doc*. If the file didn't exist, DOS would create it, just as it would in the previous example, which used the > symbol.

You can redirect input and output from and to devices as well as files, and you can redirect both the input and output of a program. For example, to tell the Sort command to read its input from the file LIST.DOC and write its output to the printer (PRN), you would type *sort < list.doc > prn*.

Rather than redirecting output to a file or device, you can send the output of a command or program to the input of another command or program by separating the program or command names with a vertical bar (¦). Because the programs or commands are logically connected, this connection is called a *pipe*.

Pipes are used primarily with the filter commands: Find, More, and Sort. These commands read standard input and write to standard output, so they can be combined through redirection and pipes in a variety of useful ways. For example, *dir ¦ sort* sends the output of the Directory command to the input of the Sort command.

You can combine redirection and piping: For example, you could pipe the output of the Directory command to the Sort command, pipe the output of the Sort command to the Find command and, finally, redirect the output of the Find command to the printer by typing *dir ¦ sort ¦ find /v "<D" > prn*.

INSTALL
(CONFIGURATION COMMAND)
Load a Command from CONFIG.SYS
Versions 4.0 and later

The Install command loads into memory the command file for any of the following four DOS commands: Fastopen, Keyboard (keyb), National Language Support Functions (nlsfunc), and Share. Once loaded, these command files remain in memory until you restart your computer. Install helps DOS manage your computer's use of memory.

install=<path><cmdfile> <cmdparms>

<path> is the path to the command file. In version 4, it is C:\DOS (on a fixed disk), unless a different directory was specified when DOS was installed.

<cmdfile> is the name of the command file to be installed. You must include the extension (COM or EXE).

<cmdparms> represents the parameters, if any, of the command to be installed.

Example

If you're using a fixed disk, the version 4 installation program uses the Install command to specify that DOS keep track of the last *x* files opened on drive C. The command is in your CONFIG.SYS file and looks something like this (assuming that all DOS files are stored in the directory C:\DOS):

```
INSTALL=C:\DOS\FASTOPEN.EXE C:=(50,25)
```

To tell DOS to keep track of the last 30 files, edit the command so it looks like the following:

```
INSTALL C:\DOS\FASTOPEN.EXE C:=(30,15)
```

JOIN
Join a Disk Drive to a Directory
Versions 3.0 and later

Page 321
The Join command connects one disk drive to an empty directory on a second drive. DOS then treats the disk in the joined drive as if it were a directory on the disk in the drive to which it is joined.

join <drive> <pathname> /D

<drive> is the drive that is to be joined to a directory on the second drive. The complete directory structure of <drive> is joined, starting at the root. Once you join <drive> to a directory on another drive, you cannot use the letter of <drive> in any DOS command.

<pathname> is the drive letter and path name of the drive and directory to which <drive> is to be joined. The directory must be in the root directory. If the directory doesn't exist, the Join command creates it; if the directory does exist, it must be empty. You cannot join <drive> to the root directory of another drive.

/D disconnects any join involving <drive>. The specified directory remains on the disk until it is removed with a Remove Directory command (rd).

If you omit all parameters (type just *join*), DOS displays any joins in effect.

Note: You should avoid using the Assign, Backup, Diskcopy, Format, Restore, and Substitute commands on a drive to which another drive is joined. If you want to use one of these commands, or if you need to use the drive that is joined, delete the join with the /D parameter. Join cannot be used with a network drive.

Examples

To join drive B to C:\DRIVEB:

```
C:\DOS>join b: \driveb
```

To delete the join from the preceding example:

```
C:\DOS>join b: /d
```

Assume that you joined drive A to C:\DRIVEA and drive B to C:\DRIVEB. To display the joins in effect:

```
C:\DOS>join
```

DOS displays:

```
A: => C:\DRIVEA
B: => C:\DRIVEB
```

KEYB
Select a Keyboard Layout
Versions 3.3 and later

Page 394

The Keyboard command (keyb) selects a keyboard layout that matches the layout used in the country you specify. Keyb replaces the Keyb*xx* command used in releases through 3.2. If you have one of those versions of DOS, refer to the entry KEYB*xx*, following this one.

keyb <country>,<code-page>,<kbdfile> /ID:<kbdid>

<country> is one of the following two-letter keyboard codes:

Country	Keyboard Code	Code Page(s)	Keyboard ID
Belgium	be	850,437	120
Canada (French)	cf	863,850	058
Denmark	dk	850,865	159
Finland	su	850,437	153
France	fr	437,850	120,189
Germany	gr	437,850	129
Italy	it	437,850	141,142
Latin America	la	437,850	171
Netherlands	nl	437,850	143
Norway	no	850,865	155
Portugal	po	850,860	163
Spain	sp	437,850	172
Switzerland (French)	sf	850,437	150
Switzerland (German)	sg	850,437	000
Sweden	sv	437,850	153
United Kingdom	uk	437,850	168,166
United States	us	437,850	103

<code-page> is a three-digit number that specifies the code page that DOS is to use. For more information on code pages, refer to Appendix D.

<kbdfile> is the name of the system file that contains the keyboard layouts. If you don't specify <kbdfile>, DOS assumes that the file is named KEYBOARD.SYS and that it is stored in your \DOS directory if you're using version 4 from a fixed disk, or in the root directory of the system disk if you're using diskettes or version 3.3.

/ID/:<kbdid> is a three-digit code that specifies a keyboard layout to be used when a country has more than one keyboard ID, as listed in the preceding table. If you don't specify /ID:<kbdid>, and more than one keyboard ID is listed for the country specified, DOS assumes the first keyboard ID listed. (Version 4)

If your computer was manufactured for use in the United States, you can return to the United States keyboard after entering a Keyb command by pressing Ctrl-Alt-F1. To return to the keyboard you defined with the Keyb command, press Ctrl-Alt-F2.

Examples

To select the French keyboard layout and code page 850, and to let DOS assume that the keyboard definition file is KEYBOARD.SYS:

```
C:\>keyb fr,850
```

To specify the French keyboard layout, let DOS assume the value for the code page, and tell DOS that the keyboard definition file is in the directory C:\MYDOS:

```
C:\>keyb fr,,c:\mydos\keyboard.sys
```

Notice the two commas following *fr*; if you omit <code-page>, you must still type the comma that would follow, to show DOS that you omitted it.

To display the currently active keyboard code and its code page, as well as the code page currently being used by CON:

```
C:\>keyb
```

If you had selected the United States keyboard and code page 850 for the keyboard and console, DOS would respond:

```
Current keyboard code: US  code page: 850
Current CON code page: 850
```

KEYB*xx*
Select a Keyboard Layout
Version 3.2, IBM releases 3.0 through 3.2

Page 383

The Keyboard command (keyb*xx*) in versions of DOS prior to 3.3 loads a program that DOS keeps in memory to change the keyboard layout to match the keyboard used in a particular country.

If you specify a keyboard layout other than the one you normally use, you can return to the layout DOS assumes by pressing Ctrl-Alt-F1. You can also switch back to the other keyboard layout by pressing Ctrl-Alt-F2.

The Keyb*xx* command has six forms, one for each keyboard that DOS supports. Each begins with *keyb*; you replace the *xx* with one of the following two-letter codes:

Description	Code	Typed as
Dvorak keyboard (non-IBM versions of DOS)	dv	keybdv
France	fr	keybfr
Germany	gr	keybgr
Italy	it	keybit
Spain	sp	keybsp
United Kingdom	uk	keybuk

Example

To select the French keyboard layout:

```
C>keybfr
```

LABEL
Change or Delete the
Volume Label of a Disk
Versions 3.1 and later, IBM releases 3.0 and later

Page 104

The Label command displays, adds, changes, or deletes the volume label of a disk. In version 4 of DOS, you can assign a volume label when you format a disk with the /V:<label> parameter of the Format command. In versions that include the Label command, you can add, change, or remove the volume label at any time.

The Label command has two parameters:

label <drive><newlabel>

<drive> is the letter, followed by a colon, of the drive containing the disk whose volume label is to be affected.

<newlabel> is the volume label you want to assign to the disk in <drive>. The label can be up to 11 characters long; it can include any characters that are valid for a file name, plus a blank space. If you specify <newlabel>, DOS assigns the label to the disk in <drive>, whether or not the disk already has a volume label. If you omit <newlabel> (type just *label*, or *label* plus a drive letter), DOS displays the volume label (if there is one) of the disk in the current or specified drive, then prompts you to type a new volume label or to press Enter. If you press Enter and the disk already has a volume label, DOS asks if you want to delete the current label.

Note: You cannot use the Label command on a network drive. You should also avoid using it on a drive affected by the Assign or Substitute commands. If you just want to display the volume label of a disk, use the Volume (vol) command.

Examples

To assign the volume label CLIENT LIST to the disk in drive A:

```
C:\DOS>label a:client list
```

To display the volume label of the disk in drive A:

```
C:\DOS>label a:
```

DOS responds:

```
Volume in drive A is CLIENT LIST
Volume Serial Number is 3F68-1AFF
Volume label (11 characters, ENTER for none)?
```

If you type a label, DOS renames the disk. If you press Enter, DOS displays:

```
Delete current volume label (Y/N)?
```

Type *y* and press Enter to delete the volume label, or type *n* and press Enter to leave it unchanged.

LASTDRIVE
(CONFIGURATION COMMAND)
Define the Highest Drive Letter
Versions 3.0 and later

Page 315

The Lastdrive configuration command specifies the highest drive letter that DOS recognizes as valid. In version 4, the installation program includes the command *lastdrive=e* in your file of configuration commands. In versions prior to 4, if CONFIG.SYS doesn't contain a Lastdrive command, the highest drive letter DOS recognizes is E. The Lastdrive command is used to specify a higher letter (up to Z) if more than five drive letters are needed—for example, because the computer uses many simulated disk drives (virtual disks or RAM disks), or because a large fixed disk is divided into sections, each referred to by a different drive letter.

lastdrive=<letter>

<letter> specifies the highest drive letter that DOS recognizes. It can be any letter from A through Z. If <letter> specifies fewer disk drives than the actual number attached to the computer, DOS ignores the Lastdrive command.

Example

To allow eight drive letters, you would include the following command in CONFIG.SYS:

```
lastdrive=h
```

MD (MAKE DIRECTORY)
Make a New Directory
Versions 2.0 and later

Page 136

The Make Directory command (md or mkdir) creates a new subdirectory.

md   <drive><path>

<drive> is the letter, followed by a colon, of the drive containing the disk on which the directory is to be created. If you omit <drive>, DOS creates the directory on the disk in the current drive.

<path> is the path name of the subdirectory to be created. If <path> begins with a backslash (\), DOS makes the new directory a subdirectory of the root directory of

the disk in the current or specified drive; if <path> doesn't begin with a backslash, DOS makes the new directory a subdirectory of the current directory. There is no absolute limit to the number of levels of subdirectories you can create, but a good practical limit is about four or five; beyond this, a multilevel directory structure can become more confusing and unwieldy than helpful. The maximum length of a path name from the root directory is 63 characters, including backslashes.

Note: Because the Assign, Join, and Substitute commands mask the real identities of directories, you shouldn't create directories when those commands are in effect.

Examples

To create a subdirectory named WP in the *current* directory of the current drive:

```
C:\ENG>md wp
```

To create a subdirectory named WP in the *root* directory of the current drive:

```
C:\DOS>md \wp
```

To create a subdirectory named WP in the directory \MKT of the disk in drive A:

```
C:\DOS>md a:\mkt\wp
```

MEM (MEMORY)
Display Memory Use
Versions 4.0 and later

Page 112

The Memory command displays the amount of memory installed and available for use, including extended and expanded memory. It can also display the name, location, size, and type of each program in memory.

mem /PROGRAM /DEBUG

/PROGRAM specifies that the name, location, size, and type of each program in memory be displayed.

/DEBUG specifies that additional detail beyond that provided by the /PROGRAM parameter be included in the report.

Examples

Assume that your system has 640 K of regular memory and 3.5 MB of extended memory; that you have installed ANSI.SYS, a mouse driver, and a 1000 K (1 MB) RAM disk in extended memory; and that your CONFIG.SYS file also contains *buffers=32*, *files=32*, and *lastdrive=m*. To display just the amount of memory installed and available, type the Mem command with no parameters:

```
C:\DOS>mem
    655360 bytes total memory
    654336 bytes available
    562112 largest executable program size

   3538944 bytes total extended memory
   1867776 bytes available extended memory
```

This report provides the same sort of information as the memory report of the Check Disk command; *bytes available* refers to the amount of installed memory actually available to programs (including DOS), and *largest executable program* size refers to the amount of memory available after DOS, various buffers, device drivers, and resident programs are installed (it's the same number as the *bytes free* number in the Check Disk memory report). Similarly, the two numbers for extended memory show the amount of extended memory installed and the amount available for use after DOS has installed RAM disks and other features you can put in extended memory.

To display the name, size, location, and type of each program in memory, add the /PROGRAM parameter:

```
C:\DOS>mem /program
```

Address	Name	Size	Type
-------	--------	------	------
000000		000400	Interrupt Vector
000400		000100	ROM Communication Area
000500		000200	DOS Communication Area
000700	IBMBIO	002540	System Program
002C40	IBMDOS	0088D0	System Program
00B510	IBMBIO	006A50	System Data
	ANSI	001190	DEVICE=
		000640	FILES=
		000100	FCBS=
		004290	BUFFERS=
		0001C0	LASTDRIVE=
		000CD0	STACKS=
011F70	COMMAND	001A20	Program
0139A0	IBMDOS	000030	-- Free --
0139E0	COMMAND	000400	Environment
013DF0	MOUSE	000090	Environment
013E90	MOUSE	002890	Program
016730	MEM	0000F0	Environment
016830	MEM	012F60	Program
0297A0	IBMDOS	076450	-- Free --

```
 655360 bytes total memory
 654336 bytes available
 562112 largest executable program size

3538944 bytes total extended memory
1867776 bytes available extended memory
```

You probably won't have much need for this detailed report. The locations (addresses) and sizes are in hexadecimal, but you can still recognize some familiar names such as ANSI.SYS and FILES. IBMBIO and IBMDOS refer to the hidden files that IBM's release of DOS uses on the system disk, and COMMAND refers to COMMAND.COM, the program that accepts your commands and passes the instructions along to DOS.

The report produced by the /DEBUG parameter is similar to the /PROGRAM report, but it shows further detail by listing the names of the system device drivers in IBMBIO.COM.

MODE
Control Device Mode
Versions 3.2 and later, IBM releases 1.0 and later

The Mode command is used in several different ways to enable DOS to work with the display and with printer and communications ports. In versions 3.3 and later, the Mode command is also used to set code-page information that enables DOS to display and print accented and foreign-language characters. Mode has eight basic uses:

- Set display characteristics, such as monochrome instead of color, or 40 columns instead of 80 columns.

- Set number of display lines. (Version 4)

- Set keyboard repeat rate. (Version 4)

- Set communications parameters for a serial communications port.

- Set line length and width for a parallel printer attached to a parallel port or tell DOS to use a printer attached to a parallel port other than LPT1.

- Connect a serial printer by redirecting output from a parallel port (such as LPT1) to a serial port (such as COM1).

- Check the status of system devices.

- Prepare and select code pages for national language support. (Versions 3.3 and later)

Each of these uses is described separately in the following entries.

MODE
Set Display Characteristics
Versions 3.2 and later, IBM releases 2.0 and later

Page 115

This form of the Mode command selects a display adapter, either monochrome or color/graphics. If you select a color/graphics adapter, you can also set the width of the display and enable or disable color. If the image on a display isn't centered, you can use Mode to shift the image left or right and display a test pattern.

mode   <method>,<shift>,T

<method> selects the monochrome or color/graphics adapter and specifies the width and color characteristics of the display attached to the color/graphics adapter. <method> can be specified as one of the following values:

Value	Characteristics
mono	Monochrome display adapter
40	Color/graphics adapter, 40-column display
80	Color/graphics adapter, 80-column display
co40	Color/graphics adapter, color enabled, 40-column display
co80	Color/graphics adapter, color enabled, 80-column display
bw40	Color/graphics adapter, color disabled, 40-column display
bw80	Color/graphics adapter, color disabled, 80-column display

<shift> can be specified as either *l* or *r* to shift left or right an off-center image on a display attached to the color/graphics adapter. The image is shifted two columns if the display width is 80 characters, one column if the display width is 40 characters. <shift> has no effect on an EGA or VGA display, or on a display attached to a monochrome display adapter.

T displays a test pattern after shifting the image so that you can see if the display is centered. It also displays a prompt asking if you can see the leftmost (or rightmost) character in the pattern. If you reply *n*, the Mode command shifts the image and displays the prompt again, continuing until you reply *y*. DOS then returns to the system prompt.

Examples

To select the display attached to the color/graphics adapter, enable color, and set the display to 80 columns:

```
C>mode co80
```

To select the display attached to the color/graphics adapter, disable color, set the display to 80 columns, shift the display two columns to the right, and display a test pattern:

```
C>mode bw80,r,t
```

Note the commas.

To select the display attached to the monochrome display adapter:

```
C>mode mono
```

MODE
Set Display Lines
Versions 4.0 and later

Page 113

This form of the Mode command lets you specify whether 40 or 80 columns and 25, 43, or 50 lines should be displayed on the screen. The command is effective only if the line DEVICE=ANSI.SYS (preceded by a path if necessary) is included in your CONFIG.SYS file, and if the display attached to your system can display the number of lines you specify. You can set either columns or lines, or both, with the command.

mode con cols=<columns> lines=<lines>

CON is the name of the console device; the display is the output portion of CON (the keyboard is the input portion of CON).

cols=<columns> specifies the number of columns in a line. <columns> can be either 40 or 80.

lines=<lines> specifies the number of lines on the screen. <lines> can be 25, 43, or 50.

Note: If you specify 43 or 50 lines and an application program, such as a word processor, resets the display to 25 lines whenever it returns to DOS, you can add the /L parameter (DEVICE=ANSI.SYS /L) to the DEVICE=ANSI.SYS command in CONFIG.SYS to tell DOS to maintain the number of lines you specified. Some application programs may not operate properly if you do this; in that case, remove the /L parameter from the DEVICE=ANSI.SYS command and reset the display to the number of lines you prefer with the Mode command. You can avoid the need to enter the Mode command each time by starting the application program with a batch file that ends with a Mode command that sets the number of display lines to the number you prefer.

Example

To set the number of display lines to 43 and leave the number of columns unchanged:

```
C:\DOS>mode con lines=43
```

MODE
Set Keyboard Repeat Rate
Versions 4.0 and later

Page 113

This form of the Mode command lets you control how long the keyboard waits when you hold down a key before starting to repeat, and how quickly the character is repeated. You must specify both parameters.

mode con rate=<speed> delay=<pause>

CON is the name of the console device; the keyboard is the input portion of CON (the display is the output portion of CON).

rate=<speed> specifies the speed of the repeat action. <speed> can be from 1 through 32. A value of 1 specifies the slowest rate, about 2 repetitions per second; 32 specifies the fastest rate, about 30 repetitions per second.

delay=<pause> specifies how long the keyboard should wait, after you press a key, before starting to repeat. <pause> represents units of a quarter of a second, and can range from 1 through 4; a value of 1 causes a delay of 0.25 second, and a value of 4 causes a delay of one second.

Example

To set the keyboard repetition rate to 10 and the delay to 0.5 second, type:

```
C:\DOS>mode con rate=10 delay=2
```

MODE
Set Serial Communications Parameters
Versions 3.2 and later, IBM releases 1.1 and later

Page 118

This form of the Mode command sets the communications parameters for a serial communications port. The parameters are separated by commas. If you omit any parameters, enter a comma for each so that DOS can assume values for them. The following form of this command applies to all versions of DOS; changes for version 4 are on the next page.

mode <port> <baud>,<parity>,<databits>,<stopbits>,P

<port> is the name of the serial port whose communications parameters are to be set. If you're using 3.2 or an earlier version of DOS, <port> can be COM1 or COM2. If you're using 3.3 or a later version, <port> can be COM1, COM2, COM3, or COM4.

<baud> is the baud rate; it can be 110, 150, 300, 1200, 2400, 4800, or 9600. If you're using version 3.3 or a later version, you can specify 19200 on a system capable of such speed. You must specify <baud>, but need not enter the entire number; you can type only the first two digits if you want.

<parity> can be *o* for odd, *e* for even, or *n* for none; if you don't specify <parity>, DOS assumes *e*.

<databits> is the number of electrical signals used to represent one character (such as *a*). <databits> can be 7 or 8; if you don't specify <databits>, DOS assumes 7.

<stopbits> is the number of electrical signals that mark the end of a character. It can be 1 or 2. If you do not specify <stopbits> and <baud> is 110, DOS assumes 2; otherwise, DOS assumes 1.

P, in versions through 3.3, tells DOS to continuously try to send output to the serial port if the device attached to the port is not ready to receive data (for example, if the device is busy or not turned on). Specify P when a printer is attached to the serial port. If DOS is waiting for the printer and you want to return to the system prompt, press Ctrl-C to cancel the continuous retries.

Version 4 adds several additional values for the parameters of this form of the Mode command. It also lets you specify the parameters—either as a name followed by an equal sign and a value, in any order with no separating commas, or (as in the previous form) as just the values, separated by commas in the defined sequence.

mode <port> baud=<rate> data=<databits> parity=<type>
stop=<stopbits> retry=<action>

<port> is the name of the serial port whose communication parameters are to be set. <port> can be COM1, COM2, COM3, or COM4.

baud=<rate> specifies the baud rate. <rate> can be any of the values listed for <baud>, above.

data=<databits> specifies the number of electrical signals used to represent one character (such as *a*). <databits> can be 5, 6, 7, or 8. If you don't specify <databits>, DOS assumes 7.

stop=<stopbits> specifies the number of electrical signals that mark the end of a character. <stopbits> can be 1, 1.5, or 2. If you don't specify <stopbits>, DOS assumes 1 unless the baud rate is 110, in which case DOS assumes <stopbits> to be 2.

parity=<type> specifies the sort of error checking to be performed. <type> can be none, odd, even, mark, or space. If you don't specify parity, DOS assumes *e*.

retry=<action> specifies what the Mode command should respond when DOS requests the status of the serial port and the port is busy. Possible values are E (error), B (busy, which has the same effect as the P parameter in earlier versions of DOS), and R (ready). If you don't specify <action>, the Mode command assumes R; unless the instructions for a program suggest otherwise, don't specify this parameter.

Example

To set COM1 to 1200 baud, 8 data bits, no parity, and 1 stop bit, letting DOS assume a value for retries, type:

```
C:\DOS>mode com1 1200,n,8,1
COM1: 1200,n,8,1,-
```

If you're using version 4, you could also type:

```
C:\DOS>mode com1 baud=1200 stop=1 data=8 parity=none
COM1: 1200,n,8,1,-
```

To set COM2 to 2400 baud and no parity, let DOS assume values for data bits and stop bits, and specify continuous retries, type:

```
C:\DOS>mode com2 2400,n,,,p
COM1: 2400,n,7,1,p
```

If you're using version 4, you could also type:

```
C:\DOS>mode com2 baud=2400 retry=b parity=none
COM1: 2400,n,7,1,b
```

MODE
Set Parallel Printer Width and Spacing
Versions 3.2 and later, IBM releases 1.0 and later

Page 116

This form of the Mode command sets the number of characters per line and the number of lines per inch for a printer attached to a parallel port. The parameters are separated by commas. If you omit a parameter, be sure to enter the comma to show that you omitted it.

mode <printer> <width>,<spacing>,P

<printer> is the name of the parallel printer port whose width and spacing are to be set. <printer> can be LPT1, LPT2, or LPT3.

<width> is the maximum number of characters that can be printed on a line. It can be 80 or 132; if you don't specify <width>, DOS assumes 80.

<spacing> is the number of lines printed per inch. It can be 6 or 8; if you don't specify <spacing>, DOS assumes 6.

P, in versions prior to 4, tells DOS to continuously try to send output to the printer, even if the printer is busy or not ready. If DOS is waiting for the printer and you want to return to the system prompt, press Ctrl-C to cancel continuous retries.

Version 4 lets you specify the parameters—either as a name followed by an equal sign and a value, in any order with no separating commas, or (as in the previous form) as just the values in the defined sequence, separated by commas.

mode <printer> cols=<width> lines=<spacing> retry=<action>

<printer> is the name of the parallel printer port: LPT1, LPT2, or LPT3.

cols=<width> specifies the maximum number of characters that can be printed on a line—80 or 132, as described above for <width>.

lines=<spacing> specifies the number of lines printed per inch—6 or 8, as described above for <spacing>.

retry=<action> specifies what the Mode command should respond when DOS requests the status of the parallel port and the port is busy. Possible values are E (error), B (busy, which has the same effect as the P parameter in earlier versions of DOS), R (ready), and N (none). If you don't specify <action>, the Mode command assumes N; unless the instructions for a program suggest otherwise, don't specify this parameter.

Example

To set LPT1 to 132 characters per line and 8 lines per inch, letting DOS assume a value for retries, type:

```
C:\DOS>mode lpt1: 132,8
LPT1: not rerouted
LPT1: set for 132
Printer lines per inch set
No retry on parallel printer time-out
```

If you're using version 4, you could also type the command as:

```
C:\DOS>mode lpt1: lines=8 cols=132
```

To set LPT2 to 8 lines per inch and specify continuous retries, type:

```
C:\DOS>mode lpt2: ,8,p
LPT1: not rerouted
Printer lines per inch set
Resident portion of MODE loaded
Infinite retry on parallel printer time-out
```

If you're using version 4, you could also type the command as:

```
C:\DOS>mode lpt1: lines=8 retry=b
```

MODE
Redirect Parallel Printer Output
Versions 3.2 and later, IBM releases 1.1 and later

Page 120

This form of the Mode command redirects output from a parallel port to a serial port. Before using a serial printer, you must set the communications parameters of the serial port as described previously under the heading ''MODE: Set Serial Communications Parameters,'' and then redirect output from a parallel port to the serial port with the following form of the Mode command:

mode <printer>=<port>

<printer> is the name of the parallel printer whose output is to be redirected. <printer> can be LPT1, LPT2, or LPT3.

<port> is the name of the serial communications port to which the parallel printer port is to be redirected. If you're using 3.2 or an earlier version of DOS, <port> can be COM1 or COM2. If you're using version 3.3 or later, <port> can be COM1, COM2, COM3, or COM4.

To cancel redirection, omit the equal sign and <port> from the Mode command. That is, type just *mode <printer>*.

Examples

To redirect output from LPT1 to COM2:

```
C:\DOS>mode lpt1:=com2:
```

To cancel redirection of LPT1:

```
C:\DOS>mode lpt1:
```

MODE
Check Device Status
Versions 4.0 and later

Page 121

Beginning with version 4, this form of the Mode command enables you to request a report on the status of any or all devices on your system.

mode <device> /STATUS

<device> is the name of the device you want to check on, such as CON, LPT1:, or COM1:. If you omit <device>, DOS reports on all the devices it recognizes.

/STATUS tells DOS you want to check on device status. You can abbreviate this parameter as */sta*, and you can omit it from the command altogether unless you are checking on a parallel printer whose output you've redirected.

Example

To check the status of a parallel printer attached to LPT1: whose output has been redirected to COM2:, with no retries if the port is busy:

```
C:\DOS>mode lpt1: /sta
Status for device LPT1:
-----------------------
LPT1: rerouted to COM2:
RETRY=NONE
Code page operation not supported on this device
```

(The last line means that the device has not been set up for international language support, as described in the following entries.)

MODE
Preparing a Code Page
Versions 3.3 and later

Page 397

This form of the Mode command defines the code page or code pages to be used with a hardware device. To use this form of the Mode command, you must already have installed code-page switching; for details, see Appendix D.

mode <device> cp prepare=((<code-page>) <font-file>)

<device> is the name of the device for which the code page or code pages are to be prepared. It can be CON, PRN, LPT1, LPT2, or LPT3.

<code-page> is the code page to be used with <device>. If you specify more than one code-page number, separate them with blanks. Note that the code-page numbers are enclosed in their own set of parentheses. You can use the following code-page numbers: 437 (United States); 850 (Multilingual); 860 (Portuguese); 863 (Canadian French); 865 (Nordic), or any other that represents a valid code-page information file.

<font-file> is the name of the code-page information file that contains the font information for <device>. A code-page information file has the extension CPI. The following font files are included in the IBM release of versions 3.3 and later (if you use a different release, your version may include others):

EGA.CPI	Enhanced graphics adapter (EGA) or PS/2
4201.CPI	IBM Proprinter and Proprinter XL
4208.CPI	IBM Proprinter X24 and Proprinter XL24 (version 4)
5202.CPI	IBM Quietwriter III printer
LCD.CPI	IBM PC Convertible liquid crystal display (LCD)

Example

To prepare code pages 437 and 850 for an EGA or compatible display, specifying EGA.CPI as the code-page information file:

```
C:\DOS>mode con cp prepare=((437 850) c:\dos\ega.cpi)
```

MODE
Selecting a Code Page
Versions 3.3 and later

Page 397

This form of the Mode command selects a code page for a device. To use this form of the Mode command, you must already have installed code-page switching; for details, see Appendix D.

mode <device> cp select=<code-page>

<device> is the name of the device for which the code page is to be selected. It can be CON, PRN, LPT1, LPT2, or LPT3.

<code-page> is the three-digit number of the code page to be used with <device>. You can use the following code-page numbers: 437 (United States); 850 (Multilingual); 860 (Portuguese); 863 (Canadian French); 865 (Nordic), or any other that represents a valid code-page information file. <code-page> must be one previously prepared with the *cp prepare* option of the Mode command.

Example

To select code page 850 for the console:

```
C:\DOS>mode con cp select=850
```

MODE
Displaying the Code Page Status
Versions 3.3 and later

Page 398
This form of the Mode command displays the status of the code pages. To use this form of the Mode command, you must already have installed code-page switching; for details, see Appendix D.

mode <device> cp /STATUS

<device> is the name of the device whose code-page status is to be displayed. It can be CON, PRN, LPT1, LPT2, or LPT3.

/STATUS is optional. Include it if you want.

Example

To display the status of the console device:

```
C:\DOS>mode con cp
```

MODE
Restoring a Code Page That Was Lost
Versions 3.3 and later

Page 398
This form of the Mode command restores a code page that was selected for a device, then erased from memory. To use this form of the Mode command, you must already have installed code-page switching; for details, see Appendix D.

mode <device> cp refresh

<device> is the name of the device whose most recently selected code page is to be restored. It can be CON, PRN, LPT1, LPT2, or LPT3.

Example

To restore the most recently selected code page for the printer that is attached to the LPT2 port:

```
C:\DOS>mode lpt2: cp refresh
```

MORE
Display a File One Screenful at a Time
Versions 2.0 and later

Page 251

The More filter command reads standard input (normally the keyboard) and sends lines to standard output (normally the display); after each screenful of lines it displays the line —*More*— and waits for you to press a key.

Because the input and output of the More command can be redirected, input can also come from a file, a device other than the keyboard, or the output of another command. Likewise, you can redirect the output of the More command to a file or a device other than the display.

Thus, by redirecting or piping output to the More command, you can display a file one screenful at a time, pressing a key to see the next screenful. To stop displaying, you press Ctrl-Break. The More command has no parameters:

more

Examples

To display the current directory one screenful at a time:

```
C:\DOS>dir | more
```

To display the file REPORT.DOC one screenful at a time, the More command can be used in either of two ways. The first uses the redirection symbol < to get input from the file REPORT.DOC:

```
C:\MKT\WP>more < report.doc
```

The second pipes output from the Type command to the More command:

```
C:\MKT\WP>type report.doc | more
```

NLSFUNC (NATIONAL LANGUAGE SUPPORT FUNCTION)
Support National Language and Conventions
Versions 3.3 and later

Page 393

The National Language Support Function command (nlsfunc) tells DOS the path and file name of the file that contains country-specific information, such as date format, time format, and currency symbol. You must enter the Nlsfunc command before you can use the Change Code Page (chcp) command.

nlsfunc <country-file>

<country-file> is the name of the country information file (COUNTRY.SYS in most versions of DOS). If you omit <country-file>, DOS assumes the file is the one specified in the Country configuration command in CONFIG.SYS; if there is no Country configuration command in CONFIG.SYS, DOS assumes that the file is named COUNTRY.SYS and looks for it in the root directory of the current drive.

Example

If you use national language support regularly and you have version 4 of DOS, add an Install command naming NLSFUNC.EXE to your CONFIG.SYS file. For example, to specify C:\DOS\COUNTRY.SYS as the country information file, add the following command to CONFIG.SYS:

```
INSTALL C:\DOS\NLSFUNC.EXE C:\DOS\COUNTRY.SYS
```

If you use national language support occasionally, the following command (typed at the system prompt C:\>) specifies C:\DOS\COUNTRY.SYS:

```
C:\>nlsfunc c:\dos\country.sys
```

Finally, if you have version 3.3 of DOS and use national language support regularly, put the preceding Nlsfunc command in AUTOEXEC.BAT.

PATH
Define the Command Path
Versions 2.0 and later

Page 145

The Path command tells DOS where to search for a command file (a file whose extension is COM, EXE, or BAT) that isn't in the current directory. A command path becomes part of the DOS environment, so it is available to every program DOS carries out during a work session on your computer.

path <drive><path> ;

<drive> is the letter, followed by a colon, of the drive containing the disk on which you want DOS to look for command files.

<path> is the path name of the directory that you want DOS to search for command files. You can enter a series of path names, separated by semicolons. If you omit <path> but include the semicolon, DOS deletes any paths in effect.

If you enter the Path command with no parameters (type just *path*), DOS displays the current command path. If no path has been specified, DOS displays *No path*.

Include a Path command in AUTOEXEC.BAT if application programs or batch files on your fixed disk are stored in separate subdirectories.

Examples

To tell DOS to search the root directory and the directories named \DOS, \WORD, and \EXCEL of the current drive for command files:

```
C:\>path c:\;c:\dos;c:\word;c:\excel
```

To display the command path:

```
C:\>path
```

For the command path in the preceding example, DOS responds:

```
PATH=C:\;C:\DOS;C:\WORD;C:\EXCEL
```

To delete the command path:

```
C:\>path ;
```

PAUSE (BATCH COMMAND)
Temporarily Stop a Batch File
Versions 1.0 and later

Page 260

The Pause batch command displays the message *Press any key to continue . . . (Strike a key when ready . . .* in versions before 4) and waits for you to press a key before carrying out any more commands. You can cancel a batch file while it is paused by pressing Ctrl-C.

The Pause command also lets you include a message to be displayed before *Press any key to continue. . .*

pause <message>

<message> is the message to be displayed before *Press any key to continue. . .*

Examples

To temporarily stop the batch file:

```
pause
```

To echo the message *Put data disk in drive B* and temporarily stop a batch file before the *Press any key to continue . . .* message:

```
@echo off
echo Put the data disk in drive B and
pause
```

When DOS carries out the commands in the batch file, it displays the following messages and waits for any key to be pressed:

```
Put the data disk in drive B and
Press any key to continue . . .
```

PRINT
Print a File

The Print command loads the DOS Print program, which manages a queue of files waiting to be printed. The print program, also known as a *print spooler,* can print the files in the queue while another program is running. It does this by using small portions of the computer's processing time.

The Print command is used in two forms. You use the first when you load the print program and set up its operating characteristics, and you use the second to manage the contents of the print queue. These forms are described separately in the following entries.

PRINT
Set Operating Characteristics
Versions 2.0 and later

Page 84

The first time you enter the Print command after you start DOS, you can define the operating characteristics of the print program with the command:

**print /D:<printer> /Q:<size> /B:<size> /S:<slice>
/M:<max> /U:<wait>**

/D:<printer> specifies the name of the print device. If you do not specify <printer> in the first Print command you enter after starting the system, DOS prompts you for the device name by displaying *Name of list device [PRN]:.* You can specify LPT1, LPT2, LPT3, COM1, COM2, AUX, or PRN. If you're using version 3.3 or later, you can also specify COM3 or COM4. If you press Enter without specifying a device, DOS assumes PRN. If you use /D to name the print device, it must be the first parameter in the Print command. (Versions 3.0 and later)

/Q:<size> specifies how many files can be in the print queue. The range is 4 through 32; if you don't specify /Q:<size>, DOS assumes 10.

/B:<size> specifies the number of bytes, up to 16,000, in the print buffer (an area of memory used for data by the Print program). If you don't specify /B:<size>, DOS assumes 512 bytes. (Versions 3.0 and later)

/S:<slice> specifies the number of times each second (number of time slices) that Print is allowed to control the computer. <slice> can be from 1 through 255; if you don't specify /S:<slice>, DOS assumes 8. (Versions 3.0 and later)

/M:<max> specifies the length of each time slice, measured in ticks of the computer's internal timer. <max> can be from 1 through 255; if you don't specify /M:<max>, DOS assumes 2. (Versions 3.0 and later)

/U:<wait> specifies how many timer ticks Print waits before giving up its time slice if the printer is busy or unavailable. If you don't specify /U:<wait>, DOS assumes 1. (Versions 3.0 and later)

Because DOS assumes values for all these parameters, you needn't use any of them unless you want to change these assumed values. Depending on such factors as how often you use the Print command, how many files you typically put in the print queue, the average length of the files you print, and the size of your printer's buffer, you may be able to improve overall system performance by experimenting with some of the values that DOS assumes.

Example

To specify COM1 as <printer>, 2048 as the buffer size, 100 time slices per second, and 255 timer ticks for each time slice:

```
C:\DOS>print /d:com1: /b:2048 /s:100 /m:255
```

Note: Remember that you define these characteristics the first time you enter a Print command. Your AUTOEXEC.BAT file might already contain a Print command. To change the operation of the Print command, edit your AUTOEXEC.BAT file and restart your computer.

PRINT
Manage the Print Queue
Versions 2.0 and later

Page 81

Files are placed in the print queue in the order in which you specify them in the Print command, and they are printed in the same order. You can add files to and delete files from the print queue in the same command.

DOS continues printing a file until it reaches an end-of-file marker (Ctrl-Z), then stops, even if it has not reached the actual end of the file, and goes on to the next file in the queue. After printing a file, DOS advances the paper to the top of the next page.

print <filename> /P /C /T

<filename> is the name of the file to be added to or deleted from the print queue. You can use wildcard characters to print a set of files with similar file names or extensions, and you can specify more than one file in a single Print command, separating the file names with blanks. In versions 3.0 and later, you can also include a path name.

/P adds to the print queue the preceding and all subsequent files in the command line up to a /C parameter. If you enter a Print command with a file name but no other parameter, DOS assumes /P.

/C deletes from the print queue the preceding and all subsequent files in the command line up to a /P parameter. If one of the deleted files is being printed, DOS prints *File canceled by operator*, sounds the printer's bell (if there is one), and advances the paper to the top of the next page.

/T terminates printing. DOS deletes all files from the print queue, cancels any file being printed, prints *All files canceled by operator*, sounds the printer's bell, and advances the paper to the top of the next page.

If you enter the Print command with no parameters, DOS displays the names of the files in the print queue.

Examples

To add all files in the current directory with the extension DOC (or as many as the queue will hold) to the print queue:

```
C:\MKT\WP>print *.doc
```

To remove the file named REPORT.DOC from the print queue and at the same time add the files named SLSRPT.DOC and SLSFCST.DOC to the print queue:

```
C:\MKT\WP>print /c report.doc /p slsrpt.doc slsfcst.doc
```

To cancel printing and remove all files from the print queue:

```
C:\MKT\WP>print /t
```

PROMPT
Set the System Prompt
Versions 2.0 and later, IBM releases 2.1 and later

Page 316

The Prompt command defines the system prompt, which DOS normally displays as the current drive letter, followed by a greater-than sign (such as *C>*). If you change the system prompt, you can include any character DOS can display, plus such items of system information as the time, date, current drive, and current directory.

prompt <string>

<string> is a string that defines the new prompt. It can contain any character DOS can display, plus any number of the following two-character codes, which tell DOS to include specific information in the prompt (each code must begin with a dollar sign):

Code	Information Displayed
$t	The time
$d	The date (preceded by the day of the week)
$p	Current directory of the current drive
$v	DOS version number
$n	Current drive
$g	A greater-than sign (>)
$l	A less-than sign (<)
$b	A vertical bar (¦)
$q	An equal sign (=)
$h	A backspace (which erases the previous character)
$e	An Escape character
$_ (underscore)	Start a new line
$$	A dollar sign ($)

If any other character follows the $, DOS ignores both characters.

If you enter a Prompt command with no parameters, DOS resets the system prompt to the standard version.

Examples

Each of the following examples shows both a Prompt command and the prompt it produces (<space> represents pressing the spacebar once):

To set the system prompt to display the word *Command* followed by a colon:

```
C:\DOS>prompt Command:<space>
```

DOS displays:

```
Command: _
```

To set the system prompt to the time—with six backspaces to erase seconds and hundredths of seconds—followed by a blank, the date, and a colon:

```
C:\DOS>prompt $t$h$h$h$h$h$h<space>$d:<space>
```

DOS displays:

```
16:07 Mon 10-16-1989: _
```

To set the system prompt to the date, time, and current directory on separate lines:

```
C:\DOS>prompt $d$_$t$_$p<space>
```

DOS displays:

```
Mon 10-16-1989
16:07:31.56
C:\DOS _
```

RAMDRIVE.SYS
Create a Virtual or RAM Drive in Memory
Versions 3.2 and later

The device driver RAMDRIVE.SYS is used with the Device configuration command to create a virtual disk drive in your computer's memory. This file is in Microsoft's releases of DOS from version 3.2. The equivalent file in IBM's releases of DOS is called VDISK.SYS. Because the examples in this book are based on IBM's releases of DOS, virtual disks are discussed in the entry VDISK.SYS. Refer to that entry if your system includes RAMDRIVE.SYS.

RECOVER
Recover Files from a Damaged Disk
Versions 2.0 and later

The Recover command attempts to reconstruct files from a disk that has damaged sectors or a damaged directory. It names the recovered files FILE*nnnn*.REC, where *nnnn* is a sequence number that starts with 0001. Recovered files may include extraneous material at the end, which you'll need to edit out of the file.

   The Recover command excludes data from all damaged sectors; recovered files may or may not be complete and may or may not be usable by an application program. Files can be recovered from subdirectories, but they are placed in the root directory of the disk, not in the subdirectory in which they were originally saved.

Note: Recover cannot be used on a network, nor with a drive affected by a Join or Substitute command.

   recover <filename>

   <filename> is the name of the file to be recovered. If you specify a drive letter rather than a file name, DOS assumes that the directory of the disk in the drive is damaged and recovers the directory as a single file containing the names of the files it

originally contained. The original directory is erased, however, so don't use this form of the command unless you're sure the directory is unusable.

Examples

To recover the file named REPORT.DOC in the current directory of the current drive:

```
C:\MKT\WP>recover report.doc
```

To recover as many files as DOS can fit into the root directory of the disk in drive B:

```
C:\DOS>recover b:
```

REM (BATCH COMMAND)
Include a Remark in a Batch File
Versions 1.0 and later

Page 229

The Remark batch command (rem) lets you include remarks in a batch file. Remarks are displayed if echo is on and are not displayed if echo is off.

rem <remark>

<remark> is the remark.

Example

The following batch command includes the remark *This batch file requires the data disk* in a batch file:

```
rem This batch file requires the data disk
```

REMOVE DIRECTORY (RD)
Remove a Directory
Versions 2.0 and later

Page 144

The Remove Directory command (rd or rmdir) removes a subdirectory. You cannot remove the current directory or the root directory, nor can you remove a directory that contains files.

rd <drive><path>

<drive> is the letter, followed by a colon, of the drive containing the disk with the directory to be removed.

<path> is the path name of the directory that is to be removed.

Note: Because the Assign, Join, and Substitute commands can mask the actual subdirectory names, you shouldn't remove a directory with the RD command when any of these commands are in effect.

Examples

The following examples assume that the current directory is C:\.

To remove the subdirectory C:\MKT:

```
C:\>rd mkt
```

To remove the subdirectory C:\MKT\WP:

```
C:\>rd \mkt\wp
```

To remove the subdirectory A:\WORD\LETTERS:

```
C:\>rd a:\word\letters
```

RENAME (REN)
Change the Name of a File
Versions 1.0 and later

Page 73

The Rename command (ren) changes the name of a file or a set of files. The renamed file must be in the same directory as the original, and can't be given the name of an existing file in the same directory.

rename <oldname> <newname>

<oldname> is the name of the file to be renamed.

<newname> is the new name to be assigned to the file. DOS ignores any drive letter or path name. If <newname> is the same as the name of an existing file, DOS responds *Duplicate file name or file not found* and leaves <oldname> unchanged.

Examples

To change the name of the file REPORT.DOC to FINALRPT.DOC:

```
C:\MKT\WP>ren report.doc finalrpt.doc
```

To change the name of the file FINALRPT.SAV to FINALRPT.DOC:

```
C:\MKT\WP>ren finalrpt.sav *.doc
```

To change the names of all files named REPORT in the directory D:\MKT\WP to the name FINALRPT, keeping the same extension:

```
C:\>ren d:\mkt\wp\report.* finalrpt.*
```

REPLACE
Replace or Add Files on a Disk
Versions 3.2 and later

Page 163

The Replace command lets you copy files selectively, either by replacing files that already exist on the target disk or by adding files to the target. The Replace command can also search subdirectories on the target disk for files to be replaced.

replace <source> <target> /A /S /R /P /W /U

<source> is the name of the file to be copied. You can use wildcard characters to copy a set of files with similar file names or extensions.

<target> specifies where <source> is to be copied. You can include a drive letter and path name, but not a file name.

/A (for *add*) copies only the files on <source> that don't exist on <target>. This lets you add files to <target> without replacing files that already exist. If you don't specify /A, only files specified in <source> that also exist in <target> are copied. If you specify /A, you cannot specify /S or /U.

/S applies the Replace command to all subdirectories contained in <target>. If you specify <target> as the root directory of a disk, the Replace command is applied to every subdirectory on the disk. If you specify /S, you can't specify /A.

/R replaces read-only files on <target>.

/P prompts for confirmation before replacing or adding each file.

/W waits and prompts you to press a key before the Replace command begins. This gives you a chance to put in the correct diskette before starting to replace or add files on it.

/U replaces only files on the target disk or directory that are older than their counterparts on the source disk or directory.

When it finishes, Replace sets *errorlevel* to one of the following values:

0	Completed normally.
1	There was an error in the command line (versions 3.3 and earlier).
2	No files were found to replace.
3	The source or destination path name was entered incorrectly or does not exist.
5	A read-only file was encountered on <target> but the /R parameter was not included in the command.
8	Not enough memory.
11	Command line error (version 4).
15	The command includes an invalid drive letter.

You can check this value with the *errorlevel* option of the If batch command and use the outcome of the replace procedure to control which subsequent commands are carried out in a batch file.

Examples

To replace all files whose extension is DOC in the directory C:\MKT\WP and all its subdirectories with the files whose extension is DOC on the disk in drive A and prompt for confirmation before each file is copied:

```
C:\>replace a:*.doc c:\mkt\wp /s /p
```

To add all files from the disk in drive A whose extension is DOC and that don't exist in the current directory on the disk in the current drive:

```
C:\MKT\WP>replace a:*.doc /a
```

RESTORE
Restore Backed-Up Files
Versions 2.0 and later

Page 176

The Restore command copies files that were backed up with the Backup command, restoring them from the backup disk to the original disk. Files are restored to the directories from which they were backed up, so the same directory structure must exist on the disk to which the files are restored. If you have a series of backup diskettes, DOS prompts for them, as they are needed, in the same sequence in which they were backed up with the Backup command.

The Restore command includes a number of parameters that help you fine-tune the restoration procedure, but not all parameters are available in all versions of DOS. Check the documentation that came with your version of DOS to determine which parameters you can use.

restore <drive> <path><filename> /S /P /B:<date> /A:<date> /M /N /E:<time> /L:<time>

<drive> specifies the drive that contains the backup disk from which files are to be restored. If you don't specify a drive letter, the files are restored from the disk in the current drive.

<path> and <filename> specify the file to be restored. You can use wildcard characters to restore a set of files with similar names or extensions. If you don't specify a path name, the files are restored to the current directory.

/S restores files in all subdirectories in the specified directory.

/P causes DOS to prompt for confirmation before restoring a read-only file, a hidden file, or a file that has changed since it was backed up. This lets you protect files that you have updated since you backed them up, and avoid replacing read-only and system files (IBMBIO.COM and IBMDOS.COM, or IO.SYS and MSDOS.SYS, depending on whose version of DOS you're using) with backup copies from a different version of DOS.

/B:<date> restores only files that were created or changed on or before <date>.

/A:<date> restores only files that were created or changed on or after <date>.

/M restores only files that have been changed since they were backed up.

/N restores only files that don't exist on the target.

/E:<time> restores only files that were created or changed at or earlier than <time>.

/L:<time> restores only files that were created or changed at or later than <time>.

When it is finished, Restore sets one of the following *errorlevel* values:

0	Completed normally.
1	No files were found to restore.
2	Some files were not restored because of file-sharing conflict.
3	The restore process was canceled because the user pressed Ctrl-C or Ctrl-Break.
4	A system error occurred and the restore process was stopped.

You can check this value with the *errorlevel* option of the If batch command and thus use the outcome of the restore procedure to control which subsequent commands are carried out in a batch file.

Warning: Trying to restore files that were backed up when an Assign, Substitute, or Join command was in effect can damage the directory structure of the disk.

Examples

To restore the file named REPORT.DOC from the disk in drive A to the directory \MKT\WP (from which it was backed up) on the disk in drive C:

```
C:\DOS>restore a: c:\mkt\wp\report.doc
```

To restore all files in the root directory and all subdirectories on the disk in drive A to the same subdirectories on the disk in drive C:

```
C:\DOS>restore a: c:\ /s
```

To restore all files with the extension DOC from the disk in drive A to the directory named \MKT\WP on the disk in drive C, prompting for confirmation if the file has changed since it was backed up or if the file is hidden or read-only:

```
C:\DOS>restore a: c:\mkt\wp\*.doc /p
```

SELECT
Start the Installation Program
Versions 4.0 and later

Starting with version 4, the Select command starts the DOS installation program, which prompts you for information about how to set up your operating system and then installs DOS either on your fixed disk or on diskettes. Because the questions include language and keyboard-layout preferences, the DOS diskettes created by the installation program are country-specific, maintaining consistency with the earlier version of the Select command.

The DOS version 4 Install diskette contains an AUTOEXEC.BAT file that automatically starts this version of the Select program. To start the program, put the DOS Install diskette in drive A and turn the system on (or, if the system is running, press Ctrl-Alt-Del). For more information on installing version 4, refer to Appendix B.

SELECT
Create a Country-Specific System Diskette
Version 3.3, IBM releases 3.0 through 3.3

Page 389

The Select command creates a system diskette tailored to the date format and keyboard layout of a particular country.

select <source> <target> <country> <keyboard>

<source> is the letter, followed by a colon, of the drive that contains the DOS system diskette; it must include the system files, COMMAND.COM, the Format command, and the Xcopy command. <source> must be either drive A or drive B; if you don't specify <source>, DOS assumes drive A. (Versions 3.2 and 3.3)

<target> is the letter, followed by a colon, of the drive that contains the target diskette. If you don't specify <target>, DOS assumes drive B. (Versions 3.2 and 3.3)

<country> is the three-digit code, corresponding to the long-distance telephone prefix, of the country whose date and time format you want to use.

<keyboard> is the two-letter code for the keyboard layout you want to specify.

Valid country and keyboard codes through version 3.3 are as follows (not all are available in all versions of DOS):

Country	Country Code	Keyboard Code
Australia	061	US
Belgium	032	BE
Canada (English)	001	US
Canada (French)	002	CF
Denmark	045	DK
Finland	358	SU
France	033	FR
Germany	049	GR
International (English)	061	—
Israel	972	—
Italy	039	IT
Latin America	003	LA
Middle East (Arabic)	785	—
Netherlands	031	NL
Norway	047	NO
Portugal	351	PO
Spain	034	SP
Sweden	046	SV
Switzerland (French)	041	SF
Switzerland (German)	041	SG
United Kingdom	044	UK
United States	001	US

When you create a system diskette with the Select command, DOS also creates a CONFIG.SYS file and an AUTOEXEC.BAT file containing Date, Time, and Version commands. In version 3.2, if you specify a country whose keyboard file is not on the source diskette, DOS prompts you to insert the correct diskette. Once a country-specific diskette is created, you can use it to start DOS with the date format and keyboard layout appropriate to that country.

Example

To create a system diskette for France and the French keyboard layout:

```
select 033 fr
```

SET
Change or Display
An Environment Variable
Versions 2.0 and later

The Set command changes or displays the value assigned to an environment variable. The environment is an area of memory in which DOS keeps track of such information as the command path and definition of the system prompt. You can also use the Set command to define replaceable parameters for use with batch files, but it's unlikely to be needed in your everyday use of DOS. Its primary use is by people who write their own programs. If you need more information on this command, refer to the documentation that came with your version of DOS.

SHARE
Allow Files To Be Shared
Versions 3.0 and later

The Share command allows files to be shared by more than one program. If your computer is part of a network, you must enter a Share command before joining the network. Consult with the administrator of your network for information on how to use the Share command.

   If your computer isn't part of a network, you probably don't need to use the Share command.

SHELL (CONFIGURATION COMMAND)
Specify the Command Processor
Versions 2.0 and later

The Shell configuration command specifies the command processor—the program that receives your instructions at the keyboard and relays them to the appropriate DOS program—that DOS is to use. Unless you specify otherwise with a Shell command, DOS uses the program named COMMAND.COM. If you need to use a different command processor, the program requiring it should give you instructions on its use.

Note: The Shell command is not the same command that starts the DOS Shell in version 4. To start the version 4 Shell, you type dosshell *at the system prompt.*

SHIFT (BATCH COMMAND)
Move Batch Parameters One Position Left
Versions 2.0 and later

Page 283

The Shift batch command moves the command-line parameters entered with a batch command one position to the left; the leftmost parameter is lost, and all other parameters move one position left. You can use the Shift command to process more than 10 replaceable parameters in a batch file.

   shift

Example

The following batch file, named SHIFT _ IT.BAT, uses the Shift command to process as many parameters as you can enter in the command line. The line numbers are shown only for reference:

```
 1: @echo off
 2: echo %0
 3: shift
 4: :start
 5: if "%0"=="" goto all_done
 6: echo %0 %1 %2
 7: shift
 8: shift
 9: shift
10: goto start
11: :all_done
12: echo ALL DONE
```

The Echo command in line 2 displays the name of the batch file, and the Shift command in line 3 shifts all command-line parameters one position to the left; the previous %0 (the name of the batch file) is lost, what was %1 becomes %0, what was %2 becomes %1, and so forth. Line 5 checks the leftmost parameter to see if there is one. If there isn't, the command *goto all _ done* ends the batch file. If there is a leftmost parameter, line 6 displays the three leftmost parameters, lines 7 through 9 shift the parameters three positions to the left, and line 10 goes back to repeat the process.

   Entering the SHIFT _ IT batch command with the following parameters produces the display shown below:

```
C>shift_it 1 2 3 4 5 6 7 8 9 10 11 12 13 14 15
shift_it
1 2 3
4 5 6
7 8 9
10 11 12
13 14 15
ALL DONE
```

SORT
Arrange Lines of a File
Versions 2.0 and later

Page 245

The Sort filter command reads lines from standard input, arranges (sorts) them in alphabetic or numeric order, and writes the sorted lines to standard output.

In version 2, uppercase and lowercase letters are treated separately, so that *Zurich* comes before *aardvark* in a sorted list. In versions 3.0 and later, however, uppercase and lowercase letters are treated identically, so that *aardvark* comes before *Zurich*. Also in versions 3.0 and later, accented characters are treated like their alphabetic equivalents, so that â, ä, à, and å, for example, are all grouped with the letter A.

The input and output of the Sort command normally come from the keyboard and go to the display. Both, however, can be redirected from or to a file or device, or piped from or to another command. For example, you can redirect input to a file to sort the lines of the file, then redirect the output to another file to store the sorted version on disk. The largest file that the Sort program can handle is 63 K. If you redirect both the input to and the output from the Sort command to a file, use different file names; sorting a file to itself can destroy the contents of the file.

sort /R /+<column>

/R sorts the file in reverse order (Z to A instead of A to Z, or highest number to lowest number).

/+<column> specifies the column on which the sorting is to be based; if you don't specify /+<column>, DOS assumes 1.

Examples

To sort the lines of a file named CLIENTS.LST and display the result:

```
C:\MKT>sort < clients.lst
```

To sort the file CLIENTS.LST in reverse order, placing the result in the file named CLIENTS.SRT:

```
C:\MKT>sort /r < clients.lst > clients.srt
```

To pipe the output of the Directory command to a Sort command that sorts the entries in reverse order by file size (starting with column 14 of the Directory command output), then print the result:

```
C:\>dir ¦ sort /r /+14 > prn
```

STACKS
(CONFIGURATION COMMAND)
Reserve Memory for
Temporary Program Use
Versions 3.2 and later

The Stacks configuration command tells DOS how much memory to reserve for its own temporary use. Some application programs may require a Stacks command in CONFIG.SYS, and should tell you how to do it; otherwise, you shouldn't need to use this command.

SUBSTITUTE (SUBST)
Treat a Directory as a Disk Drive
Versions 3.1 and later

Page 320

The Substitute command (subst) tells DOS to treat a subdirectory as if it were an additional disk drive in your system. This lets you use subdirectories with an application program that doesn't recognize path names, because you can substitute a drive letter for a path to a subdirectory.

subst <drive> <pathname> /D

<drive> is the letter, followed by a colon, of the drive to be substituted for <pathname>. <drive> cannot be the current drive. If you specify <drive>, you must also specify <pathname>.

<pathname> is the path to the subdirectory for which <drive> is to be substituted; <pathname> must begin at the root directory (start with \). If you include a drive letter in <pathname>, it must be different from the letter you specified for <drive>. You must specify at least a backslash to name the root directory.

/D deletes a substitution, returning the drive letter to its original meaning. Do not use this parameter from within the substituted drive or directory.

If you enter the Substitute command with no parameters (type just *subst*), DOS displays all substitutions in effect.

If you substitute a drive letter for one subdirectory, then want to substitute the same drive letter for a different subdirectory, you must first delete the original substitution.

If you want to use several subdirectories, enter a Substitute command for each subdirectory and use a different drive letter for each. If you need drive letters beyond E (the highest letter DOS recognizes unless you specify otherwise), add or edit a Lastdrive configuration command in CONFIG.SYS to tell DOS the highest drive letter.

Note: Because the Substitute command masks the actual type of disk drive from DOS, you shouldn't use the Assign, Backup, Diskcomp, Diskcopy, Fdisk, Format, Join, Label, or Restore commands when a substitution is in effect. Because the Substitute command can mask the true directory structure, you should also avoid using the Change Directory, Make Directory, Remove Directory, and Path commands when a substitution is in effect. If you want to use one of these commands, delete the substitution. The Substitute command cannot be used with a network drive.

Examples

Suppose your word processor doesn't recognize path names, but you want to keep the word-processing program in a directory named \WP and some word-processing files in a subdirectory named \MKT\WP. The following Substitute command lets you use drive letter E to represent the subdirectory:

```
C:\>subst e: \mkt\wp
```

To display any substitutions in effect:

```
C:\>subst
```

For the preceding example, DOS would display:

```
E: => C:\MKT\WP
```

To delete the substitution created by the first example:

```
C:\>subst e: /d
```

SWITCHES
(CONFIGURATION COMMAND)
Block Enhanced Keyboard Functions
IBM releases 4.0 and later

Page 316

The Switches configuration command prevents DOS from using the additional keys on the enhanced keyboard. You would most likely need the Switches command only if pressing one of the additional keys on the enhanced keyboard caused problems with one of your application programs.

switches=/K

/K tells DOS not to use the enhanced keyboard functions.

SYSTEM (SYS)
Transfer System Files
Versions 1.0 and later

The System command (sys) copies the DOS system files—IO.SYS and MSDOS.SYS or IBMBIO.COM and IBMDOS.COM, depending on whose version of DOS you're using—from the disk in the current drive to a formatted disk. The system files are hidden and have special storage requirements. You don't see them in the output of the Directory command, but they must be present on any disk from which you want to start DOS. The System command does not copy COMMAND.COM, which must also be on a startup disk; you must copy COMMAND.COM with the Copy command.

You use the System command to transfer the DOS system files to a fixed disk, to a formatted blank diskette, or to a disk (such as an application diskette) on which space has been reserved especially for these files. You can also use the System command to replace existing system files with a newer version, if the new system files will fit into the space occupied by the older files.

> **sys <source> <drive>**

<source> specifies where the system files are to be copied from. You can specify a drive letter and a directory path name. If you don't specify <source>, DOS copies the system files from the current drive. (Version 4)

<drive> is the letter of the drive, followed by a colon, that contains the disk to which the system files are to be copied. In versions prior to 4, the system files themselves must be on the disk on the current drive.

Note: The System command cannot be used on a network drive.

Example

To copy the system files from the disk in drive C to a diskette in drive A:

```
C:\DOS>sys a:
```

TIME
Change or Display the System Time
Versions 1.0 and later

Page 15

The Time command displays the time maintained by DOS, to the hundredth of a second, and prompts you to enter a new time. The time is displayed and entered according to a 12-hour or a 24-hour clock, depending on the customs of the country specified in the Country command in CONFIG.SYS. If you're using version 4 in a country, such as the United States, that normally uses a 12-hour clock, you can specify the time in 12-hour format, followed by an *am* or *a* or a *pm* or *p* (for example, *3:15 p* or *3:15 pm*), or in 24-hour format (for example, *15:15* for 3:15 P.M.).

The command form here shows the traditional United States format (hours:minutes:seconds).

time   <hh:mm><:ss> <.xx>

<hh:mm> is the new time to be set. <hh> is the hour (1 through 24 or 1 through 12 A.M. or P.M.) and <mm> is minutes (0 through 59). <hh> and <mm> are separated by a colon (:).

<:ss> specifies seconds (0 through 59), preceded by a colon (:). If you don't specify <:ss>, DOS assumes 0.

<.xx> specifies hundredths of a second (0 through 99), preceded by a decimal point (.). If you don't specify <.xx>, DOS assumes 0.

If you enter the Time command with no parameter (type just *time*), DOS displays the current time and prompts you to enter the new time. You can either enter the new time, or just press the Enter key to leave the time unchanged. If your system does not keep the time current when the computer is switched off, consider putting Date and Time commands in your AUTOEXEC.BAT file.

Note: The Time command might not permanently change the system clock on computers with built-in or add-on clock/calendars. If you have a system with a built-in clock/calendar (such as the IBM PC/AT or a compatible) and the Time command does not permanently change the time, use the SETUP program on your Diagnostics disk. If you have an add-on clock/calendar, use the software that came with the clock/calendar card.

Examples

To set the time to 6:00 A.M.:

```
C:\DOS>time 6:00
```

If you're using version 4, you could also type:

```
C:\DOS>time 6:00a
```

To set the time to 6:00 P.M.:

```
C:\DOS>time 18:00
```

If you're using version 4, you could also type:

```
C:\DOS>time 6:00p
```

To display the current time and respond to the prompt for a new time:

```
C:\DOS>time
```

DOS responds:

```
Current time is  6:02:01.60p
Enter new time: _
```

Or, if you're not using version 4:

```
Current time is 18:02:01.60
Enter new time: _
```

Type the new time or press the Enter key to leave the current time unchanged.

TREE
Display a Directory Structure
Versions 3.2 and later, IBM releases 2.0 and later

Page 146

The Tree command shows the structure of a disk or directory by displaying the directory and subdirectory names and, optionally, the names of the files in each directory. In version 4, the Tree command diagrams the structure of a disk or a multilevel directory by using line-drawing and box-drawing characters. Before version 4, the output is simply a list of directory names and, if requested, file names.

tree <drive><path> /F /A

<drive> is the letter of the drive, followed by a colon, that contains the disk whose directory structure is to be displayed.

<path> is the path to a specified directory. If you omit <path>, DOS displays the current directory of the current drive.

/F displays a list of the files in each directory.

/A specifies that an alternate character set (plus signs, hyphens, and vertical bars) be used to draw the tree diagram so that it can be printed by printers that don't support the IBM extended character set. (Version 4)

Note: You can also display a list of the directories and files on a disk with the /V option of the Check Disk command.

Examples

Assume that the root directory of the disk in drive C contains four directories: DOS, MKT, MFG, and ENG; \MKT and \ENG, in turn, contain subdirectories named WP and EXCEL. To display this directory structure, type:

```
C:\>tree
```

Beginning with version 4, DOS displays the following diagram:

```
Directory PATH listing for Volume FIXED DISK
Volume Serial Number is 1608-5A30
C:.
├────DOS
├────MKT
│        ├────WP
│        └────EXCEL
├────MFG
└────ENG
         ├────WP
         └────EXCEL
```

To print the diagram using the alternate character set, add the /A parameter and redirect the output to the printer:

```
C:\>tree /a > prn
```

DOS prints the following diagram:

```
Directory PATH listing for Volume FIXED DISK
Volume Serial Number is 1608-5A30
C:.
+---DOS
+---MKT
¦   +---WP
¦   \---EXCEL
+---MFG
\---ENG
    +---WP
    \---EXCEL
```

To display the directory structure of the disk in drive B, including all file names and pausing after each screenful:

```
C:\DOS>tree b: /f ¦ more
```

TYPE
Display a File
Versions 1.0 and later

Page 65

The Type command sends a file to standard output. If you don't redirect standard output, the file is displayed.

type <filename>

<filename> is the file to be sent to standard output. The Type command doesn't accept wildcard characters.

Note: Some files include characters other than alphabetic and numeric characters and punctuation marks. Program files are one example; another is a word-processed document that includes special formatting codes designed to be read by programs, rather than by people. If you use the Type command to display such a file, you'll probably see unintelligible characters and hear occasional beeps. Don't worry; your computer can handle the display, even though the results might be meaningless to you.

Examples

To display the file named REPORT.DOC in the current directory:

```
C:\MKT\WP>type report.doc
```

To print the file REPORT.DOC from the directory \MKT\WP on the disk in drive A:

```
C:\DOS>type a:\mkt\wp\report.doc > prn
```

VDISK.SYS
Define a Virtual Disk Drive
IBM releases 3.0 and later

Page 310

Note: The equivalent of VDISK.SYS in other versions of DOS is RAMDRIVE.SYS, available in versions 3.2 and later. The following description applies to both virtual-disk programs; differences between VDISK.SYS and RAMDRIVE.SYS are noted where appropriate.

VDISK.SYS and RAMDRIVE.SYS are programs that create a virtual disk in memory. To install a virtual disk, you must include a Device command in CONFIG.SYS that names VDISK.SYS or RAMDRIVE.SYS and specifies the size and characteristics of the virtual disk.

You can create more than one virtual disk by including in CONFIG.SYS a Device command for each virtual drive. DOS assigns the first available drive letter to a virtual drive; if you need a drive letter higher than E, include or modify a Lastdrive configuration command in CONFIG.SYS that specifies the highest drive letter you need.

In most machines, a virtual drive reduces the amount of available memory. If you're using VDISK.SYS with an IBM Personal Computer AT or a machine compatible with it, you can create the virtual drive in extended memory. If you're using version 4 of DOS, you can also create a virtual drive in expanded memory if your computer is so equipped.

If you're using RAMDRIVE.SYS and your computer is equipped with either extended memory (as in the IBM PC/AT and compatibles) or if your computer contains an expanded memory board that complies with the Lotus/Intel/Microsoft Expanded

Memory Specification, you can tell DOS to create a virtual disk in extended or expanded memory.

The format and parameters for VDISK.SYS and RAMDRIVE.SYS are described separately here.

For VDISK.SYS, the form of the command is:

device=vdisk.sys <size> <sector> <directory> /E:<sectors> /X:<sectors>

vdisk.sys is the name of the file that contains the virtual-disk program. If VDISK.SYS isn't in the root directory of the system disk, you must include the path name and, if necessary, the drive letter of the directory that contains VDISK.SYS.

<size> specifies the size, in kilobytes, of the virtual disk. It can range from 1 to the total available memory; if you don't specify <size>, DOS assumes 64. If you specify more than the total available memory, DOS reduces <size> to 64. If <size> would leave less than 64 K of memory available, DOS reduces <size> to leave 64 K. If less than 64 K is available for the virtual disk, DOS displays an error message and doesn't create the virtual disk.

<sector> specifies the size of each sector, in bytes. <sector> can be 128, 256, or 512; if you don't specify <sector>, DOS assumes 128.

<directory> specifies how many directory entries the root directory can hold. <directory> can range from 2 through 512; if you don't specify <directory>, DOS assumes 64. Each entry requires 32 bytes; if the entries you specify require a fraction of a sector, DOS increases the number of entries to fill the final sector. If the virtual disk isn't large enough to contain the directory, DOS reduces the directory one sector at a time until it fits; if DOS reduces the directory to 1 sector and the directory still doesn't fit, DOS displays an error message and doesn't create the virtual disk.

/E:<sectors> specifies that the virtual disk is to be installed in extended memory; you can specify this parameter only if you're using a computer in which extended memory has been installed. <sectors> specifies the highest number of sectors that VDISK transfers to DOS at a time. <sectors> can be from 1 through 8; if you don't specify <sectors> (enter the parameter as just /E), DOS assumes 8. If you use /E:<sectors>, you cannot use /X:<sectors>.

/X:<sectors> specifies that the virtual disk is to be installed in expanded memory; you can specify this parameter only if you're using a computer in which expanded memory has been installed. <sectors> specifies the highest number of sectors that VDISK transfers to DOS at a time. <sectors> can be from 1 through 8; if you don't specify <sectors> (enter the parameter as just /E), DOS assumes 8. The /X parameter might not be able to work with some hardware. If you use /X:<sectors>, you cannot use /E:<sectors>. (Version 4)

The program RAMDRIVE.SYS is similar to VDISK.SYS in the way you tell DOS to create a virtual disk. The format of the command is also similar, but it is not identical—especially in the values DOS assumes.

The command for RAMDRIVE.SYS is:

device=ramdrive.sys <size> <sector> <directory> /E /A

ramdrive.sys is the name of the file that contains the virtual-disk program. You must include a drive letter and path name if RAMDRIVE.SYS is not in the root directory of the system disk.

<size> is the size of the virtual disk in kilobytes. You can specify from 16 up to the total amount of memory; if you don't specify <size>, DOS assumes 64.

<sector> is the size of each sector, in bytes. You can specify 128, 256, 512, or 1024. If you don't specify <sector>, DOS assumes 512 in version 4, 128 in earlier versions.

<directory> specifies how many entries the root directory can hold. You can specify from 4 through 1024; if you don't specify <directory>, DOS assumes 64. DOS adjusts the directory size to fill a partial sector.

/E tells DOS to use extended memory for the virtual disk. If you use /E, you cannot use /A.

/A tells DOS to use expanded memory for the virtual disk. If you use /A, you cannot use /E.

Examples

The following examples show equivalent Device commands for VDISK.SYS and RAMDRIVE.SYS. Such commands would be included in CONFIG.SYS.

To create a 64 K virtual drive with the values that DOS assumes if VDISK.SYS or RAMDRIVE.SYS is in the root directory of the system disk:

```
device=vdisk.sys
```

or

```
device=ramdrive.sys
```

To tell DOS to look for VDISK.SYS (or RAMDRIVE.SYS) in the directory named \DOS on drive C, and to create a 360 K virtual drive with 256-byte sectors and room for 112 directory entries:

```
device=c:\dos\vdisk.sys 360 256 112
```

or

```
device=c:\dos\ramdrive.sys 360 256 112
```

To create a 1 MB (1000 K) virtual drive with 512-byte sectors and room for 128 directory entries in extended memory:

```
device=vdisk.sys 1000 512 128 /e
```

or

```
device=ramdrive.sys 1000 512 128 /e
```

VER (VERSION)
Display the DOS Version Number
Versions 2.0 and later

Page 316

The Version command (ver) displays the DOS version number, which consists of the major version number, a period, and the minor version number (such as 3.30).

The Version command has no parameters.

ver

Example

To display the DOS version number:

```
C:\DOS>ver
```

For IBM's version 4, DOS responds:

```
IBM DOS Version  4.00
```

VERIFY
Verify Data Written to Disk
Versions 2.0 and later

The Verify command turns the verify feature of DOS on or off. The verify feature confirms that data is correctly written to disk. Storing data on a disk takes a bit longer when Verify is on. Setting Verify on is equivalent to using the /V parameter of the Copy command. DOS assumes Verify is off unless you specify otherwise.

verify on off

on turns Verify on.
off turns Verify off.

If you enter a Verify command with no parameters (type just *verify*), DOS displays the current status of Verify (*VERIFY is on* or *VERIFY is off*).

Examples

To turn Verify on:

```
C:\DOS>verify on
```

To turn Verify off:

    C:\DOS>verify off

To display the status of Verify:

    C:\DOS>verify

DOS responds:

    VERIFY is off

or

    VERIFY is on

VOL (VOLUME)
Display the Volume Label of a Disk
Versions 2.0 and later

Page 105

The Volume command (vol) displays the volume label of a disk.

vol <drive>

<drive> is the letter of the drive, followed by a colon, containing the disk whose volume label is to be displayed. If you omit <drive>, DOS displays the volume label of the disk in the current drive.

Example

To display the volume label of the disk in the current drive:

    C:\DOS>vol

If the disk's volume label is FIXED DISK, DOS responds as follows (the volume serial number is included beginning with version 4):

    Volume in drive C is FIXED DISK
    Volume Serial Number is 1608-5A30

If the disk has no volume label, DOS responds:

    Volume in drive A has no label
    Volume Serial Number is 3433-1BC6

XCOPY
Copy Files and Directories Selectively
Versions 3.2 and later

Page 165

The Xcopy command lets you copy only files whose archive attribute is on, or files that have changed since a particular date. You can also use the Xcopy command to copy files not only from the source directory but also from all the subdirectories it contains; if the corresponding subdirectories don't exist on the target disk or directory, the Xcopy command creates them. Xcopy is thus particularly useful in duplicating a directory structure from one disk to another.

xcopy <source> <target> /A /M /E /P /S /V /W /D:<date>

<source> is the name of the file to be copied. You can use wildcard characters to copy a set of files with similar file names or extensions. You must include <source>, specifying at least a drive letter.

<target> specifies where <source> is to be copied. You can include any combination of drive letter, path name, and file name.

/A copies only those files whose archive attribute is on, but leaves the archive attribute unchanged.

/M copies only those files whose archive attribute is on, then turns off the archive attribute of the source files. Turning the archive attribute off is useful for backup procedures because it tells DOS (or any other program, such as a backup utility) that the file hasn't been changed since it was last backed up, and therefore doesn't need to be archived again.

/E creates subdirectories on <target> even if they are empty on <source>. If you use /E, you must also use /S.

/P prompts for confirmation before copying each file specified in <source>.

/S applies the Xcopy command to all subdirectories contained in <source>. If you specify <source> as a drive letter or as the root directory of a disk, the Xcopy command is applied to every subdirectory on the disk.

/V verifies that the copy of the file on <target> was stored correctly. This option can slow the operation of the Xcopy command somewhat, but it's good insurance if you're copying critical data and must be certain that it was copied correctly.

/W waits and prompts you to press a key before the Xcopy command begins. This gives you a chance to put in the correct diskette before starting to copy files.

/D:<date> copies only files whose date of creation or last change (as displayed by the Directory command) is the same as or later than <date>.

Examples

To copy all the files whose archive attribute is on from the directory C:\MKT\WP to the disk in drive A and turn off the archive attribute of the source files:

```
C:\>xcopy \mkt\wp a: /m
```

To copy all the files whose archive attribute is on from the directory C:\MKT\WP and all subdirectories that contain files to the disk in drive A and turn off the archive attribute of the source files:

```
C:\>xcopy \mkt\wp a: /s /m
```

To copy all the files that have changed since October 16, 1989, from the directory D:\MKT\WP and all subdirectories that contain files to the disk in the current drive, prompting for confirmation before each copy:

```
C:\>xcopy d:\mkt\wp /d:10-16-89 /s /p
```

To copy all the files and directories on the disk in drive A to the disk in drive B, including all empty subdirectories:

```
C:\>xcopy a:\ b:\ /s /e
```

XMAEM.SYS
Emulate IBM PS/2 80286
Expanded Memory Adapter
Versions 4.0 and later

XMA2EMS.SYS
Manage Lotus-Intel-Microsoft
Expanded Memory
Versions 4.0 and later

XMAEM.SYS and XMA2EMS.SYS are device drivers that enable DOS and application programs to use memory beyond the normal maximum of 640 K. Because these programs are for use by specific computer models and memory expansion boards, follow the instructions in the manual that came with your computer or memory expansion board when using these commands.

INDEX

VAN WOLVERTON

A professional writer since 1963, Van Wolverton has had bylines as a newspaper reporter, editorial writer, political columnist, and technical writer. He wrote his first computer program—one that tabulated political polls—for the *Idaho State Journal* in Pocatello, Idaho, in 1965. His interest in computers and writing have been intertwined ever since. As a computer professional, Wolverton has worked at IBM and Intel and has written software documentation for the major national software companies, including Microsoft Corporation. He is also the author of the bestselling **SUPER-CHARGING MS-DOS** and a contributor to **THE MS-DOS ENCYCLOPEDIA**. Wolverton and his wife, Jeanne, live in a twenty-first century log cabin near Alberton, Montana.

OTHER TITLES FROM MICROSOFT PRESS

SUPERCHARGING MS-DOS®, 2nd ed.
Van Wolverton

"If you want to learn how to make DOS jump through hoops, this is probably where you want to start." *MicroTimes*

When you're ready to go beyond the basics, you're ready for SUPERCHARGING MS-DOS. You'll discover how to get the maximum in efficiency and productivity from your PC. And you'll learn to customize your screen and printer output, create a RAM disk to improve the performance of your applications, work with DEBUG, and create useful batch files. Van Wolverton shows you exactly how to do all this and more.
$19.95   Order Code 86-96973

SUPERCHARGING MS-DOS®, 2nd ed. (Software Version)
Van Wolverton

Now you can save hours of typing and still enjoy Van Wolverton's helpful batch files and useful menu system with the book/disk version of SUPERCHARGING MS-DOS. This book is a complete tutorial and reference, and the companion disk features ready-to-run versions of all the programs and batch files contained in the book. Learn at your own speed but enjoy the benefits right away!
$34.95   Order Code 86-97013

QUICK REFERENCE GUIDE TO MS-DOS® COMMANDS, revised ed.
Includes version 4
Van Wolverton

Forgotten how to remove a directory? Sort a file? Compare a disk? Use the built-in DOS text editor? Here's a handy alphabetic reference — with examples — to all DOS, batch, configuration, and Edlin commands. Instant answers to all your DOS questions.
$5.95   Order Code 86-97047

QUICK REFERENCE GUIDE TO HARD DISK MANAGEMENT
Van Wolverton

Here is the core information you'll need to prepare your hard disk for use, configure DOS for your system, organize your files and directories, create timesaving batch files, and back up and maintain your hard disk. If you're the owner of an IBM PC, PS/2, or compatible and want the efficiency of a well-managed hard disk, this guide is for you.
$5.95   Order Code 86-96353

RUNNING MICROSOFT® EXCEL
The Cobb Group

Here is the most complete and authoritative guide to Microsoft Excel for Windows that you'll find anywhere. No matter what your level of expertise — seasoned spreadsheet user, beginning or occasional Microsoft Excel user, or longtime Lotus 1-2-3 user — RUNNING MICROSOFT EXCEL will be your primary source of information, advice and tutorials. Authored — and published — by the Microsoft Excel experts.
$24.95   Order Code 86-96197

MICROSOFT® EXCEL BUSINESS SOURCEBOOK
Charles W. Kyd

If you prefer learning-by-doing, then the MICROSOFT EXCEL BUSINESS SOURCEBOOK is for you. Simply turn to any one of the more than 150 practical applications in the book. Each application contains all the key information you need to create it and customize it — formulas, formats, range names, column widths, row heights, and more. Also included are tips on understanding Microsoft Excel's built-in formulas and functions, spreadsheet auditing and debugging, and a handy quick reference guide to Microsoft Excel commands. Start using Microsoft Excel today.
$24.95   Order Code 86-96452

RUNNING WINDOWS
Nancy Andrews and Craig Stinson

With this attractively designed, hands-on introduction, you'll be using Microsoft Windows in no time at all. Learn how to master the built-in applications and desktop accessories, switch among applications, transfer information and graphics between applications, and keep several tasks open and ready to work on. RUNNING WINDOWS — suddenly it's much clearer.
$19.95   Order Code 86-96346

LEARN WORD NOW
Janet Rampa

Designed as an accelerated learning program, LEARN WORD NOW is the ideal guide for those new to word processing or simply new to Microsoft Word. The step-by-step approach — augmented by dozens of screen shots and examples — will have even novice users up and running in no time at all.
$19.95   Order Code 86-96445

Microsoft Press books are available wherever fine books are sold. Credit card orders can be placed by calling 1-800-638-3030 (in Maryland call collect 824-7300).

The manuscript for this book was prepared and submitted to Microsoft Press in electronic form. Text files were processed and formatted using Microsoft Word.

Cover design by Thomas A. Draper
Interior text design by Microsoft Press
Illustrations by Rick van Genderen and Doug Ranney

Text composition by Microsoft Press in Times Roman with display in Times Roman Bold, using the Magna composition system and the Linotronic 300 laser imagesetter.